Dietrich Bonhoeffer

Letters and Papers
from Prison

The Enlarged Edition

Edited by
EBERHARD BETHGE

A TOUCHSTONE BOOK
Published by Simon & Schuster

TOUCHSTONE
Rockefeller Center
1230 Avenue of the Americas
New York, NY 10020

Translated from the German *Widerstand und Ergebung:
Briefe und Aufzeichnungen aus der Haft* (Munich: Christian
Kaiser Verlag, 1970). The translation incorporates the text
of the third English edition produced by Reginald Fuller,
Frank Clark and others; additional material by John Bowden.

First Touchstone Edition 1997

TOUCHSTONE and colophon are registered
trademarks of Simon & Schuster Inc.

Manufactured in the United States of America

19   20

Library of Congress Cataloging in Publication data is available

ISBN-13: 978-0-684-83827-4
ISBN-10:   0-684-83827-3

Contents

Preface to New Edition

I have delayed a long time before interfering with the make-up of *Letters and Papers from Prison* as it was planned and brought into being in 1950-1. At that time, my primary intention was to make available to a group of people who were interested in Bonhoeffer some short, specifically theological, meditations from Tegel. Extracts had been transcribed for a few friends even before the end of the war, and there were a couple of copies in my desk. But what were the theological considerations without their setting in the circumstances of the time? I had to guard against the misunderstanding that this was a tractate or monograph by Bonhoeffer on a chosen theme and not authentic correspondence. So other parts of Bonhoeffer's letters to his parents and to me were added – and the whole became a book.

Nevertheless, I was extremely cautious about including passages about personal relationships or relationships within the family and about deciphering any such references. Thus, for example, to begin with hardly a single reference to Bonhoeffer's fiancée appeared. The decision whether or not to publish accounts of this aspect of the period in Tegel had to be left to her. Of course, even then the fate of the author of the correspondence from Tegel and his attitude towards it played a decisive part in the selection of passages from the letters which did not have an immediate bearing on theology.

Whatever I expected to happen as a result of the publication of the letters has meanwhile been completely put in the shade by the reception that has actually been given to them throughout the world. The situation to which the book is addressed has now undergone a fundamental change. When a short while ago the English publishers of *Letters and Papers from Prison* undertook a complete revision of the translation, the reason they gave for this expensive course of action was that the book was now included among the 'religious classics'.

In the two decades since the book was planned, there have been increasingly urgent inquiries as to whether it would not also be possible to make available any objections, counter-questions or suggestions that Bonhoeffer may have received by letter while he was in Tegel. Such requests have so far remained unfulfilled, because I have felt that the replies to Bonhoeffer's correspondence which have been preserved are seldom on anything like the same level as Bonhoeffer's own theological reflections. There is good reason for this point of view even today. Nevertheless, those who seek a more complete picture are probably right, particularly now that there is an increasingly clear recognition that Bonhoeffer's theology is interwoven with the course of his life and that the forces which gave rise to it are being studied much more deeply.

The new edition called for on the occasion of the twenty-fifth anniversary of Bonhoeffer's death, on 9 April 1970, finally led me to propose a considerable expansion. After a quarter of a century, personal and family considerations have retreated into the background. The significance of the action and thought of this man has long since left the private sphere.

Bonhoeffer's own letters to his family and his friend now appear in much greater detail than hitherto, and for the first time extracts have been printed from letters written to him by his family and his friend. Finally, the volume puts in context notes on the interrogations, hitherto inaccessible, on which a first commentary has been made in my biography.[1] The sketch of the last days of Bonhoeffer's life, a preliminary study for the biography, which appeared at the end of earlier editions, is now to be found in the biography itself; in this new edition it has been replaced by Karl-Friedrich Bonhoeffer's reminiscence of the time spent in prison by members of his family. This and some other pieces give aspects of Bonhoeffer's experience, as well as the historical and theological passages, a new setting in the context of the war years.

These more comprehensive selections have been put as far as possible in strict chronological order. It seemed most natural to divide the imprisonment into periods, following the decisive points of the legal investigations. It was these that determined Bonhoeffer's existence in prison. Thus we have:

I The phase of the preliminary investigations;

II The continually vain waiting for a date for the trial;

III The period of hope for the overthrow of Hitler and the 'ditching' of the charge;

IV The time after the catastrophe.

These developments are seldom alluded to directly in the material, but they form a continual background to the communications. Inside, in his cell in Tegel, Bonhoeffer was able to do nothing; but outside, the family was able to exert its influence by constantly interfering secretly with the course of the investigation or trying to have it dropped. None of this, of course, was put on paper. The new basis for division is not a theological one. In this book, such a division cannot either be extracted or established.

The reader should note how strongly the censorship of those letters which were not smuggled out has affected both the way in which they are written and what they say; this is true above all of the first months at Tegel. Thus, for example, in letters from Bonhoeffer's mother there are sentences which she would never have written in normal circumstances, such as references to the age of Bonhoeffer's parents, assertions of innocence, questions about imaginary attacks of asthma and other comments about aspects of illness.

Although the picture of the period of Bonhoeffer's engagement is now much more vivid than it was before, his correspondence with his fiancée will still be missed. However, she herself has kept control over the disposal of the letters. In this respect, therefore, we are restricted to an attractive article, written in English, by Maria von Wedemeyer, which contains some quotations from letters written to her.[2]

Substantially extended notes have been provided for the new edition. They give information about family relationships, biographical details and the history of the time. They also decipher codes in the correspondence and add the words of biblical passages and hymns that are mentioned.

There can be no doubt that the expansion has noticeably shifted accents in comparison with the earlier edition. The private element has been heightened. This may even give rise to the impression that the period of the letters and some of the things that have been said in the meantime have been moved even further into the past. Nevertheless, the reader will also find that he can encounter at greater depth an authentically attested piece of the history of our time, which is also part of the history of Christian devotion and theology. Here is an account of the life lived by some conscientious Christians and others at a greater remove from belief, when the dilemma of both an external and an internal destruction came upon them. It was at precisely that point that Bonhoeffer's visions of a future Christianity took shape.

Special thanks are due to Rotraud Forberg, who deciphered the whole of the Tegel correspondence for this new edition of the text and prepared the final typescript. Otto Dudzus, Ernst Feil and Ulrich Kabitz gave considerable advice about the selection. My wife shared the work of revising and editing.[3]

February 1970   Eberhard Bethge

NOTES

1. Eberhard Bethge, *Dietrich Bonhoeffer: A Biography,* Collins and Harper & Row 1970. Hereafter referred to as DB.

2. Reprinted here as the Appendix, pp. 412ff.

3. In the text, insertions by the editor are marked by square brackets and omissions by triple dots.

Prologue

After Ten Years

A Reckoning made at New Year 1943[1]

Ten years is a long time in anyone's life. As time is the most valuable thing that we have, because it is the most irrevocable, the thought of any lost time troubles us whenever we look back. Time lost is time in which we have failed to live a full human life, gain experience, learn, create, enjoy, and suffer; it is time that has not been filled up, but left empty. These last years have certainly not been like that. Our losses have been great and immeasurable, but time has not been lost. It is true that the knowledge and experience that were gained, and of which one did not become conscious till later, are only abstractions of reality, of life actually lived. But just as the capacity to forget is a gift of grace, so memory, the recalling of lessons we have learnt, is also part of responsible living. In the following pages I should like to try to give some account of what we have experienced and learnt in common during these years – not personal experiences, or anything systematically arranged, or arguments and theories, but conclusions reached more or less in common by a circle of like-minded people, and related to the business of human life, put down one after the other, the only connection between them being that of concrete experience. There is nothing new about them, for they were known long before; but it has been given to us to reach them anew by first-hand experience. One cannot write about these things without a constant sense of gratitude for the fellowship of spirit and community of life that have been proved and preserved throughout these years.

No ground under our feet

One may ask whether there have ever before in human history been people with so little ground under their feet – people to whom every available alternative seemed equally intolerable, repugnant, and futile, who looked beyond all these existing alternatives for the source of their strength so entirely in the past or in the future, and who yet, without being dreamers, were able to await the success of their cause so quietly and confidently. Or perhaps one should rather ask whether the responsible thinking people of any generation that stood at a turning-point in history did not feel much as we do, simply because something new was emerging that could not be seen in the existing alternatives.

Who stands fast?

The great masquerade of evil has played havoc with all our ethical concepts. For evil to appear disguised as light, charity, historical necessity, or social justice is quite bewildering to anyone brought up on our traditional ethical concepts, while for the Christian who bases his life on the Bible it merely confirms the fundamental wickedness of evil.

The 'reasonable' people's failure is obvious. With the best intentions and a naïve lack of realism, they think that with a little reason they can bend back into position the framework that has got out of joint. In their lack of vision they want to do justice to all sides, and so the conflicting forces wear them down with nothing achieved. Disappointed by the world's unreasonableness, they see themselves condemned to ineffectiveness; they step aside in resignation or collapse before the stronger party.

Still more pathetic is the total collapse of moral *fanaticism*. The fanatic thinks that his single-minded principles qualify him to do battle with the powers of evil; but like a bull he rushes at the red cloak instead of the person who is holding it; he exhausts himself and is beaten. He gets entangled in non-essentials and falls into the trap set by cleverer people.

Then there is the man with a *conscience*, who fights single-handed against heavy odds in situations that call for a decision. But the scale of the conflicts in which he has to choose – with no advice or support except from his own conscience – tears him to pieces. Evil approaches him in so many respectable and seductive disguises that his conscience becomes nervous and vacillating, till at last he contents himself with a salved instead of a clear conscience, so that he lies to his own conscience in order to avoid despair; for a man whose only support is his conscience can never realize that a bad conscience may be stronger and more wholesome than a deluded one.

4

From the perplexingly large number of possible decisions, the way of *duty* seems to be the sure way out. Here, what is commanded is accepted as what is most certain, and the responsibility for it rests on the commander, not on the person commanded. But no one who confines himself to the limits of duty ever goes so far as to venture, on his sole responsibility, to act in the only way that makes it possible to score a direct hit on evil and defeat it. The man of duty will in the end have to do his duty by the devil too.

As to the man who asserts his complete *freedom* to stand foursquare to the world, who values the necessary deed more highly than an unspoilt conscience or reputation, who is ready to sacrifice a barren principle for a fruitful compromise, or the barren wisdom of a middle course for a fruitful radicalism – let him beware lest his freedom should bring him down. He will assent to what is bad so as to ward off something worse, and in doing so he will no longer be able to realize that the worse, which he wants to avoid, might be the better. Here we have the raw material of tragedy.

Here and there people flee from public altercation into the sanctuary of private *virtuousness*. But anyone who does this must shut his mouth and his eyes to the injustice around him. Only at the cost of self-deception can he keep himself pure from the contamination arising from responsible action. In spite of all that he does, what he leaves undone will rob him of his peace of mind. He will either go to pieces because of this disquiet, or become the most hypocritical of Pharisees.

Who stands fast? Only the man whose final standard is not his reason, his principles, his conscience, his freedom, or his virtue, but who is ready to sacrifice all this when he is called to obedient and responsible action in faith and in exclusive allegiance to God— the responsible man, who tries to make his whole life an answer to the question and call of God. Where are these responsible people?

Civil courage?

What lies behind the complaint about the dearth of civil courage? In recent years we have seen a great deal of bravery and self-sacrifice, but civil courage hardly anywhere, even among ourselves. To attribute this simply to personal cowardice would be too facile a psychology; its background is quite different. In a long history, we Germans have had to learn the need for and the strength of obedience. In the subordination of all personal wishes and ideas to the tasks to which we have been called, we have seen the meaning and the greatness of our lives. We have looked upwards, not in servile fear, but in free trust, seeing in our tasks a call, and in our call a vocation. This readiness to follow a command from 'above' rather than our own private opinions and wishes was a sign of legitimate self-distrust. Who would deny that in obedience, in their task and calling, the Germans have again and again shown the utmost bravery and self-sacrifice? But the German has kept his freedom – and what nation has talked more passionately of freedom than the Germans, from Luther to the idealist philosophers? – by seeking deliverance from self-will through service to the community. Calling and freedom were to him two sides of the same thing. But in this he misjudged the world; he did not realize that his submissiveness and self-sacrifice could be exploited for evil ends. When that happened, the exercise of the calling itself became questionable, and all the moral principles of the German were bound to totter. The fact could not be escaped that the German still lacked something fundamental: he could not see the need for free and responsible action, even in opposition to his task and his calling; in its place there appeared on the one hand an irresponsible lack of scruple, and on the other a self-tormenting punctiliousness that never led to action. Civil courage, in fact, can grow only out of the free responsibility of free men. Only now are the Germans beginning to discover the meaning of free responsibility. It depends on a God who demands responsible action in a bold venture of faith, and who promises forgiveness and consolation to the man who becomes a sinner in that venture.

Of success

Although it is certainly not true that success justifies an evil deed and shady means, it is impossible to regard success as something that is ethically quite neutral. The fact is that historical success creates a basis for the continuance of life, and it is still a moot point whether it is ethically more responsible to take the field like a Don Quixote against a new age, or to admit one's defeat, accept the new age, and agree to serve it. In the last resort success makes history; and the ruler of history repeatedly brings good out of evil over the heads of the history-makers. Simply to ignore the ethical significance of success is a short-circuit created by dogmatists who think unhistorically and irresponsibly; and it is good for us sometimes to be compelled to grapple seriously with the ethical problem of success. As long as goodness is successful, we can afford the luxury of regarding it as having no ethical significance; it is when success is achieved by evil means that the problem arises. In the face of such a situation we find that it cannot be adequately dealt with, either by theoretical dogmatic arm-chair criticism, which means a refusal to face the facts, or by opportunism, which means giving up the struggle and surrendering to success. We will not and must not be either outraged critics or opportunists, but must take our share of responsibility for the moulding of history in every situation and at every moment, whether we are the victors or the vanquished. One who will not allow any occurrence whatever to deprive him of his responsibility for the course of history—because he knows that it has been laid on him by God—will thereafter achieve a more fruitful relation to the events of history than that of barren criticism and equally barren opportunism. To talk of going down fighting like heroes in the face of certain defeat is not really heroic at all, but merely a refusal to face the future. The ultimate question for a responsible man to ask is not how he is to extricate himself heroically from the affair, but how the coming generation is to live. It is only from this question, with its responsibility towards history, that fruitful solutions can come, even if for the time being they are very humiliating. In short, it is much easier to see a thing through from the point of view of abstract principle than from that of concrete responsibility. The rising generation will always instinctively discern which of these we make the basis of our actions, for it is their own future that is at stake.

Of folly

Folly is a more dangerous enemy to the good than evil. One can protest against evil; it can be unmasked and, if need be, prevented by force. Evil always carries the seeds of its own destruction, as it makes people, at the least, uncomfortable. Against folly we have no defence. Neither protests nor force can touch it; reasoning is no use; facts that contradict personal prejudices can simply be disbelieved – indeed, the fool can counter by criticizing them, and if they are undeniable, they can just be pushed aside as trivial exceptions. So the fool, as distinct from the scoundrel, is completely self-satisfied; in fact, he can easily become dangerous, as it does not take much to make him aggressive. A fool must therefore be treated more cautiously than a scoundrel; we shall never again try to convince a fool by reason, for it is both useless and dangerous.

If we are to deal adequately with folly, we must try to understand its nature. This much is certain, that it is a moral rather than an intellectual defect. There are people who are mentally agile but foolish, and people who are mentally slow but very far from foolish – a discovery that we make to our surprise as a result of particular situations. We thus get the impression that folly is likely to be, not a congenital defect, but one that is acquired in certain circumstances where people *make* fools of themselves or allow others to make fools of them. We notice further that this defect is less common in the unsociable and solitary than in individuals or groups that are inclined or condemned to sociability. It seems, then, that folly is a sociological rather than a psychological problem, and that it is a special form of the operation of historical circumstances on people, a psychological by-product of definite external factors. If we look more closely, we see that any violent display of power, whether political or religious, produces an outburst of folly in a large part of mankind; indeed, this seems actually to be a psychological and sociological law: the power of some needs the folly of the others. It is not that certain human capacities, intellectual capacities for instance, become stunted or destroyed, but rather that the upsurge of power makes such an overwhelming impression that men are deprived of their independent judgment, and – more or less unconsciously – give up trying to assess the new state of affairs for themselves. The fact that the fool is often stubborn must not mislead us into thinking that he is independent. One feels in fact, when talking to him, that one is dealing, not with the man himself, but with slogans, catchwords, and the like, which have taken hold of him. He is under a spell, he is blinded, his very nature is being misused and exploited. Having thus become a passive instrument, the fool will be capable of any evil and at the same time incapable of seeing that it is evil. Here lies the danger of a diabolical exploitation that can do irreparable damage to human beings.

But at this point it is quite clear, too, that folly can be overcome, not by instruction, but only by an act of liberation; and so we have come to terms with the fact that in the great majority of cases inward liberation must be preceded by outward liberation, and that until that has taken place, we may as well abandon all attempts to convince the fool. In this state of affairs we have to realize why it is no use our trying to find out what 'the people' really think, and why the question is so superfluous for the man who thinks and acts responsibly – but always given these particular circumstances. The Bible's words that 'the fear of the Lord is the beginning of wisdom' (Ps. 111.10) tell us that a person's inward liberation to live a responsible life before God is the only real cure for folly.

But there is some consolation in these thoughts on folly: they in no way justify us in thinking that most people are fools in all circumstances. What will really matter is whether those in power expect more from people's folly than from their wisdom and independence of mind.

Contempt for humanity?

There is a very real danger of our drifting into an attitude of contempt for humanity. We know quite well that we have no right to do so, and that it would lead us into the most sterile relation to our fellow-men. The following thoughts may keep us from such a temptation. It means that we at once fall into the worst blunders of our opponents. The man who despises another will never be able to make anything of him. Nothing that we despise in the other man is entirely absent from ourselves. We often expect from others more than we are willing to do ourselves. Why have we hitherto thought so intemperately about man and his frailty and temptability? We must learn to regard people less in the light of what they do or omit to do, and more in the light of what they suffer. The only profitable relationship to others – and especially to our weaker brethren – is one of love, and that means the will to hold fellowship with them. God himself did not despise humanity, but became man for men's sake.

Immanent righteousness

It is one of the most surprising experiences, but at the same time one of the most incontrovertible, that evil – often in a surprisingly short time – proves its own folly and defeats its own object. That does not mean that punishment follows hard on the heels of every evil action; but it does mean that deliberate transgression of the divine law in the supposed interests of worldly self-preservation has exactly the opposite effect. We learn this from our own experience, and we can interpret it in various ways. At least it seems possible to infer with certainty that in social life there are laws more powerful than anything that may claim to dominate them, and that it is therefore not only wrong but unwise to disregard them. We can understand from this why Aristotelian–Thomist ethics made wisdom one of the cardinal virtues. Wisdom and folly are not ethically indifferent, as Neo-protestant motive-ethics would have it. In the fullness of the concrete situation and the possibilities which it offers, the wise man at the same time recognizes the impassable limits that are set to all action by the permanent laws of human social life; and in this knowledge the wise man acts well and the good man wisely.

It is true that all historically important action is constantly overstepping the limits set by these laws. But it makes all the difference whether such overstepping of the appointed limits is regarded in principle as the superseding of them, and is therefore given out to be a law of a special kind, or whether the overstepping is deliberately regarded as a fault which is perhaps unavoidable, justified only if the law and the limit are re-established and respected as soon as possible. It is not necessarily hypocrisy if the declared aim of political action is the restoration of the law, and not mere self-preservation. The world *is*, in fact, so ordered that a basic respect for ultimate laws and human life is also the best means of self-preservation, and that these laws may be broken only on the odd occasion in case of brief necessity, whereas anyone who turns necessity into a principle, and in so doing establishes a law of his own alongside them, is inevitably bound, sooner or later, to suffer retribution. The immanent righteousness of history rewards and punishes only men's deeds, but the eternal righteousness of God tries and judges their hearts.

A few articles of faith on the sovereignty of God in history

I believe that God can and will bring good out of evil, even out of the greatest evil. For that purpose he needs men who make the best use of everything. I believe that God will give us all the strength we need to help us to resist in all time of distress. But he never gives it in advance, lest we should rely on ourselves and not on him alone. A faith such as this should allay all our fears for the future. I believe that even our mistakes and shortcomings are turned to good account, and that it is no harder for God to deal with them than with our supposedly good deeds. I believe that God is no timeless fate, but that he waits for and answers sincere prayers and responsible actions.

Confidence

There is hardly one of us who has not known what it is to be betrayed. The figure of Judas, which we used to find so difficult to understand, is now fairly familiar to us. The air that we breathe is so polluted by mistrust that it almost chokes us. But where we have broken through the layer of mistrust, we have been able to discover a confidence hitherto undreamed of. Where we trust, we have learnt to put our very lives into the hands of others; in the face of all the different interpretations that have been put on our lives and actions, we have learnt to trust unreservedly. We now know that only such confidence, which is always a venture, though a glad and positive venture, enables us really to live and work. We know that it is most reprehensible to sow and encourage mistrust, and that our duty is rather to foster and strengthen confidence wherever we can. Trust will always be one of the greatest, rarest, and happiest blessings of our life in community, though it can emerge only on the dark background of a necessary mistrust. We have learnt never to trust a scoundrel an inch, but to give ourselves to the trustworthy without reserve.

The sense of quality

Unless we have the courage to fight for a revival of wholesome reserve between man and man, we shall perish in an anarchy of human values. The impudent contempt for such reserve is the mark of the rabble, just as inward uncertainty, haggling and cringing for the favour of insolent people, and lowering oneself to the level of the rabble are the way of becoming no better than the rabble oneself. When we forget what is due to ourselves and to others, when the feeling for human quality and the power to exercise reserve cease to exist, chaos is at the door. When we tolerate impudence for the sake of material comforts, then we abandon our self-respect, the flood-gates are opened, chaos bursts the dam that we were to defend; and we are responsible for it all. In other times it may have been the business of Christianity to champion the equality of all men; its business today will be to defend passionately human dignity and reserve. The misinterpretation that we are acting for our own interests, and the cheap insinuation that our attitude is anti-social, we shall simply have to put up with; they are the invariable protests of the rabble against decency and order. Anyone who is pliant and uncertain in this matter does not realize what is at stake, and indeed in his case the reproaches may well be justified. We are witnessing the levelling down of all ranks of society, and at the same time the birth of a new sense of nobility, which is binding together a circle of men from all former social classes. Nobility arises from and exists by sacrifice, courage, and a clear sense of duty to oneself and society, by expecting due regard for itself as a matter of course; and it shows an equally natural regard for others, whether they are of higher or of lower degree. We need all along the line to recover the lost sense of quality and a social order based on quality. Quality is the greatest enemy of any kind of mass-levelling. Socially it means the renunciation of all place-hunting, a break with the cult of the 'star', an open eye both upwards and downwards, especially in the choice of one's more intimate friends, and pleasure in private life as well as courage to enter public life. Culturally it means a return from the newspaper and the radio to the book, from feverish activity to unhurried leisure, from dispersion to concentration, from sensationalism to reflection, from virtuosity to art, from snobbery to modesty, from extravagance to moderation. Quantities are competitive, qualities are complementary.

Sympathy

We must allow for the fact that most people learn wisdom only by personal experience. This explains, first, why so few people are capable of taking precautions in advance – they always fancy that they will somehow or other avoid the danger, till it is too late. Secondly, it explains their insensibility to the sufferings of others; sympathy grows in proportion to the fear of approaching disaster. There is a good deal of excuse on ethical grounds for this attitude. No one wants to meet fate head-on; inward calling and strength for action are acquired only in the actual emergency. No one is responsible for all the injustice and suffering in the world, and no one wants to set himself up as the judge of the world. Psychologically, our lack of imagination, of sensitivity, and of mental alertness is balanced by a steady composure, an ability to go on working, and a great capacity for suffering. But from a Christian point of view, none of these excuses can obscure the fact that the most important factor, large-heartedness, is lacking. Christ kept himself from suffering till his hour had come, but when it did come he met it as a free man, seized it, and mastered it. Christ, so the scriptures tell us, bore the sufferings of all humanity in his own body as if they were his own – a thought beyond our comprehension – accepting them of his own free will. We are certainly not Christ; we are not called on to redeem the world by our own deeds and sufferings, and we need not try to assume such an impossible burden. We are not lords, but instruments in the hand of the Lord of history; and we can share in other people's sufferings only to a very limited degree. We are not Christ, but if we want to be Christians, we must have some share in Christ's large-heartedness by acting with responsibility and in freedom when the hour of danger comes, and by showing a real sympathy that springs, not, from fear, but from the liberating and redeeming love of Christ for all who suffer. Mere waiting and looking on is not Christian behaviour. The Christian is called to sympathy and action, not in the first place by his own sufferings, but by the sufferings of his brethren, for whose sake Christ suffered.

Of suffering

It is infinitely easier to suffer in obedience to a human command than in the freedom of one's own responsibility. It is infinitely easier to suffer with others than to suffer alone. It is infinitely easier to suffer publicly and honourably than apart and ignominiously. It is infinitely easier to suffer through staking one's life than to suffer spiritually. Christ suffered as a free man alone, apart and in ignominy, in body and spirit; and since then many Christians have suffered with him.

Present and future

We used to think that one of the inalienable rights of man was that he should be able to plan both his professional and his private life. That is a thing of the past. The force of circumstances has brought us into a situation where we have to give up being 'anxious about tomorrow' (Matt. 6.34). But it makes all the difference whether we accept this willingly and in faith (as the Sermon on the Mount intends), or under continual constraint. For most people, the compulsory abandonment of planning for the future means that they are forced back into living just for the moment, irresponsibly, frivolously, or resignedly; some few dream longingly of better times to come, and try to forget the present. We find both these courses equally impossible, and there remains for us only the very narrow way, often extremely difficult to find, of living every day as if it were our last, and yet living in faith and responsibility as though there were to be a great future: 'Houses and fields and vineyards shall again be bought in this land' proclaims Jeremiah (32.15), in paradoxical contrast to his prophecies of woe, just before the destruction of the holy city. It is a sign from God and a pledge of a fresh start and a great future, just when all seems black. Thinking and acting for the sake of the coming generation, but being ready to go any day without fear or anxiety – that, in practice, is the spirit in which we are forced to live. It is not easy to be brave and keep that spirit alive, but it is imperative.

Optimism

It is wiser to be pessimistic; it is a way of avoiding disappointment and ridicule, and so wise people condemn optimism. The essence of optimism is not its view of the present, but the fact that it is the inspiration of life and hope when others give in; it enables a man to hold his head high when everything seems to be going wrong; it gives him strength to sustain reverses and yet to claim the future for himself instead of abandoning it to his opponent. It is true that there is a silly, cowardly kind of optimism, which we must condemn. But the optimism that is will for the future should never be despised, even if it is proved wrong a hundred times; it is health and vitality, and the sick man has no business to impugn it. There are people who regard it as frivolous, and some Christians think it impious for anyone to hope and prepare for a better earthly future. They think that the meaning of present events is chaos, disorder, and catastrophe; and in resignation or pious escapism they surrender all responsibility for reconstruction and for future generations. It may be that the day of judgment will dawn tomorrow; in that case, we shall gladly stop working for a better future. But not before.

Insecurity and death

In recent years we have become increasingly familiar with the thought of death. We surprise ourselves by the calmness with which we hear of the death of one of our contemporaries. We cannot hate it as we used to, for we have discovered some good in it, and have almost come to terms with it. Fundamentally we feel that we really belong to death already, and that every new day is a miracle. It would probably not be true to say that we welcome death (although we all know that weariness which we ought to avoid like the plague); we are too inquisitive for that – or, to put it more seriously, we should like to see something more of the meaning of our life's broken fragments. Nor do we try to romanticize death, for life is too great and too precious. Still less do we suppose that danger is the meaning of life – we are not desperate enough for that, and we know too much about the good things that life has to offer, though on the other hand we are only too familiar with life's anxieties and with all the other destructive effects of prolonged personal insecurity. We still love life, but I do not think that death can take us by surprise now. After what we have been through during the war, we hardly dare admit that we should like death to come to us, not accidentally and suddenly through some trivial cause, but in the fullness of life and with everything at stake. It is we ourselves, and not outward circumstances, who make death what it can be, a death freely and voluntarily accepted.

Are we still of any use?

We have been silent witnesses of evil deeds; we have been drenched by many storms; we have learnt the arts of equivocation and pretence; experience has made us suspicious of others and kept us from being truthful and open; intolerable conflicts have worn us down and even made us cynical. Are we still of any use? What we shall need is not geniuses, or cynics, or misanthropes, or clever tacticians, but plain, honest, straightforward men. Will our inward power of resistance be strong enough, and our honesty with ourselves remorseless enough, for us to find our way back to simplicity and straightforwardness?

The view from below[2]

There remains an experience of incomparable value. We have for once learnt to see the great events of world history from below, from the perspective of the outcast, the suspects, the maltreated, the powerless, the oppressed, the reviled – in short, from the perspective of those who suffer. The important thing is that neither bitterness nor envy should have gnawed at the heart during this time, that we should have come to look with new eyes at matters great and small, sorrow and joy, strength and weakness, that our perception of generosity, humanity, justice and mercy should have become clearer, freer, less corruptible. We have to learn that personal suffering is a more effective key, a more rewarding principle for exploring the world in thought and action than personal good fortune. This perspective from below must not become the partisan possession of those who are eternally dissatisfied; rather, we must do justice to life in all its dimensions from a higher satisfaction, whose foundation is beyond any talk of 'from below' or 'from above'. This is the way in which we may affirm it.

NOTES

1. Given to Hans von Dohnanyi, Hans Oster and Eberhard Bethge at Christmas, 1942. One copy was kept under the roof-beams of Bonhoeffer's parents' house in Charlottenburg, Marienburger Allee 43.
2. This final paragraph was probably written at the end of 1942 (or in autumn 1943?), and is unfinished. It may well have been planned as part of 'After Ten Years'. The German text does not appear in the new German edition of *Letters and Papers*, but in *Gesammelte Schriften* II, p. 441 (*Miscellaneous Papers* of Bonhoeffer, published in 4 vols, 1958–61). It appears here at the suggestion of Eberhard Bethge and by kind permission of Christian Kaiser Verlag, Munich.

I

Time of Interrogation

April to July 1943

Dear Dietrich,

I wanted to send you a greeting from us and to tell you that we're always thinking of you. We know you, and so we are confident that everything will turn out well – and, we hope, soon. Amidst all our present disquiet, the cantata 'Praise the Lord' which you produced for my seventy-fifth birthday[1] with the two younger generations of the family remains a splendid memory and one that we want to keep alive. I hope that we shall be able to talk with you soon. Loving greetings from mother, Renate and fiancé[2] and

your old Father

After receiving permission we sent you on Wednesday 7th a parcel with bread and other food, a blanket and a woollen vest, etc.

To his parents [Tegel] 14 April 1943

Dear parents,

I do want you to be quite sure that I'm all right. I'm sorry that I was not allowed to write to you sooner, but I was all right during the first ten days too.[3] Strangely enough, the discomforts that one generally associates with prison life, the physical hardships, hardly bother me at all. One can even have enough to eat in the mornings with dry bread (I get a variety of extras too). The hard prison bed does not worry me a bit, and one can get plenty of sleep between 8 p.m. and 6 a.m. I have been particularly surprised that I have hardly felt any need at all for cigarettes since I came here; but I think that in all this the psychic factor has played the larger part. A violent mental upheaval such as is produced by a sudden arrest brings with it the need to take one's mental bearings and come to terms with an entirely new situation – all this means that physical things take a back seat and lose their importance, and it is something that I find to be a real enrichment of my experience. I am not so unused to being alone as other people are, and it is certainly a good spiritual Turkish bath. The only thing that bothers me or would bother me is the thought that you are being tormented by anxiety about me, and are not sleeping or eating properly. Forgive me for causing you so much worry, but I think a hostile fate is more to blame than I am. To set off against that, it is good to read Paul Gerhardt's hymns and learn them by heart, as I am doing now. Besides that, I have my Bible and some reading matter from the library here, and enough writing paper now.

You can imagine that I'm most particularly anxious about my fiancée[4] at the moment. It's a great deal for her to bear, especially when she has only recently lost her father and brother in the East. As the daughter of an officer, she will perhaps find my imprisonment especially hard to take. If only I could have a few words with her! Now you will have to do it. Perhaps she will come to you in Berlin. That would be fine.

The seventy-fifth birthday celebrations were a fortnight ago today. It was a splendid day. I can still hear the chorale that we sang in the morning and evening, with all the voices and instruments: 'Praise to the Lord, the Almighty, the King of Creation. . . . Shelters thee under his wings, yea, and gently sustaineth.' That is true, and it is what we must always rely on.

Spring is really coming now. You will have plenty to do in the garden; I hope that Renate's wedding preparations are going well. Here in the prison yard there is a thrush which sings beautifully in the morning, and now in the evening too. One is grateful for little things, and that is surely a gain. Good-bye for now.

I'm thinking of you and the rest of the family and my friends with gratitude and love,   your Dietrich

When you have the chance, could you leave here for me slippers, bootlaces (black, long), shoe polish, writing paper and envelopes, ink, smoker's card, shaving cream, sewing things and a suit I can change into? Many thanks for everything.

The Judge Advocate of the War Court   Berlin-Charlottenburg 5,
StPL. (RKA)III 114/43   20 April 1943
                                      Witzlebenstrasse 4–10
                                      Telephone: 30 06 81

To
Professor Dr Bonhoeffer

In the action against your son Dietrich *Bonhoeffer*, you are informed, in reply to your letter of 17 April 1943, that the application for permission to visit is refused.

Stamp of the War Court 18
F.d.R.
Signature   By order
Army Inspector of Justice   signed   Dr Roeder

From Karl-Friedrich Bonhoeffer[5]   Leipzig, 23 April 1943

Dear Dietrich,
One doesn't always think of the most obvious things first. I've
only just learnt in Berlin that it is possible to write to you and in
this way at least to give you an indication in your isolation that
people are thinking about you. One has a great many heartfelt
questions, but this note cannot be more than the need to tell you
all kinds of inconsequential matters. Of course we all very much
hope that by now you will soon have the time of testing behind
you and will soon be released again. I've often been in Berlin during the last two weeks. You need not worry about the parents; of
course they are very shaken, but full of confidence and trust that
the matter will soon come out all right; a substantial part of our
conversations has been concerned with what you are to do when
you come out. But you will have to talk about the question,
too . . .

I'm brooding on a manuscript which I really wanted to get ready for publication in the Easter holidays, but my thoughts often go astray and end up with you. Keep your spirits up. All the best.

Ever your Karl-Friedrich

From Hans von Dohnanyi[6] Sacrow bei Potsdam[7]
Good Friday [23 April] 1943

My dear Dietrich,
I don't know whether I shall be allowed to send you this greeting, but I want to try. The bells outside are ringing for worship, and memories flood back of the marvellous, profound hours that we spent together in the garrison church, and those many joyful, happy, untroubled Easters with children, parents, brothers and sisters. You will feel the same, and one needs a great deal of strength to master these memories. You cannot know how much it oppresses me that I am the cause of this suffering that you, Christel, the children, our parents now undergo; that because of me, my dear wife and you have been deprived of freedom. *Socios habuisse malorum* may be a comfort, but *habere* is an infinitely heavy burden.[8] And that mistrustful question 'Why?' keeps forming itself on my lips. If I knew that all of you, and you in particular, were not thinking of me reproachfully, a weight would be lifted from my spirit. What wouldn't I give to know that the two of you were free again; I would take everything upon myself if you could be spared this testing. It was marvellous that I could see you;[9] I have also been allowed to speak to Christel, but what can one say in the presence of other people? How immeasurably difficult, impossible it is to open one's heart . . . You know me well. We are, I feel, more than 'just' relatives by marriage, and you know what my wife is to me. I simply *cannot* be without her, when she has shared everything with me hitherto. That I am not allowed now to endure what has been laid upon us with her – who can fathom what that means? It certainly does not further the *case*; I am completely taken aback.

I'm reading the Bible a good deal now; it is the only book that does not keep making my thoughts stray. This morning Matthew 26–28, Luke 22–24, Psalms 68 and 70. I have never before been so struck by the remarkable divergences between the two evangelists; how much I would like to talk them over with you.

I hear from Ursel[10] that the children are in Friedrichsbrunn.[11] Our idea of a perfect holiday is *there*.

I want you to know that I'm grateful to you for everything that you have been and are to my wife, my children and myself. So good-bye.   Your Hans

To his parents   [Tegel] Easter Day, 25 April 1943

Dear parents,
At last the tenth day has come round, and I'm allowed to write to you again; I'm so glad to let you know that even here I'm having a happy Easter. Good Friday and Easter free us to think about other things far beyond our own personal fate, about the ultimate meaning of all life, suffering, and events; and we lay hold of a great hope. Since yesterday it has been marvellously quiet in the house. I heard many people wishing each other a happy Easter, and one does not begrudge it anyone who is on duty here – it's a hard job. In the stillness now I can also hear your Easter greetings, if you're together with the family today and thinking of me.

Good Friday was Maria's birthday. If I didn't know how bravely she bore the death of her father, her brother and two cousins of whom she was particularly fond, last year, I would be really alarmed about her. Now Easter will comfort her, her large family will be there to support her, and her work in the Red Cross will occupy all her time. Give her my love, tell her that I long for her very much, but that she is not to grieve, but to be as brave as she has always been. She is still so very young – that is the hard thing.

First of all, I must thank you very much for all the things that you brought me and for father's and Ursel's greetings. You can't imagine what it means to be suddenly told: 'Your mother and sister and brother have just been here, and they've left something for you.' The mere fact that you have been near me, the tangible evidence that you are still thinking and caring about me (which of course I really know anyway!) is enough to keep me happy for the rest of the day. Thank you very much indeed for everything.

Things are still all right, and I am well. I'm allowed out of doors for half an hour every day, and now that I can smoke again, I even forget sometimes, for a little while, where I am! I'm being treated well, and I read a good deal – newspapers, novels, and above all the Bible. I can't concentrate enough yet for serious work, but during Holy Week I at last managed to work solidly through a part of the passion story that has occupied me a great deal for a long time – the high-priestly prayer. I've even been able to expound to myself a few chapters of Pauline ethical material; I felt that to be very important. So I really have a great deal to be very thankful for.

How are things with you? Are you still enjoying the masses of glorious birthday flowers? What are your plans for travelling? I'm rather afraid that now you won't be going into the Black Forest, good and necessary though that would have been. And on top of everything there are now the preparations for Renate's wedding. I want to make it clear that it is my express wish that Ursel should not postpone the date by a single day, but should let Renate get married as soon and as happily as possible; don't let her worry. Anything else would only distress me. Renate knows all the good wishes for her in my thoughts, and how much I share her joy. In recent years we have really learnt how much joy and sorrow can and must fill the human heart at one and the same time. So, the sooner the better. Do give her my love.

I would also very much like to know how things are with Maria's grandmother.[12] Please do not conceal it from me if she has died. Maria and I have both hung on her a great deal.

Now a couple of requests: I would very much like the brown, or better still the black boots with laces. My heels are going. My suit is very much in need of cleaning; I would like to give it to you and to have the other brown one instead. I also need a hairbrush, lots of matches, a pipe with tobacco, pouch and cleaners, and cigarettes. Books: Schilling, *Morals*, Vol. II and a volume of Stifter. Excuse me for troubling you. Many thanks.

It is surprising how quickly the days pass here. I can hardly believe that I have been here three weeks. I like going to bed at eight o'clock (supper is at four), and I look forward to my dreams. I never knew before what a source of pleasure that can be; I dream every day, and always about something pleasant. Before I go to sleep I repeat to myself the verses that I have learnt during the day, and at 6 a.m. I like to read psalms and hymns, think of you all, and know that you are thinking of me.

The day is over now, and I hope you are feeling as peaceful as I am. I've read a lot of good things, and my thoughts and hopes have been pleasant too. But it would put my mind very much at rest if one day Maria were quietly with you. Give this letter to her to read – and also to Renate.[13] I always have the short notes from father and Ursel in front of me, and I keep reading them.

Good-bye for now, and excuse all the worry that I'm causing you. Greetings to all the rest of the family. Love and thanks with all my heart,   your Dietrich

From his mother   Charlottenburg
Wednesday after Easter [28 April] 1943
25th anniversary of Walter's death[14]

My dear Dietrich,

. . . I was outside yesterday with Susi[15] and brought you the things. I hope I've sent roughly what you wanted. You must see that you keep your strength up, too. We've just had a letter from you, and are eagerly waiting for the next. It all happened too suddenly. Who would have thought it possible that such a thing could happen to you! We are trying to get rid of our old idea that being in prison is a disgrace; it makes life unnecessarily difficult. We have to realize that in our difficult times a good deal of mistrust influences people's opinions of a man; it may be very difficult to avoid it. But we are convinced that when you hear the charges that

27

are laid against you, you will be in a position to exonerate yourself.

Today Ursula is at Renate's home and is getting it ready. She is rather sad that everything cannot be as beautiful as she would like to make it. I want to go there too at the end of the week, to see how and whether I can help with some of my old things. May God continue to bless you in these hard times. Father joins me in sending his love.

Your Mother

The splendid flowers from father's seventy-fifth birthday have now gone. So everything has its time and its end . . .

From Rüdiger Schleicher[16]   Charlottenburg, 29 April 1943

Dear Dietrich,

Easter is over, and everyday life now has its due. We have missed you very much in the past days. We've chiefly been working in the garden and music has taken a back place. But it has not been absent altogether: I played quartets on Sunday evening; but that was almost all, and above all the beginning of Sunday morning didn't really come off, because the children aren't here.

Above all, you ought to know that our thoughts are with you. Though I know that you have strength enough to put up with all the difficulties and dangers of life, I want to tell you so once again. I hope and wish that you will be able to enjoy in freedom a spring that is becoming increasingly more beautiful.

All goes well with us. Hans-Walter[17] writes most contentedly from his aircraft radio operator's school at Nachod. Ursel is vigorously getting ready for Renate's wedding, which is to take place on 15 May, as I expect you already know. Hans-Walter will get leave for it. The three girls are still in Friedrichsbrunn with Bärbel, Klaus and Christoph.[18] We now expect them at the weekend; their accounts from up there were very enthusiastic.

We all send you our love. Keep well. All the best.

Ever your Rüdiger

Dear parents,
Many thanks for the letters from mother, K. Friedrich and Rüdiger.
I'm so glad that you are at ease and confident, and also that K.
Friedrich can be with you frequently. I'm sure that it is good for me
personally to undergo all this, and I believe that no more is laid
upon any man than he can receive the strength to bear. The hardest
thing for me is that you must bear the burden too, but the way in
which you do it is again infinitely cheering and a great strength to
me. I'm very pleased that Maria has written to you so bravely and
so full of confidence. How one lives entirely on a basis of trust!
Without trust, life is impoverished. I'm now learning every day
how good it always was being with you; in addition, I'm learning
to practise myself what I have said to other people in sermons and
books.

I've now had four weeks in prison; and whereas I was able
from the outset to accept my lot consciously, I'm now getting
used to it in a kind of natural and unconscious way. That is a relief,
but it raises problems of its own, for one rightly does not want to
get used to being in this position; I think you will feel the same
way about it.

You want to know more about my life here. To picture a cell
does not need much imagination – the less you use, the nearer the
mark you will be. At Easter the *Deutsche Allgemeine Zeitung*[20]
brought out a reproduction from Dürer's *Apocalypse*, which I
pinned up on the wall; and some of Maria's primulas are still here
too. Our day lasts fourteen hours, of which I spend about three
walking up and down the cell – several kilometres a day, besides
half an hour in the yard. I read, learn, and work. I particularly
enjoyed reading Gotthelf again, with his clear, wholesome, serene
style. I'm getting on all right and keeping well.

The wedding at the Schleicher's will soon be here now, and I
won't be able to write again before then. I've lately been reading
in Jean Paul that 'the only joys that can stand the fires of adversity
are joys of home'. If they both understand that – and I think that
they understand it very well – then I can see nothing but great good

fortune for this marriage, and I'm already looking forward one day to sharing the joys of their home. Very soon, they ought to read together Jeremias Gotthelf's *Money and Spirit*; it is better than any speeches I could give them. I would like to give them the spinet, which already half belongs to them, and also, as I've already said to Ursel, my contribution to the piano, as much as they need. I hope they will get it soon. I wish them a very happy day with all my heart and will be there with them with many happy thoughts and wishes. I would so like it if they in turn could think of me only with happy thoughts, memories and hopes. Precisely at the time when one is having rather hard personal experiences, one can ensure that the real joys of life – and a wedding is certainly one of those – keep their due proportions. Here in the quietness I hope that one day we shall all be together to celebrate my and Maria's wedding day – when? At the moment that seems fanciful, but it's a splendid hope and a great one. It's all rather a lot for Ursel; how much I would like to help her move and plan. Now she has all the trouble over me on top of everything else. Much love to everyone at home, and especially to the happy couple. Congratulations to the Schleicher parents on their twentieth wedding anniversary.[21] They ought to take a couple of photographs!

Now once again thanks for everything that you brought, for all your trouble, consideration and love – Wednesday is always such a specially good day, and how I look forward to it! – and a few requests: a clothes brush, mirror, towel, face-cloth, and if it keeps being so cold (it seems to be warmer today) a warm shirt and long socks; also Holl, *Church History*, the volume on the West, and something to smoke, whatever is going, and some matches. I don't understand, either, why you can't find my suit and jacket.

I suppose that everyone now knows about the engagement. But it's still in the family? According to my count 'the immediate family' on both sides adds up to more than eighty people, so it will probably not remain a secret for long. My main concern is to observe Maria's mother's wishes. Special thanks to Maria for her greetings. It's splendid that things are better with her grandmother; she, too, has a heavy burden to bear with five sons and grandsons killed and seven still out there. Special greetings to her; I'm sure she's thinking of me. Unfortunately I won't be able to thank aunt Elisabeth[22] for the Bach cantatas. Please remember me to her as well.

I often think here of that lovely song of Hugo Wolf's, which we have sung several times lately:

> *Über Nacht, über Nacht kommt Freud und Leid*
> *und eh' du's gedacht, verlassen dich beid',*
> *und gehen dem Herren zu sagen,*
> *wie du sie getragen.*[23]

It all turns on that 'how', which is more important than anything that happens to you from outside. It allays all the anxieties about the future which sometimes torment us. Thank you again very much for remembering me every day, and for all that you are doing and putting up with on my account. My best wishes to the family and friends. Tell Renate to have a really happy wedding with no sad thoughts, and to rest assured that even here I can join in all her happiness. I'm allowed to send the next letter on the 15th, so I shall be writing on the day before the wedding.

By the way, if I'm here on Wednesday, I will give you the dirty washing straight away, otherwise it has to wait here a whole week. I always have to be present when your parcel is unpacked.

I hope that every worry will soon be removed from you and all of us. With all my heart,   your grateful Dietrich

I've just heard that one of my sisters has been here with the parcel. Once again, many thanks. I see from the contents that my letter of the 25th has still not reached you; I'm very sorry for your sakes. But probably it often takes a long time. Write often! The cigars seem to come from Stettin.[24] Many thanks.

To Hans von Dohnanyi   [Tegel] 5 April 1943[25]

My dear Hans,
Your letter so surprised, delighted and moved me that I could not refrain, at the very least, from attempting to reply to it. Whether

this letter reaches you does not lie within my power; but I hope it fervently. For you must know that there is not even an atom of reproach or bitterness in me about what has befallen the two of us. Such things come from God and from him alone, and I know that I am one with you and Christel in believing that before him there can only be subjection, perseverance, patience – and gratitude. So every question 'Why?' falls silent, because it has found its answer. Until recently, until father's seventy-fifth birthday, we have been able to enjoy so many good things together that it would be almost presumptuous were we not also ready to accept hardship quietly, bravely – and also really gratefully. I know that it is more difficult for you because of Christel and the children; but I know Christel well enough to be troubled only for a moment over her inner disposition; her one wish will be that you do not worry about her. I now want you to know – not to burden you, but simply to delight you and to enable you to share my joy – that since January I have been engaged to Maria von Wedemeyer. Because of the deaths of her father and brother, it was not to be mentioned until the summer, and I was only to tell my parents. It's a severe trial for Maria, but mother writes that she is brave, cheerful and confident, so that is a very great encouragement to me. I am convinced that this experience is good for the two of us, even if it is still so incomprehensible. So rejoice with me!

I'm reading, learning and working a great deal – and systematically – and have a quiet time in the morning and the evening to think of all the many people, at home and in the field, whom one would and should commend each day to God. I need not say that now you and Christel have a special place among them. No, you must not and need not worry about us at all; another has now taken this worry from you. What we cannot do, we must now simply let go of and limit ourselves to what we can and should do, that is, be manly and strong in trust in God in the midst of our suffering. I expect you know that song by Hugo Wolf:

> *Über Nacht, über Nacht kommt Freud und Leid*
> *und eh' du's gedacht, verlassen dich beid',*
> *und gehen dem Herren zu sagen,*
> *wie du sie getragen.*

Keep well and in good spirits. I think with gratitude of the many good hours with you at home, making music, walking, enjoying the garden, playing and talking. The children are in good hands with their grandparents and they are old enough to know what sort of behaviour they owe themselves and you.

God bless you. I think of you faithfully each day.

Your Dietrich

Notes

I [26]

Separation from people   8 May 1943
        from work
        from the past
        from the future
        from marriage
        from God

Different mental attitudes towards the past . . . *forgetting*, . . . caesuras. Experiences
Fulfilled or unfulfilled according to *history*

self-deception, idealizing of the past and of the present. Realism instead of illusion
Overcoming memories!
        selfpity
Amusement – passing the time
        for the one who has overcome, humour

Smoke in the emptiness of time
Memory for what is possible, although incorrect

—

The significance of illusion

—

Experience of the past – preservation, thanks, regret
Consciousness of time   not just the *results*
                           present
                           and therefore past?
Novalis   *Possessions*   Gen. 3, Eccles. 3
                                           Rev. 10   Matt. 6
                                           Saying of the month and
                                               Ps. 31.16

In expectations (youth) slowly – uphill, but then falls away quickly

old woman lets time glide by   What is freedom?
peacefully, similarly in great danger Formal love
. . . composure   On freedom
                                    in prison
Waiting – but e.g. quite composed for *death*
Time of *day* – peasant, but not 'the' time
Experience of time as experience of *separation* – engaged couple
                                                      from God
Past   Why all over in 100 years and not:
until recently was everything good?   No *possession* which
outlasts time, no *task*

—

Flight before the experience of time in dreams, terror on awakening
here in the dream past = future, timeless
Teeth of time – the gnawing of time
healing time – scarring [illegible]
Emptiness of time despite all that fills it. 'Filled' time very different
                                                      Love

II [27]

Saying of the month[28] – time as help – as torment, as enemy.
                    Boredom as an expression of despair.

Ps. 31.16[29]
Time

34

Beneficence of time: forgetting, healing
Separation – from past and future
>'he is not strong who is not firm in need'

Waiting
Boredom
Fortune   Prov. 31. 'laughs at the day to come'[30]
Work   Matt. 6 take no thought . . .
      What still determines the present, is uppermost
      in the memory, is short for . . . whereas
      an event lying equally far away can be infi-
      nitely far

Continuity with past and future interrupted

—

Dissatisfaction
Tension
Impatience
Longing
Boredom
sick – profoundly alone
Indifference
Urge to do something, change, novelty
Being blunted, tiredness, sleep – on the other hand [illegible]
Order
Fantasy, distortion of past and future
Suicide, not because of consciousness of guilt but because basically
I am already dead, draw a line,
Summing up
Is the memory better for joyful impressions? Why is that? A past
grief stands under the sign of its being *overcome*, only griefs that
have not been overcome (unforgiven sin) are always fresh and
tormenting to the memory.

Overcoming in *prayer*

From his father to the Judge Advocate of the War Court
[Charlottenburg] 9 May 1943

To the Judge Advocate of the War Court

In the preliminary enquiry against my son Dietrich Bonhoeffer I asked for permission to visit on 17 April 1943. My request was refused by the Judge Advocate of the War Court on 20 April (StPL RKA III 114/43). I repeat this request for my wife and myself since my son has now been under investigation for five weeks. I would point out that for more than thirty years I have been a member of the Senate concerned with sanitary measures within the army. I believe that I can claim to be trustworthy enough to keep within the bounds of the regulations that are in force during a visit to my son. I can say the same of my wife.

Karl Bonhoeffer

From the Judge Advocate of the War Court to his father

The Judge Advocate of the War Court   Berlin-Charlottenburg 5,
StPL (RKA) III 114/43   Witzlebenstrasse 4–10
                                                             10 May 1943
                                                   Telephone: 30 06 81
To
Professor Dr Bonhoeffer

For the present you and your wife cannot yet be granted permission to visit as the investigations do not make this seem expedient.

Drafted:
Signature   By order
Army Inspector of Justice   signed   Dr Roeder

My dear Dietrich,

. . . On Saturday it's the wedding, and we intend to celebrate it happily in accordance with your express wishes. You are right; if a heart is rightly disposed, sorrow and joy must have a place in it. The evening before, Bärbel will bring the garland of roses and little Christine will be the *Märkerin* and bring salt and bread. All the young people will sing them that beautiful old folk-song of Simon Dachs', 'Aennchen of Tharau'. Dorothee will bring the garland of myrtle. I expect that there will be some chamber music, too.

We're only getting together after the supper. The wedding, I mean the betrothal, is at 2.30, followed by a simple meal at the Schleichers. For this, Ursel has cleared out Christine's room, decorated it with some pictures from your room and laid the table. It's amazing how many things have a place side by side in heart and senses . . .

God bless you.   Your Mother

From Karl-Friedrich Bonhoeffer   [Leipzig] 15 May 1943

Dear Dietrich,

Your letters from prison are always a great joy to us. We longingly wait until the ten days are up and you can write to us again; or rather, we quietly hope that the next letter will be overtaken by your own reappearance. For it is gradually getting time for you to be let out.

I've learnt from your letters that you are secretly engaged. You cannot imagine how much that delighted me. I'm in principle sorry for any unmarried man, ridiculous though this confession may seem. But your case, in my view, was a very special one. You are not one of those who are by nature destined to be a bachelor, and precisely in the difficulties which your calling brings with it today, you need a good, wise and competent wife. Ursel has since told me many nice things about your young fiancée, and the parents, who probably knew of it beforehand, are also very pleased about her. So I hope that I too will soon have an opportunity to get to know her. Thinking of your fiancée, though, your present situation must be particularly irksome, and I'm really amazed at the equanimity with which you accept it as misfortune without any reproaches.

Today it's the wedding at the Schleichers, and at your wish it has become a real feast. Hans-Walter, whom we had here in the house recently for a couple of hours on his way through, tanned and looking well fed, is coming on leave. I'm very pleased about that for Ursel's sake. All is well with us. Keep as well as you can and make sure that you come out soon, so that you aren't cheated of the whole of this wonderful spring.

Many greetings from us all.

Your Karl-Friedrich

To his parents   [Tegel] 15 May 1943

Dear parents,

By the time you get this letter, all the final preparations and the wedding itself will be over, as will my own bit of longing to be there myself . . . I'm looking back today in gratitude for the happy times that we have had, and am happy about them all. I'm anxious to hear what the text of the sermon was; the best I can think of is Romans 15.7;[31] I've often used it myself. What splendid summer weather they're having; I expect this morning's hymn was Paul Gerhardt's 'The golden sun'. After a lengthy interval, I received your letter of the 9th very quickly, on 11 May. Many thanks for it. Anyone for whom the parental home has become so much a part of himself as it has for me feels specially grateful for any message from home. If only we could see each other or talk together for a short time, what a great relief it would be.

Of course, people outside find it difficult to imagine what prison life is like. The situation in itself – that is each single moment – is perhaps not so very different here from anywhere else; I read, meditate, write, pace up and down my cell – without rubbing myself sore against the walls like a polar bear. The great thing is to stick to what one still has and can do – there is still plenty left – and not to be dominated by the thought of what one cannot do, and by feelings of resentment and discontent. I'm sure I never realized as clearly as I do here what the Bible and Luther mean by 'temptation'. Quite suddenly, and for no apparent physical or psychological reason, the peace and composure that were supporting one are jarred, and the heart becomes, in Jeremiah's expressive phrase, 'deceitful above all things, and desperately corrupt; who can understand it?' It feels like an invasion from outside, as if by evil powers trying to rob one of what is most vital. But no doubt these experiences are good and necessary, as they teach one to understand human life better.

I'm now trying my hand at a little study on 'The feeling of time', a thing that is specially relevant to anyone who is being held for examination. One of my predecessors here has scribbled over the cell door, 'In 100 years it will all be over.' That was his way of trying to counter the feeling that life spent here is a blank; but there is a great deal that might be said about that, and I should like to talk it over with father. 'My time is in your hands' (Ps. 31) is the Bible's answer. But in the Bible there is also the question that threatens to dominate everything here: 'How long, O Lord?' (Ps. 13).

Things continue to go well with me, and I must be grateful for the past six weeks. I'm particularly pleased that Maria's mother has been with you. Is there any news yet of Konstantin in Tunisia?[32] That's going through my head a great deal as I think of Maria and the family. If only it isn't too long before I see Maria again and we can get married! We need a cease-fire really soon; there are all sorts of other earthly wishes that one has.

The parcel of laundry has just been brought again. You've no idea what a joy and strength even this indirect link is. Many thanks, and please thank Susi very specially for all the help that she is giving you now. I'm also very pleased that you have got the asthma sweets again; they are most acceptable. I've already made myself a mirror here. I would be grateful for some ink, stain

39

remover, laxative, two pairs of short underpants, a cellular shirt and the repaired shoes, collar studs. Once the sun has burnt itself into the thick walls it certainly becomes very hot, but so far it is still very pleasant. I hope that father has not given up smoking altogether by now in my favour! Also, many thanks for the Jeremias Gotthelf. In a fortnight I would very much like his *Uli der Knecht*. Renate has it. By the way, you really ought to read his *Berner Geist*, and if not the whole of it, at least the first part; it is something out of the ordinary, and it will certainly interest you. I remember how old Schöne[33] always had a special word of praise for Gotthelf, and I should like to suggest to the Diederich Press that they bring out a Gotthelf day-book. Stifter's background, too, is mainly Christian; his woodland scenes often make me long to be back again in the quiet glades of Friedrichsbrunn. He is not so forceful as Gotthelf, but he is wonderfully clear and simple, and that gives me a great deal of pleasure. If only we could talk to each other about these things. For all my sympathy with the contemplative life, I am not a born Trappist. Nevertheless, a period of enforced silence may be a good thing, and the Roman Catholics say that the most effective expositions of scripture come from the purely contemplative orders. I am reading the Bible straight through from cover to cover, and have just got as far as Job, which I am particularly fond of. I read the Psalms every day, as I have done for years; I know them and love them more than any other book. I cannot now read Psalms 3, 47, 70, and others without hearing them in the settings by Heinrich Schütz. It was Renate[34] who introduced me to his music, and I count it one of the greatest enrichments of my life.

Many congratulations to Ursel on her birthday; I think of her a lot. Greetings to all the family and friends and especially to the young couple. I hope Maria will come to you soon. I feel myself so much a part of you all that I know that we live and bear everything in common, acting and thinking for one another, even though we have to be separated. Thank you for all your love and concern and loyalty day by day and hour by hour.

Your Dietrich

A Wedding Sermon from a Prison Cell

May 1943

Eph. 1.12: '*We who . . . have been destined and appointed to live for the praise of his glory.*'

It is right and proper for a bride and bridegroom to welcome and celebrate their wedding day with a unique sense of triumph. When all the difficulties, obstacles, hindrances, doubts, and misgivings have been, not made light of, but honestly faced and overcome – and it is certainly better not to take everything for granted – then both parties have indeed achieved the most important triumph of their lives. With the 'Yes' that they have said to each other, they have by their free choice given a new direction to their lives; they have cheerfully and confidently defied all the uncertainties and hesitations with which, as they know, a lifelong partnership between two people is faced; and by their own free and responsible action they have conquered a new land to live in. Every wedding must be an occasion of joy that human beings can do such great things, that they have been given such immense freedom and power to take the helm in their life's journey. The children of the earth are rightly proud of being allowed to take a hand in shaping their own destinies, and something of this pride must contribute to the happiness of a bride and bridegroom. We ought not to be in too much of a hurry here to speak piously of God's will and guidance. It is obvious, and it should not be ignored, that it is your own very human wills that are at work here, celebrating their triumph; the course that you are taking at the outset is one that you have chosen for yourselves; what you have done and are doing is not, in the first place, something religious, but something quite secular. So you yourselves, and you alone, bear the responsibility for what no one can take from you; or, to put it more exactly, you, Eberhard, have all the responsibility for the success of your venture, with all the happiness that such responsibility

41

involves, and you, Renate, will help your husband and make it easy for him to bear that responsibility, and find your happiness in that. Unless you can boldly say today: 'That is *our* resolve, *our* love, *our* way', you are taking refuge in a false piety. 'Iron and steel may pass away, but *our* love shall abide for ever.' That desire for earthly bliss, which you want to find in one another, and in which, to quote the medieval song, one is the comfort of the other both in body and in soul – that desire is justified before God and man.

Certainly you two, of all people, have every reason to look back with special thankfulness on your lives up to now. The beautiful things and the joys of life have been showered on you, you have succeeded in everything, and you have been surrounded by love and friendship. Your ways have, for the most part, been smoothed before you took them, and you have always been able to count on the support of your families and friends. Everyone has wished you well, and now it has been given to you to find each other and to reach the goal of your desires. You yourselves know that no one can create and assume such a life from his own strength, but that what is given to one is withheld from another; and that is what we call God's guidance. So today, however much you rejoice that you have reached your goal, you will be just as thankful that God's will and God's way have brought you here; and however confidently you accept responsibility for your action today, you may and will put it today with equal confidence into God's hands.

As God today adds his 'Yes' to your 'Yes', as he confirms your will with his will, and as he allows you, and approves of, your triumph and rejoicing and pride, he makes you at the same time instruments of his will and purpose both for yourselves and for others. In his unfathomable condescension God does add his 'Yes' to yours; but by doing so, he creates out of your love something quite new – the holy estate of matrimony.

God is guiding your marriage. Marriage is more than your love for each other. It has a higher dignity and power, for it is God's holy ordinance, through which he wills to perpetuate the human race till the end of time. In your love you see only your two selves in the world, but in marriage you are a link in the chain of the generations, which God causes to come and to pass away to his glory, and calls into his kingdom. In your love you see only the heaven of your own happiness, but in marriage you are placed at a post of responsibility towards the world and mankind. Your love is your own private possession, but marriage is more than something personal – it is a status, an office. Just as it is the crown, and not merely the will to rule, that makes the king, so it is marriage, and not merely your love for each other, that joins you together in the sight of God and man. As you first gave the ring to one another and have now received it a second time from the hand of the pastor, so love comes from you, but marriage from above, from God. As high as God is above man, so high are the sanctity, the rights, and the promise of marriage above the sanctity, the rights, and the promise of love. It is not your love that sustains the marriage, but from now on, the marriage that sustains your love.

God makes your marriage indissoluble. 'What therefore God has joined together, let no man put asunder' (Matt. 19.6). God joins you together in marriage; it is his act, not yours. Do not confound your love for one another with God. God makes your marriage indissoluble, and protects it from every danger that may threaten it from within and without; he wills to be the guarantor of its indissolubility. It is a blessed thing to know that no power on earth, no temptation, no human frailty can dissolve what God holds together; indeed, anyone who knows that may say confidently: What God has joined together, *can* no man put asunder. Free from all the anxiety that is always a characteristic of love, you can now say to each other with complete and confident assurance: We can never lose each other now; by the will of God we belong to each other till death.

God establishes a rule of life by which you can live together in wedlock. 'Wives, be subject to your husbands, as is fitting in the Lord. Husbands, love your wives' (Col. 3[18, 19]). With your marriage you are founding a home. That needs a rule of life, and this rule of life is so important that God establishes it himself, because without it everything would get out of joint. You may order your home as you like, except in one thing: the wife is to be subject to her husband, and the husband is to love his wife. In this way God gives to husband and wife the honour that is due to each. The wife's honour is to serve the husband, to be a 'help meet for him', as the creation story has it [Gen. 2.18]; and the husband's honour is to love his wife with all his heart. He will 'leave his father and mother and be joined to his wife' [Matt. 19.5], and will 'love her as his own flesh'. A wife who wants to dominate her husband dishonours herself and him, just as a husband who does not love his wife as he should dishonours himself and her; and both dishonour the glory of God that is meant to rest on the estate of matrimony. It is an unhealthy state of affairs when the wife's ambition is to be like the husband, and the husband regards the wife merely as the plaything of his own lust for power and licence; and it is a sign of social disintegration when the wife's service is felt to be degrading or beneath her dignity, and when the husband who is faithful to his wife is looked on as a weakling or even a fool.

The place where God has put the wife is the husband's home. Most people have forgotten nowadays what a home can mean, though some of us have come to realize it as never before. It is a kingdom of its own in the midst of the world, a stronghold amid life's storms and stresses, a refuge, even a sanctuary. It is not founded on the shifting sands of outward or public life, but it has its peace in God, for it is God who gives it its special meaning and value, its own nature and privilege, its own destiny and dignity. It is an ordinance of God in the world, the place in which – whatever may happen in the world – peace, quietness, joy, love, purity, discipline, respect, obedience, tradition, and, with it all, happiness may dwell. It is the wife's calling, and her happiness, to build up for her husband this world within the world, and to do her life's work there. How happy she is if she realizes how great and rich a task and destiny she has. Not novelty, but permanence; not change, but constancy; not noisiness, but peace; not words, but deeds; not commands, but persuasion; not desire, but possession – and all these things inspired and sustained by her love for her husband –, that is the wife's kingdom. In the Book of Proverbs we read [31.11 ff.]: 'The heart of her husband trusts in her, and he will have no lack of gain. She does him good, and not harm, all the days of her life. She seeks wool and flax, and works with willing hands. . . . She rises while it is yet night and provides food for her household and tasks for her maidens. . . . She opens her hand to the poor, and reaches out her hands to the needy . . . Strength and dignity are her clothing, and she laughs at the time to come . . . Her children rise up and call her blessed; her husband also, and he praises her . . . Many women have done excellently, but you surpass them all.' Again and again the Bible praises, as the supreme earthly happiness, the fortune of a man who finds a true, or as the Bible puts it, a 'virtuous' or 'wise' woman. 'She is far more precious than jewels' [Prov. 31.10]. 'A virtuous woman is the crown of her husband' [Prov. 12.4]. But the Bible speaks just as frankly of the mischief that a perverse, 'foolish' woman brings on her husband and her home.

Now when the husband is called 'the head of the wife', and it goes on to say 'as Christ is the head of the church' [Eph. 5.23], something of the divine splendour is reflected in our earthly relationships, and this reflection we should recognize and honour. The dignity that is here ascribed to the man lies, not in any capacities or qualities of his own, but in the office conferred on him by his marriage. The wife should see her husband clothed in this dignity. But for him it is a supreme responsibility. As the head, it is he who is responsible for his wife, for their marriage, and for their home. On him falls the care and protection of the family; he represents it to the outside world; he is its mainstay and comfort; he is the master of the house, who exhorts, punishes, helps, and comforts, and stands for it before God. It is a good thing, for it is a divine ordinance when the wife honours the husband for his office's sake, and when the husband properly performs the duties of his office. The husband and wife who acknowledge and observe God's ordinance are 'wise', but those who think to replace it by another of their own devising are 'foolish'.

God has laid on marriage a blessing and a burden. The blessing is the promise of children. God allows man to share in his continual work of creation; but it is always God himself who blesses marriage with children. 'Children are a heritage from the Lord' (Ps. 127.3), and they should be acknowledged as such. It is from God that parents receive their children, and it is to God that they should lead them. Parents therefore have divine authority in respect of their children. Luther speaks of the 'golden chain' with which God invests parents; and scripture adds to the fifth commandment the special promise of long life on earth. Since men live on earth, God has given them a lasting reminder that this earth stands under the curse of sin and is not itself the ultimate reality. Over the destiny of woman and of man lies the dark shadow of a word of God's wrath, a burden from God, which they must carry. The woman must bear her children in pain, and in providing for his family the man must reap many thorns and thistles, and labour in the sweat of his brow. This burden should cause both man and wife to call on God, and should remind them of their eternal destiny in his kingdom. Earthly society is only the beginning of the heavenly society, the earthly home an image of the heavenly home, the earthly family a symbol of the fatherhood of God over all men, for they are his children.

God gives you Christ as the foundation of your marriage. 'Welcome one another, therefore, as Christ has welcomed you, for the glory of God' (Rom. 15[7]). In a word, live together in the forgiveness of your sins, for without it no human fellowship, least of all a marriage, can survive. Don't insist on your rights, don't blame each other, don't judge or condemn each other, don't find fault with each other, but accept each other as you are, and forgive each other every day from the bottom of your hearts.

Your home will be a pastor's home. From it, light and strength will have to go out into many other homes. The pastor undertakes a life of special discipline. The husband must bear alone much that belongs to his ministry, since the ministry is his and must, for the sake of God, be a silent one. So his love for his wife must be all the greater, and he must be all the more concerned to share with her what he may. And as a result the wife will be able to lighten the husband's burden all the more, stand by his side, give him help. As fallible human beings, how can they live and work in Christ's community if they do not persevere in constant prayer and forgiveness, if they do not help each other to live as Christians? The right beginning and daily practice are very important indeed.

From the first day of your wedding till the last the rule must be: 'Welcome one another . . . for the glory of God'.

That is God's word for your marriage. Thank him for it; thank him for leading you thus far; ask him to establish your marriage, to confirm it, sanctify it, and preserve it. So your marriage will be 'for the praise of his glory'. Amen.

From Susanne Dress   [Dahlem] 15 May 1943

Dear Dietrich,

Every week, when I leave the things outside for you at Tegel, I am always pleased to hear that you are well and almost have the feeling that I have visited you. Simply being near to you matters a great deal, even though one is continually aware with gratitude how little outward separation has to do with inward togetherness. Today we've been celebrating Renate's wedding; the twenty years since Ursel and Rüdiger were married has passed very quickly. Tine[35] is now as old as I was then. So the bridesmaids were very young. Michael and Cornelie bore the train, Andreas and Walter[36] scattered flowers. The three brothers and sisters of Eberhard were all there, and Hans-Walter had leave . . .

We have window-panes and shutters again; now the painter has to come. The last alert was very peaceful here, and went very quickly. By the time I had the children down below, the worst shooting was over . . .

With much love from   your Suse

From Karl-Friedrich Bonhoeffer   Leipzig, 30 May 1943

Dear Dietrich,

A week ago today I was in Berlin, on my way through to Hamburg, where I had work to do. I managed things particularly well, as this was the very day on which your fiancée and her mother had planned to visit the parents; so I got to know her earlier than I had expected. It must be very remarkable for you that she is now being introduced to the family without your being there. These are rather crazy times. As you can imagine, we all liked her very much. She had a great deal to say about what she was doing in Hanover. Apparently she is one of those people who look round for the hardest and most strenuous service and take no consideration for themselves at all. Her self-assurance and modesty in this made a great impression on me. I was very cross with her for saving her week's ration of butter for you and for not keeping the few coffee beans which she had been given by a patient for her nights of duty. I think that I acted as you would have done. Her mother also seems to be a special woman. I accompanied her a little way into town and we talked a bit about the two families on the way. At any rate, now that I know the circle into which you are to move, I can once again give you special congratulations. By the way, as far as I can see, no one outside the family knows yet.

But how are you? Are you getting used to it? One cannot imagine it all if one has not experienced it – and once you are outside, you will probably soon forget again what it was like. Did you freeze over the last few weeks? It was quite cold in the rooms, if one could not move about. I hope that this really is the last letter that I shall have to write to you in prison. So far we have not said anything about it to the children. I think that they feel it rather comic that I now have biscuits baked and sweets made for my journeys to Berlin.

Much love from Grete[37] and myself.

Your Karl-Friedrich

To his parents   [Tegel] Ascension Day, 4 June 1943

Dear parents,
I had just written you a long letter when the post brought the letters from Maria and her mother and with them a quite indescribable joy into my cell. Now I must begin the letter all over again and ask you above all to write to both of them and thank

them straight away. You can imagine how frustrated I feel not to be able to do that myself.[38] Maria writes so happily about her day with you. How hard it must be despite all the love you have shown her; it is a wonder how she bears up under it all – and for me an incomparable example and a piece of good fortune. The feeling that I cannot do anything to help her would often be unbearable did I not know that I can really have a quiet mind about her. For her sake much more than for mine, I do hope that this hard time does not last too long. But I'm certain and therefore grateful that one day these very months will be supremely important for our marriage. I can hardly say how moved I was by the letter from Maria's mother. Since the first day of my imprisonment I have been tormented that I have had to add one more trouble to all the grief of the past year; now she has made this very affliction that has come upon us the occasion for shortening the time of waiting and thus making me happy. I am really very shamed by this great confidence, this graciousness and generosity. I'm so grateful, and will never forget her for what she has done. This is the fundamental attitude that I have always detected in all the households of this family, and it moved me a great deal long before I suspected anything of my future good fortune. Now I know from your and Karl-Friedrich's letters that you, too, are fond of Maria; but that could hardly be otherwise. She will be a very good daughter-in-law to you, and will surely soon feel as at home in our family as I have for years in her own. I'm very pleased that Karl-Friedrich accompanied Maria's mother into town and so got to know her a bit; and it was very nice of him to tell Maria off for me about stinting herself on her rations – she really needs them herself with all her hard work.

Thank you very much for your letters. They are always too short for *me*, but of course I understand! It is as though the prison gates were opened for a moment, and I could share a little of your life outside. Joy is a thing that we want very badly in this solemn building, where one never hears a laugh – it seems to get even the warders down – and we exhaust all our reserves of it from within and without.

Today is Ascension Day, and that means that it is a day of great joy for all who can believe that Christ rules the world and our lives. My thoughts go out to all of you, to the church and its services, from which I have now been separated for so long, and also to the many unknown people in this building who are bearing their fate in silence. I repeatedly find that these and other thoughts keep me from taking my own little hardships too seriously; that would be very wrong and ungrateful.

I've just written a little more about 'The feeling of time'; I'm very much enjoying it, and when we write from personal experience, we can write more fluently and freely. Thank you very much, father, for Kant's *Anthropologie*, which I've read through; I didn't know it. There was a great deal that was interesting in it, but it has a very rationalist rococo psychology, which simply ignores many essential phenomena. Can you send me something good about forms and functions of memory? It's a thing that interests me very much in this connection. Kant's exposition of 'smoking' as a means of entertaining oneself is very nice.

I'm very glad that you are now reading Gotthelf; I'm sure you would like his *Wanderungen* – just as much. I think Susi has them. For serious reading I have been very glad to read here Ulhorn's great *History of Christian Philanthropy*; Holl's *Church History* reminds me of his seminars.

I read some of Stifter almost every day. The intimate life of his characters – of course it is old-fashioned of him to describe only likable people – is very pleasant in this atmosphere here, and makes one think of the things that really matter in life. Prison life in general brings one back, both outwardly and inwardly, to the simplest things of life; that explains why I could not get on at all with Rilke. But I wonder whether one's understanding is not affected by the restrictive nature of life here?

Now it's Friday, and in the meantime your *wonderful* spring parcel has just come with the first produce of the garden. Once again, very many thanks to you and everyone who shared in it for this and for everything that has come beforehand. How long will you continue to be put to all this trouble and worry for me – who knows?

I would very much like Hoskyns, *The Riddle of the New Testa-*

ment, when it's convenient (over my bed), and some cotton wool; it's sometimes quite noisy at night.

These days I keep hoping for a letter from you. Always write everything that you know about Maria. It's good that Karl-Friedrich and the Schleichers were there recently; the Schleichers also know the older Bismarck sister,[39] and perhaps you still remember her brother Max, my confirmation candidate from Stettin, who was killed? Always send greetings to Maria's grandmother!

Hardly an hour passes when my thoughts do not stray from my books to all of you. To see each other again in freedom is an unimaginably splendid thought. Until then we must go on being patient and confident. I'm so sorry that you aren't travelling and can't get a holiday. Is everything all right with you? All is well with me; I'm better again, have enough to eat, sleep fairly well and time keeps passing more quickly. Love to all the family, the children and friends. With love and many thanks,   your Dietrich

From his parents   Charlottenburg, 8 June 1943

Dear Dietrich . . .
I get down to science less often than I would like; in the evening I sometimes read Gotthelf's *Berner Geist* to mother. Recently I've had an invitation to have a sound film made of myself for the 'Film Archive of Personalities' which has recently been instituted in the Ministry of Propaganda, to 'preserve a picture of me for later times'. I think that it will be enough if my picture is preserved in the family. Warmest greetings,   Father

Dear Dietrich,
I wanted to add a greeting too, so that you also have it at Whitsun. The festivals will be particularly hard to feel in your situation, I expect. I will write at length when your letter comes. We think of you so much and I write to you daily in my thoughts, but one must not overburden the censor. May you have a blessed Whitsun. With all my heart.   Your Mother

My dear boy,

. . . Another parcel is going off to you tomorrow; we fill it with all our love. Each one thinks about what he can contribute, even the little ones. So today there are the few sweets. They all ask after you so much: when *are* you coming back? We're so grateful that you're healthy. After Whitsun we're going to try again to see you at the Judge Advocate's, as we did last time. Perhaps it will be possible. We aren't really vexed in any way, but it really is taking Dr Röder too long. Anyway, I hope that it will be allowed. I wanted to send you Reuter's *Ut mine Stromtid*, but couldn't find it, so I'm now sending the *Festungstid* . . .

I long to hug you.   Your Mother

From Karl-Friedrich Bonhoeffer   [Leipzig] 12 June 1943

Dear Dietrich,

. . . What is one to tell you? Perhaps that despite everything we have plans for the summer and I have booked Grete and the children into Templeburg again for three weeks . . . Perhaps I shall go walking for a couple of days, if that is still possible with the billeting and does not use up too many calories. One cannot run up a great appetite . . .

A small volume of Gerhard Ritter, *Weltwirkung der Reformation* (1942), has just come to hand; I've read it with great interest and have also read parts of it to Grete in the evenings. Next time I am in Berlin, I will try to find out whether you already know it, and then put it in the parcel; also perhaps a collection of articles on modern physics, or rather natural philosophy, which has just appeared. I must read the latter rather better, though, to be able to judge whether you will get anything out of it. Christoph recently ended a letter to Hans with the phrase, 'Here's to a speedy reunion'. To the same intent we both send best greetings and our love.

Your Karl-Friedrich

Dear parents,
Well, Whitsuntide is here, and we are still separated; but it is in a
special way a feast of fellowship. When the bells rang this morning, I longed to go to church, but instead I did as John did on the
island of Patmos, and had such a splendid service of my own, that
I did not feel lonely at all, for you were all with me, every one of
you, and so were the congregations in whose company I have kept
Whitsuntide. Every hour or so since yesterday evening I've been
repeating to my own comfort Paul Gerhardt's Whitsun hymn
with the lovely lines 'Thou art a Spirit of joy' and 'Grant us joy-
fulness and strength', and besides that, the words 'If you faint in
the day of adversity, your strength is small' (Prov. 24), and 'God
did not give us a spirit of timidity but a spirit of power and love
and self-control' (II Tim. 1). I have also been considering again the
strange story of the gift of tongues. That the confusion of tongues
at the Tower of Babel, as a result of which people can no longer
understand each other, because everyone speaks a different language, should at last be brought to an end and overcome by the
language of God, which everyone understands and through which
alone people can understand each other again, and that the church
should be the place where that happens – these are great momen-
tous thoughts. Leibniz grappled all his life with the idea of a
universal script consisting, not of words, but of self-evident signs
representing every possible idea. It was an expression of his wish
to heal the world, which was then so torn to pieces, a philosophical
reflection on the Pentecost story.

Once again all is silent here; one hears nothing but the tramp of
the prisoners pacing up and down in their cells. How many comfortless and un-Whitsun-like thoughts there must be in their
minds! If I were prison chaplain here, I should spend the whole
time from morning till night on days like this, going through the
cells; a good deal would happen.

Once again, many thanks for the letters from you, Karl-
Friedrich and Ursel. You're all waiting, just as I am, and I must
admit that in some part or other of my subconscious mind I had

53

been hoping to be out of here by Whitsuntide, although I'm always deliberately telling myself not to envisage any particular date. It will be ten weeks tomorrow; as mere laymen we did not imagine that 'temporary' confinement would amount to this. But after all, it is a mistake to be as unsuspecting in legal matters as I am; it brings home to one what a different atmosphere the lawyer must live in from the theologian; but that is instructive too, and everything has its proper place. All we can do is to wait as patiently as may be, without getting bitter, and to trust that everyone is doing his best to clear things up as quickly as possible. Fritz Reuter puts it very well: 'No one's life flows on such an even course that it does not sometimes come up against a dam and whirl round and round, or that people never throw stones into the clear water. Something happens to everyone, and he must take care that the water stays clear, and that heaven and earth are reflected in it' – when you've said that, you've really said everything.

It was really an enormous delight that you were both below here the day before yesterday to deliver the Whitsun parcel. It's remarkable how knowing that you were near once again brought everything very close, home and all your life. Sometimes it seems so unreal and distant. Thank you very much, and also for the parcel, which again was extremely welcome. I was particularly pleased with the yellow food; it keeps so well.

Again I've had a marvellous letter from Maria. The poor girl has to keep on writing without getting a direct response from me. That must be hard, but I delight in every word about her and every small detail interests me because it makes it easier to share in what she is doing. I'm so grateful to her. In my bolder dreams I sometimes picture our future home. My study on 'The feeling of time' is practically finished; now I'm going to let it lie for a while and see what it looks like later.

It's Whit Monday, and I was just sitting down to a dinner of turnips and potatoes when your parcel that Renate brought as a Whitsuntide present arrived quite unexpectedly. I really cannot tell you what happiness such things give one. However certain I am of the spiritual bond between all of you and myself, the spirit always seems to want some visible token of this union of love and remembrance, and then material things become the vehicles of spiritual realities. I think this is analogous to the need felt in all religions for the visible appearance of the Spirit in the sacrament. Special thanks to Renate for this great delight; every day I wish her much joy in her marriage and in her work. It's splendid that they've got a piano; one of the specially fine moments of being free will be to make music with them again. I'm most grateful for anything that one can smoke.

Now let's hope very much that everything will soon be finished. Love to Maria and the family.

I'm always thinking of you in love and gratitude.

Your Dietrich

From his mother [Charlottenburg] 15 June 1943

Dear Dietrich,

. . . None of us can imagine how you could have got into such a position when you are so outspokenly law-abiding in your attitude. We just cannot find any solution to the riddle. So we keep returning to the comforting conviction that everything will soon have to be cleared up and that you will be with us again.

We're going to ask for another permission to visit today; we very much want to see you again and find out how you are bearing your long imprisonment, especially because of your asthma. I hope that we shall get the permission. We are quite old people, and the pressure on father in addition to his strenuous work is rather a considerable one. How could we ever have imagined the evening of our life, after so much work in the profession and in the family, in this way . . .[40]

This time I will bring you grandfather Hase's *Ideals and Errors*. I've asked grandmother for the book about the old Kleist-Retzow.

Now God bless you; we all send our love. You're always in my thoughts.

Your Mother

Outlines of Letters

[On his own exemption]

Please allow me to take up your time once again in this way, chiefly so that I shall really have done everything possible for a speedy clarification of my case. I would like to try once again to put my views on what seems to me to be the very important question of my exemption through the *Abwehr*. Perhaps I will succeed better, writing quietly, in stating matters clearly; in the interrogation I sometimes forget to say important things. I would also like to add a few points on this question which have not been discussed so far. Before I do that, I would like to tell you that I am grateful to you for describing the situation to me so openly in the last interrogation. The interlude with General Oster's remark for a while must have put me in a quite dreadful light as far as you were concerned, and I am glad that everything has now been sorted out. Perhaps there are other things that I do not know which still stand in the way of clarifying the proceedings over my release and burden me so much. I am the last person to want to dispute that in an activity as strange and new to me as *Abwehr* service, and as complicated, mistakes could creep in. You will therefore, your honour, understand that it is very important to clarify *whether* mistakes have really been made here, and if so, *who* has made them. It is not only a personal concern, but also involves my relatives and my profession.

In your words, there is a suspicion that my exemption was procured in order to extricate me from the Gestapo who, in September 1940, prohibited me from speaking in public and required me to report regularly. If I have understood you rightly, this would be supported by: 1. circumstances of time; 2. remarks of mine concerning Dibelius;[42] 3. remarks made by my brother-n-law. I would like to reply to these in turn.

First, a general comment: if I had been afraid that after the imposition of the prohibition against speaking and the requirement to report, the Gestapo would want to take still further measures against me, and if I had wanted to avoid them, then it would not have been exemption but call-up that would have been the appropriate course. But I had no reason at all to fear further measures by the Gestapo, *first* because the measures already taken against me seemed rather to have been part of a wider preventative action by the Gestapo against the whole of the Confessing Church – at that time about 6 prohibitions against speaking were issued almost simultaneously in quite different parts of the Old Prussian Church with exactly the same reasons. I could not imagine that they were directed against me personally; the Gestapo have not confronted me with a single 'disruptive' sermon or lecture. *Secondly*, to avoid all further conflict, I had withdrawn to the mountains of Bavaria, to write a large academic work. I had also reported this to the Gestapo, as I was obliged, and really had nothing more to fear in that regard. On the church side, it had been reported to me that there was some interest in the fact that I was following my book *The Cost of Discipleship* with an account of a 'concrete evangelical ethics', and previously I had worked predominantly as an academic theologian; as a result, I could also satisfy the church with my activity at that time. Of course, I felt the prohibition against preaching and lecturing to be very hard, but after the rejection of my application I could not reckon with a lifting of the prohibition for the time being, and in fact that has not happened even now. So since that time my activity in the church has been limited to the above-mentioned academic work, and I have kept strictly to the terms of the prohibition against my speaking in public. At that time I resolved to transport my whole library to Munich and to take up permanent residence there, but with the uncertainty over the duration of the war and the time of my call-up I kept putting off the very costly and difficult execution of this decision. It was my brother-in-law who offered me the possibility of using my church contacts in the *Abwehr*. Despite considerable inner hesitations, I took advantage of it because it gave me the chance of making a contribution to the war that I had sought since its outbreak, and did so in my status of theologian. I have kept saying that I would have much preferred to work as an army chaplain, but in the meantime that has not proved possible. A view that I have reached over the years in my activity in German congregations abroad is that for a great many people the church is the last and firmest support for Germany and that for these reasons the church has a quite decisive part to play in the field and at home, even in wartime.

On 1.   I do not dispute that the fact that my exemption for the *Abwehr* followed a few months after the prohibition against speaking was a great inner relief to me. I saw it as a welcome opportunity to rehabilitate myself in the face of the state authorities, which was very opportune, in view of the damaging charge that had been made against me and that I considered to be quite unjustified. The awareness that I was being used by a military department was, therefore, of great personal significance to me. I made a great personal sacrifice for this possibility of rehabilitation and for my activity in the service of the nation, namely surrendering all my ecumenical contacts for military purposes. I also believe that this thought of rehabilitation also played some part with my brother-in-law. He knows me well enough personally to be aware that the political charge bore no relation to my whole inner attitude; he also knows how much suffering it caused me. Though, as he has said recently, our good personal relationship was quite emphatically based on the view that service questions and personal questions had to be kept quite separate; that sometimes verged on the pedantic.

The fact that, as you said, my age group was called up in Schlawe[43] in autumn 1940 was and is unknown to me; presumably it happened after my stay there in September 1940; I think it quite improbable that my brother-in-law and General Oster had known about it. But it surprises me in that I know that a colleague in my age group from the Schlawe district, who was a sergeant and liable for call-up, continued to work in his community until 1941. It may be that the chief of the conscription department there had considerable understanding of the task of the church at home and postponed the call-up of this colleague further at the request of the superintendent. Perhaps I might also add that if I had really been concerned simply to be exempted for church work, this could certainly have been arranged at that time in Schlawe at the request of the superintendent.[44] In January 1941, however, I received exemption not for church work, but expressly for service in the *Abwehr*, and if external technical hitches had not kept happening at the last moment, I would have been almost uninterruptedly on *Abwehr* journeys and would hardly have had any more time for my academic church work. I could not personally think of any reason for objections to my exemption for the *Abwehr*, as it was expressly confirmed to me that Admiral Canaris had wished and commanded this. When I occasionally asked whether my record with the Gestapo might not cause difficulties for the *Abwehr*, I was told [crossed out: we work with enemies, Communists, Jews, why not also with the Confessing Church] that these things were nothing to do with military purposes, and besides, the *Abwehr* worked with all kinds of people who were useful to them. This set my mind fully at rest.

On 2. Over the last years it has always been difficult for me to give any information about my present activity when meeting colleagues, and for that very reason I have largely avoided them, as my family and my colleagues can themselves testify. Where people have known and asked me about my relationship with my brother-in-law, e.g. General Superintendent Dibelius, Superintendent Diestel, I have always said to them – as arranged with my brother-in-law – that I was in the service of the OKW[45] in Munich and abroad. These were church matters, as the OKW was interested in ecumenical questions. Even Dibelius could not *know* that I was in the service of the military *Abwehr*, but could only guess it; I have deliberately never told him. Even before him I had to preserve the fiction that my work was predominantly concerned with the church, because – quite apart from the need for absolute secrecy – of the other pastors. This sort of thing could be talked about among them and do me personal damage. I therefore thought it important that my exemption should be looked upon in this way in church circles. That this put me and the military department concerned in a rather remarkable light could not be helped. Dibelius will therefore have meant his words in that sense.

On 3. Of course, I do not know what kind of remarks my

brother-in-law may have made about me to third parties. But I do know that e.g. he did not want Schm[idhuber][46] to learn anything about the military assignments that I received directly from the Admiral; he did not think very much of Schm.'s discretion. This went so far that his first reaction to the news that my name had come under suspicion in church circles in Switzerland was that Schm. had probably been indiscreet. But I think it quite possible that in Schm.'s case, Doh[nanyi] played his cards close to his chest. I myself have certainly often expressed my delight about the possibility given to me to foster ecumenical relations. It is in the end the same thing as when a student or a chemist is sent abroad, can do work that interests him there and at the same time has to fulfil particular military tasks.

Finally, a couple of personal remarks on the matter:

It certainly cannot have the force of proof for you – but perhaps you will believe me personally, and this is the hope in which I speak, that it is hard for me to see how earlier conflicts with the Gestapo, which, as I profoundly believe, have arisen from a purely church attitude, have now led to the point when I can be thought capable of such a severe failing in the obvious duties of a German towards his people and nation. I still cannot believe that this charge has really been made against me. If this had been my attitude, would I have found my fiancée in an old officers' family, all of whose fathers and sons have served as officers since the beginning of the war, some with the highest distinction, and have made the greatest sacrifices? My fiancée has lost both her father and her brother at the front. If that were the case, would I have cancelled all the engagements that I had made in America and have returned immediately upon the outbreak of war to Germany, where I had to expect to be called up straight away? Would I have offered myself as an army chaplain immediately after the outbreak of war? If anyone wants to learn something of my conception of the duty of Christian obedience towards the authorities, he should read my exposition of Romans 13 in my book *The Cost of Discipleship*. The appeal to subjection to the will and the demands of authority for the sake of Christian conscience has probably seldom been expressed more strongly than there. That is my personal attitude to these questions. I cannot judge how far such personal arguments have any legal significance, but I cannot imagine that one can simply pass over them.

[On Operation 7]   10 June 1943

Please permit me to add two further points which occurred to me after today's interrogation, when I was reflecting on the Friedenthal affair.[47] 1. As far as I know, the gentleman who carried on negotiations with Frl. Friedenthal was a Dr Arnold: my brother-in-law told me that on some later occasion. Moreover, as far as I know, my brother-in-law himself spoke to her. 2. Frl. Friedenthal looked me up briefly one day during the course of the summer and asked me whether I thought that she could legitimately undertake the task that she assumed would be assigned to her. At that time I answered in the affirmative.

[In the margin: She was speaking only of the fact and not the *content* of the task, of which I did not learn anything, even later.]

Please believe me that these two points really did occur to me afterwards. I often find it difficult to follow the tempo of your questioning, probably because I am not used to it, but I really have no interest in doing other than relating the whole matter as it took place. Ultimately I too am solely concerned with the earliest possible clarification. I very much hope that you will take these words from me.

Heil Hitler!

Yours faithfully,   Dietrich Bonhoeffer

[Further remarks on Operation 7]

The chief point concerns the date[48] of my conversation with my brother-in-law. Perhaps you remember from the interrogation that my first reaction to the question of date was, 'At any rate, it was a long time ago'; I then uncertainly mentioned spring 1942 and you immediately confirmed this, so I regarded this information as correct. Meanwhile it has become quite clear to me that this date, which seemed to me to be too near, must be completely wrong. I infer this from two things: my brother-in-law occasionally said to me that the carrying through of the whole action lasted more than a year. I further recall that during my long illness, i.e. in autumn 1941, my brother-in-law told me on the occasion of a visit to my room that the Friedenthal affair was now under way. Accordingly, the first discussion of this matter took place a considerable while back. I also now remember that Dr Schmidhuber was once concerned with the affair and that on one of his visits to Switzerland he asked Köchlin,[49] to whom he wanted to be introduced by me, about obtaining an entry visa for Frl. Fr.

How it came about I cannot recollect, despite all my efforts, and I simply cannot remember any more the situation in which the matter was discussed with Schm., whether it was discussed by myself or by my brother-in-law, whether in Berlin or Munich or by letter. I think that there are only two possibilities: either this request to Schm. arose in connection with the intentions of the military branch – in that case it may be that my brother-in-law rather than I spoke with Schm., or it went back to the fact that I had learnt that Frl. Friedenthal wanted to go abroad to relatives in Switzerland and that I thereupon discussed this question with Schm. But in the latter case, it seems very remarkable that I cannot remember having discussed the matter personally with Schm. At any rate, the two must have been very close together in time, and I think I can remember that since I was concerned with her case, Frl. Fr. had instructions from the *Abwehr* branch to be at their disposal. My brother-in-law would probably remember; I do not believe that at that time Schm. was already informed of the plans of the *Abwehr*, as the whole matter was handled very secretly. As I last saw Köchlin on my second visit to Switzerland in August 1941 and never talked about this matter with K., I in fact assume that Schm.'s journey took place after August 1941. But it would also be conceivable that by chance I never entered into conversation with K. on this matter. I later learnt in some way from Schm. that K. had made direct contact with Frl. Fr.

Anyway, in my recollections I feel that the case fits in well with the planned *Abwehr* action. Nor will I deny for a moment that in this whole affair a Christian and charitable element always played a part.

The reason why my recollections of the whole Friedenthal case are so inaccurate is probably that both K. and the *Abwehr* dealt directly with Frl.Fr., so that in both instances I served only once as a go-between, and that in an affair which was of very little concern to me, because, as I have said, I hardly knew Frl.Fr. personally. Besides, Frl.Fr. is to be regarded as a 'Non-Aryan' and not as a 'Jewess', as like Dr Arnold she never wore a star.

And now, your honour, I would like to put a question to you. I hope that you will excuse me for my complete lack of orientation in legal matters. I simply cannot understand why you allow me to persist, for example, in a mistake like that over the date of my discussion with my brother-in-law, which makes all my remarks inaccurate and unclear and is no help to anyone. The person being interrogated only finds himself in the painful position of having to make corrections afterwards, thus giving the impression that he had previously wanted to make a false statement. I am convinced that you have your reasons for this form of interrogation, but for anyone who has no intention of speaking untruths it is at any rate very disturbing and oppressive afterwards. It may sound like a feeble excuse, but you will know better than I from your experience that people's memories function very differently, and that some people simply need certain outward props to their memory to be able to reconstruct a situation accurately. Without these, everything escapes one and that is an extremely unpleasant position.

I regret having caused you trouble with this long letter, but I hope that I have now said really everything that I know about these matters.

As to your question about the extent to which my brother-in-law contributed to my journeys . . . I can with certainty remember only the following contributions: 1 sleeper supplement,

Berlin–Munich; 1 D train supplement, second class, Munich to Ettal; 1 journey Schlawe to Berlin, winter 39/40; 1 round trip Ettal–Munich–Ettal (Gürtner's funeral).

[On exemption for pastors of the Confessing Church][50]

Dear Judge Advocate,

I am really sorry to keep troubling you in this way, but I must not omit to tell you something that seems important to me, and so I ask you to be so kind as to excuse this demand on your time also. When you read to me yesterday parts of letters to my brother-in-law that I had long forgotten, I was at first tremendously shocked by the word 'threaten' in connection with Niesel's[51] call-up, and cannot understand how I could have come to use such an expression; I must concede that taken by itself it really does make a very unpleasant impression.

1. Had a man like Niesel had a church authority recognized and appointed by the state, it would certainly have declared him to be indispensable on church grounds alone.

2. Only a church that is inwardly strong in faith can fulfil its hard task to the homeland during a war, which consists in the summons to unswerving (?) trust in God, to strong inward resistance, to perseverance, to firm confidence and [indecipherable] personal pastoral care to Germans fighting in the homeland [indecipherable]. I intended it as a service to the German people in the war when I advocated a strong church – within the bounds of present possibilities. I believe that in this war, too, the German people to a large extent still desire the service of the church, and I see with fear and shame how feebly and weakly, on the whole, we are equipped, and how as a result our people have lost spiritual powers which are so necessary if they are to survive.

People may think what they like about the Confessing Church, but there is one thing of which it cannot be accused without being completely misunderstood: no one in it would at any time regard 'call-up' as something 'threatening'. The hundreds of voluntary registrations by young ministers of the Confessing Church and the great sacrifices made from their ranks speak clearly enough to the contrary. Even I have hardly spoken to a single minister of the Confessing Church who would not have regarded his call-up as an inner liberation from the heavy pressure of political suspicion which has burdened the Confessing Church and gladly have seized it as a long-sought opportunity to prove his inner attitude and readiness for sacrifice as a soldier. Pastor Niemöller's voluntary registration for military service right at the beginning of the war has not been without its effect on the Confessing Church. I may say all this as one who knows the young generation of pastors in the Confessing Church and has been more closely associated with them than most other ministers. Precisely because these facts are so irrefutable and because we can have a clear conscience about them, I have felt able and indeed compelled to plead in an urgent individual case – as in that of Niesel – that a pastor should be preserved for church service and the homeland, provided that this can be justified on military grounds. This latter point was not within my competence to judge, so as a result I approached my brother-in-law about it. Two things led me to do so:

I know that even religious people can judge the church very differently, but in times of war no one should want to dispute that the motive of its conviction and its action is love of the German people and a wish to serve it – particularly during the war – to the best of its ability.

Since the beginning of the war I have argued in a number of long conversations with Minister Gürtner,[52] whom I knew personally, for a settlement of the church dispute and a common effort by the different forces of the Protestant church; I submitted suggestions for this to Dr Gürtner and he discussed them with the Minister for Religious Affairs, Herr Kerrl. The latter showed interest and approval. In December 1940, Dr Gürtner accompanied me on a walk at Ettal which lasted for several hours, in the course of which he said that he hoped that the matter would reach a satisfactory settlement and told me in detail how that might come about. His death a month later, and the illness and death of

Minister Kerrl, shattered these hopes. It was an attempt to bring about peace in the church during the war so as to release its greatest strength for the war effort. This attempt, despite its failure, meant that I may feel that I have done everything in my power to bring about as harmonious and strong a contribution by the church to the war as possible.

Although this may seem to be little related to the matter, I wanted very much to have said it at some point so that you, your honour, could judge my personal attitude on this question.

[On travelling]

Now, finally, a word about my stays in Berlin. I had to be in Berlin regularly for the following official reasons.
1. Before and after every journey.
2. To prepare certain journeys, some of which took a considerable time (see below).
3. I was expressly told that I was to be at the disposal of Admiral C[anaris] for special commissions, and I was often asked for addresses, commendations and advice.

The following details should be added: Preparation for my planned Scandinavian trip in June 1941 kept me in Berlin from April to July 1941 inclusively. This was because of discussions with the pastor at the Swedish embassy, journeys to the embassy, addresses and advice which I had to get from [crossed out: Dibelius, Diestel] Protestant ministers. Immediately after the failure of this proposed journey I had to apply for my second visa for Switzerland in Munich, and I travelled to Switzerland in August. After my return, further trips to Paris and Spain were planned – I recently forgot to mention this – but they did not materialize because of my protracted illness, which I contracted in Berlin. I was not capable of travelling again before the middle of January, beginning of February. From March to July 1942 I was on official journeys with only brief interruptions. These also had to be prepared in Berlin. The intention was that this travelling should be continued in the autumn to the Balkans and to Switzerland. This plan failed to come off with Schm[idhuber]'s disappearance. So at the request of my brother-in-law I remained in Berlin until the matter was cleared up, as otherwise I would have had to sit about in Munich doing nothing. The situation was so unclear at that time that every day I was expecting to be sent back to Munich and on journeys. I myself repeatedly urged that I should be allowed to travel again, as the military inactivity was getting too long for me. It was no fault of mine that this did not come about. My stay in Berlin was always notified to my military superiors and to my Munich home. I could be reached within the hour and in practice was always reached immediately in urgent matters, both through urgent calls to my landlady in Munich[53] and through the Berlin office of the *Abwehr*. My parents can attest how much I disliked this state of permanent uncertainty about my travelling plans. On my side, there was no week after January 1943 in which I was not told that the next week I would have to go to Munich and then travel, though this was always called off again soon afterwards; in effect I was kept on tenterhooks without knowing how long this state would last.

I have already mentioned the personal reasons why I was glad to remain in Berlin, namely my books which I needed for work, and my elderly parents, whom I did not like to leave all alone unnecessarily, particularly during air-raids.

[On the charge of damaging the war effort]   [2 August 1943]

Your honour,
You have allowed me to write to you once again, and I want to do that today, probably for the last time before the trial. In the three days which have passed since you informed me that charges would be laid against me I have attempted, on your advice, to think quietly through the whole complex of questions once again. I do not want to trouble you with personal matters; I need not tell you what the mere fact of my being charged with damaging the war

effort means for myself, my profession and my family; you know my professional and personal circumstances well enough. If the law requires the charge, it must happen; I understand that. The reason why I did not expect it is perhaps that I did not know the text of the law and also that I have felt myself to be innocent of the charge of damaging the war effort and still feel the same way, even after looking again at what you said to me on Friday.

The results of my consideration are, in brief, as follows: My exemption for service in the *Abwehr* in essence amounts to conscription into the *Abwehr*. I could not have made the journeys intended by the *Abwehr* had I served in the *Abwehr* as an enlisted man; in that case I would have lost the disguise which was absolutely necessary for my journeys. That I came to do my war service with the *Abwehr* and not the armed forces is, in my opinion, exclusively the responsibility of those who regarded my contacts abroad as being so numerous and important that they claimed me for this service; i.e. Admiral Canaris must really decide about that, as he himself ordered that I was to be used for the *Abwehr*. However, it is also my own personal conviction that I could do greater service to the nation by making use of my contacts abroad than elsewhere. You know, your honour, that I am not well up in matters of law, but I cannot suppress the question whether there is not a regulation to the effect that in war each man is to be put where he makes the greatest contribution for the nation. A chemist is left in his laboratory if he has special knowledge not possessed by anyone else. Be that as it may, at any rate, these are the reasons why I worked for the *Abwehr* – without any doubt about the rightness of my activity. And I must pass on the responsibility for this to those who engaged me.

Now about my letter to my brother-in-law in the matters of Niesel, Wolf[54] and Jannasch.[55] I can at least understand that it may seem strange if one reads it without taking into account the personal relationship between myself and my brother-in-law. For me it was part of one of the numerous purely personal conversations in which for many years I had been telling my brother-in-law of church matters and difficulties and had occasionally been asking his advice. In this case it was a question of asking personal advice as to whether any help could be offered in this or that difficulty. In the Jannasch case I even told the father, who had lost his other son shortly before and was with me in great distress, explicitly that things could not be changed in any way. Was it really impermissible to ask my brother-in-law about the matter once again, personally? This is the context – i.e. that of a quickly written personal letter – in which the words 'there is a *threat* of call-up' are to be understood; a stranger could certainly misunderstand them or take objection to them, but my brother-in-law certainly did not misunderstand them. One need only ask him how he took the expression; [illegible] was the difficulty 'threatening' the church. A plea to my brother-in-law on church matters would never have seemed impermissible to me, especially as he alone was responsible for working out all the military possibilities; it would never have occurred to me to press anything on him or to suggest anything to him that he thought irresponsible. My brother-in-law will confirm to you at any time that in these affairs it was exclusively a matter of questions and reports; I never pressed him to do anything. Finally, I always kept in mind the significance of the church for the war effort at home and felt myself inwardly justified in presenting such things to my brother-in-law. He knew this and understood it well. I will not disclaim responsibility for having spoken up for the church even during the war, where this seemed to me to be in the interest of church and nation; and I confidently believe that what I have done can be answered for and defended before the law also. Perhaps you will believe me when I say that I have too high an opinion of the law to want to see casuistry or stretching of points for my personal sake. I believe that in my own case, prosecution and defence are at least agreed on this basic attitude.

Finally, may I add something that hardly needs saying? If my work for the *Abwehr* should no longer be regarded as important, I would immediately hold myself ready for any other service. But that is not a matter that I have to decide.

Dear parents,

I'm beginning this letter today, though I hope that I shall be seeing you in person tomorrow. In the week after Whit Sunday I had a great many letters, which pleased me very much. First of all yours, which is always such a great comfort, though I cannot get over the fact that you have now had to suffer so long under my misfortune; then Maria's letter, which made me well content with its fabulous dreams of the future; even Hans-Walter has found time for a letter to me in his short, duty-free moments – I'm particularly grateful to him for it. Splendid that he is now so near to Berlin.

Christoph wrote so nicely in his letter from Sakrow – I do hope that the children will soon be relieved of this burden – and in the last parcel little Michael even sent his sweets to his godfather in prison. He is not to do it again, but I'm sure that this sacrifice – and it really is a sacrifice for such a small boy – will be remembered, and that he is as glad about it as I am. When I am free again, I will do something that he particularly wants; ask him to think what that might be. And Karl-Friedrich has written again so nicely; I think I've already said thank-you for Ursel's letter. I see from the parcels that the whole family keeps sharing in them – and the children and Maria's family. I want them all to know how grateful I am. It is a real help. What a blessing it is, in such distressing times, to belong to a large, closely-knit family, where each trusts the other and stands by him. When pastors were arrested, I sometimes used to think that it must be easiest for those of them who were unmarried. But I did not know then what the warmth that radiates from the love of a wife and family can mean in the cold air of imprisonment, and how in just such times of separation the feeling of belonging together through thick and thin actually grows stronger. I was very pleased about Walter's[56] induction; I forgot a while ago to send him good wishes for that and for his birthday; I'm also very pleased for Susi, who was so attached to the community and has done so much for it.

Letters from mother and grandmother have just come. Thank you very much. From what you say about strawberries and raspberries, school holidays and plans for travel, I begin to feel that summer has really come. Time is not of much account here. I'm glad the weather is mild. A little while ago a tomtit had its nest with its ten little ones in a recess in the yard here. I enjoyed going to look at it every day till some cruel fellow went and destroyed the lot and left some of the tomtits lying on the ground, dead; I can't understand it. When I walk in the yard I get a great deal of pleasure from a small ant-hill and from the bees in the lime-trees. I sometimes think of the story of Peter Bamm, who was on a lovely island where he met all kinds of people, good and bad. He dreamt in a nightmare that a bomb might come and destroy everything, and the first thing that occurred to him was what a pity it would be for the butterflies! Prison life brings home to one how nature carries on uninterruptedly its quiet, open life, and it gives one quite a special – perhaps a sentimental – attitude towards animal and plant life, except that my attitude towards the flies in my cell remains very unsentimental. In general, a prisoner is no doubt inclined to make up, through an exaggerated sentimentality, for the soullessness and lack of warmth in his surroundings; and perhaps he may react too strongly to anything sentimental that affects him personally. The right thing for him to do then is to call himself to order with a cold shower of common sense and humour, to avoid losing his sense of proportion. I believe it is just here that Christianity, rightly understood, can help particularly.

You, father, know all this quite well from your long experience of prisoners. I am not yet sure what the so-called prison psychosis is, though I am getting a pretty good idea.

I'll send you my smoker's card back as soon as possible; I'm hardly getting any cigarettes here now, only very bad pipe tobacco. Maria's and mother's cigarettes were glorious.

I've much enjoyed reading grandfather's *Ideals and Errors*;[57] I also enjoyed *Indian Summer*. You must read Stifter's *Waldsteig* and Gotthelf's *Uli* sometime; very rewarding!

I've just come back and have seen Maria – an indescribable surprise and joy. I knew about it only a minute beforehand. It's still like a dream – really an almost unimaginable situation – what will we think of it one day? What one can say at such a time is so trivial, but that's not the main thing. It was so brave of her to come; I wouldn't have dared to suggest it to her. It's so much more difficult for her than for me. I know where I am, but for her it is all unimaginable, mysterious, terrifying. Think how things will be when this nightmare is over! And now Maria's and mother's letters have just come, to make my joy complete and as an echo of this morning. How good things still are! Tell them that I say this to myself every day.

We shall probably be able to see each other next week. I'm looking forward to that very much. Maria so enjoys being with you, and speaks of the Schleichers so happily. I'm very grateful for that. Much love to all the family and friends. I'm always thinking of you.

Ever your grateful Dietrich

From his mother   [Charlottenburg] 27 June 1943

Dear Dietrich,

We were very glad that you were able to see Maria again and to talk with her, though at the same time I was rather worried that there would not be enough time for us. But perhaps it will be a good thing if we get used to that a bit; and we were told by Captain Maetz[58] that we would have a chance to see you at the beginning of next week. Maria was quite thrilled by the reunion and of course she had to tell us all about it . . . I expect Maria has also told you about us, as she said.

At the moment we're wondering whether we should not have the best of our pictures rolled up and put in a less dangerous place. A man from the museum would help us. Our air-raid shelter is already so full anyway. And now its only window is to be walled in. As father is over seventy, I expect that I shall remain upstairs with him, come what may. If the window is closed in, one cannot get out with the things. I'm also wondering about all your books in the attic; I would very much like to send away the most important of them, too, but I cannot decide about them by myself. Can you perhaps write a list with rough details of what is where?

Perhaps your absence will now really not last much longer. One finishes each week in disappointment with the thought 'and again not', and who knows at our time of life how many weeks one still has left? They say that war years count double. I have the feeling that they count 'fourfold' . . .

With much love.   Your Mother

To his parents   [Tegel] Sunday, 3 July 1943

Dear parents,
When the bells of the prison chapel start ringing at about six o'clock on a Saturday evening, that is the best time to write home. It's remarkable what power church bells have over human beings, and how deeply they can affect us. So many of our life's experiences gather round them. All discontent, ingratitude, and selfishness melt away, and in a moment we are left with only our pleasant memories hovering round us like gracious spirits. I always think first of those quiet summer evenings in Friedrichsbrunn, then of all the different parishes that I have worked in, then of all our family occasions, weddings, christenings, and confirmations – tomorrow my godchild[59] is being confirmed! – I really cannot count all the memories that come alive to me, and they all inspire peace, thankfulness, and confidence. If only one could help other people more!

During the past week I've done a good deal of quiet work, and have read some good books, as well as some letters from you and Maria; and now today there is your magnificent parcel. It makes me a bit uneasy that the windows of your air-raid shelter are to be walled in. I don't think you ought to have that done in any circumstances. It's the only way out, and this was surely not the intention. I've had a word with the captain here; he has successfully offered resistance. This is only the systematic carrying out of a regulation which does not fit your house at all. Rüdiger ought to be able to help you there. I can understand that you want to stay

73

up during the alerts, but it makes me uneasy and must be straightened out. A thick layer of sandbags could be built up in front of the window.

It's certainly sad to part with the good paintings, but perhaps it's the right thing to do, now that the attacks seem to be getting so brutal. I hope that I really will be able to see to my books myself, to spare you the trouble. Perhaps the large Rembrandt portfolios should be stored away now.

Maria has been writing to me about setting up house; it's made me tremendously happy. I find the sketches of the furniture in her room most attractive. I'm glad that she can be at home for a while, for everybody's sake . . .

Just to keep you up to date with things, and not because I think that it's really worth mentioning, I ought to report my lumbago. It's not bad, but it's already lasted more than three weeks; it's a bit of a nuisance. The stone floor is probably the cause. There is everything imaginable here, ray treatment and footbaths, but nothing is any use.

I've now been in prison three months. I remember hearing Schlatter say, in his lectures on ethics, that it was one of the duties of a Christian citizen to take it patiently if he were held for investigation. That meant nothing to me at the time, but in the past few weeks I have thought of it several times, and now we must wait calmly and patiently as long as we have to, just as we have done up to now. I am dreaming more than ever that I have been released and am back home with you.

The day lilies have been simply lovely; their cups open slowly in the morning and bloom only for a day; and the next morning there are fresh ones to take their place. The day after tomorrow they will all be over.

I've just come back from visiting time. Once again it was marvellous; I am so grateful for it. My thoughts are particularly with Renate . . . I'm so pleased. By the way, Goethe's mother was barely eighteen when he came into the world. Special greetings to her. Greetings, too, to all the family; I don't think that there is anyone of whom I don't think once a day. I was particularly pleased to hear that things are going so well with grandmother again. If only you can soon get rid of the worry and travel. That's my constant wish. Once again, thank you for everything, and much love from   your Dietrich

From his father   Charlottenburg, 11 July 1943

Dear Dietrich,

. . . Have you found anything useful in Heidegger's *Phenomenology of Time-Consciousness*? It is difficult, almost too difficult reading for a clinical psychiatrist. You will find it less hard as you are up in the latest philosophy. I prefer Stifter's *Nachsommer* that you recommended. The chapter about the stay reminds me very much of *Great-grandfather's Portfolio*, where he also introduces a visit to a strange house with a charming garden scene. Maria wrote that she had asked for permission to visit. I hope her wish is granted. We hope for a letter from you soon. Mother sends her love. She will be writing very soon. Much love,   Father

From his mother   Charlottenburg, 14 July 1943

Dear Dietrich,

Your letter of the 5th only arrived today. They say that it is no longer being sent via Florastrasse, and yet it took so long. But it was good that we found you fit and well when we visited you in the meantime.

Don't worry yourself about the air-raid shelter. I have spoken with the NCO in charge of the matter and he will arrange a gas door and gas window that can be opened and shut. Of course there is still a lot of work, as we first have to clear everything out . . .

Father, the family and friends all send their love and continually wish you all the best. With much love.   Your Mother

From Karl–Friedrich Bonhoeffer [Leipzig] 11 July 1943

Dear Dietrich,

Hope refuses to be put to shame! Every time I sit down to write to you, I hope that you will not get the letter but will have come out in the meanwhile. Since I last had business in Berlin the parents have spoken with you; I expect that it was the event from which you have been living in the last week. I was very glad that the impression that you made on them set their minds at rest and evidently did them good.

At the moment I'm a grass widower. Grete went off to Tempelburg with the children the day before yesterday. The train left with them all standing together in the corridor in a dreadful crush. They all spent a day and a night with the parents in Berlin; I hope that it wasn't just a strain, but also brought them a degree of pleasure. It was quite an invasion. I'm enjoying the complete quietness and lack of interruptions and have spent the day working over my lecture again and 'modernizing' it. I also worked in the garden for a couple of hours. Our pear tree hadn't borne fruit before and we were going to cut it down last year, but this year there is fruit all over it. The pears are dangling down vertically from the thin branches right at the top of the tree and are now bound to break off at the first storm. I've built a tall framework round the tree from clothes props and other things nailed together and hope that this will save some fruit and the tree. The crop of berries isn't bad this year, either, but they aren't sweet because there hasn't been enough sun. That at least is a consolation for you: you haven't lost too much sunshine recently . . .
Warmest greetings.   Your Karl–Friedrich

To his parents   [Tegel] Sunday, 24 July 1943

Dear parents,

So you came here yesterday in all the heat to bring me the parcel! I hope it was not too much of an effort for you. Thank you very much for coming, and for all the things that you brought. The summer produce is particularly welcome here, of course. Fancy the tomatoes being ripe already! Just lately I've been feeling the warmth for the first time. It's not too uncomfortable here in the cell, especially as I keep fairly still most of the time. But one longs more and more for fresh air. I should just like to spend an evening in the garden again. Of course, it is good to have half an hour's walking every day, but it's not enough. I suppose the various things associated with a cold – aches, catarrh, and so on – won't go till I can get into the fresh air again. The flowers are always a great blessing; they bring some colour and life into this dreary cell. Thank you very much for your letters with the news of the family. I hope that everyone has had good holidays; they all need them. I had another very nice letter from Susi, which pleased me very much. She is quite right; this time of separation first makes it clear that often we take too little trouble to get together in normal times. Precisely because we do not feel it necessary to 'cultivate' the obvious family relationships, many things are often neglected, and that is a pity. Thanks, too, to Walter for his card. I'm particularly grateful to Susi again for bringing the parcel so often; it's such a chore for her. Still, despite all the trouble you have with the parcel, I do want you to know that I savour each bit of it with very great thankfulness and with a really good appetite. So far I've kept in very good fettle as a result. I always arrange things so that it lasts exactly a week, and in this way I have a good remembrance of you which gives me strength. Even at breakfast I feel surrounded by you all, and that is all the better, as inwardly I find that the morning is the most difficult time of the day for me to get over.

Two splendid letters from Maria and one from her mother – dated the 27 June! perhaps it's been lying around somewhere? – have given me great delight. Let Maria ride as much as she wants; I'm glad about that and only envy her it. From her refusal to take up my suggestion that she should give me riding lessons I assume that she regards me as a hopeless case – but perhaps she's even wrong about that!? If, though, she should think that riding is not suitable for a pastor, I beg to differ . . .

In my reading I'm now living entirely in the nineteenth century.

During these months I've read Gotthelf, Stifter, Immermann, Fontane, and Keller with new admiration. A period in which people could write such clear and simple German must have had quite a healthy core. They treat the most delicate matters without sentimentality, the most serious without flippancy, and they express their convictions without pathos; there is no exaggerated simplifying or complicating of language or subject matter; in short, it's all very much to my liking, and seems to me very sound. But it must have meant plenty of hard work at expressing themselves in good German, and therefore plenty of opportunity for quiet. By the way, the last Reuters were as fascinating as ever; I'm delighted and surprised at their equipoise, which often extends to the language itself. An author's style is often enough to attract or repel the readers.

Special thanks, too, for the trouble you take over something to smoke and to all the kind donors of cigarettes.

How are things with Renate? Please give her my love and thank her very much for her greetings.

Each time I write, I hope it will be my last letter to you from prison. Of course, this really becomes more likely every day; and one gradually gets sick of being here. I do so wish for all of us that we could have a few more of the lovely summer days together.

Father, have you really allowed yourself to be included in the 'Film of Personalities'? That would be very nice. And surely in that way we could get a series of good photographs of you?

So once again, many thanks for everything that you keep doing. Much love to Maria, mother, grandmother and the new in-laws, and of course to all the rest of the family. Love and thanks,

your Dietrich

From his father   Charlottenburg, 28 July 1943

Dear Dietrich,

I've been wanting to write to you all day and something has always been getting in the way. In this respect you are more master of your time, so even in your situation there are places where one can speak of freedom. There was a telephone call here early this morning to say that Maria will be allowed to talk with you the day after tomorrow. We are both very pleased. My letter will only reach you after you've talked to her, so I need not report what we and the rest of the family are doing. You will hear the essential news from her. On Sunday the Leipzig party and the Schleichers are coming back from Tempelburg; I expect we shall have another large but amusing invasion unless the Leipzig party continue their journey in the evening. Emmi[60] has already come back with her three and Suse's time at Friedrichsbrunn will also be coming to an end soon. Spring and summer are passing. We think of you a great deal these hot days in your cell under the roof. One small comfort to us is the memory of those hot September days when we visited you in Barcelona,[61] when you visited us in the early morning you asked whether we had frozen in the night. You would have taken the blanket, whereas we spent the night wondering how to protect ourselves from the heat.

You will soon have been out there for four months. I trust that we can now hope that things have been satisfactorily cleared up and that we shall soon have you with us again. It would be fine if we could spend some time together at Friedrichsbrunn. But one dare not think of such idylls in this troubled, bomb-threatened time. It's very beautiful even in the garden; if only mother hadn't to cope with the whole housekeeping, one could be quite content with it. It is very often the case – I keep hearing it from patients – that people are glad to be home again because in the end they can feed themselves better then. Of course there is nothing to beat a walk through the woods at Friedrichsbrunn and a fine afternoon in the fields, and I hope that I shall experience that once again. Much love from mother and   your Father

[Pencil note from D. Bonhoeffer in the margin of the letter: air-raid protection, travel, Reuter, Captain on leave, Hans cannot take the heat!]

Dear parents,

At today's interview at the War Court Dr Roeder gave me permission to write to you and Rüdiger Goltz[62] about my defence.[63] As I don't know Rüdiger's address in Bavaria, I wanted to ask you to get in touch with him. I think that it is questionable whether he can take the case himself because of the damage to his leg, which as far as I know has become much worse again. But he will surely be able to recommend a suitable person. Dr Roeder thought that the counsel for the defence would need one day for the brief, one day for discussion with me and one for the trial, i.e. three days. That is not very much. But I expect that you, father, know many lawyers, too. I'm sure that you know Dr Sack from the Lubbe trial.[64] However, it's questionable whether such a big name would take on a case that seemed to him to be so petty, and besides, he is said to be frightfully dear. I only wanted to remind you; I cannot judge myself. I have in mind a quiet, experienced, older man, not tied up in church politics, whom one can trust as a person and in whom one can confide one's case. I know no one myself,[65] but you'll find the right person. It would be good if you could clear up the matter soon.

By the way, I'm now allowed to write to you every four days; that is very splendid for me. I think that I will always alternate between you and Maria.

Many thanks for everything and please don't be worried. Love to you and the family. Your Dietrich

NOTES

1. 31 March 1943.

2. Renate Schleicher, grand-daughter of Karl Bonhoeffer, and Eberhard Bethge.

3. For several months the censor only allowed letters to his parents, at ten-day intervals.

4. Maria von Wedemeyer, from the Pätzig estate in the Neumark.

5. Older brother, Professor of Physical Chemistry, at that time in Leipzig.

6. A supreme court judge, at that time a 'special leader' with the military *Abwehr* (Military Intelligence Department) in Berlin. He was married to Bonhoeffer's sister Christine; husband and wife were arrested together on 5 April 1943, the latter being held for several weeks. Dohnanyi was murdered on 9 April 1945.

7. Written in the WUG (Wehrmacht Investigation Prison) for officers, Berlin-Moabit, Lehrter Strasse 64.

8. i.e. To *have had* companions in trouble is a comfort, but to *have* them is a burden (quotation from Vergil, *Aeneid*).

9. Bonhoeffer was confronted by Dohnanyi and his wife Christel during the investigations.

10. Ursula Schleicher, Dietrich Bonhoeffer's sister, who lived with her family next door to the parents' house, Marienburger Allee 42.

11. Summer house of the Bonhoeffer parents at Friedrichsbrunn, in the east Harz.

12. Ruth von Kleist-Retzow in Klein-Krössin, see DB, pp. 358f.

13. This is really a reference to Eberhard Bethge. Bonhoeffer avoided mentioning him directly during the first six months in Tegel, so as not to draw attention to the relationship between them and Bethge's exemption from military service, also for the *Abwehr*.

14. Brother, killed in France in 1918.

15. Youngest sister, wife of the Dahlem pastor Prof. Lic. Walter Dress.

16. Bonhoeffer's brother-in-law, ministerial adviser and Professor of Air Law in Berlin, arrested 4 October 1944, murdered 23 April 1945.

17. Son of the Schleicher couple.

18. Renate, Dorothee and Christine Schleicher; Barbara, Klaus and Christoph von Dohnanyi.

19. A slip of the pen; it has to be 4 May 1943.

20. A national, middle-class daily newspaper, at one time close to Stresemann; not all its contents had yet been brought into line.

21. The wedding took place on the twentieth anniversary of the Schleicher parents' wedding day.

22. E. von Hase in Breslau, sister of Bonhoeffer's mother.

23. 'Over night, over night, come joy and sorrow, and before you know it, both leave you and go to the Lord, to say how you have borne them.'

24. From Fritz and Margret Onnasch; the husband was a pastor in the Pomeranian council of brethren and had been inspector of studies in Finkenwalde and Köslin.

25. A slip of the pen; it has to be 5 May 1943.

26. Written on a leaf from a registration pad from the guard room at Tegel on which his father had made notes about utensils and food that he had brought for his son, see DB, p. 735.

27. Undated page from a notebook.

28. May 1943: 'Always be prepared to make a defence to anyone who calls you to account for the hope that is in you' (I Peter 3.15b).

29. 'My time is in your hands.'

30. Prov. 31.25.

31. 'Welcome one another, therefore, as Christ has welcomed you, for the glory of God.'

32. Son of Hans Jürgen von Kleist-Retzow in Kieckow, grandson of Ruth von Kleist-Retzow, cousin of Maria von Wedemeyer.

33. Richard Schöne, neighbour and cousin of the Bonhoeffer family, General Director of the Berlin museums.

34. Eberhard Bethge is meant.

35. Christine Schleicher.

36. Michael and Andreas Dress, Cornelie and Walter Bonhoeffer. The latter were children of Dr Klaus Bonhoeffer, syndic at Lufthansa in Berlin, and Emmi, née Delbrück.

37. Grete Bonhoeffer, née von Dohnanyi.

38. The authorities only allowed him to write to his fiancée after the conclusion of the first phase of the investigation, at the end of July, 1943.

39. Ruth-Alice, née von Wedemeyer, from Pätzig, wife of Klaus von Bismarck.

40. The whole letter is written with an eye to the censor.

41. Composed between June and August 1943. To serve his own defence as well as to conceal a far-reaching conspiracy, true details usually appear in a fictitious context; see DB, pp. 714ff.

42. General Superintendent Otto Dibelius, at that time under suspension, in Berlin.

43. One of the two church groups in Further Pomerania, in which Bonhoeffer trained candidates in a collective pastorate until March 1940; this was his official residence, from which he had to report to the police.

44. Superintendent Eduard Block.

45. Supreme Military Command.

46. Attorney at law and Portuguese consul in Munich. He was a member of the *Abwehr* department there and was arrested as early as October 1942.

47. Fräulein Friedenthal, a colleague in the provisional governing body of the Confessing Church, was one of a group of Jews whom Canaris and Dohnanyi evacuated safely to Switzerland on the pretext that they were *Abwehr* agents. Dr Arnold was the spokesman of the group. For 'Operation 7', see DB, pp. 651–53, 721.

48. By means of a late date, Roeder wanted to prove that von Dohnanyi and Bonhoeffer had sabotaged the Reich policy of deportation. Bonhoeffer therefore had to prove that this date lay before the beginning of the deportation in October 1942, in Berlin; see DB, pp. 721f.

49. President of the Swiss Evangelical Church Alliance, who was approached for an affidavit and for help for the Jews to be rescued.

50. On the draft outline of the letter to his parents dated 24 June 1943 (Thursday).

51. Wilhelm Niesel, at that time in the Old Prussian Council of Brethren and, *inter alia*, a director of training.

52. See DB, pp. 593f.

53. His cousin, Christine, Countess Kalckreuth.

54. Ernst Wolf, at that time Professor of Church History in Halle, member of various Councils of Brethren.

55. Wilhelm Jannasch, at that time pastor and member of the National Council of Brethren, on behalf of whose son Bonhoeffer had intervened.

56. Prof. Walter Dress as pastor in Dahlem.

57. Bonhoeffer means his great-grandfather, the church historian Karl August von Hase, and his autobiography *Ideale und Irrtümer*, 7th ed., 1917.

58. Commandant of the Wehrmacht Interrogation Prison at Tegel.

59. Marianne Leibholz, daughter of Dietrich Bonhoeffer's twin sister Sabine and Gerhard Leibholz, Professor of International Law, at that time in Oxford.

60. Wife of Klaus Bonhoeffer.

61. 1928, see DB, p. 73.

62. Rüdiger Graf von der Goltz, lawyer and state adviser, son of a sister of Bonhoeffer's mother.

63. See DB, p. 724. Bonhoeffer is indicating his excellent contacts to the censor.

64. See DB, pp. 198f.

65. A hint that none of the lawyers associated with the Confessing Church in general and Martin Niemöller in particular, e.g. Horst Holstein, should be involved in his political, military trial.

II

Waiting for the Trial

August 1943 to April 1944

Dear parents,

I'm really very happy and thankful that I can write to you oftener now, as I'm afraid you must be worrying about me, first because of the heat in my cell just under the roof, and secondly because of my asking for a lawyer. Your wonderful parcel has just come with tomatoes, apples, bottled fruit, thermos flask, etc., and the cooling salt, which is fantastic – I never knew there was such a thing. What trouble you have taken for me again. Please don't worry; I've often had to put up with worse heat in Italy, Africa, Spain, Mexico, and, almost the worst of all, in New York in July 1939; so I've a fairly good idea what to do about it. I don't eat or drink much,[1] I sit quietly at my desk, and so manage to work unhindered. From time to time I refresh my body and soul with your lovely things. I don't want to ask to be moved to another floor, as that would not be fair to the other prisoner who would have to come into my cell, probably without such things as tomatoes; and besides, it does not make much difference whether the temperature in the cell is 34 or only 30. Unfortunately I know that Hans always finds the heat trying; I'm sorry about that. One sees again and again how much easier it is to put up with a thing if one knows it cannot be changed, than if there seems to be a chance of relief round the corner.

About my request for a lawyer to defend me, I very much hope that this has not caused you any great anxiety, but that you are waiting, as I am, for things to take their course. You really mustn't imagine that I am uneasy or depressed. Of course, this has been a disappointment for me, as I suppose it has been for you too. But in a way I feel freer now that I know my case will soon be finally cleared up, after we have been kept waiting for so long. I'm expecting more information any day.

It doesn't matter if Rüdiger Goltz cannot now make himself available so quickly. Dr Roeder expressed the opinion that it is a case that any decent lawyer can cope with, and if he's a competent, warm-hearted, respectable man who also can argue quietly and with distinction, keeping the tone that has so far been maintained in the proceedings[2] – and you can best judge that – I am fully in agreement. Personally, I really have the feeling that one best says oneself what one has to say; but for legal matters, which I do not understand, I imagine that a lawyer is necessary.

I sometimes wonder whether you wouldn't do better for the immediate future to go to Sakrow in case of possible alerts.[3] Maria also suggested Pätzig, but communications there are so complicated and I don't imagine that you will want to travel before my case is settled. Wouldn't it be sensible for Renate to stay a while in the country with her mother-in-law and for her husband to try to arrange his work to fit in with that? It's only an hour's journey. But perhaps all my anxieties, as so often, are quite unnecessary. I hope so!

Once again I've been reading a number of good things. *Jürg Jenatsch* brought back youthful memories and gave me a good deal of pleasure and interest. On historical matters I found the work about the Venetians very instructive and arresting. Will you please send me some Fontane: *Frau Jenny Treibel, Irrungen und Wirrungen,* and *Stechlin*? This concentrated reading of the last few months will be very useful for my work; one often learns more about ethics from such books as these than from text-books. I like Reuter's *Kein Hüsung* as much as you do, mother. I expect I've finished the Reuters now – or have you anything else particularly good?

By the way, another thought has struck me about the lawyer: it would be a good thing if the man could spare some time for me, and wasn't too hasty. I think he should be like a doctor, who shouldn't give the impression that he has a great many things to do.

I've just eaten a couple of the marvellous tomatoes from the garden for my lunch, and thought of the work you've had in picking them. But they've really ripened most gloriously. Very many thanks. And thank you, father, for your letter. I don't suppose that any one of us loves Friedrichsbrunn less than anyone else. Just think, it's thirty years this year since you bought it. I very much hope for a couple of fine days there with you. Perhaps it will also cure my lumbago.

I've already been allowed to write to Maria again since I saw her. I was very glad about that. I'm always so fearfully sorry about her going to court. But I found her looking better.

Are these hot days especially trying for Renate's condition? I would be very sad about that. Many greetings to her and her husband, and of course to all the family. The other day I read this pretty verse in *Der Grüne Heinrich*:

> *Und durch den starken Wellengang*
> *der See, die gegen mich verschworen,*
> *geht mir von Euerem Gesang,*
> *wenn auch gedämpft, kein Ton verloren.*[4]

With much love and good confidence,

your grateful Dietrich

I've just read the appeal for evacuation; couldn't you at least spend the night in Sakrow for a while? The others will all have made their plans already. It's really very annoying to have to sit here unnecessarily at the moment and wait. I hope we shall see each other soon!

D.

To his parents   [Tegel] 7 August 1943

Dear parents,
This letter is now going to you again instead of to Maria, as originally planned. I don't know whether it is right to send letters to her with my present address on the envelope. All that sort of thing gets talked about in the village,[5] and there could be someone there who knows what Tegel, Seidelstrasse 39, means. I would rather that Maria were spared that. Besides, at the moment she is not even at home, and I want to be all the more careful not to put her in a position which I cannot look after from here. She already has enough to put up with. So I'm waiting until I hear from her what she thinks about it all. This having to wait for everything is the dominating feature of my present condition, and the nearer

one hopes to be getting to the end, the more difficult it is to be patient.

The heat has broken now, and once again I'm sitting at the table in my jacket. But I would like to thank you again for having eased the hot days so much for me. The journey to Tegel was always a great chore for you, I know.

I wonder whether you are still very much occupied with air-raid precautions. After all that has been in the papers lately, one cannot help thinking out the whole matter afresh. I just remember that we talked once about the beams in the cellar and were rather doubtful about them; were not some alterations going to be made in the central beam? I wonder whether you are still thinking of it, and whether you can get anyone to help with the work. I think it might be very difficult now. How I should love to help you with it myself. Do tell me all about it; I'm interested in every detail.

What plans do my brothers and sisters have for the children? Will you be going to Sakrow, at least for nights?

To drag myself from these thoughts, at least for a short while, I've recently been reading Hauff's fairy tales with great satisfaction. One is transported into a quite different world; the only thing is that one is always afraid of being aroused from the realm of fantasy and dreams to all too sober reality! I would very much like to read Lichtenstein again; I've a Reclam edition at home. The small print would not trouble me.

At heart I keep hoping day by day that you will not have to go to Tegel so often, and will at last be able to have the holidays that you need so much in peace.

I've just been reading the regulation requiring the possession of copper vessels to be reported. This will include my Spanish brassaro; but it should be noted that it is a work of art from the eighteenth century. It is remarkable how indifferent one becomes to such things in our time.

The books of mine that I would very much like to be put in safe keeping are the Vilmar, Schlatter and Calvin, and perhaps also the old pictures in my room; but please do not take too much trouble over them. One can always buy books again afterwards, and *above all else* you must preserve your strength these days; compared with that, everything else is really quite unimportant.

Meanwhile, Sunday is also almost over, and I face the new week with great expectation.[6] I hope, too, that post will soon come from you and Maria. I don't think I've told you that every day, when I get tired of reading and writing, I work on a chess problem; I enjoy it very much. If you come across some good little work on the subject, perhaps with set problems, I should be grateful; but don't put yourselves out over it; I shall manage all right.

Once again, please give my love to all the family and please let me know soon about all your plans and about everything that you decide. Please discuss with Maria what she thinks about the post, and give her all my love. I'm thinking of you all very much. With many thanks,   Dietrich

From Karl-Friedrich Bonhoeffer   [Leipzig] 8 August 1943

Dear Dietrich,

. . . I don't want to keep [the children] here. Instead, on Monday they're all going into the Harz mountains, to Friedrichsbrunn. I think it's now time to prepare for air raids, and children don't belong in the kind of mess produced by a heavy attack. Recently I had my Hamburg colleague[7] here at home for a couple of days as a lodger. He arrived with a small suitcase. He had stood the first three heavy attacks in the centre of the city, then had slept for a night outside in the open air and had not returned to the city. So he was washed up in our direction. Now he's returned again to see to his things. I only hope that Berlin does not get it as long as you are still 'sitting' there. But one cannot ignore *the* possibility. Travelling conditions are now the most difficult imaginable, so I limit my official journeys as much as possible and am also in Berlin less often. In these circumstances it's not a pleasant feeling to separate oneself from the family. One does not know how often we shall be able to see each other. But we mustn't forget that there are only a very few families in Europe today who have been able to keep together this far, and be grateful that we have managed up till now. What the future will be like is in any case beyond human foretelling . . .

All the best. Don't lose patience. We all hope very much that we shall see you soon.   Your Karl-Friedrich

From his mother   Charlottenburg, 11 August 1943

Dear Dietrich,

. . . Your most important books have now been brought down from the attic into the cellar, and yesterday also your gramophone and the records. The Dürer prints are outside. Of course we missed your planning and your help very much . . .

We had such a warm and friendly invitation into the country from Maria's mother, for ourselves or any of the grandchildren. But we don't want to go until your case has been cleared up. If it gets too chaotic we shall perhaps sleep outside.[8] Father doesn't want to leave his work, despite his seventy-five years. He will only agree to the film for 'the personalities' that the propaganda ministry wants to make of him when his children are no longer in prison, and I can understand that. If the attacks come, look after yourself, too, as well as you can. Make sure that you get a helmet and have enough water to dampen a towel which you should make into a hood and put over your head; get your blanket from your room, make it wet and wrap it round you and make your shoes, etc. wet; that is said to be the most important thing if one has to go through fire. On Sunday we were with Paul von Hase[9] and his wife at such a display of phosphorus bombs. There are more attractive things. I had a very nice letter from Maria. You will get a dear, brave wife and that is a great joy to us. She wanted to come to Berlin now that she has finished her cure there, but I dissuaded her strongly; I don't think her mother will allow it. She wants to help me, but if she came I would just have one more worry . . .

Now may God continue to bless you and bring us all together in his grace. Father and I are always thinking of you.

Your Mother

To his parents   [Tegel] 17 August 1943

Dear parents,

I'm enclosing an authority for Rüdiger, in case he can still arrange it; I expect that you will have heard from him in the meantime. Of course, I will understand if he does not want to go away as far as Berlin for such a matter, especially at present and with ten children to look after. But you will probably have talked with him about Dr Wergin.[10]

The hour with you yesterday was again indescribably beautiful; thank you very much indeed for coming. I think that you especially, father, could look a bit better than you do. Why don't you do as I do for a while, and go to sleep at 8.00 p.m. or, failing that, at 9.00 p.m., and have a good rest in the afternoon into the bargain? All your work, the inadequate food, disturbed nights and on top of everything your worry about me – it's too much. It's for that reason in particular that I'm so troubled by the continual postponement of the decision. In more normal times, four weeks is nothing, but in these uncertain times, with the threat of the bombs, every day is long. Still, as one may assume that the speediest settlement possible must be to everyone's advantage, I'm quietly hoping that we shall come to the end even more quickly. Above all, please don't worry about me more than you can help. I'm keeping my end up, and my mind is quite calm. What a good thing it is to know from previous experience that we are really not upset at all by air raids. I'm very glad that Dr Roeder's courts are to stay in Berlin.[11] I imagine that for men in responsible positions it is not a very attractive proposition to go out of Berlin now. Anyway, you – like myself – have something better to do than to be thinking all the time about possible raids. Prison life gives one, almost as a matter of course, a certain detachment from the actions and excitements of the day.

I forgot to mention the birthdays on the 22nd[12] and the 28th.[13] I would very much like to do something for Susi, who has so often had trouble with my parcel, but the only thing that I can think of is a last bottle of sweet wine, which I have and would very much like to give her. The Schleichers would probably like the new one-volume Bible, bound in thick, light-brown leather, which is in the air-raid shelter; please put it on the birthday table and tell them both that I am thinking of them with affectionate best wishes. How much I would love to be there! But this trial of my patience is still not at an end. As long as one doesn't lose sight of the greater issues in these small disappointments that one keeps on experiencing, one soon sees how trivial one's own personal privations are.

For the last fortnight I've been waiting in such uncertainty day by day[14] that I've hardly felt equal to any serious work; but I'm going to try now to get down to some more writing. Some weeks ago I sketched the outlines of a play,[15] but meanwhile I've realized that the material is not suitable for drama; and so I shall now try to rewrite it as a story. It's about the life of a family, and of course there is a good deal of autobiography mixed up in it.

I would very much like some rough paper and my watch; the other one suddenly stopped yesterday. It's going again now, but it's too risky for me suddenly to be left without a watch. And please could you buy me N. Hartmann's *Systematic Philosophy*, Verlag Kohlhammer 1943. I can now use the personal library here, which has all sorts of good things, so I need less from you. But if you can dig out Stifter's *Witiko*, that would be splendid. – I was very touched when the Schleichers sent me the rabbit liver a little while ago. A real piece of meat is very welcome in all this spoon-fodder; I'm also very grateful to them for biscuits, peaches and cigarettes. Do you by any chance still have a spot of tea? I can occasionally get boiling water here.

The death of the three young pastors[16] grieves me very much. I should be grateful if their relatives could be told in some way that I cannot write to them now; otherwise they would not understand my not doing so. Of all my pupils, those three were closest to me. It's a great loss, both for me personally and for the church. More than thirty of my pupils must have fallen by now, and most of them were among my best.

I'm again very grateful to Karl-Friedrich for his letter; they're always especially nice. Hans-Christoph[17] also wrote very nicely about my engagement, but he does so as though it had already been published. Perhaps someone should tell uncle Hans that that hasn't happened yet. There is no greater delight here in my cell than letters.

I quite forgot to ask after uncle Paul.[18] Have you really expressed my sympathy after the death of his mother? Do give him my kindest regards.

Once again, thank you for everything. The day when we shall meet again in freedom gets closer and closer, and it will be one of those days which we shall never forget all our lives. Many greetings to all the family. Write again soon. The next letter is going to Maria again.

I'm always thinking of you.   Your grateful Dietrich

From his mother   [Sakrow] 22 August 1943

My dear Dietrich,
We've just come out again over the weekend and are sitting on deck-chairs by the water enjoying the stillness. With moving in the house and getting some things out before the air raids that are expected, we've had a great deal to do recently. Father's books and your most important books are now in the air-raid shelter and the store room, and a number of your portfolios and belles-lettres are with father's on the shelves that have become empty. Your wardrobe upstairs is quite empty. I sent another parcel to Pätzig and brought yet another out here. Our walls, too, are almost completely empty. We have taken many pictures out of their frames and the frames are in the garage. Similarly, all the good carpets have been taken away. You wouldn't like the house

now. Neither do I! But what's the use? One does what one can. Otherwise we're waiting . . .

God bless you and all of us in this difficult and uncertain time.

Your Mother

To his parents   [Tegel] 24 August 1943

Dear parents,

Well, you had a rough passage last night. I was very relieved when the Captain sent word to me that you were all right. My cell is high up, and the window is kept wide open during alerts, so one has a very clear view of the ghastly firework display on the south side of the city; and without the least feeling of anxiety for myself, I do feel most strongly at such times how utterly absurd it is for me to be kept waiting here doing nothing. I thought the *Brüdergemeinde* text for this morning was most appropriate: 'And I will give peace in the land, and you shall lie down, and none shall make you afraid.'[19]

On Sunday night I stupidly got gastric catarrh; yesterday I had a temperature, 38, but today it is normal again. I've only just got up to write this letter, and shall be going straight back to bed as a precaution; I don't want to be ill on any account.[20] As such cases are not catered for here, I was very glad of your rusks and a packet of biscuits that I kept by me for emergencies. A medical orderly also gave me some of his white bread, so I am getting along quite well. One ought to have something of the kind here in case of need, and perhaps also a small packet of semolina or oat flakes, which could be cooked in the sick bay. By the time you get this letter, it will all be over and done with.

Thank you very much, mother, for your letter of the 11th, which arrived yesterday, the 23rd. It's perhaps quite a good thing that you saw such a display with uncle Paul Hase. In these days he will have his hands full as city commandant. Letters also came yesterday from Maria and her mother while I was lying in bed. That was particularly cheering. I'm really very pleased that Maria has offered you help, mother. I cannot decide from here whether you should have refused it. It's so difficult to put oneself completely in the situation. I keep trying to do it, but I don't know enough of the details.

I've been able to work very well again during the last week, and was in full swing when this stupid interruption occurred. Incidentally, I'm reading the *Microbe Hunters* with great pleasure; as K. Friedrich sent it, I assume that it is scientifically reliable. It's a very impressive history of research. – Well, I really can't think of anything else to write, so I'll lie down again. Can I ask you again for some *envelopes*? I've only three left. Please don't let the letter worry you. I didn't want to miss it, even if it is rather shorter. I shall definitely be better by the day after tomorrow. Greetings once again to the birthday children. Tell them how much I'm thinking of them and how I would love to be there.

With love to you and the whole family.

Your grateful Dietrich

Special greetings to Christel. I'm always particularly sorry for her on the air-raid nights, and for the children.

From Karl-Friedrich Bonhoeffer [Friedrichsbrunn[21]] 30 August 1943

Dear Dietrich,

As you see, at the moment I'm in Friedrichsbrunn. Grete is up here with the children and Suse is also here with hers, and we are now seeing whether we can equip the house for the winter. We have to get a sufficient quantity of coal, wood and petrol, and that is not easy. One runs from one office to another and fights. In addition, the question of school is still completely obscure and there is no satisfactory solution for the two older children. So it is still an open question whether we shall stay up here. In any case, however, it's certainly a good thing to take as many precautions as possible and to make it possible to live here; we always have to count on the possibility that one of our large family will be forced to live here.

You went through a heavy attack a week ago; we heard it from the distance in Leipzig. At any rate, we believe that what we heard at night was Berlin. We were, of course, thinking especially of you. By the time you get this letter you may have been visited by more attacks. If only you could be let out at last . . .

Do you have time and peace of mind in your cell to do some work on your own account, or is the time completely lost for you as far as academic work is concerned? Can I get you books from the university library? So far I've kept avoiding this question, as I thought that by the time I had an answer you would be out again. Even this disappointment does not prevent me from hoping the same thing again. When I can get a few quiet minutes from the tumult of children I've been studying a little book on the structure and function of the brain. I read recently that the offspring of wild animals born in the zoo have a smaller brain that their contemporaries born wild in natural surroundings. An effect of imprisonment which will perhaps interest you – excuse the feeble joke. At any rate, one does not notice this aspect in your letters. They are always a great delight to us. They're always sent on to me by the parents or Maria. Something must be due again in the next few days.

Much love from us all. Get as much good out of this time as you can.

Your Karl-Friedrich

From his parents   Charlottenburg, 30 August 1943

My dear Dietrich,
Your last letter was dated 7 August. How can that be possible? It must be something to do with the moving of the War Court to Torgau. But it's very distressing. And I expect that the same thing will have happened with our letters, and you will have been without news. We will now apply for permission to visit and hope that it comes soon. I keep reading your last letter through and am glad

that you share our confidence that this time which is so difficult for you and us parents will soon come to an end. I'm glad too that you keep your head and your spirits high. But the summer is almost over. Do you think, though, that a couple of fine autumn days up there in Friedrichsbrunn are in store for us? Of course we're moving all sorts of things in the house and we often miss a strong hand. Things don't look very nice here any more . . .

God bless you. We keep entrusting you to him.

Your Mother

31 August 1943

Dear Dietrich,

I just want to add a word to mother's letter. She has already told you that here, too, the day passes with moving things and putting them away to a greater degree than is good for peaceful work and inner rest. It has become a perpetual state of moving things round which is particularly unpleasant because one really cannot see how long it will last. Once it gets to the stage that one can say of oneself *omnia mecum porto*, it will become much simpler. I've taken up my sessions again, but they are by no means over-full. Those outside are afraid of the journey into unsafe Berlin and those who live here have 'no time for nerves', as old Heim used to say, in their concern for their possessions. The thick end will come later, when people have time to think about their bodies once more.

We've heard nothing of you for a long time. That is probably because of the competition of the letters to Maria. I hope all is well again with your health. Maria has told us of her visit out there to you. She's a brave person. I'm glad that she gets on well with mother and that they are fond of each other. I hope that our patience will not be tried too much longer. And I hope that we can talk to you soon.   Affectionately, your Father

Dear parents,

As you will already have heard two days after my previous letter, through Maria, who to my great surprise was allowed to pay me a visit, I am in good health once again. Aspirin for fever and charcoal for the afflictions that go with it are my sovereign remedies, and with the help of your great thermos flasks I was mobile again soon afterwards. I didn't even need to deny myself the glorious liver sausage. Many thanks for the trouble you took. I've now even been prescribed white bread, so please, mother, don't deny yourself any for my sake.

Maria's visit here was marvellous, and I was so pleased that she had principally come on your account. I'm dreadfully sorry that Renate had bomb damage in her new house, and it's frightful for Ursel too, after all the trouble she had getting it ready. Can I suggest to Renate that she tries to buy two pewter plates and two pewter mugs at my expense; sometimes you can find this sort of thing at the place where we got her the pewter tureen for her wedding. It would please me very much if she could do this; instead, she won't get anything for her birthday. I really would like her to do this.

Unfortunately I haven't had any bright ideas at all about Christoph's birthday; I would very much like to give him something nice. Would *You and the Weather* interest him? It's among my books. Perhaps, too, it would be possible to find him something else in Plahn's bookshop?[23] Could you call there some time? They have always served me very well. At any rate, give him my greetings; I hope that next time we shall be able to celebrate a satisfactory birthday together. This time of trial is really very hard for the children. But he's already astonishingly sensible and knows the sort of attitude he should have towards his parents. Meanwhile you will have had the birthday at the Schleichers'; of course you were very much in my thoughts.

For the last few days I've again been able to work well and write a good deal. When I find myself back in the cell after a few hours of complete absorption in my work, it takes me a moment or two to get my bearings again. The fact of my being here is hard to credit even now, however much I get used to the external conditions. I find it quite interesting to watch this gradual process of accustoming and adapting myself. A week ago I was given a knife and fork for my meals – a new provision – and they seemed almost unnecessary, as it had become so much a matter of course for me to use a spoon for spreading my bread and so on. On the other hand, I think there are some things that are so irrational, e.g. the actual state of being in prison, that it is impossible, or at least very difficult, to get used to them. That kind of thing needs a conscious effort if it is to be accepted. I expect there are psychological works on the subject.

Delbrück's *World History* is very good reading, only it seems to me to be more a history of Germany. I've finished *The Microbe Hunters*, and enjoyed it very much. I've also been reading some more of Storm, though without being very much impressed by it on the whole. I hope you will bring me some more of Fontane or Stifter. It's a nuisance that the letters now always take so long, usually 10–12 days. As we are only 10 kilometres apart, that seems rather generous. Nevertheless, it's always the greatest joy to get a letter. I've now been told that as Dr Roeder is evidently not in Berlin I am to send my letters to Maria via your address. So she must go on having patience for a little longer. I'm so sorry for her. But I hope that I shall not have to write too many more letters from here. I think that five months' uncertainty and waiting are enough, and for you too. The summer is nearly over. But there will still be fine days in September and October. Much love to all the family. I long so much to see them all again. Above all, all of you keep well until then.

With all my heart,   your grateful Dietrich

Dear Dietrich,

Yesterday we got your letter of 24 August, in which you wrote of the attack the previous night. Those are impressions that you will not forget all your life. You owe them to being there in Tegel, as in our air-raid shelter you certainly would not have seen that terrifyingly beautiful scene in the air from your open window up there. How much I understand your incomprehension about your situation at such moments, when you have to look on ineffectually and cannot help anyone, in the best years of your manhood . . . Meanwhile there has been another heavy attack, the day before yesterday; by chance we were spending the night at Christel's, in Sakrow, and even from there we were able to have quite a different view of it from that at home. We saw that our neighbourhood was in great danger round the Heerstrasse, but we were really quite composed in the face of what couldn't be altered. We were only heavy-hearted about the Schleichers near us. When we went home the next morning, we saw many fine houses destroyed in the Heerstrasse; the station was burning and there were some fire bombs in Lötzenerallee. There was blast damage in Soldauer, Kurländer and Marienburgerstrasse, windows and roofs broken in two. We only lost a kitchen window and there was some damage to the ceiling in the baggage room next to your room. It has been worse in Charlottenburg and Moabit, and I expect they're what we saw burning. Unfortunately there's been the same damage at Susi's as before, if not worse, with damage to the windows and doors that was caused by a high explosive bomb which came down on the Sehring's house. We were there the whole morning helping to move, so that one could at least get in and out. Then we packed up some more things and took them with us in an estate car, as this neighbourhood is almost always getting it. I expect that Susi will come to Berlin this week if Grete is up there again with the children. – Nothing has happened with Klaus . . .

God bless you. Father joins me in sending love.

Your Mother

Dear Dietrich,

You've been shut up now for six months. I never believed it would last so long. I hope that at least the time is now going quicker than it did. Through some organizational mistake I no longer get your letters sent on from Berlin, which I'm very sorry about. But I'm still in Berlin quite often and then hear the latest news about you.

I'm sitting here a grass widower again. Grete is up in Friedrichsbrunn with the children . . . Tomorrow I'm going up there for a couple of days. When I think how much I look forward to seeing them all again, I can just about imagine how you must long to be free once more. If it still goes on lasting all too long I will put in an application for permission to visit you – provided that I don't get in the way of a visit that you would prefer more. Now that the most beautiful time of year is almost over and everywhere outside looks grey and gloomy you may perhaps miss your freedom less.

Many greetings and all the best.   Your Karl-Friedrich

From Christoph von Dohnanyi   [Sakrow near Potsdam]
4 September 1943

Dear Uncle Dietrich,

We're back home again. We had to help at Uncle Walter's.[24] He's had bad luck again. He already had one lot on 1 March, but today everything is all over the place. No wonder. Four high explosive bombs fell near him and with those the blast is so strong that people fly out of their beds. With four, of course, it can be quite unpleasant. An Australian baled out in a little wood near the grandparents. He was found asleep by his parachute and was caught straightaway by Herr Schröter. His parachute is still lying in the wood, not far from the grandparents' house. I can't imagine how a man can go on sleeping in such a situation.

It was a good thing that the grandparents were spending the night with us, as it always saves the nerves (as the grown-ups put it).

They're coming again today. That's good. I must go down. I have to finish the letter quickly as a lot of help is needed. Pictures, washing, carpets, shoes, everything you can think of is dragged round to us. If we can clean it up a bit that's some use. But it's not very probable.

Uncle Klaus wants to come tomorrow. I hope something comes of it. Then the family will all be nicely together again. A pity, though, that it's not quite complete. But that, too, will happen again. Then we shall have the party that we're all longing for. Till then we have to wait patiently. Some time the day will quite definitely come.

The best part of autumn is now over. The last apple fell from the tree yesterday. It was immediately eaten by me. Unfortunately the wasps had already had quite a good bite out of it, but that's not altogether a bad sign. Soon the pears will be ripe, and then it will be better again.

This week we have to get the potatoes in. I'm agog to see how many there are. By and large they say that the crop is nothing special. But it varies a good deal.

Now I must stop, because they're going to collect the post particularly early today. You don't know what will happen in the night.

I hope, first, that you have an undisturbed night and, secondly, that you have all you need for your 'well-being'. With much love,

your grateful Christoph

To his parents   [Tegel] 5 September 1943

Dear parents,
I don't think there is any need for us to compare notes about the night before last. I shall never forget looking through the cell window at the horrible night sky. I was very relieved to hear from

the Captain the next morning that you were safe. I'm very sorry that Susi has had damage a second time and now has to move house. She also has a load to bear. What a good thing that the children weren't there! And I'm very relieved that Maria does not have to be in Berlin. Wouldn't now be a good time for you at least to spend the nights in Sakrow?

It's remarkable how we think at such times about the people that we should not like to live without, and almost or entirely forget about ourselves. It is only then that we feel how closely our own lives are bound up with other people's, and in fact how the centre of our own lives is outside ourselves, and how little we are separate entities. The 'as though it were a part of me' is perfectly true, as I have often felt after hearing that one of my colleagues or pupils had been killed. I think it is a literal fact of nature that human life extends far beyond our physical existence. Probably a mother feels this more strongly than anyone else. There are two passages in the Bible which always seem to me to sum the thing up. One is from Jeremiah 45: 'Behold, what I have built I am breaking down, and what I have planted I am plucking up . . . And do you seek great things for yourself? Seek them not . . . but I will give your life as a prize of war . . .'; and the other is from Psalm 60: 'Thou hast made the land to quake, thou hast rent it open; repair its breaches, for it totters.'

I do want to thank you and everyone else involved for the last parcel. I never forget, and remind myself every day, of all the thoughts, trouble and sacrifice that such a parcel always demands. Precisely for that reason it is always not only an outward help, but also a great inward one, too. It was really very nice of the Schleicher girls to send me some of their sweets, but I think that they really need them very much themselves. I'm also more than grateful to Hans-Walter for his gift of tobacco. Of course I recognized grandmother's biscuits, and the greetings from Pätzig are naturally part of it all, and daily direct my thoughts towards the time to which we all look forward. It makes me very happy to imagine Maria sewing and working away at her trousseau – really making preparations for the day. I can't do anything here but wait, hope and look forward to it. It would be wonderful if the letters weren't so long on the way. Something has probably gone wrong. Your last letter is dated 11 August!, Maria's the 16th. That's really too long. I would like, for instance, to know Maria's plans, and also how the great Berlin evacuation has gone with them.[25] I wish you would let me know whether you have had the anti-shrapnel trench dug, and whether it would not be possible for you to have an exit made from the cellar to the trench. That is what Captain Maetz has done. How are things with Renate? Aren't these alarm nights particularly bad for her condition, even if she is out there at Sakrow for them?

I'm still getting on all right. I have been moved two floors lower because of the raids, and now it is very nice to have a direct view from my window on to the church towers. Last week I was able to write quite well again. The only thing I miss is open air exercise, on which I depend very much for any useful work. But it won't be long now, and that is the main thing.

Much love to Maria. Tell her to be patient a little while longer and stay in Pätzig or in Kl. Reetz[26] and not to worry. And love to all the family. Please don't tire yourselves out too much with the alerts, have a rest in the afternoon and eat as well as you can. I'm always thinking of you all.   Your grateful Dietrich

From Christoph von Dohnanyi   [Sakrow] 7 September 1943

Dear Uncle Dietrich,
It's now three days since I wrote to you last time. Not much has happened in this short time. As I think I've already told you, the grandparents and uncle Klaus were here on Sunday. Uncle Klaus only came later. He had a visit which kept him from eight in the evening until half past seven the next morning.[27] So he spent the day sleeping. They all stayed the night with us and then went back home again early on Monday.

Tomorrow we can all go to visit father. It's really very splendid that it's happened exactly on my birthday. It's my second visit since father went away. This evening Eberhard is coming home again. The English have attacked Kade;[28] 38 farms were burnt out. But nothing's happened to Eberhard's mother. It's really going a bit far when they go out into the country and smash it flat.

Yesterday I got myself into a bit of a smash. As I caught it right on the ankle, I couldn't cycle to school. I hope it's all right in the morning again, so that I can go to see father. I must do that whatever happens. I can't think of anything else to write to you, but I'll write again soon.

All the best.   Your grateful Christoph

From Renate Bethge   Sakrow, 8 September 1943

Dear Uncle Dietrich,[29]
We so much wished that you would be able to visit us soon in our beautiful house.[30] We really expected you from week to week. You would have had many well-known things to discover, I expect, but the way in which they had all blended together and were now arranged, the pictures and the books, would certainly have been a great delight to you. And now you will no longer be able to inspect them. Everything is in such a mess and scattered all over the place. In the meantime, you too have had to wait and wait, have had to tell yourself so often that your help would have been so useful in the turmoil, and I'm sure have often been anxious in the air raids because you have not been able to know straight away whether everything has gone well with us. We certainly hoped to see you again on the birthday. We celebrated it with lots of good things at the parents', with mother-in-law, the parents, aunt Christel, the grandparents and Bärbel. And you had such nice greetings and wishes arranged. Thank you very much. We also discovered the beautiful pigskin Bible with great delight. Even there you come upon the most beautiful presents. Did you also prompt Maria to the heartening greeting by telling her how much something like that would be cherished? Unfortunately my husband had to go travelling again in the evening. He has a heavy programme, so I am often alone. But things are well with us.

With me, in fact, they are going much better again, except that unfortunately I cannot keep on with the Conservatory from here. Of course it's difficult that we cannot now settle anywhere properly. There are many difficulties on all sides . . . It's very nice that we can have Bärbel's room at aunt Christel's for the moment. In that way we still have a small domain of our own. It's difficult with the scattered things, especially the books. When there is work to be done one never knows where the tools now are, in the Burchhardthaus cellar, with the parents, in Kade, in Bärbel's room or in aunt Christel's cellar. But things are still really good with us. The question of furniture has not yet been solved. The piano, which is quite especially beautiful, is coming to the parents' . . .

Did you know that your publisher, Lempp, has died? Apparently quite suddenly. Ebeling held a quite excellent memorial service for Erich Klapproth. Fritz[31] held the one in Köslin for Winfried Krause. All these happenings will make your seclusion particularly difficult. We would love to talk to you about everything. It will come about very soon. At any rate, we hope and wish very much for it. You are, though, to be envied for one thing in your awful position – for the many good things that you've read. These last weeks have quite taken it out of us. The music has been very quiet; even I don't get down to much practice. Now best wishes from us both; I hope all is well with you.

Your Renate

To his parents   [Tegel] 13 September 1943

Dear parents,
Last time I said I should like to have more letters, and in the last few days I've been delighted to have a whole sheaf of them. I almost seem to be like Palmström, who ordered 'a quarter's mixed correspondence'. But seriously, a day when there are letters is a very noticeable change from the usual monotony. Now that the permission to visit has also come, things really are looking up.

After the tiresome postal delays of recent weeks I've felt very grateful for that. I was glad that you seemed to be looking a little better when you came, but what worries me most about the whole business is that this year you've missed the holiday that you so badly needed. You really must go away for a time before winter, and it would be best of all if I could go with you. Today letters came from you and from Karl-Friedrich, dated 3 September, and Christoph has even written twice. It was very nice indeed of him, and I'm most grateful. It will, of course, have been an enormous chore for you to have moved my things away without my help. Thank you very much.

It's a strange feeling to be so completely dependent on other people; but at least it teaches one to be grateful, and I hope I shall never forget that. In ordinary life we hardly realize that we receive a great deal more than we give, and that it is only with gratitude that life becomes rich. Its very easy to overestimate the importance of our own achievements in comparison with what we owe to others.

The stormy happenings in the world in the last few days[32] go right through one, and I wish I could be doing useful service somewhere or other, but at present that 'somewhere' must be in the prison cell, and what I can do here makes its contribution in the unseen world, a sphere where the word 'do' is quite unsuitable. I sometimes think of Schubert's *Münnich* and his crusade.

For the rest, I'm reading and writing as much as I can, and I'm glad to say that I've never had a moment's boredom in the five months and more that I've been here. My time is always fully occupied, but in the background there is always the feeling, from morning till night, of waiting for something. A few weeks ago I asked you to get me some books that have just been published: N. Hartmann's *Systematic Philosophy* and *The Age of Marius and Sulla*, published by Diederich; now I should also like *German Music* by R. Benz. I shouldn't like to miss these things, and I should be glad to be able to read them while I am still here. Karl-Friedrich wrote about a book on physics, written for the general reader, and said he would send it to me. Klaus, too, sometimes discovers books that are worth reading. I've practically finished everything that I want to read here. I may have another try at Jean Paul's *Siebenkäs* or *Flegeljahre*; I have them in my room. I might not bring myself to read them later on, and there are many well-read people who think highly of him. In spite of several attempts, I've always found him too long-winded and affected. But as we're now in mid-September, I hope these wishes will already be out of date before they are fulfilled.

Another brief greeting has just come from Christoph. I've already such a great longing to see him and all the children again. They will have changed over these months. Christoph fulfils his duties as a godchild much better than I do mine as a godfather; but I'm already looking forward to doing with him something that he really wants.

If you speak to Maria or see her, please give her my love. Many thanks to grandmother for her letter. Greetings to all the family – and the children. Thank you for everything,   your Dietrich

Where is it that Karl-Friedrich has been called? Is he accepting? Some notepaper, please!

From the Judge Advocate of the War Court

The War Court   Torgau, Ziethen Barracks
StPL (RKA)   [deleted: Berlin-Charlottenburg 5
III/114/43   Witzlebenstrasse 4–10
                                  Telephone 38 06 81]
                                   16 September 1943

Stamp: Wehrmacht Interrogation Prison
       Branch office
       23 September 1943
       Ac.: 83.23g
signed. Mz

Order

The legal attorney Dr Kurt Wergin of Berlin W 35, Woyrsch-strasse 8, is permitted as the chosen defender of pastor Dietrich Bonhoeffer, §323 Abs.4 MStGO§51 GStVO.

The President	The Judge Advocate
of the Reich War Court	by order
as Chief Judge	signed Dr Lotter
signed Bastian	Reich War Attorney
Admiral	

From his mother   Charlottenburg, 20 September 1943

My dear Dietrich,

. . . I don't think that anything will now come of our trip to the little house[33] for a couple of days this summer or autumn. Very sad. I sometimes think that I will go up there once again for a week with father. With all his work and his seventy-five years he hasn't had a day's relaxation for a year. But he can't make up his mind to it until your case is sorted out, and I feel the same way. It will be all the finer if it then becomes possible again, and then this time your Maria will be coming, too. She has made such a kind offer to give me some help in the house now, but I would have no peace of mind and a very bad conscience in the air raids, whereas as things are I'm absolutely calm. There's no sense in a slit trench if it isn't supported at the sides, and the wood isn't to be had. Walter was in such a trench during the last heavy attack and when the bombs fell near him the sand came over him and the sides collapsed, so he won't go into another one. Eberhard is now in Spandau, at the Seeckt barracks . . .[34]

Father wants to ask for permission to visit again. It helps one on a bit further if we've seen each other and talked. By the way, I have Hartmann's *Systematic Philosophy* and will bring it next time.

III

We're pleased that you've just written a family story, and we're very eager to read it sometime later. Unfortunately I can't get hold of the chess book you wanted anywhere, nor Stifter's *Witiko*. If you wanted to have Fontane's *Journeyings through the Mark*, that would be there. I'll go on looking for the other books. Your bookshelves upstairs have now been completely cleared and everything has been moved down below, including the pictures and what was in the cupboards. When one sees all the damage to the roofs round about, it's best that way, though of course everything has got thoroughly mixed up. In Kade,[35] too, a number of fire bombs have been dropped on the barns. That place was supposed to be safe. Little Renate sent a mass of things out there. But that's how it goes; one cannot plan for anything at all. Perhaps it's quite a good thing, as otherwise there would be even more unrest among families. Father wants to add a greeting. I'm always thinking of you.   Your Mother

Mother hasn't left me much room. But she's told you all the important news, so that all that remains is for me to send you best wishes. I'm drying tobacco leaves at the moment. I hope you will be out again by the time they're smokable. Zacharias[36] has kept bringing me cigarettes from his own planting, which tasted very good. Warmest greetings.   Your Father

Testament[37]

In the event of my death . . .
I can give my parents nothing but thanks. I write these lines in the grateful consciousness of having lived a rich and full life, in the assurance of forgiveness and in prayer for all those named here.

Berlin, 20 September 1943   Dietrich Bonhoeffer

Eberhard is not to distress himself over my burial. I am quite happy if Ebeling, Rott, Kanitz, Schönherr, Dudzus, Fritz,[38] Walter,[39] Asmussen, Dibelius, Böhm, Jannasch or Lokies see to it.

To his parents   [Tegel] 25 September 1943

Dear parents,
Yesterday, mother, you left another splendid parcel for me. Your imagination really is inexhaustible; the warm food in the thermos flask was a special surprise – and it was marvellous; but thank you and everyone else who contributed for everything else. I do hope that you will soon be spared this trouble. The rain seems to have gradually settled in outside, and to match it I have a running cold, and my lumbago is back. I think that the reason is simply the lack of fresh air. The brief half hour, from which the hasty NCO is very fond of docking a few minutes, because otherwise he cannot get his duty done, is far too little, especially if one catches chills as easily as I do. That's only a burden because it prevents one from doing the only things that one can do here, reading and writing. But it's not serious, and certainly shouldn't make you worry. It's just a nuisance, and quite incidental.

A very nice letter came from Renate a few days ago; I'm very grateful to her for it. It's now become a real wartime marriage for her to endure, with many deprivations and difficulties. But the two of them will not lose heart as easily as all that. At any rate, they had a couple of very good months together. Perhaps I will soon face a similar decision.[40] If one can foresee that we can be together for at least a couple of months, then I would be in favour of marriage; on the other hand, I think that only a two-day honeymoon is too short, particularly for the woman, so I think it better to wait – but how long? Still, one can only make a decision about these questions when the time comes, and not beforehand. I'm so sorry for Maria, with the shocking delay over my case. Who could have envisaged it in April? I wish very much that one were told at the outset how long a business like this is likely to last. Even in my work here there is a good deal that I could have done differently and more profitably. In fact, people being as they are, every week, every day is precious. Although it may sound paradoxical, I was really glad yesterday when at last permission for a lawyer and then the warrant for my arrest came. So it seems that the apparently purposeless waiting will soon be over. At the same time, being in custody for so long has brought me experiences that I shall never forget. I keep reading the unusual books that you brought me from Karl-Friedrich with great delight, in between my work proper. For the rest, I'm doing some writing, and noticing that I also enjoy doing free-lance, non-theological writing. But I'm realizing for the first time how difficult the German language is and how easily one can murder it.

Many thanks to Ursel for what she sent recently. But she should really use *all* of it for her two soldier sons!

On reading this letter through, I think it sounds a bit disgruntled. That is not what I intend, and it wouldn't represent my state of mind. Much as I long to be out of here, I don't believe a single day has been wasted. What will come out of my time here it's still too early to say; but something will come of it. –

Please give my love to Maria, to all the family and the children. I've only had Renate's letter recently. Keep well in these autumn days. With all my love and thanks,   your Dietrich

From Christoph von Dohnanyi   [Sakrow] 28 September 1943

Dear Uncle Dietrich,
Today I've taken something to father. Then after I'd bought something else in town, I went home again about mid-day.

My flute teacher has now come back again. He's been in Spain. I can go to him tomorrow. He lives in Steglitz. That's not exactly the best place for air raids. He takes his fourteen flutes – I believe that's the number he has – with him into the cellar each time there's an alert.

Our little goat – I believe that you were here when she was born – is growing with tremendous speed; already she's almost as big as the old one. The two of them are making quite a lot of work. First there is clearing out the stalls, and secondly the question of fodder is not at all easy to solve. We can't give the animals our own potatoes. They have to be outside a great deal and eat greenstuff. They're both very fond of that, and afterwards the old one always gives much better milk. However, as a result the garden is losing its attractiveness. Still, milk today is more important than an attractive garden and two into one won't go.

Now I have to stop and clean up those stalls, which are already very messy.

All the best.   Your grateful Christoph

From his parents   [Charlottenburg] 3 October 1943

Dear Dietrich,
Your letter of 31 August came the day before yesterday – a record: one month for a distance of 13 kilometres! – evidently as a result of the move of the Reich War Court to Torgau. That is a pity. I hope that the request for permission to visit will not take so long. I asked for it about ten days ago. Tomorrow it's six months since we had your arrest, with the flowers from my seventy-fifth birthday celebrations still around. It's good news to us that you have the capacity to concentrate on your work, at least for a time, to such a degree that you can quite forget the situation of the moment. I'm eager to read your study on the experience of time. When one lives with certain dates in mind, as we do from Friday to Friday, when we take your weekly parcel, the weeks seem short, and in reminiscences what has been experienced seems to go quickly back into the past. Perhaps the latter is something to do with old age, but perhaps it is also connected with the abundance of new impressions with which one is confronted in the present times. I'm not particularly good at being able to work. Too many things come upon one. The garden is now taking less time. We shall be picking three apples and no pears. On the other

hand, the vintage is a good one this time. I think that we shall be able to see to a sample for you on Friday.

Yesterday the day was filled with glass work. We had to nail in the panes ourselves and put the putty on, after the glass man had shown us. It looks easier than it is. Still, we now have everything in order except for one pane in the dining-room. Mother will write to you on the other side about the family and the house and give you all the news. Warmest greetings and good courage for the rest of your time of trial.   Your Father

Dear Dietrich,

It is a handicap to writing letters when one assumes that they will be outdated by the course of events before they reach the person to whom they're sent. For instance, I would very much like to give you some advice about what to do for your catarrh; I see that you have it from your request for some Ems pastilles. But as unfortunately they aren't to be had any more, the question doesn't arise. I only hope that you can get some advice from a doctor . . .

You can't imagine how difficult it is to get the Fontane and the Stifter. Renate says that you had two volumes of Stifter in your library, and *your* Fontane. But I haven't any possibility of getting anything out of your library anyway, as we took everything from the attic down to father on the ground floor and on to the first floor, where it is piled up in cupboards. When I saw how often it was that the top floor of a house was burnt out, I didn't really want to do it, but resolved to. I can, however, send Raabe's *Hungerpastor* to you. Let me know what Stifter and Fontane you already have there; the things often go to Hans, and then I'm no longer in the picture about where they were . . . Always let me know what you want. I would so like to make your position as comfortable as possible within our powers. It really is a quite improbable situation for members of our family. But I can say one thing. I have always been proud of my eight children, and I am now, more than ever, when I see the dignity and respect they maintain in such an indescribable situation. I'm also convinced, though, that this time of trial for your patience has a meaning for you, and go on entrusting you to the divine guidance. He will make things well. So we must go on waiting and working, to make this evil time pass quickly. That is sometimes a blessing of work. Thank God you can do some in the intellectual sphere; there is no lack of work for me here at home and with the family, and I will be cheerful as long as I can.

All the best, my good boy.   Your old Mother

To his parents   [Tegel] 4 October 1943

Dear parents,
Many thanks for your letter of the 20 September, which arrived here simultaneously with one from Maria of the 2 September . . ., three days ago! Could you please let Maria know straightaway that I've only just received her letter; otherwise she won't understand why I haven't replied to it; a later one, dated 13 September, arrived earlier.

Outside it's lovely autumn weather, and I wish that you – and I with you – were at Friedrichsbrunn, and also Hans and his family, who are all so specially fond of the cottage. But how many people must there be in the world today who cannot have their wishes met? I certainly don't agree with Diogenes that the greatest happiness is the absence of desire, and that the best place to live in is a tub; why should we be fooled into believing that kind of thing? But I do believe that it may be good for us, especially when we are young, to have to wait for what we want, although we ought not to go so far as to give up wishing for anything and grow apathetic. But I'm in no danger of that at present . . .

A letter from Christoph has just come. It's surprising how he keeps thinking of writing. What a view of life a fourteen-year-old must get when he has to write to his father and godfather in prison for months on end. He cannot have many illusions about the world now; I suppose all these happenings mean the end of his childhood. Please thank him very much for his letter; I'm greatly looking forward to seeing him again.

I am glad you were able to get hold of Hartmann's *Systematic*

Philosophy. I'm getting down to it properly, and it will keep me busy for several weeks, if the interruption that I hope for does not occur in the meantime.

Maria wrote so nicely about her hours with you in her last letter. She feels very much at home with you, and of course I'm infinitely glad about that. Thank you very much for always making things so pleasant for her. I would find the thought that she should relieve you of the household work very attractive, mother, thinking of my return also; I believe that the worst time for air raids is past, but of course I wouldn't want to take the responsibility.

I'm looking forward to the next visit that you've applied for. Can't one of the family come with you some time? How are things with Renate and her husband now? Of course I'm thinking of them a great deal. Please give my love to them and all the others. With much love,   your grateful Dietrich

Would you please try to get for me: Ortega y Gasset, 'System der Geschichte' and 'Vom römischen Imperium', two articles which appeared in 1943 from the Deutsche Verlagsanstalt, Stuttgart.

To his parents   [Tegel] 13 October 1943

Dear parents,
I have in front of me the gay bunch of dahlias that you brought me yesterday; it reminds me of the lovely hour that I was able to have with you, and of the garden, and in general of how beautiful the world can be in these autumn days. One of Storm's verses that I came across the other day just about expresses this mood, and keeps going through my head like a tune that one cannot get rid of:

> *Und geht es draussen noch so toll,*
>   *unchristlich oder christlich,*
> *ist doch die Welt, die schöne Welt*
> *so gänzlich unverwüstlich.*[41]

All that is needed to bring that home to one is a few gay autumn flowers, the view from the cell window, and half an hour's 'exercise' in the prison yard, where there are, in fact, a few beautiful chestnut and lime trees. But in the last resort, for me at any rate, the 'world' consists of a few people whom I should like to see and to be with. The occasional appearances of you and Maria, for a brief hour as though from a great distance, are really the thing for which and from which I principally live. If, besides that, I could sometimes hear a good sermon on Sundays – I sometimes hear fragments of the chorales that are carried along by the breeze – it would be still better. By the way, Karl-Friedrich or Ursel ought to apply some time for permission to accompany you on one of your visits; that would be a great delight.

I was very pleased about your last letter of 3 October, which came with surprising speed. In the meantime you have convinced yourselves that things go well with me, and I really thought that this time you looked a little better. Thank you very much for the grapes from the garden; they certainly are excellent and I'm only sorry, father, that you yourself are not eating them now.

I've again been doing a good deal of writing lately, and for the work that I have set myself to do, the day is often too short, so that sometimes, comically enough, I even feel that I have 'no time' here for this or that less important matter! After breakfast in the morning (about 7 o'clock) I read some theology, and then I write till midday; in the afternoon I read, then comes a chapter from Delbrück's *World History*, some English grammar, about which I can still learn all kinds of things, and finally, as the mood takes me, I write or read again. Then in the evening I am tired enough to be glad to lie down, though that does not mean going to sleep at once.

When will Maria come to you now? Mother, why don't you simply hand over the housekeeping to her, even if only for a while? It would be a sort of holiday for you, and I imagine that Maria will do it brilliantly. I'm so sorry that you and she have troubled yourselves unnecessarily with the fur. But in the warm white sweater and the ski suit I really feel quite warm, although it's only 12 degrees inside. How long will we have to keep on writing letters? On the 26th, the birthdays of Christel and Renate will be very much in my thoughts. Each of them celebrates with their own particular worries. It is also, by the way, the anniversary of Max Wedemeyer's[42] death.

Much love to all the family. My desire to see them all again grows greater week by week. Greetings, too, to aunt Elisabeth. Take care of yourselves in the cold weather!

Much love.   Your grateful Dietrich

From his father to the Presidents of the War Court
[Charlottenburg] 17 October 1943

I request you to arrange the release of my son pastor Dietrich Bonhoeffer from prison. He has been in prison since the beginning of April. I need not say that it would be a great joy to my wife and myself, who are both old people, if we had him with us at the festival. At one time, on the occasion of a visit to the prison, Judge Advocate Roeder indicated that it was envisaged that the proceedings would be closed by the middle of July. We hear that the investigations have now been closed for some time and with a member of my family there could be no question that in the event of a release from prison he would evade the proceedings. We therefore hope that our request can be granted. From the personality of my son I am also convinced that he has not committed any offence that could justify further imprisonment.

                                                         Karl Bonhoeffer

To his parents   [Tegel] 22 October 1943

Dear parents,
I'm told that Suse has just been here with little Michael, to leave your parcel. Thank you, and her, very much for it. I hope the

prison didn't make too great an impression on the little boy; a child like that has as yet no standards by which to judge such things, and he may imagine that things are blacker for me than they are. I was really distressed not to be able to give him a friendly welcome and talk to him; it would certainly have reassured him. No doubt Suse's point of view is that we ought not deliberately to keep children away from the experiences that life brings us; and I think that's right in principle. But when they are eighteen, how different they will be from what we were – not too disillusioned and bitter, I hope, but actually tougher and stronger because of all that they've been through. Please give Michael my best thanks for his bunch of flowers.

It seems as if my affairs are now beginning to move, and I'm very glad of it; it's all the more unnatural that I can't discuss my concerns with you now, as I used to. But I don't think it can be very much longer now. Anyway, you mustn't suppose that I'm giving all my time to this business; that's not so at all, and I think there is no need for it. The last few days and weeks have been quiet, and I've been using them to do as much work as possible; unfortunately I never get through quite as much as I set out to during the day. I've had the great advantage of being able lately to read through undisturbed, and compare with each other, the great German educational and cultural novels, *Wilhelm Meister*, *Der Nachsommer*, *Der Grüne Heinrich*, *Der Hungerpastor* (at present I'm on *Die Flegeljahre*), and I shall enjoy the recollection of them for a long time. I found it very useful, too, to read the *World History*. I still like Hartmann's *Systematic Philosophy* very much; it's a very handy survey. So I can feel as if I had been given a term at a university with a series of good lectures. Of course, any creative output of my own has suffered badly; but I'm now looking forward tremendously to the day when I shall again be in touch, not only with ideas and fictitious figures, but with real people and all our many daily problems; it will be a very radical change.

How are things with you? Is Else[43] away? What are the Schleichers doing?

Have you any news from Calabria of Hans-Christoph?[44] I'm getting on all right, and am enjoying the last warm days of the year, as far as that's possible. Thank you very much for every-thing. I hope your anxiety will soon be over now; it's high time. Many thanks to Karl Friedrich for his letter. I hope I shall soon see him on a visit. It would be very good. With good confidence, love to you and all the family,   your grateful Dietrich

When is Maria coming to you? She wrote to me today that she was going to Kniephof to spend a while with her sister Bismarck.[45] She says that you spoilt her too much and that I am to tell you. But I think it's very nice.

From his father   [Charlottenburg] 23 October 1943

Dear Dietrich,
I hope that we shall soon be able to talk to you again out there. I've asked for permission to visit with a special request for a regular fortnightly rotation. I hope that this will be allowed and then soon overtaken by your release. It's a shame that these fine warm autumn days are passing by us and millions of other people without our being able to enjoy them freely. It's a good thing that there still seem to be warm days for our soldiers in the East, too. In this way the winter will be shortened a bit . . .

It will not be long before I can send you some tobacco of my own make. But I will mark it in some way so that you know it and can throw it away if it's unusable.

Warmest greetings.   Your Father

To his parents   [Tegel] 31 October 1943

Dear parents,
Once again, very many thanks for your visit. If only it could be rather more often and longer! With the size of our family, there is not enough time to ask about each one singly. But the main

thing is that you and all the others are getting along tolerably well. It's obvious now that everyone has his particular worries and a great deal of work, though in your old age you really have the right to feel this rather less. Instead of we younger ones being able to make some things easier for you and to relieve you of some of the burden, it's unfortunately quite the other way round.

Once again, very many thanks for the parcel; I know well enough how [much] care and thought it always costs you. You recently wrote, mother, about the way in which it always puts you out when something is forgotten; please don't let that happen. First, in fact, it's hardly ever that anything *is* forgotten – on the contrary, everything is always much finer than I could believe possible; secondly, I know full well all the things that you have to think about now. I would really be sorry if afterwards you had the slightest worry about something that never gives me anything but great joy. So very many thanks, and please pass them on to Ursel and all the others who share in it.

Today is Reformation Day, a feast that in our time can give one plenty to think about. One wonders why Luther's action had to be followed by consequences that were the exact opposite of what he intended, and that darkened the last years of his life, so that he sometimes even doubted the value of his life's work. He wanted a real unity of the church and the West – that is, of the Christian peoples, and the consequence was the disintegration of the church and of Europe; he wanted the 'freedom of the Christian man', and the consequence was indifference and licentiousness; he wanted the establishment of a genuine secular social order free from clerical privilege, and the result was insurrection, the Peasant's War, and soon afterwards the gradual dissolution of all real cohesion and order in society. I remember from my student days a discussion between Holl and Harnack as to whether the great historical intellectual and spiritual movements made headway through their primary or their secondary motives. At the time I thought Holl was right in maintaining the former; now I think he was wrong. As long as a hundred years ago Kierkegaard said that today Luther would say the opposite of what he said then. I think he was right – with some reservations.

Now another request. Would you please order for me *Lesebuch der Erzähler*, by Wolf Dietrich Rasch (Kiepenheuer, 1943), *Die Ballade*, by Wilhelm von Scholz (Theodor Knaur, 1943), and *Briefe der Liebe aus 8 Jahrhunderten*, by Friedrich Reck-Malleczewen (Keil, 1943)? There may not be a great number of copies printed, so they will have to be ordered at once.

A short time ago my rheumatism was so bad that for a few hours I couldn't get up from my chair without help, or even lift my hands to feed myself. But they at once gave me electrical treatment in the sick-bay, and it's much better now, though I haven't been entirely free of it since May. Is there anything I can do about it later? How good that you've found a regular receptionist!

Please give my love to all the family and the children. I'm hoping every day for a speedy reunion with you.

Your grateful Dietrich

The letter from grandmother Kleist arrived yesterday.

From his father   [Charlottenburg] 5 November 1943

Dear Dietrich,
Your Reformation Day letter has come with a pleasant turn of speed. We received it today. I've ordered the books that you wanted. The bookseller didn't have them in stock, but he will send them as soon as he has them . . .

Unfortunately the blooms on our fine dahlias were nipped by the frost last night. I've managed to save the last rose for mother's desk. It's seven months today since you were imprisoned. It's a comforting thought for us to know that you can work and are able to divide your day up into parts. That will help to make the rest of this trial tolerable for you. As far as your rheumatism is concerned, November is not exactly the best month for getting rid of it. Perhaps you can take a yellow tablet of aspirin or nelutrin three times a day. I don't know whether the latter can be had, though. I expect that when you are back in normal conditions and can move about more in the fresh air, you will get rid of it. We've just had a short alert. It's considerate of them to come so early. We are still up and hope for an undisturbed night . . .

Affectionately, your Father

To his parents   [Tegel] 9 November 1943

Dear parents,
Now the dismal autumn days have begun and one has to try to get light from within. Your letters always help with this; recently they've been coming through with astonishing speed. Once again, your last parcel was particularly fine. I was very surprised and pleased with the Stifter anthology. As it consists mainly of extracts from his letters, it's almost all new to me. My overriding interest for the last ten days has been *Witiko* which, after my giving you so much trouble to hunt for it, was discovered in the library here – a place where I shouldn't really have expected it. Most people would find its thousand pages, which can't be skipped but have to be taken steadily, too much for them, so I'm not sure whether to recommend it to you. For me it's one of the finest books I know. The purity of its style and character-drawing gives one a quite rare and peculiar feeling of happiness. One really ought to read it for the first time at the age of fourteen, instead of the *Kampf um Rom*, and then grow up with it. Even today's good historical novels, e.g. those by Gertrud Bäumer, can't compare with it – it's *sui generis*. I should very much like to have it, but it would hardly be possible to get hold of it. So far, the only historical novels that have made a comparable impression on me are *Don Quixote* and Gotthelf's *Berner Geist*. I've again failed to make anything of Jean Paul; I can't get over the feeling that he is vain and affected. He must have been rather unattractive personally, too. It's fine to go through literature like this on voyages of discovery, and one does discover some quite surprising things, even after so many years' reading. Perhaps you've further suggestions to make?

A few days ago I got Rüdiger's letter, for which I thank him very much. The programme of the Furtwängler concert that he went to did make me wish I could have been there. I hope I won't forget what's left of my technique while I'm here. I sometimes feel a real craving for an evening of music – trio, quartet, or singing; one would like to hear something different from the voices in this building. After more than seven months here one has had more than enough of it. But of course, that's only to be expected, and there is no need to mention it to you. What is not a matter of course is that I'm all right here in spite of everything, that I can experience pleasures of one kind or another, and that with it all I keep my spirits up – and so I'm very thankful every day. Maria is to come on a visit tomorrow. I keep encouraging her along from month to month and ask her to be patient, but it's indescribably difficult for her.

I hope I shall see you again soon and that I shall get a letter in the meanwhile. Give my love to all the family. Many thanks to Anna[46] for the cigarettes. Keep well, and don't worry about me. 'Good work . . .'[47]

Much love.   Your grateful Dietrich

And many thanks for the chess book!

To his parents   [Tegel] 17 November 1943

Dear parents,
While I'm writing this letter, on Repentance Day, the Schleichers, so Ursel told me, are all listening to the B Minor Mass. For years now I've associated it with this particular day, like the St Matthew Passion with Good Friday. I well remember the evening when I first heard it. I was eighteen, and had just come from Harnack's seminar, in which he had discussed my first seminar essay very kindly, and had expressed the hope that some day I should special-ize in church history. I was full of this when I went into the Phil-harmonic Hall; the great *Kyrie Eleison* was just beginning, and as

it did so, I forgot everything else – the effect was indescribable. Today I'm going through it, bit by bit, in my mind, and I'm glad the Schleichers can hear it, as it's my favourite work of Bach.

Ursel's visit this morning was a great delight. I'm most grateful to her for it. It's always so comforting to find you so calm and cheerful despite all the unpleasantness you have to put up with as a result of my imprisonment. You, mother, wrote recently that you were proud that your children behaved 'respectably' in such a grim situation. In fact we've all learnt it from the two of you, especially when you were so completely calm during serious illnesses in the family and didn't give anything away. So it has probably become a legacy. Ursel told me a great deal about everyone; it was really time that we met again after these long months, during which so much has happened that affects us both. Now I *very much* hope that Eberhard's request for a visit will be granted before he goes on active service. Even if that should not be the case, we both know that we are bound together in our thoughts day by day. I'm very pleased for Renate that he has got this leave,[48] and hope that Hans-Walter will soon get his long-deserved leave also.

There's nothing much new to report about myself. It's nearly evening now, and it's quiet in the building, so I can pursue my thoughts undisturbed. During the day I keep on finding out again the different degrees of noise with which people do their work; I suppose that's how nature has endowed them. A fortissimo just outside my cell is hardly the right background for serious study. I've very much enjoyed re-reading Goethe's *Reinecke Fuchs* this last week. You might enjoy it again too.

What are the prospects for some jewellery for Maria? I would so like to get something for her if I were free again. But I expect that it will be very difficult. Once again, many thanks to Ursel for the flask with the splendid cocoa and to Tine[49] for the milk which she sacrificed for it. And very many thanks for the biscuits. From week to week I hope for an end to this trial of patience. I also feel that it is gradually becoming too great a burden for Maria to bear. But it can't be much longer.

I hope you have a very good first Sunday in Advent with the

children. I shall be thinking of you very much; I hope the Schleichers have a couple of good musical evenings in the old style. It's good that Renate now plays the piano part better than I do. Good-bye, and above all keep well! Much love to all the family. With all my love.   Your grateful Dietrich

To Eberhard Bethge   [Tegel][50] 18 November 1943

Dear Eberhard,

As you are in the neighbourhood, I simply must take the opportunity of writing to you. I expect you know that I haven't even been allowed to have the pastor to see me here; but even if he had come – I'm really very glad that I have *only* the Bible – I wouldn't have been able to speak to him in that way which is only possible with you.

You can't imagine how much I worried during the first weeks of my imprisonment in case your wedding plans had been shattered. I prayed a great deal for you and Renate, and thanked God for every day on which I had good news of you. Your wedding day *really* was a day of joy for me, like few others. Later in September it was a great torment not to be able to support you.[51] But the certainty that so far you have been guided with such unbelievable friendship made me quite confident that God intends things to be very well with you.

And now, after these long months without worship, penitence and eucharist and without the *consolatio fratrum* – once again be my pastor as you have so often been in the past, and listen to me. There is so infinitely much to report, that I would like to tell both of you, but today it can only be the essentials, so this letter is for you alone . . . So let me tell you a little that you ought to know about me. For the first twelve days, during which I was segregated and treated as a felon – up to now the cells on each side of me have been occupied almost solely by handcuffed men awaiting death – Paul Gerhardt was an unexpectedly helpful standby, and so were the Psalms and Revelation. During this time I have been preserved from any serious spiritual trial. You are the only person who knows how often *accidie, tristitia*, with all its menacing consequences, has lain in wait for me; and I feared at the time that you must be worrying about me on that account. But I told myself from the beginning that I was not going to oblige either man or devil in any such way – they can do what they like about it for themselves; and I hope I shall always be able to stand firm on this.

At first I wondered a good deal whether it was really for the cause of Christ that I was causing you all such grief; but I soon put that out of my head as a temptation, as I became certain that the duty had been laid on me to hold out in this boundary situation with all its problems; I became quite content to do this, and have remained so ever since (I Peter 2.20; 3.14).[52]

I've reproached myself for not having finished my *Ethics* (parts of it have probably been confiscated), and it was some consolation to me that I had told you the essentials, and that even if you had forgotten it, it would probably emerge again indirectly somehow. Besides, my ideas were still incomplete.

I also felt it to be an omission not to have carried out my long-cherished wish to attend the Lord's Supper once again with you. I wanted to tell you once again how grateful I am that you . . . bore with such patience and tolerance all the things with which I have sometimes made life hard for you. I ask you for forgiveness, and yet I know that we have shared spiritually, although not physically, in the gift of confession, absolution, and communion, and that we may be quite happy and easy in our minds about it. But I did just want to tell you this.

As soon as it was possible, apart from my daily work on the Bible (I've read through the Old Testament two and a half times and learnt a great deal), I began to do some non-theological work. An essay on 'The feeling of time'[53] originated mainly in the need to bring before me my own past in a situation that could so easily seem 'empty' and 'wasted'. Our past is always kept before us by thankfulness and penitence. But more of that later.

Then I started on a bold enterprise that I've had in mind for a long time: I began to write the story of a contemporary middle-class family.[54] The background for this consisted of all our innumerable conversations on the subject, and my own personal experiences; in short, it was to present afresh middle-class life as we know it in our own families, and especially in the light of Christianity. It tells of two families on terms of friendship living in a small town. Their children grow up, and as they gradually enter into the responsibilities of official positions, they try to work together for the good of the community as mayor, teacher, pastor, doctor, engineer. You would recognize many familiar features, and you come into it too. But I haven't yet got much further than the beginning, mainly because the repeated false forecasts of my release have made it difficult for me to concentrate. But the work is giving me great pleasure. Only I wish I could talk it over with you every day; indeed, I miss that more than you think. I may often have originated our ideas, but the clarification of them was completely on your side. I only learnt in conversation with you whether an idea was any good or not. I long to read to you some of what I've written. Your comments on details are so much better than mine. Perhaps that seems to be mad presumption?!

Incidentally, I've written an essay on 'What is "speaking the truth"?'[55], and at the moment I'm trying to write some prayers for prisoners;[56] it's surprising that there are none, and perhaps these may be distributed at Christmas.

And now for my reading. Yes, Eberhard, I'm very sorry that we did not get to know Stifter together; it would have helped us very much in our talks, but we shall have to put it off till later. But I've a great deal to tell you about that. Later? When and how will it come about? To be on the safe side, I've made my will and given it to my lawyer. In it, I've left almost everything I have to you. But first Maria must be allowed to look for something that she would like in remembrance. If this should happen, please be very good to Maria, and if possible, write to her in my stead from time to time, just a few kind words, as you can do so well, and tell her gently that I asked you to. But perhaps – or certainly – you are now going into greater danger. I shall be thinking of you every day and asking God to protect you and bring you back. Please take with you anything of mine that you need; I'm only too pleased to know it's with you. And please provide yourself with as much of the food that has come for me as you need. That's a thought that would comfort me very much.

There is so much that I would very, very much like to hear of you. Sometimes I've thought that it is really very good for the two of you that I'm not there. At the beginning it's not at all easy to resolve the conflict between marriage and friendship; you're spared this problem, and later it won't exist. But that's only a private and passing thought; you mustn't laugh at it.

I wonder whether, if I'm not condemned, but released and called up, it might be arranged for me to get to your neighbourhood. That would be fine! Anyway, if I should be condemned (one never knows), don't worry about me. It really doesn't worry me at all, except that in that case I shall probably be kept here for a few more months longer 'on probation', and that's really not pleasant. But there is a great deal that isn't pleasant! The thing for which I should be condemned is so unexceptionable that I should only be proud of it. But I hope that, if God preserves us, we shall at least be able to celebrate Easter happily together. And then, *sub conditione Jacobea*, I shall baptize your child!

And now, Eberhard, good-bye. I don't expect a long letter from you. You've little time now. But let's promise to remain faithful in interceding for each other. I shall ask that you may have strength, health, patience, and protection from conflicts and temptations. You can ask for the same things for me. And if it should be decided that we are not to meet again, let us remember each other to the end in thankfulness and forgiveness, and may God grant us that one day we may stand before his throne praying for each other and joining in praise and thankfulness.

God protect you and Renate and all of us. Faithfully,

your grateful Dietrich

. . . By the way, I've heard that Warsaw is frightfully dear.[57] Take as much as you can with you; if you need money, feel free to draw 1000 marks of mine. I can't use it. Do you always get my letters to my parents to read? See that they send them to you. I'm finding here (I expect you are, too) that the most difficult thing is getting up in the morning (Jer. 31.26!).[58] I'm now praying quite simply for freedom. There is such a thing as a false composure which is quite unchristian. As Christians, we needn't be at all ashamed of some impatience, longing, opposition to what is unnatural, and our full share of desire for freedom, earthly happiness, and opportunity for effective work. I think we entirely agree about that.

Well, in spite of everything, or rather because of everything, that we are now going through, each in his own way, we shall still be the same as before, shan't we? I hope you don't think I am here turning out to be a 'man of the inner line';[59] I was never in less danger of that, and I think the same applies to you. What a happy day it will be when we tell each other our experiences. But I sometimes get very angry at not being free yet!

My wedding plans: if I am free and still have at least a couple of months before I'm called up, I want to get married. If I have only two or three weeks free before the call-up, then I want to wait until the end of the war. What an engagement we've had! Maria is astounding! You don't think that's too much to ask? If only we had seen each other at least a couple of times in January! I don't know why Maria has to put up with so much hardship, young as she is. I hope that it isn't too much for her, but I'm so glad to have her now. Or do you think that it would have been better and more unselfish if I had asked her after my arrest simply to wait for my release without letters and visits? I would have regarded that as unnatural, and I think that you would have done, too. Please think of her, too, when you think of me.

I was very affected by G. Seydel's[60] death. Always the best! I've borne up *well* physically with all your help . . .

That's all. We've had some incomparably good years together, and I hope that some more are before us!!   Dietrich

20 November

Your letter of 9 November has just come with so much news about which I was most delighted; but it also brought the sad news of the deaths of B. Riemer and R. August.[61] Now you've lost the last of the real friends of your youth. You will be looking more and more towards the present and the future. Thank God that you have Renate; and you yourself know well enough that behind her there is a family all of whose members count you one of themselves and will always stand by you . . .

It's also hard to think that I shall not be able to talk to you immediately I'm released. But if this really must be, we must at least write long letters for a while. We shall not forget our different experiences in a hurry! If I should still be kept in this hole over Christmas, don't worry about it. I'm not really anxious about it. One can keep Christmas as a Christian even in prison – more easily than family occasions, anyhow. Thank you especially for applying for permission to visit me; I don't expect, either, that there have been any complications this time. I certainly shouldn't have ventured to ask you to do anything about it; but as you yourself have made the move, it's much better. I really do hope it comes off. But, you know, even if it is refused, I shall be glad that you tried, and it will only make me rather more angry with certain people for the time being – and there is no harm in that (indeed, I sometimes think I am not yet angry enough about the whole business!). So in that case we will swallow even that bitter pill, for after all, we have both of us been getting used to that kind of thing lately. I'm glad I saw you just as I was arrested, and I shall not forget it. I know now that my weak attempts at looking after you are in much better hands with Renate and the best mother-in-law imaginable of all imaginable mothers-in-law (freely adapted from Leibniz) . . .

A little more about my daily routine: We get up at the same time, and the day lasts till 8 p.m.; I wear out my trousers by sitting while you wear out your soles by walking. I read the *Völkischer Beobachter* and the *Reich*,[62] and I've got to know several *very* nice people. Every day I'm taken for half an hour's walking alone, and in the afternoon they give me treatment in the sick-bay – very kindly, but unsuccessfully – for my rheumatism. Every week I get from you the most marvellous things to eat. Thank you very much for everything, and also for the cigars and cigarettes that you sent me while you were away.[63] I only hope you have plenty to eat – do you get very hungry? That would be horrid. There is nothing I miss here – except all of you. I wish I could play the G minor sonata with you[64] and sing some Schütz, and hear you sing Psalms 70 and 47; that was what you did best.

My cell is being cleaned out for me, and while it's being done, I can give the cleaner something to eat. One of them was sentenced to death the other day; it gave me a great shock. One sees a great deal in seven and a half months, particularly what heavy consequences may follow trivial acts of folly. I think a lengthy confinement is demoralizing in *every* way for most people. I've been thinking out an alternative penal system on the principle of making the punishment fit the crime; e.g., for absence without leave, the cancelling of leave; for unauthorized wearing of medals, longer service at the front; for robbing other soldiers, the temporary labelling of a man as a thief; for dealing in the black market, a reduction of rations; and so on. Why does the Old Testament law never punish anyone by depriving him of his freedom?

You must at all events indicate the preliminary work for your licenciate studies, which were not finished (Psalms lectures?). There was never any question of this, whatever happens.[65] Is your position as 'batman' to an NCO really regarded as a special honour? How unutterably comic! or is it also a nuisance? . . .

I wish you much joy and don't want you to be disturbed by any thoughts about me. I have every reason to be so infinitely grateful about everything.

Here's to a joyful reunion soon, like old times!

Your Dietrich

Those verses[66] that I wrote have also made a considerable impression here. Perhaps you would like to put the notebook in your briefcase? Of course, the rest of the letter must disappear.[67] Perhaps it will please you to hear that the prisoners and the guards here keep saying how they are 'amazed' (?!) at my tranquillity and cheerfulness. I myself am always amazed about remarks of this kind. But isn't it rather nice?

If there is *anything at all* that you could think of that would please you, it would give me the greatest delight. One of the most awful things here is that one is so hopeless about this kind of thing. Please at least help yourself occasionally to some of my bacon; tell mother that *I* asked you *very* particularly to do so! I still have plenty, and certainly don't need any in the next six weeks. If only I could share some Krössin smoked goose with you! Can one send anything?

21 November

Today is Remembrance Sunday. Will you have a memorial service for B. Riemer? It would be nice, but difficult. Then comes Advent, with all its happy memories for us. It was you who really first opened up to me the world of music-making that we have carried on during the weeks of Advent. Life in a prison cell may well be compared to Advent; one waits, hopes, and does this, that, or the other – things that are really of no consequence – the door is shut, and can be opened only *from the outside*. That idea is just as it occurs to me; don't suppose we go in very much for symbolism here! But I must tell you two other things that may surprise you: First, I very much miss meal-time fellowship. Everything that I get from you for my material enjoyment becomes here a reminder of my table-fellowship with you. So may not this be an essential part of life, because it is a reality of the Kingdom of God? Secondly, I've found that following Luther's instruction to 'make the sign of the cross' at our morning and evening prayers is in itself helpful. There is something objective about it, and that is what is particularly badly needed here. Don't be alarmed; I shall not come out of here a *homo religiosus*! On the contrary, my fear and distrust of 'religiosity' have become greater than ever here. The fact that the Israelites *never* uttered the name of God always makes me think, and I can understand it better as I go on. Did you in fact get my wedding sermon? . . . The letter has got much longer than I intended.[68] Now there are all sorts of things in it that are also intended for others. You can decide.

I'm now reading Tertullian, Cyprian, and others of the church fathers with great interest. In some ways they are more relevant to our time than the Reformers, and at the same time they provide

135

a basis for talks between Protestants and Roman Catholics.

Do you sometimes wonder why I allow so much food to be sent when I know well enough that you yourselves are short? To begin with, during the months of interrogation I thought it important to keep my strength for the sake of the cause. Later, people kept holding out the prospect of an early ending, and I wanted to keep in physical trim as much as possible for that. The same thing applies again now. Once I'm free or condemned, of course, it will stop. Anyway, I believe that on purely legal grounds my condemnation is out of the question.

22 November

If there is anything that would help Renate in her present condition, and you need money for it, please simply take as much as you need without saying any more about it. And of course that applies all the more afterwards. There is really no point in the money rotting in my account. Be glad that you bought the jewellery for Renate then. I don't think that I shall be able to get any for Maria. I've often been glad that you asked me to the civil ceremony when you did.[69] I think back to the day with great pleasure and feel that I was at the decisive moment with you. Just tell me how you get on with the soldiers, with your willingness to take no notice of false accusations – (probably a bit of your *anima naturaliter christiana*?). Two or three times here I've given people a quite colossal dressing down for indulging in only the slightest rudeness, and they were so disconcerted that they have behaved very correctly since then. I thoroughly enjoy this sort of thing, but I know it's really an impossible over-sensitiveness that I can hardly get rid of . . . It makes me furious to see quite defenceless people being unjustly shouted at and insulted. These petty tormentors, who can rage like that and whom one finds everywhere, get me worked up for hours on end. I think that you find a better equilibrium in these things. It would certainly be good for me if I could be a soldier somewhere near you. *Das Neue Lied*,[70] which I got only a few days ago, has brought back hosts of pleasant memories. You see, I am always thinking of things that I want to talk over with you, and when I start again after such a long time, I find it difficult to stop. Much that I would love to ask you and to tell you isn't even mentioned. We really must meet again soon. That really is the end. Love to you and Renate.   Your Dietrich

Do you occasionally write to mother and father? I should think that with their concern for me they would be glad of any greeting. I was very pleased about the prayer at the συνοδος.[71] Do you get round to the Bible readings, at least in the mornings?

23 November

Tonight's raid was not exactly pleasant.[72] I kept thinking of you all and especially of Renate. At such times prison life is no joke. I hope you're going back to Sakrow. I was surprised last night to see how nervy the soldiers who had been at the front were while the alert was on.

My parents have just been here and brought good news. So the long journey was not in vain. How is it that they've only managed to get through here? In the city the prospect seems to be very bad. I was so sorry that we couldn't speak together, but I was very glad to hear that nothing has happened to you. The date is 17 December. At last! Will I see the week? Can't Rüdiger ring up Speckhardt in Torgau about your permission to visit? We must also take care to see that the Captain[73] takes it here!

Testament

[Tegel][74] 23 November 1943

Dear Eberhard,
After yesterday's air raid I think it is only right that I should tell you briefly what arrangements I have made in case of my death. The notes given to the attorney might also be destroyed, so it is

137

better that someone knows about them. I hope that you will read this with your usual absence of sentimentality. It seems to me only reasonable to make the necessary provisions in case of such an eventuality . . . [There follow bequests to members of the family] You are to give a book each to Fritz, Jochen, Albrecht, Maechler, Dudzus, your brother Christoph, H. Christoph, Ebeling, Rott, Perels and if possible to uncle George Ch[ichester] . . .

So that's it. Keep this paper safely somewhere. I believe that one has to sign such a document with one's full name. So

Berlin, 23 November 1943   Dietrich Bonhoeffer

Prayers for Fellow-Prisoners

Christmas 1943

MORNING PRAYERS

O God, early in the morning I cry to you.
Help me to pray
And to concentrate my thoughts on you;
I cannot do this alone.

In me there is darkness,
But with you there is light;
I am lonely, but you do not leave me;
I am feeble in heart, but with you there is help;
I am restless, but with you there is peace.
In me there is bitterness, but with you there is patience;
I do not understand your ways,
But you know the way for me.

O heavenly Father,
I praise and thank you
For the peace of the night;
I praise and thank you for this new day;
I praise and thank you for all your goodness
and faithfulness throughout my life.

You have granted me many blessings;
Now let me also accept what is hard
from your hand.
You will lay on me no more
than I can bear.
You make all things work together for good
for your children.

Lord Jesus Christ,
You were poor
and in distress, a captive and forsaken as I am.
You know all man's troubles;
You abide with me
when all men fail me;
You remember and seek me;
It is your will that I should know you
and turn to you.
Lord, I hear your call and follow;
Help me.

O Holy Spirit,
Give me faith that will protect me
from despair, from passions, and from vice;
Give me such love for God and men
as will blot out all hatred and bitterness;
Give me the hope that will deliver me
from fear and faint-heartedness.

O holy and merciful God,
my Creator and Redeemer,
my Judge and Saviour,
You know me and all that I do.
You hate and punish evil without respect of persons
in this world and the next;
You forgive the sins of those
who sincerely pray for forgiveness;
You love goodness, and reward it on this earth
with a clear conscience,
and, in the world to come,
with a crown of righteousness.

I remember in your presence all my loved ones,
my fellow-prisoners, and all who in this house
perform their hard service;
Lord, have mercy.

Restore me to liberty,
and enable me so to live now
that I may answer before you and before men.
Lord, whatever this day may bring,
Your name be praised.
Amen.

In my sleep he watches yearning
and restores my soul,
so that each recurring morning
love and goodness make me whole.
Were God not there,
his face not near,
He had not led me out of fear.
All things have their time and sphere:
God's love lasts for ever.

Paul Gerhardt

EVENING PRAYERS

O Lord my God, thank you
for bringing this day to a close;
Thank you for giving me rest
in body and soul.
Your hand has been over me
and has guarded and preserved me.
Forgive my lack of faith
and any wrong that I have done today,
and help me to forgive all who have wronged me.

Let me sleep in peace under your protection,
and keep me from all the temptations of darkness.

Into your hands I commend my loved ones
and all who dwell in this house;

I commend to you my body and soul.
O God, your holy name be praised.
Amen.

Each day tells the other
my life is but a journey
  to great and endless life.
O sweetness of eternity,
may my heart grow to love thee;
  my home is not in time's strife.

Tersteegen

PRAYERS IN TIME OF DISTRESS

O Lord God,
great distress has come upon me;
  my cares threaten to crush me,
  and I do not know what to do.
O God, be gracious to me and help me.
Give me strength to bear what you send,
  and do not let fear rule over me;
Take a father's care of my wife and children.

O merciful God,
forgive me all the sins that I have committed
against you and against my fellow men.
I trust in your grace
and commit my life wholly into your hands.
Do with me according to your will
  and as is best for me.
Whether I live or die, I am with you,
  and you, my God, are with me.
Lord, I wait for your salvation
  and for your kingdom.
Amen.

Every Christian in his place
   should be brave and free,
with the world face to face.
Though death strikes, his spirit should
   persevere, without fear
   calm and good.
For death cannot destroy,
but from grief brings relief
   and opens gates to joy.
Closed the door of bitter pain,
   bright the way where we may
   all heaven gain.

Paul Gerhardt

[Leipzig] Sunday, 21 November 1943

Dear Dietrich,

I've just applied for permission to come to visit you. As you know, I've often toyed with the idea earlier, but I didn't know whether in so doing I might mess up another visit that you perhaps wanted more. However, people have reassured me on that point, and as in your letter of 22 October, which was forwarded on to me a couple of days ago, you also write explicitly that it would please you, I've done so. I hope it works for next time . . .

I've been using the day to think through a couple of works that I've been wanting to write for a long time. I have the feeling that time is pressing on, but that I am not getting very far forward. It's not just the empty stomach that sometimes starts rumbling and makes one get up from the desk before time. It simply is not very easy at the moment to concentrate on pure science. On the other hand, one should do so, as long as one still has windows intact, which is still the case at home. In the Institute my lecture room is now very draughty indeed and no longer usable. But we can still publish our works with hardly any restrictions. I really hope that your time in prison will soon be finished. We just cannot understand what it means to have to be alone so long.

So all the best, and perhaps we shall see each other soon.

Your Karl-Friedrich

To Eberhard Bethge   [Tegel] Friday, 26 November 1943

Dear Eberhard,

So it really came off! Only for a moment, but that doesn't matter so much; even a few hours would be far too little, and when we are isolated here we can take in so much that even a few minutes gives us something to think about for a long time afterwards. It will be with me for a long time now – the memory of having the four people[75] who are nearest and dearest to me with me for a brief moment. When I got back to my cell afterwards, I paced up and down for a whole hour, while my dinner stood there and got cold, so that at last I couldn't help laughing at myself when I found myself repeating over and over again, 'That was really great!' I always hesitate to use the word 'indescribable' about anything, because if you take enough trouble to make a thing clear, I think there is very little that is really 'indescribable' – but at the moment that is just what this morning seems to be. Karl's[76] cigar is on the table in front of me, and that is something really indescribable – was he nice? and understanding? and V.[77] too? How grand it was that you saw them. And the good old favourite 'Wolf' cigar from Hamburg, which I used to be so fond of in better times. Just by me, standing on a box, is Maria's Advent garland, and on the shelf there are (among other things) your gigantic eggs, waiting for breakfasts still to come. (It's no use my saying that you oughtn't to have deprived yourselves of them; but that's what I think, though I am glad of them all the same.) . . .

Now you've been able to convince yourself that I'm my old self in every respect and that all is well. I believe that a moment was enough to make clear to both of us that everything that has happened in the last seven and a half months has left both of us essentially unchanged; I never doubted it for a moment, and you certainly didn't either. That's the advantage of having spent almost every day and having experienced almost every event and discussed every thought together for eight years. One needs only a second to know about each other, and now one doesn't really need even that second any more. I can remember that my first visit to a prison (I went to see Fritz O.,[78] and you were with me) took it out of me terribly, although Fritz was very cheerful and nice. I hope you didn't feel like that when you were here today. You see, it would be wrong to suppose that prison life is uninterrupted torture. It certainly is not, and visits like yours relieve it for days on end, even though they do, of course, awaken feelings that have fortunately lain dormant for a while. But that doesn't matter either. I realize again in thankfulness how well off I was, and feel new hope and energy. Thank you *very* much, you yourself and all the others. When and where will I be able to visit you? Make

145

sure that you spend a long time in Lissa! We really must see each other as quickly as possible after my release. It's truly horrible that they refuse a soldier who wants to visit his closest friend. Damned bureaucrats! But one learns from everything – and for later on!

27 November

Meanwhile we've had the expected large-scale attack on Borsig.[79] It really is a strange feeling, to see the 'Christmas trees', the flares that the leading aircraft drops, coming down right over our heads. The shouting and screaming of the prisoners in their cells was terrible. We had no dead, only injured, and we had finished bandaging them by one o'clock. After that, I was able to drop off at once into a sound sleep. People here talk quite openly about how frightened they were. I don't quite know what to make of it, for fright is surely something to be ashamed of. I have a feeling that it shouldn't be talked about except in the confessional, otherwise it might easily involve a certain amount of exhibitionism; and *a fortiori* there is no need to play the hero. On the other hand, naïve frankness can be quite disarming. But even so, there's a cynical, I might almost say ungodly, frankness, the kind that breaks out in heavy drinking and fornication, and gives the impression of chaos. I wonder whether fright is not one of the *pudenda*, which ought to be concealed. I must think about it further; you've no doubt formed your own ideas on the subject.

The fact that the horrors of war are now coming home to us with such force will no doubt, if we survive, provide us with the necessary basis for making it possible to reconstruct the life of the nations, both spiritually and materially, on Christian principles. So we must try to keep these experiences in our minds, use them in our work, make them bear fruit, and not just shake them off. Never have we been so plainly conscious of the wrath of God, and that is a sign of his grace: 'O that today you would hearken to his voice! Harden not your hearts.' The tasks that confront us are immense, but we must prepare ourselves for them now and be ready when they come . . .

It began with a peaceful night. When I was in bed yesterday evening I looked up for the first time 'our' Advent hymns in the *Neues Lied*. I can hardly hum any of them to myself without being reminded of Finkenwalde, Schlönwitz, and Sigurdshof. Early this morning I held my Sunday service, hung up the Advent garland on a nail, and fastened Lippi's picture of the Nativity in the middle of it. At breakfast I greatly enjoyed the second of your ostrich eggs. Soon after that, I was taken to the sick-bay for an interview which lasted till noon. The last air raid brought some most unpleasant experiences – a land-mine 25 metres away; a sick-bay with no lights or windows, prisoners screaming for help, with no one but ourselves taking any notice of them; but we too could do very little to help in the darkness, and one has to be cautious about opening the cell doors of those with the heaviest sentences, for you never know whether they will hit you on the head with a chair leg and try to get away. In short, it was not very nice. As a result, I wrote a report of what had taken place, pointing out the need of medical attention during air raids. I hope it will be some use. I'm glad to be able to help in any way with reasonable suggestions.

By the way, I forgot to tell you that I smoked the fabulously fragrant 'Wolf' cigar yesterday afternoon during a pleasant conversation in the sick-bay. Thank you very much for it. Since the raids started, the cigarette situation has unfortunately become calamitous.

While the injured people were being bandaged, they asked for a cigarette, and the medical orderlies and I had already used up a lot beforehand; so I'm all the more grateful for what you brought me the day before yesterday. Nearly every window in the place has been blown out, and the men are sitting in their cells freezing. Although I had forgotten to open my windows when I left the cell, I found at night to my great surprise that they were undamaged. I'm very glad about that, although I'm terribly sorry for the others.

How good it is that you can be at home to celebrate Advent.

Just now you will be singing the first hymns together. It makes me think of Altdorfer's 'Nativity' and the verse

> *The crib now glistens bright and clear,*
> *The night brings in a new light here;*
> *The darkness, conquered, fades away,*
> *For faith within the light must stay.*

and also the Advent melody

though not in four-four time, but in a flowing expectant rhythm to suit the text. After this I'm going to read another of W. H. Riehl's entertaining stories. You would enjoy them, too, and they would do very well for reading aloud to the family. You must try to get hold of them some time.

Unfortunately I'm not on the same wavelength as Maria yet in the literary sphere. She writes me such good, natural letters, but she reads . . . Rilke, Bergengruen, Binding, Wiechert; I regard the last three as being below our level and the first as being decidedly unhealthy. And in fact they don't really suit her at all . . . We ought to be able to talk to each other about such things, and I don't know whether they are altogether unimportant. I would very much like my wife to be as much of the same mind as possible in such questions. But I think it's only a matter of time. I don't like it when husbands and wives have different opinions. They must stand together like an impregnable bulwark. Don't you think so? Or is that another aspect of my 'tyrannical' nature that you know so well? If so, you must tell me. The difference in our ages probably also makes itself felt in these literary matters. Unfortunately the generation of Maria and Renate has grown up with a very bad kind of contemporary literature and finds it much harder than we did to take up earlier writing. The more we have come up against the really good things, the more insipid the weak lemonade of more recent productions has become to us, sometimes almost to the point of making us ill. Can you think of a book from the belles-lettres of, say, the last fifteen years which you think has lasting value? I can't. It is partly just talk, partly striking attitudes, partly plaintive sentimentality – no insight, no ideas, no clarity, no substance and almost always bad, unfree writing. At this point I am quite determinedly a *laudator temporis acti*. Are you?

29 November

Today is quite different from all the previous Mondays. Usually on Monday mornings the shouting and swearing in the corridors is at its fiercest, but after the experiences of last week even the loudest shouters and bullies have become quite subdued – a most obvious change.

Now there's something I must tell you personally: the heavy air raids, especially the last one, when the windows of the sick-bay were blown out by the land mine, and bottles and medical supplies fell down from the cupboards and shelves, and I lay on the floor in the darkness with little hope of coming through the attack safely, led me back quite simply to prayer and the Bible. More about that later when I see you. In more than one respect my time of imprisonment is being a very wholesome though drastic cure. But the details must wait till I can tell you personally.

A box of canned food and the travelling fur have just been handed to me. I asked to be taken down straight away and hoped that I would still catch a glimpse of you; there they said that 'a young man' – (sorry about that! no one would certainly say that about me any more! or might it perhaps have been Klaus D?)[80] had left it two hours before and had gone away again immediately. Many, many thanks. It is certainly good to have a reserve ration here that one can keep against all eventualities, and the fur, too, is very welcome in the windowless house, which also makes my cell chilly. It's really wonderful how you always think of everything straightaway and also translate it into action. I think that our family is really something quite special in this respect, don't you? And how good it is that now you are included in it! When one is in a difficult situation, one can be quite sure that everything conceivable will be done to bring help and relief. You, too, can get to know that if you are anywhere outside. I believe that this helping one another is a heritage in which all the members of the family share.

I hope to get this letter off today. So I must finish. Try to stay in Lissa until after Christmas! Then perhaps we shall really be able to see each other again. What's your address? How can I reach you immediately after my release by priority call or telegram? Keep well, you and Renate! God protect you. With all my heart,
your faithful Dietrich

R.[81] was too anxious at first to finish me for good; but he has now to content himself with a most ridiculous charge, which will bring him little glory. By the way, in case you ever find yourself in prison, I think that you ought to make a code here, before you go. In the months that have passed I've learnt as never before that I owe all the alleviations and help that I get here, not to myself, but to others. On earlier occasions I've felt that you suffer somewhat under the thought that you also owe much in your life to other men. But that is quite perverse. The wish to be independent in everything is false pride. Even what we owe to others belongs to ourselves and is a part of our own lives, and any attempt to calculate what we have 'earned' for ourselves and what we owe to other people is certainly not Christian, and is, moreover, a futile undertaking. It's through what he himself is, plus what he receives, that a man becomes a complete entity. I wanted to tell you this, because I've now experienced it for myself, though not for the first time, for it was already implicit all through the years of our *vita communis*. I've certainly not received less from you than you from me.

Report on Experiences during Alerts

[28 November 1943]

The alert on 26 November led to the following experiences in the sick-bay of the Wehrmacht Investigation Prison, Tegel. As a result of one of the first bombs to fall in the neighbourhood, all the windows and black-out arrangements of the sick-bay were destroyed; a number of bottles of medicine fell out of the medicine cupboard, the floor was covered with dust and debris; the attempt to arrange a makeshift black-out failed as the bombs kept falling afresh. Shortly afterwards, a high-explosive bomb or land-mine demolished the prison wall about 25 metres away and did severe damage to the doors, windows and roof of the prison. Thereupon the prisoners under investigation, shut in their cells, began to beat wildly on the doors and scream, and the wounded cried for help. In the general tumult which arose, not to mention the explosions of bombs, it was impossible to ascertain where the wounded really were. The staff of the sick-bay opened a number of cells and discovered some minor wounds, but immediate treatment was impossible as there were no lights in the sick-bay and it would not have been possible with those who were most severely wounded. Only after the all-clear could black-out be arranged and the treatment be begun . . .

The following consequences arise:

1. If medical care is to be provided in serious cases, the construction of a hospital bunker is required.

2. Medical corps members among the prisoners for interrogation are to be allowed out to help in the sick-bay as far as is possible.

3. Measures are needed which make it possible to find the wounded as soon as possible, and in present circumstances this cannot be done. If saving lives is the main concern, then it is necessary to release as many of the prisoners from their cells as possible and to provide slit trenches immediately.

4. Furthermore, the unfavourable effect on the morale of a soldier who is shut in a cell as a prisoner under interrogation for perhaps only a small crime and who has to suffer under a heavy air

attack without prospect of help at the right time is not to be underestimated . . .

Dear parents,

Although I don't know whether and how letters are getting through at present, I want to write to you on the afternoon of the First Sunday in Advent. Altdorfer's 'Nativity' is very topical this year, showing the Holy Family and the crib among the ruins of a tumbledown house. However did he come to paint like that, against all tradition, four hundred years ago? Perhaps he meant that Christmas could and should be kept even in such conditions; in any case, that is his message for us. I like to think of your sitting with the children and keeping Advent with them, just as you used to years ago with us. Only we do everything more intensively now, as we don't know how much longer we have.

It still makes me shudder to think what a distressing night you had, with one really bad moment, without any of us with you. It really is beyond me why I should be kept behind bars like this without being able to help in any way. I do hope it will soon be over now with no more delays. All the same, please don't worry about me. We shall come out of the whole business very much strengthened.

You will know already that we've had the expected attack on nearby Borsig. Now we have the (not very Christian) hope that they won't be coming round here again just yet. It was not exactly pleasant, and when I'm released I shall make some suggestions about improving the organization here for incidents of that kind. Most surprisingly, my window-panes were unbroken, whereas nearly all the others are smashed. It makes it horribly cold for the other people. As part of the prison wall has been wrecked, there can be no more 'exercise' for the present. If only it were possible for us to hear from each other after the attacks!

It was marvellous to see you again. Many thanks for coming

and for everything that you brought with you. It's a very comforting feeling to know that you are in Sakrow for the time being. Maria is not to come to Berlin now; even if she gets permission for a visit, let's wait and see how things develop. What will happen about Renate? Presumably a confinement in Berlin is out of the question? But where will she go?

These last few days, I have been enjoying W. H. Riehl's *Stories from Olden Times*. You may remember the book from a much earlier period. Today it's just about forgotten, though it is still very pleasant and enjoyable reading; it would also be suitable for reading aloud to the children. As far as I can remember, we had a few of his works at home, but we've probably given them away since then to some collection or other.

It would be very nice if you could bring me the book on superstition. They are starting to consult cards here about the chances of a raid during the coming night. It's interesting how superstition thrives in unsettled times, and how many are prepared to listen to it, at least with half an ear. Good-bye. Much love to all the family and the children. God bless us all. Thank you for everything.   Your Dietrich

From Eberhard Bethge   [Charlottenburg] 30 November 1943

Dear Dietrich,
How shall I begin, and what can I say to show you my delight? How shall I get into much too short a letter everything I say in the imaginary conversations I have with you when walking by myself, or talking with Renate? In the midst of the chaos of the attacks and the work that they cause, seeing you was *the* event for me, and getting such a good, long letter, the first from you. I've already read it many times, and I'm only sorry not to have the same peace and quiet that you had for writing. I was astonished to find you so cheerful on Friday and looking so well. Cheerful, fresh, not at all pale, and in everything, as usual, in command of the situation, a little concerned to communicate comfort and

confidence about your situation to us, no matter what. I'm tremendously pleased that we managed the visit. And then in the afternoon I got the letter with the splendid things . . . I've heard today that I'm probably going to Merano, so I shall need less warm things. When I had to wait for Chr.[82] a whole hour outside Hans' cell, I had time as it were to devour your entire letter slowly. The biblical expression, that John ate the letter, is a very apt one, except that it didn't 'make my stomach bitter';[83] that didn't happen to Ezekiel, either.

Your letter showed me how different our two lives have been recently. In essentials I felt that military life brought me very close to you because of the loss of the ability to determine our own actions, which is so utterly unfamiliar to the two of us. I've thought of you in a new and different way since I've had to march and march endlessly in the column. And then I imagined that you would have to be beside me and how you would then have to bellow out the fatuous songs, and I had to have a good laugh at the two of us there in the silence . . .

Special thanks for the verses which you've written for me. I will most gladly take them in my briefcase on my journey into the unknown. Indeed, if only you could be a soldier with me! Here in Spandau the people were the sort that I would like to keep with. A remarkable esteem for and interest in such a curious and strange profession, especially among the eighteen- to nineteen-year-olds. In Lissa, of course, it is very different. The people are so orderly in every respect and so tedious, concerned with reliability and respectable views.[84] I'm rather alone and therefore quiet. I get very sad when I think how you've been working and writing now and I hear nothing of it – and perhaps won't for a long time. It was good that I was able to preach for so long; now I'm even to preach in Lissa, and am getting permission to do so. But the groups with which I had most contact are indeed *homines religiosi*.

Unfortunately I'm now being constantly interrupted. In the meantime it's already become 1 December, and with difficulty I have managed to extend my leave until Saturday. Will you be coming to the Lehrter Strasse before then, and shall I see you? . . .

Unfortunately no wedding sermon from you ever came into

our hands. Did you send it via R?[85] No one knows anything about it . . .

Friday, 3

Now I've got to be off. The time I earmarked today for writing some more to you was suddenly messed up, as I was again called for against all the arrangements by car, and there was a puncture, which took up all the time. I'm very sorry to have to send you this fragment, but there's nothing else I can do.

Warmest regards. I think of you a great deal and hope to see you soon.

Faithfully, with all my heart.   Your Eberhard

From his father   [Sakrow] 5 December 1943

Dear Dietrich,

I want to use this quiet Second Sunday in Advent for a letter to you. We're out here in Sakrow, which is beneficial after a week spent nailing up windows, putting in glass and unsuccessful attempts to cover up the roof with quite inadequate material – carpets and boards; there are no nails, roofing felts, hammers, etc. I have an old male nurse from my clinic to help. I hope to be able to see some or other of the patients next week. Our health is good. When one is doing manual work the coldness of the rooms is not so noticeable. Our chief concern now is to keep the central heating from freezing up. The veranda, with 22 shattered panes of glass, is the main danger spot. It's astounding how all the windows in your room are intact, although it's exposed to the side on which the high explosive bomb fell. Nevertheless, there is still a possibility of making some rooms habitable. We must be thankful for that, especially when one sees some of the destruction elsewhere in the town. My old assistant Burlage, very close to me, has been killed in his air-raid shelter with 150 others. His wife escaped because she had gone out to rescue the dog. Zutt[86] saved nothing but his case. By and large it's encouraging and surprising to see how lightly, at least for the moment, people take the loss of their possessions. Karl-Friedrich went back to Leipzig early this morning, concerned that the heavy attack on Leipzig might have caught his house; with the nearness of the water-tower, he's not unjustified in worrying. We're going to try to ring him this evening. I expect that mother wants to write, too, so I will close. I'm going to send in an application for permission to visit at the same time.

Affectionately, your father, who is quietly hoping for a Christmas together . . .

To Eberhard Bethge

[Tegel]
Advent 2 [5 December 1943]

Dear Eberhard,

I so much want to spend a quiet Sunday morning talking things over with you, and I'm so tempted by the thought that a letter like this might help you to pass a quiet solitary hour, that I will write to you, though I don't know whether, or how, or where this will reach you. Karl-Friedrich appeared here quite unexpectedly yesterday and told me that you had only gone back to Lissa yesterday. I hope the time is not too hard for you. Your boarding-school upbringing has made you much tougher about some things than I am. How and where will the two of us be keeping Christmas this time? I hope that you will manage to communicate something of the joy which you always used to bring to the group of brethren to your fellow-soldiers as well. For the calmness and joy with which we meet what is laid on us are as infectious as the terror that I see among the people here at each new attack. Indeed, I think such an attitude gives one the greatest authority, provided that it is genuine and natural, and not merely for show. People need some constant factor to guide them. We are neither of us dare-devils, but that has nothing to do with the courage that comes from the grace of God.

My thoughts and feelings seem to be getting more and more like those of the Old Testament, and in recent months I have been reading the Old Testament much more than the New. It is only when one knows the unutterability of the name of God that one can utter the name of Jesus Christ; it is only when one loves life and the earth so much that without them everything seems to be over that one may believe in the resurrection and a new world; it is only when one submits to God's law that one may speak of grace; and it is only when God's wrath and vengeance are hanging as grim realities over the heads of one's enemies that something of what it means to love and forgive them can touch our hearts. In my opinion it is not Christian to want to take our thoughts and feelings too quickly and too directly from the New Testament. We have already talked about this several times, and every day confirms my opinion. One cannot and must not speak the last word before the last but one. We live in the last but one and believe the last, don't we? Lutherans (so-called!) and pietists would shudder at the thought, but it is true all the same. In *The Cost of Discipleship* (ch. 1) I just hinted at this, but did not follow it up; I must do so later. But the logical conclusions are far-reaching, e.g. for the problem of Catholicism, for the concept of the ministry, for the use of the Bible, etc., and above all for ethics. Why is it that in the Old Testament men tell lies vigorously and often to the glory of God (I've now collected the passages), kill, deceive, rob, divorce, and even fornicate (see the genealogy of Jesus), doubt, blaspheme, and curse, whereas in the New Testament there is nothing of all this? 'An earlier stage' of religion? That is a very naïve way out; it is one and the same God. But more of this later when we meet.

Meanwhile evening has come. The NCO who has just brought me from the sick-bay to my quarters said to me as he left, with an embarrassed smile but quite seriously, 'Pray for us, Pastor, that we may have no alert tonight.'

For some time I've been taking my daily walk with a man who has been a District Orator, Regional Leader, Government Director, former member of the governing body of the German-Christian Church in Brunswick, and is at present a Party Leader in Warsaw. He has completely gone to pieces here, and clings to me just like a child, consulting me about every little thing, telling me whenever he has cried, etc. After being very cool with him for several weeks, I'm now able to ease things for him a little; his gratitude is quite touching, and he tells me again and again how glad he is to have met a man like me here. Well, the strangest situations do come about; if only I could tell you properly about them!

I've been thinking again over what I wrote to you recently about our own fear. I think that here, under the guise of honesty, something is being passed off as 'natural' that is at bottom a symptom of sin; it is really quite analogous to talking openly about sexual matters. After all, 'truthfulness' does not mean uncovering everything that exists. God himself made clothes for men; and that means that *in statu corruptionis* many things in human life ought to remain covered, and that evil, even though it cannot be eradicated, ought at least to be concealed. Exposure is cynical, and although the cynic prides himself on his exceptional honesty, or claims to want truth at all costs, he misses the crucial fact that since the fall there must be reticence and secrecy. In my opinion the greatness of Stifter lies in his refusal to force his way into man's inner life, in his respect for reticence, and in his willingness to observe people more or less cautiously from the outside but not from the inside. Inquisitiveness is alien to him. I remember once being impressed when Frau von Kleist-Kieckow told me with genuine horror about a film that showed the growth of a plant speeded up; she said that she and her husband could not stand it, as they felt it to be an impermissible prying into the mystery of life. Stifter takes a similar line. But is not this somewhat akin to the so-called English 'hypocrisy', which we contrast with German 'honesty'? I believe we Germans have never properly grasped the meaning of 'concealment', i.e. what is in the end the *status corruptionis* of the world. Kant says quite rightly in his *Anthropologie* that anyone who misunderstands or questions the significance of outward appearance in the world is a traitor to humanity.

By the way, was it you who got hold of the *Witiko* that was brought to me on Friday? Who else could it have been? Although it is painstaking rather than brilliant, I found parts of it very interesting. Thank you very much.

'Speaking the truth' (on which I have written an essay)[87]

means, in my opinion, saying how something really is – that is, showing respect for secrecy, intimacy, and concealment. 'Betrayal', for example, is not truth, any more than are flippancy, cynicism, etc. What is secret may be revealed only in confession, i.e. in the presence of God. More about that later, too.

There are two ways of dealing psychically with adversities. One way, the easier, is to try to ignore them; that is about as far as I have got. The other and more difficult way is to face them deliberately and overcome them; I'm not equal to that yet, but one must learn to do it, for the first way is a slight, though, I believe, a permissible, piece of self-deception.

Now good-bye. You're constantly in my thoughts.

Your Dietrich

From Susanne Dress   Friedrichsbrunn, 14 December 1943

Dear Dietrich,

Now I'm staying up here in the snow and the heavy frost with very little heating, and my thoughts are constantly in Berlin. I did hope so much to be at home with the children for Christmas and then arrange a visit to see you. Even more, I had hoped that you might have been back with the parents again for Christmas. But perhaps we ought to learn to hope for other things this Advent. What is the dark time round Christmas going to bring now? I was very glad to be in Berlin for those mad days, helping the parents during the day and being able to be with Walter during the attacks in the evening. Here one just hears the planes rumbling overhead and has no chance of getting any news all day. As the roads are so bad, I shall now probably have to stay here until the beginning of January. Shared life with the Leipzig brigade continues to go well. It's not so shared any more, as I'm living up here in the boys' room with my two . . . We have three beds, three chairs, two tables, one washstand, one wardrobe, one clothes stand and a stove in the room; you can cook on it if you can get enough heat underneath. At the only free place where one might be able to stand upright, Fräulein Erna, who was here, has dangled the Advent garland from the ceiling at head height. As it's already beginning to shed, one gets one's head covered with fir needles several times a day. They only get a nuisance when they slip down the back of your neck. You can imagine how cosy and pleasant it was when Walter was here! But he was so happy to be able to be with the children again that he didn't object at all . . . Christmas preparations are completely out this year . . . We wish you with all our hearts a happy Christmas and a better New Year.

    With love.   Your Suse

To Eberhard Bethge   [Tegel] 15 December 1943

Dear Eberhard,

When I read your letter yesterday, I felt as though a spring, without which my intellectual life was beginning to dry up, had begun once again to produce the first drops of water for a long, long time. Of course, that may sound to you an exaggeration; for first, in the meantime another spring has opened up for you, and moreover, you have many possibilities of replenishment. In my isolation things are quite different. I am forced to live from the past; the future which announces itself in the person of Maria still consists so very much of hints that it lies more on the horizon of hope than in the realm of possession and tangible experience. In any case, your letter set my thoughts going again, after they had grown rusty and tired during recent weeks. I had become so used to talking everything over with you that the sudden and prolonged interruption meant a profound change and a great deprivation. Now we're at least in touch again. . . . Many thanks for writing to me, and do go on writing from time to time. R[88] and Co. have smashed so much china already that we mustn't let them destroy our most important personal relationships too.

First of all a couple of external things; the wedding sermon got by mistake into the will of mine that father has, and was put away with that. Please get it from him. It's nothing special, but it was written at the time of your wedding and I would be pleased if you could read it sometime.

How is it that you've got to Forli and not to Warsaw? (Do I need to refresh your knowledge of the history of art by recalling the pictures of angels by Melozzo da Forli in the Vatican Museum?) In many respects that is better, but prepare yourself for very cold days, not much coal, bad stoves, stone floors, hills, and spring not before March or April. You will need particularly warm socks. You have the addresses of Marianne[89] and George,[90] haven't you? Do you know to whom you're coming? Are you still in any way connected with your earlier military position[91] or not any more? Learn Italian properly. More and more interpreters are needed in the many Italian prisoner-of-war camps. You ought to be able to do it in eight weeks. As it's chiefly a matter of a good ear, you will find it very easy. Did you get my *second* letter?

I expect that a smoked goose or something similar is coming in from Kl. Krössin or Kieckow for Christmas. I've one big request for you; take half and give the other half to my parents. I certainly don't want to have it here; it doesn't fit, and there is no fun at all in eating it all alone. You could send me one slice, but certainly no more. It's really very much nicer to think that you're having a good lunch together, you and Renate. I know that sounds fabulously altruistic, but it's really basically egoistic (and that sounds even more altruistic! what can we do about that? especially as people among us give the others not altruistic but only egoistic joys!) So please do what I suggest and don't offend me! Besides, you know from old that I don't make all that much of it. Hans should also have a slice; he's a fantastic admirer of smoked goose! Anyway, they are the external things.

And now I'm taking up with great pleasure your 'fireside chat' (appropriately enough the electricity has failed again, and I'm using candles). So I imagine the two of us sitting together as we used to in the old days after supper (and after our regular evening's work[92]) in my room upstairs, smoking, occasionally strumming chords on the clavichord, and discussing the day's events. I should have no end of questions to ask you, about your training, about your journey to Karolus[93] . . . And then at last I should have to start telling you that, in spite of everything that I've written so far, things here are revolting, that my grim experiences often pursue me into the night and that I can shake them off only by reciting one hymn after another, and that I'm apt to wake up with a sigh rather than with a hymn of praise to God. It's possible to get used to physical hardships, and to live for months out of the body, so to speak – almost too much so – but one doesn't get used to the psychological strain; on the contrary, I have the feeling that everything that I see and hear is putting years on me, and I'm often finding the world nauseating and burdensome. You're probably surprised now at my talking like this after all my letters; you wrote very kindly that I was making 'something of an effort' to reassure you about my situation. I often wonder who I really am – the man who goes on squirming under these ghastly experiences in wretchedness that cries to heaven, or the man who scourges himself and pretends to others (and even to himself) that he is placid, cheerful, composed, and in control of himself, and allows people to admire him for it (i.e. for playing the part – or is it not playing a part?). What does one's attitude mean, anyway? In short, I know less than ever about myself, and I'm no longer attaching any importance to it. I've had more than enough psychology, and I'm less and less inclined to analyse the state of my soul. That is why I value Stifter and Gotthelf so much. There is something more at stake than self-knowledge.

Then I should discuss with you whether you think that this trial, which has associated me with the *Abwehr* (I hardly think that has remained a secret), may prevent me from taking up my ministry again later on. At present you're the only person with whom I can discuss this question, and perhaps we shall be able to talk it over together if you're allowed to see me. Please think it over, and give me your candid opinion.

Finally, I couldn't talk about anything else with you but Maria. We've now been engaged almost a year, and so far we haven't spent even an hour alone together. Isn't that mad! . . . We have to talk and write about things which in the end aren't the most important for the two of us; every month we sit upright for an hour, side by side, as on a school bench, and then we're torn apart again

. . . Isn't that an impossible situation? And she bears up with such great self-control. It's only occasionally that something else comes through, as on the last visit, when I told her that even Christmas wasn't certain yet. She sighed and said, 'Oh, it's *too* long for me.' I know full well that she won't leave me in the lurch; it isn't 'too long' for her to hold out, but for her heart, and that's much more important. The only thing that I keep saying to myself is that it has all come about without our doing and so will probably make sense one day. As long as I don't do her wrong by asking too much of her . . .

I sometimes feel as if my life were more or less over, and as if all I had to do now were to finish my *Ethics*. But, you know, when I feel like this, there comes over me a longing (unlike any other that I experience) to have a child and not to vanish without a trace – an Old Testament rather than a New Testament wish, I suppose . . . Yes, I would tell you all this and much more, and would know that (provided that you weren't reading a newspaper or sleeping or even thinking of Renate!) you would listen to me like no one else and would give me good counsel. It may be that all my problems will blow away the moment I'm released – I hope so! Perhaps you can write me a few more words about my questions and my thoughts.

If only we could meet in freedom before you leave. But if they really intend to keep me here over Christmas, I shall keep it in my own way as a Christmas at the front, so you can have an easy mind about it. Great battles are easier to fight and less wearing than the daily guerrilla war. And I do hope you will somehow or other manage to wangle a few days' leave in February; I shall certainly be out of here by then for, to judge by the nonsense that they're bringing against me, they're bound to let me out after the trial.

I'm again working at my essay on 'What is "speaking the truth"?' I'm trying to draw a sharp contrast between trust, loyalty, and secrecy on the one hand, and the 'cynical' conception of truth, for which all these obligations do not exist, on the other. 'Falsehood' is the destruction of, and hostility to, reality as it is in God; anyone who tells the truth cynically is lying. By the way, it's remarkable how little I miss going to church. I wonder why.

Your biblical comparison with 'eating the letter' is very good. If you should get to Rome, do visit Schönhöffer[94] in the *Propaganda Fide*. – Have you found the tone among the troops very bad, or do they show you some respect? Here in the sick-bay the men are certainly very direct, but not filthy. Some of the younger prisoners seem to have suffered so much from the long solitary confinement and the long dark evenings that they have quite gone to pieces. That's another idiotic thing, locking these people in for months on end with nothing to do; it's absolutely demoralizing in every possible way.

16 December

Of course, the lawyer has left me in the lurch again. This waiting is revolting. Prisoners are like sick people and children; promises with them should be kept. It's still quite uncertain what will become of me after my release. But if you have a reasonable NCO in Italy, can't you talk with him quite openly and tell him that you have a friend and cousin whom you'd like to have with you and ask him whether he can't requisition me? That would be really splendid! Then one could withstand any situation! I'll stop, so as not to make excessive demands on your time. I wish you and Renate an incomparably splendid Christmas and a confident farewell . . . You're certainly right in describing marriage as 'what remains stable in all fleeting relationships'. But we should also include a good friendship among these stable things. Now goodbye and God bless you. I'm steadfastly thinking of you.

Your Dietrich

The lawyer is just on his way!

Dear parents,
There's probably nothing for it but to write you a Christmas letter now to meet all eventualities. Although it passes my comprehension why they may possibly still keep me here over Christmas, I've learnt in the past eight and a half months that the unexpected often happens, and that what can't be changed must be accepted with a *sacrificium intellectus,* although the *sacrificium* is not quite complete, and the *intellectus* silently goes its own way.

Above all, you mustn't think that I'm going to let myself be depressed by this lonely Christmas; it will always take its special place among the other unusual Christmases that I've kept in Spain, America, and England, and I want in later years to look back on the time here, not with shame, but with a certain pride. That's the only thing that no one can take from me.

Of course, you, Maria and the family and friends, can't help thinking of my being in prison over Christmas, and it's bound to cast a shadow over the few happy hours that are left to you in these times. The only thing I can do to help is to believe and know that your thoughts about it will be the same as mine, and that we shall be at one in our attitude towards the keeping of this Christmas. Indeed, it can't be otherwise, for that attitude is simply a spiritual inheritance from you. I needn't tell you how I long to be released and to see you all again. But for years you have given us such perfectly lovely Christmases that our grateful recollection of them is strong enough to put a darker one into the background. It's not till such times as these that we realize what it means to possess a past and a spiritual inheritance independent of changes of time and circumstance. The consciousness of being borne up by a spiritual tradition that goes back for centuries gives one a feeling of confidence and security in the face of all passing strains and stresses. I believe that anyone who is aware of such reserves of strength needn't be ashamed of more tender feelings evoked by the memory of a rich and noble past, for in my opinion they belong to the better and nobler part of mankind. They will not overwhelm those who hold fast to values that no one can take from them.

From the Christian point of view there is no special problem about Christmas in a prison cell. For many people in this building it will probably be a more sincere and genuine occasion than in places where nothing but the name is kept. That misery, suffering, poverty, loneliness, helplessness, and guilt mean something quite different in the eyes of God from what they mean in the judgment of man, that God will approach where men turn away, that Christ was born in a stable because there was no room for him in the inn – these are things that a prisoner can understand better than other people; for him they really are glad tidings, and that faith gives him a part in the communion of saints, a Christian fellowship breaking the bounds of time and space and reducing the months of confinement here to insignificance.

On Christmas Eve I shall be thinking of you all very much, and I want you to believe that I too shall have a few really happy hours, and that I am certainly not allowing my troubles to get the better of me. It will be hardest for Maria. It would be marvellous to know that she was with you. But it will be better for her if she's at home. It's only when one thinks of the terrible times that so many people in Berlin have been through lately that one realizes how much we have to be thankful for. No doubt it will be a very quiet Christmas everywhere, and the children will remember it for a long time to come. But it may perhaps bring home to some people for the first time what Christmas really is. Much love to the family, the children and all our friends. God bless us all. With much gratefulness and love.   Your Dietrich

To Eberhard Bethge   [Tegel] 18 December 1943

Dear Eberhard,
You too must at least have a letter for Christmas. I'm no longer expecting to be released. As far as I could see, I should have been released on 17 December, but the jurists wanted to take the safe course, and now I shall probably be kept here for weeks if not months. The past weeks have been more of a strain than any-

thing before that. There's no changing it, only it's more difficult to adapt oneself to something that one thinks could have been prevented than to something inevitable. But when facts have taken shape, one just has to fit in with them. What I'm thinking of particularly today is that you will soon be facing facts that will be very hard for you, probably even harder than for me. I now think that we ought first of all to do everything we can to change those facts while there's still time; and then, if we've tried everything, even though it has been in vain, they will be much easier to bear. Of course, not everything that happens is simply 'God's will'; yet in the last resort nothing happens 'without God's will' (Matt. 10.29), i.e. through every event, however untoward, there is access to God. When a man enters on a supremely happy marriage and has thanked God for it, it is a terrible blow to discover that the same God who established the marriage now demands of us a period of such great deprivation. In my experience nothing tortures us more than longing. Some people have been so violently shaken in their lives from their earliest days that they cannot now, so to speak, allow themselves any great longing or put up with a long period of tension, and they find compensation in short-lived pleasures that offer readier satisfaction. That is the fate of the proletarian classes, and it is the ruin of all intellectual fertility. It's not true to say that it is good for a man to have suffered heavy blows early and often in life; in most cases it breaks him. True, it hardens people for times like ours, but it also greatly helps to deaden them. When *we* are forcibly separated for any considerable time from those whom we love, we simply *cannot*, as most can, get some cheap substitute through other people – I don't mean because of moral considerations, but just because we are what we are. Substitutes repel us; we simply have to wait and wait; we have to suffer unspeakably from the separation, and feel the longing till it almost makes us ill. That is the only way, although it is a very painful one, in which we can preserve unimpaired our relationship with our loved ones. A few times in my life I've come to know what homesickness means. There is nothing more painful, and during these months in prison I've sometimes been terribly homesick. And as I expect you will have to go through the same kind of thing in the coming months, I wanted to write and tell you what I've learnt about it, in case it may be of some help to you. The first result of such longing is always a wish to neglect the ordinary daily routine in some way or other, and that means that our lives become disordered. I used to be tempted sometimes to stay in bed after six in the morning (it would have been perfectly possible), and to sleep on. Up to now I've always been able to force myself not to do this; I realized that it would have been the first stage of capitulation, and that worse would probably have followed. An outward and purely physical régime (exercises and a cold wash down in the morning) itself provides some support for one's inner discipline. Further, there is nothing worse in such times than to try to find a substitute for the irreplaceable. It just does not work, and it leads to still greater indiscipline, for the strength to overcome tension (such strength can come only from looking the longing straight in the face) is impaired, and endurance becomes even more unbearable . . .

Another point: I don't think it is good to talk to strangers about our condition; that always stirs up one's troubles – although we ought to be ready, when occasion arises, to listen to those of other people. Above all, we must never give way to self-pity. And on the Christian aspect of the matter, there are some lines that say

> . . . that we remember what we would forget,
> that this poor earth is not our home.

That is indeed something essential, but it must come last of all. I believe that we ought so to love and trust God in our *lives*, and in all the good things that he sends us, that when the time comes (but not before!) we may go to him with love, trust, and joy. But, to put it plainly, for a man in his wife's arms to be hankering after the other world is, in mild terms, a piece of bad taste, and not God's will. We ought to find and love God in what he actually gives us; if it pleases him to allow us to enjoy some overwhelming earthly happiness, we mustn't try to be more pious than God himself and allow our happiness to be corrupted by presumption and arrogance, and by unbridled religious fantasy which is never satisfied with what God gives. God will see to it that the man who finds him in his earthly happiness and thanks him for it does not lack reminder that earthly things are transient, that it is good for him to attune his heart to what is eternal, and that sooner or later there will be times when he can say in all sincerity, 'I wish I were home.' But everything has its time, and the main thing is that we keep step with God, and do not keep pressing on a few steps ahead – nor keep dawdling a step behind. It's presumptuous to want to have everything at once – matrimonial bliss, the cross, and the heavenly Jerusalem, where they neither marry nor are given in marriage. 'For everything there is a season' (Eccles. 3.1); everything has its time: 'a time to weep, and a time to laugh; . . . a time to embrace, and a time to refrain from embracing; . . . a time to rend, and a time to sew; . . . and God seeks again what is past.' I suspect that these last words mean that nothing that is past is lost, that God gathers up again with us our past, which belongs to us. So when we are seized by a longing for the past – and this may happen when we least expect it – we may be sure that it is only one of the many 'hours' that God is always holding ready for us. So we oughtn't to seek the past again by our own efforts, but only with God. Well, enough of this; I can see that I have taken on too much, for really in these matters I can tell you nothing that you don't know already.

Advent IV

What I wrote yesterday wasn't a Christmas letter. Today I must tell you above all how tremendously glad I am that you can spend Christmas at home.[95] That's a piece of good fortune that no one has as easily as you!

The thought that you're celebrating the fifth Christmas of the war in freedom and with Renate is so comforting, and makes me so confident for the future, that I delight in it every day. You will celebrate a very splendid and joyful feast; and after what has happened to you so far, I don't think that it will be very long before you're on leave again in Berlin. And we'll celebrate Easter again in peace, won't we?

For this last week or so these lines have kept on running through my head:

Let pass, dear brothers, every pain;
What you have missed I'll bring again.

What does this 'I'll bring again' mean? It means that nothing is
lost, that everything is taken up in Christ, although it is trans-
formed, made transparent, clear, and free from all selfish desire.
Christ restores all this as God originally intended it to be, without
the distortion resulting from our sins. The doctrine derived from
Eph. 1.10 – that of the restoration of all things, ἀνακεφαλαίωσις,
recapitulatio (Irenaeus) – is a magnificent conception, full of comfort. This is how the promise 'God seeks what has been driven
away' is fulfilled. And no one has expressed this so simply and
artlessly as Paul Gerhardt in these words that he puts into the
mouth of the Christ-child: 'I'll bring again'. Perhaps this line will
help you a little in the coming weeks. Besides that, I've lately
learnt for the first time to appreciate the hymn 'Beside thy cradle
here I stand'. Up to now I hadn't made much of it; I suppose one
has to be alone for a long time, and meditate on it, to be able to
take it in properly. Every word is remarkably full of meaning and
beauty. There's just a slight flavour of the monastery and mys-
ticism, but no more than is justified. After all, it's right to speak of
'I' and 'Christ' as well as of 'we', and what that means can hardly
be expressed better than it is in this hymn. There are also a few
passages in a similar vein in the *Imitation of Christ,* which I'm
reading now and then in the Latin (it reads much better in Latin
than in German); and I sometimes think of

from the Augustinian *O bone Jesu* by Schütz. Doesn't this passage,
in its ecstatic longing combined with pure devotion, suggest the
'bringing again' of all earthly desire? 'Bringing again' mustn't,
of course, be confused with 'sublimation'; 'sublimation' is σάρξ
'flesh' (and pietistic?), and 'restoration' is spirit, not in the sense of
'spiritualization' (which is also σάρξ), but of καινὴ κτίσις through
the πνεῦμα ἅγιον, a new creation through the Holy Spirit. I think
this point is also very important when we have to talk to people

who ask us about their relation to their dead. '*I will bring again*' – that is, we cannot and should not take it back ourselves, but allow Christ to give it back to us. (By the way, I should like the choir to sing at my funeral 'One thing I desire of the Lord', 'Hasten, God, to deliver me', and *O bone Jesu*.)

At midday on Christmas Eve a dear old man is coming here at his own suggestion to play some Christmas carols on a cornet. But some people with good judgment think it only gives the prisoners the screaming miseries, and so makes the day even harder for them; one said that the effect is 'demoralizing', and I can well imagine it. In former years the prisoners are said to have whistled and kicked up a row, no doubt to stop themselves from becoming sentimental. I think, too, that in view of all the misery that prevails here, anything like a pretty-pretty, sentimental reminder of Christmas is out of place. A good personal message, a sermon, would be better; without something of the kind, music by itself may be positively dangerous. Please don't think that I'm in any way frightened of that for myself; I'm not, but I'm sorry for all those helpless young soldiers in their cells. One will probably never quite get rid of the accumulated weight of all the oppressive experiences that come day after day, and I suppose it's right that this should be so. I'm thinking a great deal about a radical reform of the penal system, and I hope my ideas may be turned to account some day.

If this letter reaches you in time, please try to get me something good to read over Christmas. I asked for a few books some time ago, but they may not have been available. Something exciting would do quite well. And if you can get without difficulty Barth's *Doctrine of Predestination* (in sheets), or his *Doctrine of God*,[96] please have them sent to me. *Please* don't come yourself unless you have permission to visit. Your time now is short, and belongs to Renate.

Today I read the account of the travels in Palestine which old Soden did with Knopf; nothing special, but I conceived a plan to travel there with you after the war. It seems that one only gets something out of it as a theologian; for the laity too much of it is a disappointment. We'll take our wives to Italy and leave them there to wait for us. What do you think?

The propagandist with whom I walk every day is really getting more and more difficult to put up with. Whereas most people here do try to keep control of themselves, even in the most difficult cases, he has completely gone to pieces, and cuts a really sorry figure. I try to be as nice as I can to him, and talk to him as if he were a child. Sometimes he's almost comical. What is pleasanter is to hear that when I'm in the sick-bay in the afternoon the word goes round the kitchen or the garden, and the prisoners come up on some pretext or other because, they say, it's so nice to have a chat with me. Of course, that isn't really allowed, but I was pleased to hear about it, and I'm sure you will be too. But mind you don't let it get around.

This is probably the last chance we shall have for some time of writing each other uncensored letters. When I'm released I shall miss you very much; it isn't easy to imagine my first time outside. There will be many great decisions to be made, and I would need you for them. Of course I would very much like a short answer to some of the questions in my letters. Even if you haven't anything to add that might be important for me, then please let me know. I'm afraid that the time of our separation could become too long and then we wouldn't have exchanged any substantial thoughts. On the other hand, I don't want to make too many demands on your days in Berlin. Enjoy these days as much as you can, and above all come back soon and safely. It's at least a small consolation that you're going into such a beautiful and interesting neighbourhood. It will also remind you of August 1936.[97] And if you can in any way, see if you can't get me into your neighbourhood. There is a 'World Alliance' man in Florence; I was at many conferences with him. I think he's a professor;[98] a Protestant, but I've forgotten his name. You'll find him in the Annual Book of the World Alliance under 'Italy'. It's among my books. You can write to him without further ado, mentioning my name. He knows me well. Perhaps he can be of some use to you. It's always good to have someone like that at hand. If you can't find the Annual, Renate need only ring up Diestel[99] and ask him; he will know straightaway, and perhaps has other addresses. I wouldn't neglect doing it if I were you; take all these addresses in case of any eventuality. You can make some very useful contacts that way.

That's all. Read Proverbs 18.24 and don't forget it.[100] A good Christmas, a good New Year, tolerable service and above all a speedy return home. With all my heart.

Your faithful Dietrich

22 December 1943

They seem to have made up their minds that I'm not to be with you for Christmas, though no one ventures to tell me so. I wonder why; do they think I'm so easily upset? Or do they think it kinder to lull me from day to day with empty hopes? . . .[101] The English have a very suitable word for this sort of thing – 'tantalizing'. Out of pure sympathy they've been 'tantalizing' Maria and me for a couple of weeks. If you had been there, Eberhard, you would have . . . done the duty of a friend by telling me the truth. To-morrow or the day after I should be able to talk to you . . . That's an event. I must spare my parents and also Maria, but you I will not deceive in any way, nor must you deceive me. We haven't done that before, and mustn't do it ever. I won't be able to write to you again after our meeting. But I want to thank you now, today, for coming and for being there for me. If you write to Renate from Italy and can occasionally include a note for me, even if it's only a few words, you will make me very happy. Aren't there things like purification plants in lakes? You know my technical naïvete – but there is something like that, and that's what you are to me. I do want to convey to you somehow tomorrow that my attitude towards my case is unquestionably one of faith, and I feel that it has become too much a matter of calculation and foresight. I'm not so much concerned about the rather artless question whether I shall be home for Christmas or not; I think I could willingly renounce that, if I could do so 'in faith', knowing that it was inevitable. I can (I hope) bear all things 'in faith', even my condemnation, and even the other consequences that I fear (Ps. 18.29);[102] but to be anxiously looking ahead wears one down. Don't worry about me if something worse happens. Others of the brethren have already been through that. But faithless vacillation,

173

endless deliberation without action, refusal to take any risks – that's a real danger. I must be able to know for certain that I am in God's hands, not in men's. Then everything becomes easy, even the severest privation. Now it's not a matter (I think I can say this truthfully) of my being 'understandably impatient', as people are probably saying, but of my facing everything in faith. In this regard, enemies are often much less dangerous than good friends. And I feel that you're the only one who understands that. I think that Maria, too, already feels rather the same thing. If you think of me, in the next days and weeks, please do so in this way (Ps. 60.12).[103] And if you've something to say to me about it, be so good as to write it to me. I don't want to go through this affair without faith.

My own view is that I shall be released, or called up into the army, in January or February. If you can do anything – and want to – where you are about my joining you, don't let yourself be dissuaded by the suggestions of others. The only question is whether you have anyone there to whom you can speak in confidence. However, it would have to happen soon. We must learn to act differently from those who always hesitate, whose failure we know in a wider context. We must be clear about what we want, we must ask whether we're up to it, and then we must do it with unshakable confidence. Then and only then can we also bear the consequences.

Now I want to assure you that I haven't for a moment regretted coming back in 1939[104] – nor any of the consequences, either. I knew quite well what I was doing, and I acted with a clear conscience. I've no wish to cross out of my life anything that has happened since, either to me personally (would I have got engaged otherwise? would you have married? Sigurdshof, East Prussia, Ettal, my illness and all the help you gave me then, and the time in Berlin), or as regards events in general. And I regard my being kept here (do you remember that I prophesied to you last March about what the year would bring?) as being involved in Germany's fate, as I was resolved to be. I don't look back on the past and accept the present reproachfully, but I don't want the machinations of men to make me waver. All we can do is to live in assurance and faith – you out there with the soldiers, and I in my cell. – I've just come across this in the *Imitation of Christ*: *Custodi diligenter cellam tuam, et custodiet te* ('Take good care of your cell, and it will take care of you'). – May God keep us in faith.

From his father   [Sakrow] 25 December 1943

Dear Dietrich,

We hoped that perhaps we would have you at home for Christmas, and that had a bad effect on our correspondence. However, the visits made by Maria and Eberhard have kept us in the picture about your doings to some degree. Unfortunately we're still without news about our application to visit you over Christmas. The post is very variable, as one sees in other respects. Perhaps we shall already have talked to you by the time this letter arrives. The morning attack by the English that ushered in Christmas Eve was hateful; this time it has apparently brought a good deal of misfortune upon the south-eastern suburbs. Nothing has happened here. After the Dohnanyi children and Christel had been with Hans[105] in the afternoon, we had a celebration in the evening with the Schleichers and the Bethges. The Dohnanyi children had brought another splendid tree which Eberhard and Renate decorated. The children were gay and Eberhard read the Christmas epistle. It's the first time that we haven't had a tree in our house and haven't been able to have the children and grandchildren with us. You can imagine that our thoughts were very much with you and Sabine. But we were grateful to be able to be together with the children here in an undamaged house.[106] The absence of Hans and Christel cast a deep shadow and reduced little Christoph to tears by the tree, but confidence that his release had to come soon was so great that gradually cheerfulness set in again among the children. We then ate our fill together, with herring salad, goose – the gift of a patient – and poppy-seed tarts, as satisfactorily as we old ones could expect after all that we've been through in the past year . . .   Affectionately, your Father

Dear Renate and Eberhard,

It's half past nine in the evening; I've been spending a few lovely peaceful hours, and thinking very thankfully about your being able to spend the day together . . .

One of my greatest joys this Christmas is that we have again been able to exchange the *Losungen*[107] for the coming year. I had already thought of it and hoped for it, though I hardly expected that it would be possible. And now this book, which has meant so much to me in the past months, will be with us throughout next year too, and when we read it in the morning we shall think especially of each other. Many, many thanks. It was a particularly nice idea of yours to look for the beautiful book of poetry; I keep reading it and find much joy and gain in it. I was at first rather sad that I can't give you anything nice this time; but my thoughts and wishes have been closer than ever to you, if that is possible.

I should like to say something to help you in the time of separation that lies ahead. There is no need to say how hard any such separation is for us; but as I've now been separated for nine months from all the people that I'm devoted to, I should like to pass on to you something of what I have learnt. So far, Eberhard and I have exchanged all the experiences that have been important to us, and this has been a great help to us; now you, Renate, will have some part in this. You must try to forget your 'uncle' and think more of your husband's friend.

First: nothing can make up for the absence of someone whom we love, and it would be wrong to try to find a substitute; we must simply hold out and see it through. That sounds very hard at first, but at the same time it is a great consolation, for the gap, as long as it remains unfilled, preserves the bonds between us. It is nonsense to say that God fills the gap; he doesn't fill it, but on the contrary, he keeps it empty and so helps us to keep alive our former communion with each other, even at the cost of pain.

Secondly: the dearer and richer our memories, the more difficult the separation. But gratitude changes the pangs of memory into a tranquil joy. The beauties of the past are borne, not as a thorn in the flesh, but as a precious gift in themselves. We must take care not to wallow in our memories or hand ourselves over to them, just as we do not gaze all the time at a valuable present, but only at special times, and apart from these keep it simply as a hidden treasure that is ours for certain. In this way the past gives us lasting joy and strength.

Thirdly: times of separation are not a total loss or unprofitable for our companionship, or at any rate they need not be so. In spite of all the difficulties that they bring, they can be the means of strengthening fellowship quite remarkably.

Fourthly: I've learnt here especially that the *facts* can always be mastered, and that difficulties are magnified out of all proportion simply by fear and anxiety. From the moment we wake until we fall asleep we must commend other people wholly and unreservedly to God and leave them in his hands, and transform our anxiety for them into prayers on their behalf:

> With sorrow and with grief . . .
> God *will not* be distracted.

Christmas Day

I very much hope to be there when your child is born. You, Eberhard, were recently talking about names. To be honest, I must say that this question has already been going through my head. If it's a boy, I think that 'Eberhard' would be best; I like it very much when names are handed on. You still seem to be thinking of 'Dietrich'. The name is good, the model less so; it makes some degree of sense, in that it's very improbable that you would have got to know each other had I not been there. I must also confess with a degree of shame that it would please me very much . . .

Once more all my beautiful presents are arranged on the edge of my tipped-up bed, and in front of me are the pictures that I enjoy so much. I'm still relishing, almost uninterruptedly, the memory of your visit . . . It really was a *necessitas*. The mind's hunger for discussion is much more tormenting than the body's hunger for food, and there is no one but you with whom I can talk about some things and in one way. A few pregnant remarks are enough to touch on a wide range of questions and clear them up. This ability to keep on the same wavelength, to play to each other, took years to cultivate, not always without friction, and we must never lose it. It's an incredible gain, and extraordinarily helpful. What a great deal we touched on in that hour and a half, and how much we learnt from each other! Thank you very much for arranging the meeting successfully. It cost you and Renate a morning. But I think that nevertheless you were glad to do it. It *was* a *necessitas*, and now I can think of you again quite differently. By the way, your visit prompted me to a little work that perhaps I shall send you soon, and it has given me new courage and pleasure for the great work . . .

The people here did their best to give me a happy Christmas, but I was glad to be alone again; I was surprised at that, and I sometimes wonder how I shall adapt myself to company again after this. You know how I used occasionally to retire to my own room after some great celebration. I'm afraid I must have grown even worse, for in spite of all my privations I've come to love solitude. I very much like to talk with two or three people, but I detest anything like a large assembly, and above all any chatter or gossip. Maria won't have an easy time with me in that respect.

Second Day of Christmas

Today, Eberhard, you're going away. When you wake up in the morning, may God strengthen your heart and keep sadness from rising in it; may he show each of you, each day, tasks that are worth the doing (today's reading is Luke 2.17!![108]); may he smooth out all your ways and bring you together again happily; and may he also grant me the day when I see you both again. God bless you and all of us. From my heart.   Your Dietrich

. . . If you need money, *please* just take it. As much as you want – Eberhard, try to put together what the people whom you meet really believe. Presumably it can be put together in a few sentences, and it is very important for me to know . . .

You know, Eberhard, that despite all the disquietude that people give me, I know well enough how you feel about your work there. But why should we say much when we know ourselves so well? One knows that it's enough. Klaus's remark that he still hadn't had this experience is in any case not just an *ad hoc* comment; he sometimes said it before (but only in theory) . . . We are both thinking rather differently here. By the way, thank you very much for visiting Weymarn,[109] too. It will have given rise to great joy. It was really very nice of you.

To his parents   [Tegel] 25 December 1943

Dear parents,
Christmas is over. It brought me a few quiet, peaceful hours, and it revived a good many past memories. My gratitude for the preservation of yourselves and all the family in the heavy air raids, and my confidence that I shall see you again in the not too distant future, were greater than all my troubles. I lit the candles that you and Maria sent me, read the Christmas story and a few carols which I hummed over to myself; and in doing so, I thought of you all and hoped that, after all the alarms of the last few weeks, you might be able to enjoy an hour or two of peace. Your Christmas parcel was a great delight, especially great-grandfather's goblet from 1845, which is now standing on my table with evergreen in it. But the things to eat were also very fine, and will last for a while. I got interesting books and Christmas sweetmeats from the family; do thank them all very much. Maria, who was here on the 22nd, gave me the wrist-watch that her father was wearing when he was killed. That pleased me very much. She had also left a parcel for me, which was handed over early yesterday, packed in a most attractive way, with gingerbread, and greetings from her mother and grandmother. I felt rather sad that I wasn't able to give her anything; but I only want to do that when I'm free again and can give it to her myself; I told her this, and she also thought it was better that way. I'm quite sure that she will take these days of Christmas, in which she misses her father and

brother and knows that I am in prison, as calmly and as bravely as she has endured everything else so far – even if it seems to be going beyond her strength. She has learnt very early to recognize a stronger and more gracious hand in what men inflict on us.

Now I shall not even be with you on your birthday, mother, either. If only one could give you some pleasure with something! Surely everyone will try. I can only say that in these hard times we need you more than ever, and that I cannot imagine the last months of my imprisonment at all without you. The way in which the two of you have borne this blow will be an important memory for your grandchildren all their lives, and more than that. With each letter and each visit that I get from you, I'm newly thankful to you for it and will always remain so. If only you didn't make too many demands on yourself so often, and looked after your strength more carefully. That would be a real birthday wish from me to you, but I'm afraid that it will remain unfulfilled. Yet it would be such a great relief to us all.

The New Year, too, will bring a great deal of anxiety and disturbance, though I think we may on this New Year's Eve sing with greater confidence than ever that verse from the old New Year's hymn:

> *Shut fast the door of woe,*
> *In every place let flow*
> *The streams of joy and peace,*
> *That bloodshed now may cease.*[110]

I know no greater prayer or wish than that for your birthday.

Thank you for everything that you have done for me in the past year. With all my heart.   Your Dietrich

From Eberhard Bethge   Lissa,[111] 2 January 1944

Dear Dietrich,
I must try to send you another greeting and tell you how much my visit to you and your letters have inspired me. You cannot

believe how often I have read them myself, read parts of them aloud to Renate and told some of the contents to the family. I do not know how things have gone with you, but I have to report about myself, at any rate, that I left you on the 23rd almost with a light heart and feeling of freedom. Now that this had happened, parting seemed much easier, and so many, many things had been intimated at such a terrific pace. Afterwards, of course, I saw that it would have been much better had I had your letters earlier and consequently had studied the problem more thoroughly. But I hope you noticed how happy I was to talk to you at last, to hear from you directly and to read your letters. You write that, after marriage, our friendship is to be counted among the stable things of life. But that is not the case, at least as far as the recognition and consideration of others is concerned. Marriage is recognized outwardly – regardless of whether the relationship between the couple is stable or not –; each person, in this case the whole family, must take it into account and finds it the right thing that much should and must be undertaken for it. Friendship – no matter how exclusive and how all-embracing it may be – has no *necessitas*, as father put it over the question of visiting. Your letters of course go to Maria, and almost as automatically to Karl-Friedrich, but it takes an extra struggle to make the point that I have to have them too. You can understand from all that how your letters and the visit had almost a liberating effect on me. In the army, you also say, no one pays any attention to the fact that someone has a very good friend. Friendship is completely determined by its content and only in this way does it have its existence . . .

Anyway, thank you very much for everything that you said to me, for the many interesting indications of your work and the thoughts about which you write. They are very much with me now. The Old Testament, the importance of appearances, a good conscience about the good things of this earth; perhaps I shall soon find a quiet time to write more about this and send it to you. I've now another unexpected respite until the 6th because of hold-ups to military transport . . . By the way, I had a word with Lokies straightaway, on the 23rd.[112] He didn't think that there would be any problem if all cover were broken. So far no one has been able to concern themselves *seriously* with the case either among the leadership or elsewhere, because they know nothing. He didn't think that there was any marked general feeling against you; the theological confidence that you enjoy was too great and undisturbed for that . . .[113]

From Eberhard Bethge [Charlottenburg] Saturday, 8 January 1944

Dear Dietrich,
You will have heard today that I'm here again on the way through; I'm going on early tomorrow – once again the demands of a farewell. It's remarkable how little one gets used to it. So, quickly, another greeting – unfortunately a very incomplete fragment. We were so pleased to have your Christmas letter and thank you very much for your words to the two of us . . . You can't believe the tranquillity and assurance that emanates from the letters that you send to me. You have the peace there to write good long letters, and you make use of it. Otherwise no one here in Berlin has time and leisure for one another, and everyday needs make people egotistic and nervous. That's why your lines do me so much good . . . Many thanks. I wanted to say at least that much to you before I go . . .   Your Eberhard

From Eberhard Bethge   In the train to Munich
                                                  9 January 1944

Dear Dietrich,
Almost a year ago we were sitting together in the train on this same stretch of line and travelling together to Munich for the last time. It was another very good journey. You were reading Tayllerand, we ate in the dining car, I expect that I was writing to Renate again. We heard *Palestrina* and marvelled,[114] we drank coffee with Ninne[115] (I'll be going to see her in the morning) and

managed to get hold of some very good books. We worked out money and coupons together; as always, you were very generous. We had many good hopes.[116] In the meantime you've been through a great deal that we didn't suspect then. With this journey I'm bringing a completely new nine months' experience to an end. Now I want to chat about something with you before it gets dark – there are no lights on Wehrmacht trains. You've often written to me from Munich trains, by the way, more contemplatively than usual, but not at such length as your recent letters.

It has been nine months without you . . . During this time you've become much more aware of some things which have escaped me as a result of Renate's existence: a critical feeling for empty phrases, hasty and false conclusions, self-satisfaction, pietistic style, Pharisaic bourgeoisie in the church. Although you don't really say much explicitly, your ever-present ear for such things compels one to examine everything all over again . . . It seems to me that you have made many things about yourself clearer and more comprehensible, the difference in our backgrounds – yours and mine; what it meant for you to become a theologian and to be one in *this* family . . .

I admire your tone . . . I haven't yet been through such serious situations as you have. I'm not sure how well I would come to grips with the situation if I saw what is really at stake. Education and death Socratic? The educated man as the one who has no illusions and does not deceive himself in activity or does not put up with it, but who knows how to overcome in Christian faith? It's getting dark, I can't see any more. That's all for now.

Your Eberhard

Now I can go on writing. As soldiers we aren't worth lights, but this leave train has nevertheless got light in some remarkable way, so I will make good use of it. We're now skirting the Thüringian forest. Who knows when I shall get there again? If only we could correspond with each other regularly and quickly . . .

The proletarian strata 'without desires', who make themselves substitute satisfactions and allow the tension to go slack are the best-equipped warriors of today; the length of the war develops these things in a terrifying way. One really does get contemptuous in a hut of twelve people like that. How quickly men, when they make themselves 'at home', are so shamelessly at home and thus make such manageable, obedient soldiers.

I'm writing as though I were turning over the pages of your letter. Perhaps only the truly cultured man becomes homesick, and not the intellectual. What you wrote about good fortune and the cross did me good. Have you a chapter about it? Perhaps it's very important that one doesn't wrongly have a bad conscience there.

I hope that we shall soon get your wedding sermon now. It's frightful how difficult everything is now. I only dare ask your parents for something with the greatest caution. You encourage me so nicely to write some time. You've already achieved a great deal and I credit you with all kinds of midwife's arts. If I were to write, that would of course be your masterpiece with me. First, only my critical vein has developed and not my ease of expression. I still prefer to read you than to write myself . . . You've written me so many splendid things; I can never do more than touch on things, but at least I want to show you that everything is occupying me a very great deal. I'm waiting for us to see each other and talk . . .

10 January

Well, everything still isn't cleared up. Tomorrow I'm off to Verona. In the meantime I'm spending two nights at a well-known place: the Europäischer Hof.[117] Full, of course. But a reference to our, your stay here last year got me a room.

I'm now going to visit Ninne Kalckreuth, who sounded pleased to hear me on the telephone. Good-bye for now. Next it's over the Brenner. Your Eberhard

What about the anguish of Christ, about which something has to be said?

Dear Uncle Dietrich,
Many thanks for your long letter. We were really delighted with
it . . . Eberhard went off early yesterday, in the first place to
Munich. He telephoned this afternoon to say that he had to go on
to Verona tomorrow morning, and that his destination would
probably be in that area. But he doesn't know the name of the
place yet, or even whether he is now going to be a clerk, as was
first said. I'm rather worried that he will have to go still further,
because what we were told earlier was certainly not right . . .
The feeling of separation for an immeasurably long time is quite
terrible, especially the feeling of one's own utter helplessness in
the face of everything. I'm now thinking a great deal about what
you wrote to us on the subject. I hope that our patience won't be
put to the test as long as yours. Indeed, one hopes that everything
won't last much longer. What you write about your own work is
very interesting. Of course we're all very excited about it already.
It's really marvellous that you can work there in this way; I just
can't imagine myself in such surroundings. The parents have fixed
their house again enough for them to go back again today . . .
     Much love and many thanks for everything.   Your Renate

Dear Dietrich,
Of course it's still a while to your birthday, but I hear that the post
is taking such a tremendously long time that I'm writing already.
Perhaps the letter will reach you in time. Warmest congratulations; I hope that this day won't become a day of sadness. There
could be many reasons for that, and I think egotistically of the
unbridgeable distance between us. I have the impression that somehow we've celebrated your birthday less frequently than mine; I
remember mine clearly, here and there, and above all that evening
in Florence. I remember yours especially on those occasions at

Finkenwalde. On the last one I expect that you were travelling. Now we have to keep birthdays quietly in a way to which we haven't been accustomed before.

After the first two days I can give you a good report. I'm sitting near the place[118] where we saw the seven hills in the glimmering twilight after the hot car journey . . . You will . . . look back on a remarkable year that is without parallel . . .

My wishes are obvious . . . possibilities for writing; and a little more courage on your part to get things into readable form; perhaps someone who will be technically a help to you to make this laborious stage as easy as possible. By the way, when I read some passages from your letters to father,[119] he and others with him were again very impressed by your style. I can't understand why some people find it so hard to understand. It's probably the concentration that it demands . . .

Will I be able to hear again from you soon? At home everything keeps being so oppressive and agitated, whereas these two days in this country house everything has been going well and I've nothing to do but enjoy the sunshine . . .

You can think of me emptying one of the many wine glasses to drink your health!

Warmest greetings.   Your Eberhard

To his parents   [Tegel] 14 January 1944

Dear parents,
Susi has just left the parcel for me again; I'm very grateful to you and to her for it. If I had guessed that I would be here so long, I would have asked you much earlier not to take so much trouble over me and above all not to curtail your rations, short as they are, in order to send me something. Of course, each time it's a great delight to receive your parcel, but it is being gradually affected by the thought that you're not as well-fed as you should be with the strenuous work you now have to do, especially after the bomb damage. I had hoped that in the meantime you would have decided

on a rest in Pätzig; it would really be a great comfort to me if you got away from the nights of air raids, repair works and general Berlin turmoil, at least for a while, and had some relatively normal food; moreover, it would of course be a delight if you got to know the house in which I hope later on to be at home . . . If anything happens about my case any day during that time, it's easy to reach you – how marvellous it would be if I could then come with Maria to Pätzig and meet you there. I know that you're not fond of travelling and that usually it's not very useful. But perhaps it could be my birthday wish for you? Above all, you are not to overstrain yourselves; everything else is quite secondary to that!

Yesterday and today you have birthdays.[120] I expect that you will be together in the evening with K. Friedrich and Rüdiger. Today we must be thankful for each day and each hour in which we can still be together. I'm sitting by the open window, with the sunshine streaming in almost like spring, and I take this uncommonly fine start to the year for a good omen. Compared with last year, this year can only be better. – I'm getting on all right. I'm finding it a little easier to concentrate, and I'm enjoying Dilthey very much. I hope that I shall soon hear that you're on your way. Keep well. With much love from your grateful   Dietrich

From his father   [Sakrow] 16 January 1944

Dear Dietrich,
I want to use a quiet Sunday here in Sakrow to send a letter to you. Weekdays are still very disturbed by the people who make a noise near the windows, doors and on the roof. In between times patients come, and whatever else the day brings. By and large we've got to the point of being warm, and we can sit in the rooms – though not in all of them – without winter coats. I hope that it hasn't all been done in vain and that the next attack won't throw everything about again. Our house in Kurländer Allee has been designated a total write-off and the occupants have been given an

evacuation order. We're now having papers and visits about the notification of damage and compensation for rent, etc. We want to be here at night for the dark nights that are coming next. People are now interested in the rising of the moon, when beforehand they didn't give it a thought. I've noticed that I have a shameful ignorance of the phases of the moon. It seems that the English are now – unlike earlier times – afraid of the bright nights, presumably because of the night-fighters. The people at Friedrichsbrunn write that they watched an air battle during a daytime raid by the Americans; they saw aircraft crashing and prisoners being brought in – a great excitement for the Bonhoeffer and Dress children. By and large, I see that people who have gone through numerous attacks and bombings in the neighbourhood and have kept in good spirits are often affected afterwards. Their attention and their ability to concentrate suffers, they become emotionally excitable, irritable and are easily reduced to tears. This is also noticeable when one travels on the trams. A lot of time is spent searching in the house; one doesn't know what one has put away in the cellar or elsewhere, and on the whole one works more slowly. The soldiers think that sitting around doing nothing during bomb attacks at home is much more unpleasant than being in the field, where one has to take action.

I hope that we shall soon be able to talk to you again. I sent off an application about 8–10 days ago. We were very pleased about your Christmas and New Year letter, though it only reached us a few days ago. Renate got her first letter from Eberhard today, from Verona. Meanwhile he has gone further south. Our health is good. Rüdiger has reported to us that he found you looking well.

Affectionate greetings, Father

To Eberhard Bethge   [no date; sent from Tegel
                                         on 18 January 1944]
Dear Eberhard,

My thoughts have been with you constantly since you went off into the unknown. I hope that very soon I shall hear where you've ended up. It's one of those pieces of luck that almost seem to be following you around that you managed to be with Renate once again and even to bring her to Berlin, or rather, it's another instance of the goodwill that you find everywhere . . . I don't know anyone who does not like you, whereas I know a great many people who do not like me. I don't take this at all hardly for myself; wherever I find enemies I also find friends, and that satisfies me. But the reason is probably that you are by nature open and modest, whereas I am reticent and rather demanding . . .

I keep being glad to think that you were about at Christmas. No one could have filled my place better. I'm also very glad that the Dohnanyis were so pleased to have you; that's clear from letters and the remarks of Klaus, who visited me. He's become a very nice boy. These children today are much more knowledge-able and accomplished than we were at that age. I believe that a quite excellent generation may be growing up, which will be clearer, more open and less fearful than ours.

For some time I've been writing away at the little literary work that was prompted by our short meeting. But, as almost always, it's taking me more time than I expected at the beginning. I'll send it to you as soon as it's finished – if it's at all reasonable.[121] In a rather haphazard way I've recently been reading a history of Scotland Yard, a history of prostitution, finished the Delbrück – I find him really rather uninteresting in his problems –, Reinhold Schneider's sonnets – very variable in quality, some very good; on the whole all the newest productions seem to me to be lacking in the *hilaritas* – 'cheerfulness' – which is to be found in any really great and free intellectual achievement. One has always the im-pression of a somewhat tortured and strained manufacture instead of creativity in the open air. Do you see what I mean? At the moment I'm reading a gigantic English novel which goes from 1500 to today, by Hugh Walpole, written in 1909. Dilthey is also interesting me very much and for an hour each day I'm studying the manual for medical staff, for any eventuality.

This letter has been lying about for a couple of days. Mean-while Rüdiger has been to see me and told me that you first went to Verona, but after that he doesn't know where. I'm waiting for more news daily, also for W,[122] whom I've hardly seen for two weeks. You've also seen him, though, and I'm pleased about that. Over the last three days I've been reading a French novel, *Mariages* – not bad, but remarkably frank . . . I was strengthened in my conviction that the naturalistic, psychological novel is no longer adequate for us. But we would have to talk about that later.

W. is to come today. Good. I hope that the attack on Magdeburg hasn't damaged any of the places that are so much in your memories . . .

Now keep well, and overcome all the burdens on body and mind as you've been doing so far. The readings are my daily joy. Thank you for everything.   Faithfully, your Dietrich

To Renate and Eberhard Bethge   [Tegel] 23 January 1944

Dear Renate and Eberhard,
Since the ninth, my thoughts about you have taken a new shape. The fact that shortly before your parting you read the text Isa. 42.16[123] together puts these thoughts in a special light; on that day, which I knew had special significance for you, I kept reading the passages with special attention and great gratitude. That Sunday was a wrench for me as well as for you, though in a different way. It's a strange feeling to see a man whose life has in one way or another been so intimately bound up with one's own for years going out to meet an unknown future about which one can do virtually nothing. I think this realization of one's own helplessness has two sides, as you, Renate, also say: it brings both anxiety and relief. As long as we ourselves are trying to help shape someone else's destiny, we are never quite free of the question whether what we're doing is really for the other person's benefit – at least in any matter of great importance. But when all possibility of co-operating in anything is suddenly cut off, then behind any anxiety about him there is the consciousness that his life has now been placed wholly in better and stronger hands. For you, and for us, the greatest task during the coming weeks, and perhaps months,

may be to entrust each other to those hands. When I learnt yesterday, Eberhard, that you are now somewhere south of Rome, this task became much clearer to me. I am to suppress all the questions that I may keep wanting to ask myself in this connection. Whatever weaknesses, miscalculations, and guilt there is in what precedes the facts, God is in the facts themselves. If we survive during these coming weeks or months, we shall be able to see quite clearly that all has turned out for the best. The idea that we could have avoided many of life's difficulties if we had taken things more cautiously is too foolish to be entertained for a moment. As I look back on your past I am so convinced that what has happened hitherto has been right, that I feel that what is happening now is right too. To renounce a full life and its real joys in order to avoid pain is neither Christian nor human.

I'm now waiting with great excitement for your first report from out there, Eberhard. I have the feeling that to a certain degree you also see things with my eyes, just as I see things here with yours. We thus experience our different fates for each other in a kind of vicarious way. What you write from out there I will believe without hesitation, as perhaps happens in your case with my letters from here; and above all that will be the case when we can *talk* with each other again.

The news of the Nettuno landing has just come.[124] I wonder whether you are anywhere thereabouts. When things like this happen, I see that composure isn't part of my nature, but that I have to acquire it at the cost of repeated effort. In fact, natural composure is probably in most cases nothing but a euphemism for indifference and indolence, and to that extent it's not very estimable. I read in Lessing recently: 'I am too proud to consider myself unlucky. Just clench your teeth and let your skiff sail where the wind and waves take it. Enough that I do not intend to upset it myself.' Is this pride and teeth-clenching to be completely forbidden and alien to the Christian, and replaced, shall we say, by a soft composure that gives way prematurely? Is there not also a kind of composure which proudly clenches its teeth, but is quite different from a dull, stolid, rigid, lifeless, mechanical submitting-to-something-I-can't-help? I think we honour God more if we gratefully accept the life that he gives us with all its blessings, loving it and drinking it to the full, and also grieving deeply and sincerely when we have impaired or wasted any of the good things of life (some people denounce such an attitude, and think it is bourgeois, weak, and sensitive), than if we are insensitive to life's blessings and may therefore also be insensitive to pain. Job's words, 'The Lord gave etc. . . .' include rather than exclude this, as can be seen clearly enough from his teeth-clenching speeches which were vindicated by God (42.7ff.) in face of the false, premature, pious submission of his friends. Excuse me, Renate, for getting into theology again. It's one of those fragments of conversation which are unavoidable in letters between Eberhard and me. Above all I should and would have told you how glad I was to hear from you directly and also in such detail. That was a real event. How grateful I am to the train guard who lit up the Munich leave train contrary to usual custom . . . It would be good if you had a couple of photos of me with you;[125] they could eventually be used instead of visiting cards with my many acquaintances, as I can't write to all of them. Did you really make the acquaintance of Prof. Reinhold Niebuhr on that car journey with the Hennes?[126] Like Dr Leiper and Prof. Paul Lehmann, he is a good friend of mine. N. and Paul L. are also very good German speakers; that's always a help. You can always go to Cedergren's; you were their guest.[127] He now has an important post in the Red Cross. Incidentally, you can give them all special greetings from Martin.[128] I will also see that you get my letters to my parents.

I very much agree with what you say in this connection about friendship which, in contrast to marriage and kinship, has no generally recognized rights, and therefore depends entirely on its own inherent quality. It is by no means easy to classify friendship sociologically. Perhaps it is to be regarded as a sub-heading of culture and education, brotherhood being a sub-heading of church, and comradeship a sub-heading of work and politics. Marriage, work, state, and church all have their definite, divine mandate; but what about culture and education? I don't think they can just be classified under work, however tempting that might be in many ways.

They belong, not to the sphere of obedience, but to the broad area of freedom, which surrounds all three spheres of the divine mandates. The man who is ignorant of this area of freedom may be a good father, citizen, and worker, indeed even a Christian; but I doubt whether he is a complete man and therefore a Christian in the widest sense of the term. Our 'Protestant' (not Lutheran) Prussian world has been so dominated by the four mandates that the sphere of freedom has receded into the background. I wonder whether it is possible (it almost seems so today) to regain the idea of the church as providing an understanding of the area of freedom (art, education, friendship, play), so that Kierkegaard's 'aesthetic existence' would not be banished from the church's sphere, but would be re-established within it? I really think that is so, and it would mean that we should recover a link with the Middle Ages. Who is there, for instance, in our times, who can devote himself with an easy mind to music, friendship, games, or happiness? Surely not the 'ethical' man, but only the Christian. Just because friendship belongs to this sphere of freedom ('of the Christian man'?!), it must be confidently defended against all the disapproving frowns of 'ethical' existences, though without claiming for it the *necessitas* of a divine decree, but only the *necessitas* of *freedom*. I believe that within the sphere of this freedom friendship is by far the rarest and most priceless treasure, for where else does it survive in this world of ours, dominated as it is by the *three other* mandates? It cannot be compared with the treasures of the mandates, for in relation to them it is *sui generis*; it belongs to them as the cornflower belongs to the cornfield.

As to what you said about 'Christ's anguish': it comes out only in the *prayer* (as it does in the Psalms). (I have never been clear why the evangelists report this prayer, which no one can have heard. The suggestion that Jesus revealed it to the disciples during the forty days is an evasion of the difficulty. Have you any comment?)

Your reference to Socrates in connection with the theme of culture and death may be very valuable; I must think about it. The only thing I am really clear about in the whole problem is that a 'culture' that breaks down in the face of danger is no culture.

Culture must be able to face danger and death – *impavidum feriunt ruinae:* 'the ruins will strike a fearless man' (Horace) – even if it cannot 'conquer' them; what does 'conquer' mean? By finding forgiveness in judgment, and joy in terror? But we must discuss this further.

Now for the name of the child you're expecting. If it's a girl, wouldn't Sabine be very nice? You both have a good relationship to her and I think that the name itself is very attractive, rather old-fashioned, but perhaps that's its charm. I don't think that Amalie is too bad; I've also always liked the name Angelica, which I always involuntarily associate with Fra Angelico. And what do you think of Adelheid? It's comic that they're all names with a long ā. They're probably more resonant than others (or might I be influenced very personally in some way in my subconscious by Māriā?). Now I'll keep quiet about boys' names . . .

Well, that's all for today. In countless thoughts and with good wishes I'm always with you and send my greetings.

Your Dietrich

Have you paid a visit to the 'Propaganda' in Rome? What have you seen? Reminiscences of 1936 are very alive again, but you would know much more from that time than I. If you see the Laocoon again, just notice whether you don't think that the father's head may have been the model for later representations of Christ. Last time I saw this classical man of sorrows it impressed me deeply and kept me thinking for a long time. How wonderful it would be if we could be there together. You needn't worry about me. All goes well and there are a couple of really *very* nice people here, whom you must get to know some time later. If only we had got there already . . .

I've had to take a new line with the companion of my daily walks. Although he has done his best to ingratiate himself with me, he let fall a remark about the Gert[129] problem, etc., lately that has made me more offhanded and cool to him than I have ever been to anyone before; I've also arranged for him to be deprived promptly of all little comforts. Now he feels obliged to go round whimpering for a time, but it leaves me – I am surprised myself, but interested too – absolutely cold. He really is a pitiful figure, but certainly not 'poor Lazarus'.

I think that it's very nice that we are both godparents to Dieter Z.[130] Lokies' opinion was very important to me, and comforting. I would like it *very* much if I could get to see you again, Renate . . .

By the way, as far as I know, my parents were only separated once in their life, for a short time when father had to do a tour of inspection in the west during the World War! What times and marriages they were! And what different forms of *good* marriages there are! You won't be able to read *Witiko* now, with its thousand pages, but later you must read it together. Maria was also entranced by it.

I would very much like to know how and on what basis you get on with the other men. I would love to know some time if you have conversations with your comrades. Will you write about it some time? I'm getting on all right, working and waiting. Nothing has happened to shake my optimism, and I hope it's the same with you. Good-bye; may we soon meet again happily!   Dietrich

I'm already trying to work out some way of our getting together. I think that that would be very good whatever happens. Have you any possibilities? I sometimes think that if you were here, things would be very different with me. I hear only theories, nothing concrete happens. Is that 'bourgeois'? Did you feel the same thing in September? Briefly, we will do it better later on.

What will happen to Rome? The thought that it might be destroyed is a nightmare. What a good thing we saw it in peacetime! I hope I shall hear from you *soon*!

From his father   [Charlottenburg] 25 January 1944

Dear Dietrich,

If this birthday greeting is to reach you on time, I have to write it early. I hope that Maria or we shall be able to talk to you on the day . . . After the previous course of your case we can hardly assume that freedom will come to you as a birthday present, but we're convinced that it cannot be delayed much longer. It's almost a year now! We're grateful that you've borne it well so far, have retained your courage and a delight in working, and have kept well. I have no doubt that these wicked months have enriched your inner experience. To have gone through all that imprisonment means personally, for months, is something very different from having some acquaintance with it from outside and by conversation with prisoners, which has been the case with me in my observations. But that would be enough . . .

One hardly dares any longer to imagine life without the pressure that bears down on one. But that is something to do with old age, when one gradually begins to lose optimism and elasticity; in addition, there is the unproductive unrest in which one spends all the time outside regular daily work making sure of protection against night attacks. This gradually makes people tired and, I believe, would easily lead to an indolent resignation if one were not refreshed by looking at children and grandchildren. That is something for which we old ones are grateful to you young ones. I hope we shall see each other soon. Meanwhile, accept my best wishes for your birthday. May it bring you something nice, despite the unpleasant circumstances.

Affectionately, your Father

From his mother   [Charlottenburg] 27 January 1944

My dear Dietrich,
The fourth of February is approaching, and I'm thinking of how times have changed. I recall many happy children's birthdays with cakes, whipped cream, Punch and Judy shows and masquerades. It also reminds me that I'm getting old – remembering earliest days is probably a sign of that . . .

You press us so much to move away, but there is a great deal to tell against that. You are not the only reason, so to speak, why we want to stay here. Christel is very cut up,[131] and one can surely still be some help to her; and father still has a very great deal to do with patients, despite his considerable age. Doctors and patients know what sort of a person he is, and I think that that keeps him younger than if he were sitting somewhere quietly. We're out of town[132] at night for most of the time, so you needn't worry about us. We would like you to tell us whether there is anything that you would like out of the house for your birthday. Think about what you would like to have. Perhaps Minna Herzlieb's little cupboard, that Goethe gave her? I must stop. God bless you and be with you in the coming year.   Your Mother

From Renate Bethge   Sakrow, 28 January 1944

Dear Uncle Dietrich,
I want to send you warmest congratulations and all good wishes for your birthday. We really have to expect that the next year of your life will be better than the last. You yourself write that you're an optimist. We are too, of course; otherwise, how could one go on living? Thank you for the greeting which you sent us by the grandparents; I was very pleased about it and sent it on to Eberhard. I very much hope I shall get permission to visit; I've applied together with Hans-Walter, and we expect an answer any day. Hans-Walter, though, only has leave until the 2nd. In addition, the post office was bombed out last night, so there was no delivery. I hope that it wasn't there.

I've had no news of Eberhard for more than a week now . . . Of course one doesn't know what's happened to him since the landing at Nettuno. Before that, however, he wrote quite contentedly about his billet; he was in a lonely country house with fifteen men including an officer. He had the feeling that there was a very nice atmosphere. He was to have a driving test the next Monday and thought that he would then have an appointment in this direction, perhaps with some more work as a clerk. If everything has worked out like that, one could be quite content, but one can't really expect it, and the fact that there has been no post for so long is not encouraging. We're all very pleased that things are going well with you and that you can go on doing a good deal of work; but now the case really ought to come to a conclusion at last. Besides, you must be out to baptize our child. Who will see it first, you or Eberhard? . . . It's not very good that the parents still keep staying in the city; the alerts disturb mother. But father wants to stay in the house whatever happens, because he thinks that if necessary he could help to put fires out. And of course mother doesn't want to leave him all alone.

Unfortunately we have no proper present for you this time, so I've just baked you a couple of 'S'-les,[133] which I will give to Maria. Now all the best and much love, your Renate

To Eberhard Bethge [Tegel] 29 and 30 January 1944

Dear Eberhard,
Although I'm sure that you have letters from Renate every day – though they may not be handed over to you every day, so that you can't avoid the torment of waiting and the uncertainty – I expect that you enjoy every letter; and not only for that reason, but also because I find it hard not to write to you, I'm using this *quiet* Saturday afternoon, so very different from the din that we've had the last two nights,[134] to talk some things over with you. I wonder how the first few days of direct contact with war, and possibly your first personal impressions of the Anglo-Saxon opponents, whom we have so far met only in times of peace, have affected you? I find it hard to understand why we can't go through these fundamental experiences together, for later – *sub conditione Jacobea* – we shall have to ponder them together and make them fruitful for our calling. When I think of you every morning and evening, I have to try very hard not to let all my thoughts dwell on the many cares and anxieties that beset you, instead of praying

for you properly. In that connection I must talk to you some time about prayer in time of trouble; it's a difficult matter, and yet our misgivings about it may not be good. Psalm 50 says quite clearly, 'Call upon me in the day of trouble; I will deliver you, and you shall glorify me.' The whole history of the children of Israel consists of such cries for help. And I must say that the last two nights have made me face this problem again in a quite elementary way. While the bombs are falling like that all round the building, I cannot help thinking of God, his judgment, his hand stretched out and his anger not turned away (Isa. 5.25 and 9.11–10.4), and of my own unpreparedness. I feel how men can make vows, and then I think of you all and say, 'better me than one of them' – and that makes me realize how attached I am to you all. I won't say anything more about it – it will have to be by word of mouth; but when all is said and done, it's true that it needs trouble to shake us up and drive us to prayer, though I feel every time that it is something to be ashamed of, as indeed it is. That may be because I haven't so far felt able to say a Christian word to the others at such a moment. As we were again lying on the floor last night, and someone exclaimed 'O God, O God' (he is normally a very flippant type), I couldn't bring myself to offer him any Christian encouragement or comfort; all I did was to look at my watch and say, 'It won't last more than ten minutes now.' There was nothing premeditated about it; it came quite automatically, and perhaps I felt that it was wrong to force religion down his throat just then. (Incidentally, Jesus didn't try to convert the two thieves on the cross; one of them turned to him!)

I'm sorry to say that I suffered a severe loss the night before last. The man who was, to my mind, by far the most intelligent and attractive in the place was killed in the city by a direct hit.[135] I should certainly have put him in touch with you later, and we already had plans for the future. We often had interesting talks, and the other day he brought me *Daumier und die Justiz,* which I still have. He was a really educated man of working-class origin, a philosopher, and father of three children. I was very much distressed by his death.

In the last few days I've again been busy on the little work that I mentioned to you before, about the meeting of two old friends after they had been separated for a long time during the war. I hope to be able to send it to you soon. You needn't worry – it will *not* be a *roman à clef* . . .[136]

In earlier times, even one of the problems that we are now having to deal with would have been enough to take up all our time. Now we have to reduce to a common denominator war, marriage, church, profession, housing, the possible death of those nearest and dearest to us and, added to that, my present situation. No doubt most people would regard these simply as separate problems, but for the Christian and the 'cultured' man that is impossible; he cannot split up his life or dismember it, and the common denominator must be sought both in thought and in a personal and integrated attitude to life. The man who allows himself to be torn into fragments by events and by questions has not passed the test for the present and the future. In the story of young Witiko we read that he set out into the world *'um das Ganze zu tun'* (to do the whole thing); here we have the ἄνθρωπος τέλειος (τέλειος originally means 'whole' in the sense of 'complete' or 'perfect'); 'You, therefore, must be perfect (τέλειος), as your heavenly Father is perfect' (Matt. 5.48) – in contrast to the ἀνὴρ δίψυχος ('a double-minded man') of James 1.8. Witiko 'does the whole thing' by trying to adapt himself to the realities of life, by always listening to the advice of experienced people – i.e. by showing that he is one of those who are 'whole'. We can never achieve this 'wholeness' simply by ourselves, but only together with others . . .

I have just started to read Harnack's *History of the Prussian Academy*; it is very good. I'm sure he put his heart and soul into it, and he said more than once that he considered it his best book. – How are you? Do let me know. I'm still surprisingly well. I suppose it makes some difference to know that I mustn't be ill here in any circumstances. I always find enough strength and concentration for reading, but not always for writing and constructive work, except now and again. How I shall get used to living in company again I don't yet know.

That's all. The letter must go. I commend you and Renate and all of us to the grace of God. Today the gospel is Matt. 8.23, 'Why are you afraid, O men of little faith? – What sort of a man is this, that even winds and sea obey him?'

Faithfully, in daily fellowship,   your Dietrich

From Eberhard Bethge   [Rignano] 1 February 1944

Dear Dietrich,
In a few days it will be your birthday and I still don't know anything about all of you, how the last apparently dreadful attacks up to 30 January were, what happened, how things are with you and Renate. My thoughts are constantly with you all. This bit of individual life that one retains, although in other respects one is treated like the mules which climb the steep mountain paths round here without any will of their own, becomes a torment. Your thoughts that it is precisely this that is a necessary part of our condition and that in precisely this respect we must show ourselves to be what we are, bring me some comfort . . . With luck the correspondence will now start flowing a bit. My last news is from the 22nd. A letter, of course, took three weeks. The lines of communication have been destroyed to a colossal extent; built up and then smashed down again. And of course there are really very few roads which are passable at all. This problem of the march back is rather oppressive . . .

I'm very excited about the literary work.[137] I hope it will come soon. I'm chiefly occupied in studying Italian and writing letters. I took with me Burckhardt's *Renaissance* and am enjoying that very much from time to time. But great difficulty is caused for these private concerns by the unrest, constant possibility of being called away and the lack of any place of one's own to sit . . . Many greetings for your birthday. You will be reading the text for the fourth with special thoughts.[138] I wrote to Frau von Kleist a while ago from here. I wonder whether you will have a letter from me? Faithfully,   your Eberhard

By the way, Schönfeld[139] is said to be very worked up at not getting anything. I can't quite understand it, and only get hints. I've just learnt that Paton[140] died in August. You'll be sorry about that.

To Eberhard Bethge   [Tegel] 1 February 1944

Dear Eberhard,

Carpe diem – which in this case means that I take every chance of sending you a greeting. First, because I could write for weeks on end without finishing all that I have to tell you, and secondly, because one never knows how much longer things are likely to last. And since one day you will be called to write my biography, I want to put the most complete material possible at your disposal! So! Today I saw Susi, very nice and fresh and warm-hearted. It is really remarkable how a person like her, who when she was a girl seemed so little predestined to be a pastor's wife, can grow into her calling, personally and as a member of the church. She is really quite immersed in it, and that's splendid. And what were we like as youths of 17 or 18? Was it very different? And yet somehow we became pastors. How strange are the ways in which people are led to become 'Christians'! The visits are very different from each other, although of course I enjoy each one of them. The women are on the whole freer and less restrained . . . Karl-Friedrich was, of course, very nice . . . with Rüdiger, whose visit I particularly enjoyed and who really said some friendly things to me (e.g. for the state of health of my parents only the *causa*, and not the *culpa*, lay with me – of course it was Latin!), it was touching how he . . . kept coming round to talking about Maetz, so as to exclude any subject that didn't completely comply with the regulations from the start . . . I haven't seen anything of Klaus yet . . . Quite apart from anything else, I think it possible that he's inwardly too sensitive to want to expose himself to impressions here. Fortunately we've become rather more robust in this respect in our calling. Memories of 23 December [141] are still a source of joy and pride and gratitude to me.

You may know that the last few nights have been bad, especially the night of 30 January. Those who had been bombed out came to me the next morning for a bit of comfort. But I'm afraid I'm bad at comforting; I can listen all right, but I can hardly ever find anything to say. But perhaps the way one asks about some things and not about others helps to suggest what really matters; and it seems to me more important actually to share someone's distress than to use smooth words about it. I've no sympathy with some wrong-headed attempts to explain away distress, because instead of being a comfort, they are the exact opposite. So I don't try to explain it, and I think that is the right way to begin, although it's only a beginning, and I very seldom get beyond it. I sometimes think that real comfort must break in just as unexpectedly as the distress. But I admit that that may be a subterfuge.

Something that repeatedly puzzles me as well as other people is how quickly we forget about our impressions of a night's bombing. Even a few minutes after the all clear, almost everything that we had just been thinking about seems to vanish into thin air. With Luther a flash of lightning was enough to change the course of his life for years to come. Where is this 'memory' today? Is not the loss of this 'moral memory' (a horrid expression) responsible for the ruin of all obligations, of love, marriage, friendship, and loyalty? Nothing sticks fast, nothing holds firm; everything is here today and gone tomorrow. But the good things of life – truth, justice, and beauty – all great accomplishments need time, constancy, and 'memory', or they degenerate. The man who feels neither responsibility towards the past nor desire to shape the future is one who 'forgets', and I don't know how one can really get at such a person and bring him to his senses. Every word, even if it impresses him for the moment, goes in at one ear and out at the other. What is to be done about him? It is a great problem of Christian ministry. You put it very well recently when you said that people feel so quickly and so 'shamelessly at home'; I'm going to crib that expression from you, and make good use of it . . .

By the way, do you notice that uneducated people find it very difficult to decide things *objectively*, and that they allow some more or less fortuitous minor circumstance to turn the scales? It seems to me quite remarkable. I suppose one first has to take pains to *learn* to distinguish between thinking personally and thinking objectively; and, in fact, many people never learn to do so (see our professional colleagues, etc.).

2 February

Is it true that you are *north* of Rome? And at present assigned to the kitchen? I hope you will have a chance to see the city again; it must be tantalizing to be stationed outside the gates, and not be allowed to go in. It's not much consolation that you've already seen it once . . . As a lot of post has been lost in the past few nights, perhaps you didn't get my letter of 29 January? That would be a pity. I hope that in the meantime you will have had the one written jointly to you and Renate (about a week ago). How much longer I shall have to go on amusing myself in my present place of residence is still just as uncertain as it was eight weeks ago. I'm using every day to do as much reading and work as possible, for what will happen afterwards is anybody's guess. Unfortunately the one thing I can't do is to get hold of the right books, and that upsets all my plans. I really wanted to become thoroughly familiar with the nineteenth century in Germany. I'm now feeling particularly the need of a good working knowledge of Dilthey, but his books are evidently not available. It's a matter of great regret to me that I'm so ignorant of the natural sciences, but it's a gap that cannot be filled now.

My present companion, whom I have mentioned several times in my letters, gets more and more pitiable. He has two colleagues here, one of whom spends the whole day moaning, and the other literally messes his trousers whenever the alert goes, and last night even when the first warning was sounded! When he told me about it yesterday – still moaning – I laughed outright and told him off, whereupon he would have me know that one mustn't laugh at anyone in distress or condemn him. I felt that that was really going too far, and I told him in no uncertain terms what I thought of people who can be very hard on others and talk big about a dangerous life and so on, and then collapse under the slightest test of endurance. I told him that it was a downright disgrace, that I had no sympathy at all with anyone like that, that I would throw any such specimens out of the party for making it look ridiculous, and so on. He was very surprised, and I dare say he thinks me a very doubtful Christian. Anyhow, these gentlemen's behaviour is already becoming a byword here, and the result can't be exactly pleasant for them. I find all this uncommonly instructive, though it's one of the most nauseating things that I've seen here so far. I don't really think I find it easy to despise anyone in trouble, and I said so quite unmistakably, which may have made his hair stand on end; but I can only regard that as contemptible. There are 17 and 18-year-olds here in much more dangerous places during the raids who behave splendidly, while these . . . (I almost used an army term that would have surprised you) go round whimpering. It really makes one sick. Well, everyone makes a fool of himself as best he can.

I hope you won't think I've joined the ranks of the toughs; there is little enough occasion for that here, in any case. But there is a kind of weakness that Christianity does not hold with, but which people insist on claiming as Christian, and then sling mud at it. So we must take care that the contours do not get blurred.

Yesterday Susi brought me the big volume on Magdeburg Cathedral. I'm quite thrilled by the sculptures, especially some of the wise virgins. The bliss on these very earthly, almost peasant-like faces is really delightful and moving. Of course, you will know them well.

Good-bye for today, Eberhard. I'm always thinking of you faithfully.   Your Dietrich

From Karl-Friedrich Bonhoeffer   [Leipzig] 4 February 1944

Dear Dietrich,
Who would have thought that you would still be sitting in prison on your birthday! Your patience is really being put to a hard test.

I hope that at least you will be getting a visit from the parents or some of the family today? I don't imagine that Maria is in Berlin. She called me from Altenburg last Saturday, here in Leipzig. Unfortunately I'd just gone away to see Grete and the children in Friedrichsbrunn. It would have been very nice there had one not been dominated by worry for all of you in Berlin. With every attack on Berlin swarms of planes fly over the Harz so that the whole sky roars with this wild hunt. One then feels uncomfortable about every hour in which one has forgotten the suffering of all those many thousands, and has the feeling that one ought to go off straightaway to try to help. But the hard thing about the present time is that there is hardly anything one can do to help. For the few hours of freedom from work are enough, of course, to think of other people, but not to give them any real help.

I went from Friedrichsbrunn to Göttingen. I hadn't been there for ten years. People from there have been inviting me over for several years, and now at last the mobility of the bombed-out grass widower has meant that it came off at last. I gave a lecture in the Faculty of Physics on the mechanism of rhythmic reactions, and managed to interest the biologists, as I had hoped. I stayed in the Herzberger Landstrasse, diagonally opposite Sabine's old house.[142] I thought of her a good deal while I was there; ten years ago I stayed with her. She too will be with us and especially with you in all her thoughts and worries. From the scientific side, I enjoyed myself more there than I've done for a long time. It wasn't just the friendliness with which people received me everywhere. I saw a whole series of people again whose whole life is pure science, and I got to know some new ones. It really seemed as though I was 'transported into a better world'.

I'm fighting here for a labour force to put on an emergency roof to save the rest of the Institute. I run from office to office to get water and light for home, write my fingers sore to replace the burnt library books and chemical equipment and negotiate with Osram over accepting an advisory capacity. All the work that I'm really interested in gets left on one side.

Tomorrow I expect a call from Maria. Last Saturday she said that she would ring, and I'm eager to see whether she has any news. If nothing gets in the way I want to go to Berlin early the day after tomorrow.

All the best. Here's to a speedy release!

Your Karl-Friedrich

To Eberhard Bethge   [Tegel] 4 February [1944]

Dear Eberhard,

Today on my birthday morning, nothing is more natural for me than to write to you, remembering that for eight years in succession we celebrated the day together. Work is being laid aside for a few hours – it may take no harm from that – and I'm expecting a visit from Maria or my parents, although it's not yet quite certain whether it will come off. Eight years ago we were sitting at the fireside together.[143] You had given me as a present the D major violin concerto, and we listened to it together; then I had to tell you a little about Harnack and past times; for some reason or other you enjoyed that very much, and afterwards we decided definitely to go to Sweden. A year later you gave me the September Bible[144] with a lovely inscription and your name at the top. There followed Schlönwitz and Sigurdshof, and we had the company of a good many people who are no longer among us. The singing at the door, the prayer at the service that you undertook that day, the Claudius hymn,[145] for which I'm indebted to Gerhard – all those things are delightful recollections that are proof against the horrible atmosphere of this place. I hope confidently that we shall be together again for your next birthday, and perhaps – who knows? – even for Easter. Then we shall get back to what is really our life's work; we shall have ample work that we shall enjoy, and what we have experienced in the meantime will not have been in vain. We shall probably always be grateful to each other for having been able to go through this present time as we're now doing. I know you're thinking of me today, and if your thoughts include not only the past, but also the hope of a future lived with a common purpose, even though in changed circumstances, then indeed I'm very happy.

Now it won't be long before you have good news from Renate. It can't be easy to have to celebrate such a uniquely happy day among strangers who cannot help one to enjoy the occasion to the full and make it part of one's ordinary life, and to whom the climax of any happy occasion is probably *Schnapps*. I wish very much that you could meet someone who has more in common with you (as I told you, the only one here who seemed promising in that direction was killed in a raid), but I think that we, who have become more exacting than most people with regard to friendship, have more difficulty in finding what we miss and are looking for. In this respect, too, it isn't a simple matter to find a 'substitute'.

– When I was in the middle of this letter, I was called downstairs, where the first thing with which Maria greeted me was the happy news: 'Renate has a little boy, and his name is Dietrich!' Everything went well; it took an hour and a half, and mother acted as midwife, with Christel's help! What a surprise, and what a delight! I'm happier than I can tell you. And how happy you, of all people, will be. And everything went so quickly and smoothly! So now you have a son, and all your thoughts will turn towards the future, full of hope. What possibilities there may be in him! . . . Rüdiger's disposition and sensitive conscience, father's humanity – really a great many good forces have gathered together there, and it won't be long before they gradually develop. And so now he is really to be called Dietrich; I don't know what to say to that; I hope I can promise you to be a good godfather and 'great-'uncle(!), and I should be insincere if I didn't say that I'm immensely pleased and proud that you've named your first-born after me. The fact that his birthday comes one day before mine means, no doubt, that he will keep his independence *vis-a-vis* his namesake-uncle, and will always be a little ahead of him. I'm particularly pleased that the two days are so close to each other, and when he hears later on where his uncle was when he was told his name, perhaps that may leave some impression on him too. Thank you both very much for deciding to do this, and I think the others will be pleased about it too.

208

Yesterday, when so many people were showing such kindly concern for me, I completely forgot my own birthday, as my delight over little Dietrich's birthday put it right out of my head. Even the heartening little nosegay of flowers that some of my fellow inmates here picked for me remained in my thoughts by your little boy's bed. The day couldn't possibly have brought me any greater joy. It wasn't till I was going to sleep that I realized that you've pushed our family on by one generation – 3 February has created great-grandparents, grandparents, great-uncles and great-aunts, and young uncles and aunts! That's a fine achievement of yours; you've promoted me to the third generation! . . .

Renate sent me for my birthday yesterday some more lovely home-made 'S'les. Maria brought a wonderful parcel, and my parents gave me the 'Herzliebschränkchen'[146] that Goethe once gave to Minna Herzlieb. Klaus gave me Dilthey's *German Poetry and Music*; I'll tell you about it later. Are you asking mother and Christel to be godparents? I'm afraid I must stop, as I want to send the letter off. My head and my heart are so overflowing with good and happy thoughts that I simply can't put them all on paper. But you know how I think about you and try to share your joy with you and keep in close touch with you . . . Now I hope I shall soon follow your example. Good-bye, keep well; God keep and bless you both, and the little boy.   Faithfully, your Dietrich

I'm writing to Renate as well, straightaway. You can then exchange letters.

Klaus also sent me a copy of a Moravian hymn book dating from 1778; or has there perhaps been a mistake and does it come from you? It looks your sort of present; but Klaus is also very good at giving presents. I didn't really expect anything other and better than good thoughts and wishes, and for those I thank you, even if it can only be a brief thought in the turmoil of service. I hope I shall hear from you soon . . . I'm writing to you as often as possible. Of course, there may be pauses, but I hope not. All is well with me.

Dear Renate,

How can I tell you how pleased I am for you and Eberhard? . . .
I shall never forget the moment yesterday when Maria told me
first of all that you had got a boy and that he is to be called
Dietrich. After that I could really celebrate a birthday, not mine,
but little Dietrich's . . . I think that it's particularly nice that you
don't have to be in a hospital somewhere, but can be in Sakrow. If
only the planes will spare us over the next few days; I do believe
they will. One sees once again how so much that worries us beforehand can afterwards, quite unexpectedly, have a happy and simple
solution. Worries just don't matter. Tell yourself that every day
as you think of Eberhard. Things really are in a better hand than
ours.

I'm very pleased that you've called your boy Dietrich. Not
many people in my position will have a similar experience. In the
midst of all our hardships we keep experiencing an overwhelming
kindness and friendship. Hasn't that always kept happening to
Eberhard? The texts for 3 February, which you will also be reading, are fine.[147] If one day your son *sees* more of righteousness and
the power of God on earth than we do, one will be able to call him
happy. And if the text enjoins us to bow for a while in *blind* trust
under the powerful hand of God, we should do that in the hope
that the coming generation will be able to feel God's gracious
hand as well as his power.

I must stop so that the letter can get off. God bless you, Eberhard and your child.

With love,   your Dietrich

I've told Eberhard that you would also send him this letter.

Dear Eberhard,

I've been in bed for a few days with slight influenza, but I'm up again; that's a good thing, because in about a week's time I shall need to have all my wits about me.[148] Till then I shall go on reading and writing as much as I can; who knows when I shall have another chance? I had a great surprise early this morning. As I skimmed through the newspaper the name Dietrich caught my eye, and – I still didn't make the connection – right next to the name Bethge. However, it wasn't long before I took it in. Let people say what they like – there is something about the printed word; you will have felt the same thing; the objective factuality of it is once again underlined, and now the world can share in the happy event. My parents were here yesterday and told me once again about 3 February and how well everything went; even father said that the little boy looked particularly nice. What a good thing that no severe attacks took place in the first ten days; I hope that we shall be spared them for some time to come . . .

Are you having a taste of spring yet? Here the winter is just beginning. In my imagination I live a good deal in nature, in the glades near Friedrichsbrunn, or on the slopes from which one can look beyond Treseburg to the Brocken. I lie on my back in the grass, watch the clouds sailing in the breeze across the blue sky, and listen to the rustling of the woods. It's remarkable how greatly these memories of childhood affect one's whole outlook; it would seem to me impossible and unnatural for us to have lived either up in the mountains or by the sea. It is the hills of central Germany, the Harz, the Thuringian forest, the Weserberge, that to me represent nature, that belong to me and have fashioned me. Of course, there are also a conventional Harz and a hikers' Wesergebirge, just as there are a fashionable and a Nietzschian Engadine, a romantic Rhineland, a Berliners' Baltic, and the idealized poverty and melancholy of a fisherman's cottage. So perhaps 'my' central hills are 'bourgeois' in the sense of what is natural, not too high, modest and self-sufficient(?), unphilosophical, satisfied with concrete realities, and above all 'not-given-to-self-advertisement'. It would be very tempting to pursue this sociological treatment of nature some day. By the way, in reading Stifter I can see the difference between simpleness and simplicity. Stifter displays, not simpleness, but (as the 'bourgeois' does) simplicity. 'Simpleness' is, even in theology, more of an aesthetic idea (was Winckelmann right when he spoke of the 'noble simpleness' of classical art? That certainly does not apply to the Laocoon; I think 'still greatness' is very good), whereas 'simplicity' is an ethical one. One can acquire 'simplicity', but 'simpleness' is innate. Education and culture may bring 'simplicity' – indeed, it ought to be one of their essential aims – but simpleness is a gift. The two things seem to me to be related in much the same way as 'purity' and 'moderation'. One can be 'pure' only in relation to one's origin or goal, i.e. in relation to baptism or to forgiveness at the Lord's Supper; like 'simpleness' it involves the idea of totality. If we have lost our purity – and we have all lost it – it can be given back to us in faith; but in ourselves, as living and developing persons, we can no longer be 'pure', but only 'moderate', and that is a possible and a necessary aim of education and culture.

How does the Italian landscape impress you? Is there any Italian school of landscape painters, anything comparable to Thoma, or even to Claude Lorrain, Ruysdael, or Turner? Or is nature there so completely absorbed into art that it cannot be looked at for its own sake? All the good pictures that I can think of just now are of city life; I can't remember any that are purely of landscape.

13 February

I often notice here, both in myself and in others, the difference between the need to be communicative, the wish for conversation, and the desire for confession. The need to be communicative may perhaps on occasion be quite attractive in women, but I find it most repugnant in men. There is quite indiscriminate gossip, in front of all comers, about one's own affairs, no matter whether they interest or concern other people or not – simply, in fact, because one just has to gossip. It's an almost physical urge, but if you manage to suppress it for a few hours, you're glad afterwards that you didn't let yourself go. It sometimes makes me ashamed here to see how people lower themselves in their need to gossip, how they talk incessantly about their own affairs to others who are hardly worth wasting their breath on and who hardly even listen; and the strange thing is that these people do not even feel that they have to speak the truth, but simply want to talk about themselves, whether they tell the truth or not. The wish for a good conversation, a meeting of minds, is quite another matter; but there are very few people here who can carry on a conversation that goes beyond their own personal concerns. Again, the desire for confession is something quite different. I think it's infrequent here, because people are not primarily concerned here, either subjectively or objectively, about 'sin'. You may perhaps have noticed that in the prayers that I sent you the request for forgiveness of sins doesn't occupy the central place; I should consider it a complete mistake, both from a pastoral and from a practical point of view, to proceed on 'methodist' lines here. We must talk about that some day.

14 February

If it's any help to Renate now, please take some of my money and don't worry about it! It looks as if something will be decided about me in a week's time. I hope it will. If it turns out that they send me in Martin's[149] direction (though I don't think that is likely), please make your mind easy about it. I'm really not at all worried about what happens to me personally. So please don't you worry either. Good-bye, this letter must go; in thoughts, style and writing it is still considerably impaired by a head dosed with aspirin, etc. But I needn't offer excuses to you for that sort of thing. You saw me in a much weaker condition during my illness in autumn 41. So, all good wishes and loyal greetings

from your Dietrich

I'm already racking my brains about a godfather's present. Would Renate like the fur sleeping bag? She could then creep into it with the little one. At Maria's there are a great many furs, so we don't need it. Have you made any contacts with the divisional pastor?

What are the chances of being used by him or anywhere as a military chaplain? Will you try? It could be supported by Dohrmann[150] here. Write about it some time! . . .

From Eberhard Bethge   [Rignano] 15 February 1944

Dear Dietrich,

. . . I've just been seeing the eternal city again. I used what time I had, not for the Forum or the Pantheon but for St Peter's. I managed to get in with a guided party. Otherwise there were barriers up. This time Michelangelo's Pietà made a great impression on me. Probably because one already knew that it stands in a niche and is really quite small. It's certainly the work of a very young Michelangelo. I now feel that I would like to see the church again and again. Occasionally, when it's very clear, one can see the cupola towering above everything from the hill where we get supplies, etc.[151] The tour ended with an audience with the Pope, and so I saw him too. There were about forty officers and four hundred men. He spoke a few words with each of them. He looked older than I expected from the pictures. How easy it is for the Catholics now, as they can largely dispense with words and preach with their dress and their gestures! One notices how sensitive people are about false statements and how they react against them. I wasn't able to make any more visits[152] . . . we're moving our base southwards[153] to the neighbourhood of the Papal summer residence . . . This letter must go and I must be on guard. For the first time today. The traffic is now too heavy here. While I'm on watch I talk to Renate and to you.   Your Eberhard

Dear parents,

Forgive me for not having written regularly lately. I had hoped to be able to give you some definite news about my case, so I put off writing from day to day. I was first assured quite definitely that the matter would be settled by July 1943; and then, as you will remember, it was to be September at the very latest. But now it's dragging on from month to month with nothing whatever happening. I'm quite sure that if they only got down to business, the whole thing would be cleared up quite simply; and really, when one thinks of all the tasks waiting to be done outside, one is apt to feel, however hard one tries to be patient and understanding, that it is better to write no letters, but to say nothing for a time, first because disordered thoughts and feelings would only give rise to wrong words, and secondly because whatever one writes is likely to be quite out of date by the time it reaches its destination. Again and again it's something of an inward struggle to keep soberly to the facts, to banish illusions and fancies from my head, and to content myself with things as they are; for when one does not understand the external factors, one supposes that there must be some unseen internal factor at work. Besides, our generation cannot now lay claim to such a life as was possible in yours – a life that can find its full scope in professional and personal activities, and achieve balance and fulfilment. That's perhaps the greatest sacrifice that we younger people, with the example of your life still before our eyes, are called on and compelled to make, and it makes us particularly aware of the fragmentary and incomplete nature of our own. But this very fragmentariness may, in fact, point towards a fulfilment beyond the limits of human achievement; I have to keep that in mind, particularly in view of the death of so many of the best of my former pupils. Even if the pressure of outward events may split our lives into fragments, like bombs falling on houses, we must do our best to keep in view how the whole was planned and thought out; and we shall still be able to see what material was used, or was to be used, here for building.

Maria was here today on the way to her new work. It was very fine. But really everything is very hard for her. Now that Karl-Friedrich's Leipzig Institute is completely done for, will he accept the call to Berlin? I would very much like to see him here again. It's getting very depressing that things are not going better with Hans.[154] It must be grim for him not to feel in full possession of his intellectual powers. I really am very sorry. Do things seem to be well with Renate? What news does she have of her husband? Perhaps she will write to me about him some time, if she's up again . . . I got a very nice birthday letter from Ursel, for which I'm most grateful. Do go to Pätzig some time. It really would be good, and Maria's mother is so looking forward to it.

Love to all and much love to you.   Your grateful Dietrich

To Eberhard Bethge   [Tegel] 21 February 1944

Dear Eberhard,
It was an indescribable joy to hear from you! And also from Maria today, that you wrote to her on my birthday. That really was a good token of friendship. Many thanks for both. Recently I've had to think, in connection with Job ch. 1, that Satan had received permission from the Lord to separate me from my friends at this time – and that he was not going to succeed!

I heard very briefly today about the audience in the Vatican and am now immeasurably curious to hear more of it. I'm very glad that you've had this impression, though I don't expect that it corresponds completely to the old ceremonial which I experienced in 1924. Nevertheless, in contrast to the rest of your experience at present, it will have been particularly stimulating and important. I assume that some pig-headed Lutherans will put it down as a blot in your biography, and for that very reason I'm glad that you've done it . . . Otherwise there are only fragments, that I must put together into a mosaic.

About myself, I'm sorry to have to tell you that I'm not likely to be out of here before Easter. As long as Hans is ill, no changes can be taken in hand. I can't completely rid myself of the feeling that something has been too contrived and imagined and that the simplest things haven't happened yet. I'm fully convinced of the best will of all concerned, but one all too easily takes a conversation, a fancy, a hope for an action. I keep noting with amazement that in fact nothing has happened for six months, although a great deal of time and even sleep has been spent in considerations and discussions; the only thing that would have happened of itself, namely the clarification before Christmas, has been prevented. I wonder whether my excessive scrupulousness, about which you often used to shake your head in amusement (I'm thinking of our travels), is not a negative side of bourgeois existence – simply part of our lack of faith, a part that remains hidden in times of security, but comes out in times of insecurity in the form of 'dread' (I don't mean 'cowardice', which is something different: 'dread' can show itself in recklessness as well as in cowardice), dread of straightforward, simple actions, dread of having to make necessary decisions. I've often wondered here where we are to draw the line between necessary resistance to 'fate', and equally necessary submission. Don Quixote is the symbol of resistance carried to the point of absurdity, even lunacy; and similarly Michael Kohlhaas, insisting on his rights, puts himself in the wrong . . . in both cases resistance at last defeats its own object, and evaporates in theoretical fantasy. Sancho Panza is the type of complacent and artful accommodation to things as they are. I think we must rise to the great demands that are made on us personally, and yet at the same time fulfil the commonplace and necessary tasks of daily life. We must confront fate – to me the neuter gender of the word 'fate' (*Schicksal*) is significant – as resolutely as we submit to it at the right time. One can speak of 'guidance' only on the other side of that twofold process, with God meeting us no longer as 'Thou', but also 'disguised' in the 'It'; so in the last resort my question is how we are to find the 'Thou' in this 'It' (i.e. fate), or, in other words, how does 'fate' really become 'guidance'? It's therefore impossible to define the boundary between resistance and submission on abstract principles; but both of them must exist, and both must be practised. Faith demands this elasticity of behaviour. Only so can we stand our ground in each situation as it arises, and turn it to gain.

Would differences between theological and juristic existence emerge here? I'm thinking, for instance, of the extreme contrast between Klaus and Rüdiger *within* a 'legalistic', juristic approach . . . on the other hand our more flexible, livelier 'theological' approach, which has this character because in the end it is more in accord with reality.

23 February

If you have the chance of going to Rome during Holy Week, I advise you to attend the afternoon service at St Peter's on Maundy Thursday (from about 2 to 6). That is really the Good Friday service, as the Roman Catholic Church anticipates its feasts from noon on the previous day. As far as I remember (though I'm not quite certain), there is also a big service on the Wednesday. On Maundy Thursday the twelve candles on the altar are put out as a symbol of the disciples' flight, till in the vast space there is only one candle left burning in the middle – for Christ. After that comes the cleansing of the altar. At about 7 a.m. on the Saturday there is the blessing of the font (as far as I can remember, that is connected with the ordination of young priests). Then at 12 noon the Easter Alleluia is sung, the organ plays again, the bells peal, and the pictures are unveiled. This is the real celebration of Easter. Somewhere in Rome I also saw a Greek Orthodox service, which at the time – more than twenty years ago! – impressed me very much. The service on Easter Eve in the Lateran (it starts in the Baptistery) is also very famous. If you happen to be on Monte Pincio towards sunset and are near the Church of Trinità del Monte, do see whether the nuns are singing just then; I heard them once, and was very impressed; I believe it's even mentioned in Baedeker.

I wonder how far you are directly involved in the fighting where you are. I suppose it's mainly a question of air raids, as it is here. The intensification of the war in the air in about the last ten days, and especially the heavy attacks in daylight, make one wonder whether the English are probing our air power as a prelude to invasion and as a means of pinning down our land forces inside Germany.

The longer we are uprooted from our professional activities and our private lives, the more we feel how fragmentary our lives are, compared with those of our parents. The portraits of the great savants in Harnack's *History of the Academy* make me acutely aware of that, and almost sadden me a little. Where is there an intellectual *magnum opus* today? Where are the collecting, assimilating, and sorting of material necessary for producing such a work? Where is there today the combination of fine *abandon* and large-scale planning that goes with such a life? I doubt whether anything of the kind still exists, even among technicians and scientists, the only people who are still free to work in their own way. The end of the eighteenth century saw the end of the 'polymath', and in the nineteenth century intensive education replaced extensive, so that towards the end of it the 'specialist' evolved; and by now everyone is just a technician, even in the arts – in music the standard is high, in painting and poetry extremely moderate. This means that our cultural life remains a torso. The important thing today is that we should be able to discern from the fragment of our life how the whole was arranged and planned, and what material it consists of. For really, there are some fragments that are only worth throwing into the dustbin (even a decent 'hell' is too good for them), and others whose importance lasts for centuries, because their completion can only be a matter for God, and so they are fragments that must be fragments – I'm thinking, e.g., of the *Art of Fugue*. If our life is but the remotest reflection of such a fragment, if we accumulate, at least for a short time, a wealth of themes and weld them into a harmony in which the great counterpoint is maintained from start to finish, so that at last, when it breaks off abruptly, we can sing no more than the chorale, 'I come before thy throne',[155] we will not bemoan the fragmentariness of our life, but rather rejoice in it. I can never get away from Jeremiah 45. Do you still remember that Saturday evening in Finkenwalde when I expounded it? Here, too, is a necessary fragment of life – 'but I will give you your life as a prize of war'.

I've just had a very nice letter from Renate, dated 28 January, still rather anxious about you, as she had no news for a week. Happily that's now been cleared up. Are you now a clerk or a dispatch rider? or both? You've always liked lists – reminiscences of the sixth form! – and I've often enough unjustly mocked you for it. Now you will certainly make an exemplary and unique contribution. I'm very glad you've found someone more congenial than the ordinary run of people, for a companion to talk to and do things with.[156] But I should very much prefer to be in his place. I wonder whether we shall ever manage it, or whether we may perhaps keep Easter here as we used to. You see I'm not giving up hope; don't you give it up, either.

Things are again so-so with me, but as usual after these bouts of influenza, I'm still very tired, and unfortunately that hinders productive work considerably. Nevertheless, I hope that I shall soon have finished the smaller literary thing. How are you keeping up physically? What is the food like? When do you get leave? When are we going to baptize your boy? When shall we be able to talk together again, for hours at a time? Good-bye, Eberhard. Keep well! What are the Italians doing? Do you ever get any music? God bless you. I think of you every day.

Your faithful Dietrich

25.2 Can't you try some small work in the history of art down there? What do you think about my question about Laocoon as the 'man of grief'? The parents have just been here. All is in order at home.

From Eberhard Bethge   [Rignano] 22 February 1944

Dear Dietrich,
I want to use the chance of a messenger to say thanks to you once again for your letters . . . It was very reassuring to me to hear so quickly that you've been kept safe in the alarms of these days. When I see and hear the gunfire at night on my occasional jour-

neys further south,[157] I'm especially reminded of Sakrow and all of you. It's very much the same, except that it lasts longer here. So far, however, I've only experienced it rarely. Our people who've been there for a while and haven't experienced the attacks at home are quite full of it and tell every detail again and again with exaggerations. Of course I wasn't there for the worst part. Distant artillery fire affects one remarkably little. One knows what the range is, and a few kilometres beyond that the whine of shells doesn't amount to much. Of course it puts one's nerves on edge. I saw the [allied] fleet on the water in the distance; through glasses one could distinguish between large and small units, and occasionally broadsides flashed out and the noise could be heard clearly. I expect there's some colossally savage fighting there. The wider surroundings, all the beautiful and well-known places on the Alban hills and even the Papal seats, look frightful and have been thrown into complete chaos by our fighting units. Any wandering cattle are shot and 'devoured' without further ado. In some houses they have a mad rampage of destruction which ends with people indecently immortalizing themselves in the middle of the room. First of all we had to clean the house for our people there carefully from these and other traces.

I have the shortest service of any of my comrades here . . . But I must say that by and large they all behave decently towards me. A false sensitivity about turns of speech and constantly recurring pornographic expressions is quite out of place. If the talk gets round to spiritual matters, prompted by my calling, the security here and the self-assurance of the old soldiers immediately produces a long and very wordy explanation of people's own standpoint of a justificatory kind. 'Each in his own fashion' plays a large part. After an audience with the Pope, one person recently confessed to me that he was now changing from being a negative to a positive Catholic. The fact that I'm married plays some part with the Catholics; they think that it's a good thing and see celibacy as a central source of ridicule. The whole thing always takes place before a large audience. I have the impression that it's not a good thing to discuss self-justifications or contradict them too much. But there may be some false restraint here. Among them I am what

I am. There's a freethinker among us here; he never attacks me, and speaks only occasionally; he too is a soldier, and as far as I'm concerned he's only a soldier. I contradicted him. Of course, everything that I say is completely in accord with the attitude that I should maintain among people who in many things have unshaken convictions.[158] I'm advisedly cautious, and keep off things that are important to us.

I'm deeply distressed when I go past places which we saw together. For instance, the day before yesterday I was near the place where we went out together one evening with the car rattling;[159] in the end it only kept going with difficulty and we turned round. The war – and now I see the destruction and the inexorable way in which everything is drawn into it – seeks out all the most beautiful places. There is no more respect, none at all. Women and children walk along the streets hungry and beg for bread. And to think that I'm involved in all this! Most people are quite inured to it. What a task, to bring up *people* again!

I'm eager to see your work, the meeting of the two friends. I was very pleased to read the good service that *Witiko* has done you . . .

One's capacity for forgetting dangers that one has just experienced is quite remarkable. I wonder whether it is primarily a physical reaction? The danger is not completely forgotten. And unfortunately one takes the experience along as a burden into the next danger. One can feel in one's body this shaking off, this liberation, as one goes out of the war-zone.[160] I've now done it twice. Right up to the eternal city what one sees and hears is a burden. With the first houses life seems to begin, in a confused sort of way, and behind the city one almost seems to be 'at home'. After the experience of danger one tends to be more talkative than usual; if it has been really bad one does this and that zealously when one gets out of the shelter. My comrades tell how after the worst night they fooled around and jumped on the see-saw in their garden like children . . .

I must stop for today. I think of you a great deal with many wishes and prayers. Warmest greetings

from your Eberhard

Dear Eberhard,

I've nothing special to write to you today, but I don't want you to feel lonely, nor to believe for a moment that you are in any way forgotten, that one has in any way become resigned to your absence in a distant country. I want to let you know that as far as possible I'm living in a daily spiritual exchange with you; I can't read a book or write a paragraph without talking to you about it or at least asking myself what you would say about it. In short, all this automatically takes the form of this letter, even if there is really nothing 'to report'. I.e. there is, of course, enough to report, but one doesn't know where to begin and so one puts it off to the great moment of reunion. What a day it will be when you see your son for the first time (according to Maria's mother, who visited me recently, he is also said to be a bit like me, – the general view is that he looks like *you*, and that he has a particularly nice and open face), when you see Renate again – and finally, I also imagine to myself that you also look forward to being with me again and to discussing all that we've been through and learnt during a whole year. For myself at any rate, that is one of the greatest hopes for the near future. I suppose you, too, can sometimes hardly imagine that such a day will ever come. It's difficult to believe that there is any chance of our overcoming all the obstacles in our way, but 'that which tarries is all the sweeter when it comes . . .', and I must say I am entering on this new month with great hopes, and I think you are doing the same. I'm redoubling my efforts to make the best use of the last part of my time here. Perhaps your experiences, too, will be of great value to you all your life. The constant danger to which nearly all of us are at present exposed in one way or another provides a wonderful incentive to use the present moment, 'making the most of the time'. I sometimes feel that I'm living, just as long as I have something great to work for. Do you know this feeling, too? or is it rather mad? . . .

The less reflective part of your nature makes you a member of the younger generation rather than of my own, and to this extent

I can even feel as though I'm an 'uncle' towards you. What has impressed you among us older ones is, I suppose, above all the security which has come through reflection and has hardened in this way, a reflection which has not led to intellectualism and thus to disintegration and relativism, but has entered into one's whole attitude to life and not weakened, but strengthened, the impulses of life. Nevertheless, I regard 'you younger ones' as being more competent than we are. People say in America that the negroes survived because they had not forgotten how to laugh, whereas the Indians went under because they were too 'proud'. What I mean lies somewhere in this direction.

But that's all for today. This is just meant to be a brief token of the daily remembrance of your loyal   Dietrich

From Eberhard Bethge   In the south, 2 March 1944

Dear Dietrich,

I got your letter of 12 February on Sunday with great delight. Many thanks for it. Any letter from you is an event and prompts a host of questions . . . I've also just heard that by now a decision must already have been made. How long will it be before I hear anything of it? . . .

I think of you a great deal these days. It began early on Sunday when during the epistle, II Cor. 6.1–10, I saw you standing in the pulpit at Schlönwitz and remembered that splendid long sermon. That was an event for the brethren. I played the organ. I find your thoughts about the landscape very stimulating. With very few exceptions, I don't see Italian towns at all, but only the country, albeit still rather wintry. Over the Tiber valley on the hills. Here and there a village on the top of a hill, boxed up like Radicofani, which we both saw together that time in 1936 on the Via Cassia. But it *is* true; in conversation with my jurists here we confirmed that there's really no typical *Italian* landscape painting; it's always only filling or background. What interested the Italians was people and architecture, building cities. I wonder whether that is why

Italy produced Machiavelli and why the state played a decisive role alongside art at an early stage? Is it the case that in the south the landscape is an obvious abundance and there is nothing to discover there – or that nature is the enemy in the scorching heat? Is there Greek or Spanish landscape painting? I don't think so. The people who discovered the landscape here alongside antiquities, churches and cities, and painted it, were the Germans, Romantics, the generation round Kalckreuth, 1820–40. The beautiful lakes of Alba and Nemi, Rocca di papa – I've seen them all, but how ravaged! How much they've drawn here – gnarled oaks, river-valleys! I had many recollections of Klaus' beautiful portfolios of Kalckreuth and his friends, which he showed us at his house after the betrothal. Then his beautiful 'Oak Wood' in the entrance hall . . .

I've become aware of the . . . poverty of the Havel neighbourhood and its sands. Yet I would rather be there than here. The rain comes teeming down here in buckets and shortly afterwards the most splendid sun is shining, so that in a few hours the daisies spring up, large and fat, and the yellow and blue flowers along the road open. There isn't a long struggle, but it all comes with great abundance and power. And the way the soldiers go through the world, among these people and in this landscape. All they want is for the German police to be here, so that they could see order and work . . .

Some people's delight in commerce is sickening. You can find it in a person right next to sympathetic qualities: a man with whom you can talk, laugh and steal horses . . .

Many, many thanks for your decision to assign your good things to Renate. That's very nice of you. I'm rather worried that in fact you seem to be having some difficulties with your food. But if you have hard days[161] at this time, you will need everything yourself. One has heard of other such proceedings, but not this. Or aren't any people admitted anyway? I think that that will be the case. It will be bad and disturbing for the grandparents now . . .

I simply can't decide whether to ask Renate to have the child baptized now. In the normal course of events I would expect to be home in the summer and would very much like to be present. The fur sleeping bag is quite wonderful. I haven't seen the divisional pastor yet. It isn't very simple, as we're all alone here. Perhaps we shall have to wait a little longer about the military chaplaincy.

Will you be getting to see my son now, or have you to expect worse things? I'm burning for some news.

I'm thinking faithfully of you and send warmest greetings.

Your Eberhard

To his parents   [Tegel] 2 March 1944

Dear parents,

So you made the long journey once again and left a parcel for me down below, and once again I wasn't able to thank you for it myself, but had to rely on the NCO to do it properly. I hope that the permission to visit comes soon! You probably heard from Maria that I told her last time (although we don't often mention the subject) that our meals here had become rather scantier because of reduced rations, and that I was sometimes rather hungry, though that was no doubt partly because I had hardly eaten anything during the few days when I had flu.[162] Now once again you've looked after me nobly, and I must frankly admit that the world does sometimes have a different look if one has some good food inside one, and that the work goes better. All the same, I should hate to think I was depriving you of food when you have so much to do all day and need your strength more urgently than I do. Now March is here again, and still you haven't been away for a holiday. Maria's mother is expecting you eagerly. The only pity is that Maria is no longer at home. By the way, today I received her first letter from Bavaria. She is particularly fond of the cousin whose children she's teaching and in whose house she is helping; she seems to be keeping well. I hope that that is the best solution for her during the last weeks – and I really do hope that they are the last weeks – until we see each other again and can make plans together. Of course it would be best of all if we could all go to Pätzig together and then make our plans for the future together there. But after a trial of patience which has lasted so long, it's probably an almost crazy thought to wait for that.

I also got very nice birthday letters from Karl-Friedrich, Hans-Christoph and little Horn.[163] Hans-Christoph's accounts of life in Bucharest surprised me; it's still peaceful. I'm amazed that any country in Europe can still lead such a special existence today. Things have been better for him with his African and Italian divisions. Please thank them all very much.

I've been very impressed by Harnack's *History of the Prussian Academy*; it has made me feel both happy and unhappy. There are so few people now who want to have any intimate spiritual association with the eighteenth and nineteenth centuries: music tries to draw inspiration from the sixteenth and seventeenth centuries, theology from the time of the Reformation, philosophy from St Thomas Aquinas and Aristotle, and the present *Weltanschauung* from bygone Teutonic days. But who bothers at all now about the work and achievements of our grandfathers, and how much of what they knew have we already forgotten? I believe that people will one day be quite amazed by what was achieved in that period, which is now so disregarded and so little known.

Could you please get hold of Dilthey's *Weltanschauung und Analyse des Menschen seit Renaissance und Reformation* for me? How are Renate, her child and her husband? Please give them all my love.

With much love from your grateful   Dietrich

Congratulations to Hans-Walter on his 20th birthday!

From his father   [Charlottenburg] 3 March 1944

Dear Dietrich,

We got your letter yesterday. It's the same with us as with you. One thinks that by the time the letter gets into your hands we shall perhaps already have spoken and it will be out of date. That makes our writing less regular, too. We're already waiting expectantly for the next visit. Everything is much slower through having to go by Torgau.[164] Provisionally we intend to go to Pätzig on the 13th of this month . . . We're thinking of being at home for the next bright nights.[165] Going to and fro is very strenuous for mother with two lots of housekeeping . . . The Dresses are also spending nights at Sakrow now until their things are ready for moving. Suse then wants to go back to the children again. I expect that Walter will stay out there for the present. Renate, with her mother and child, and Christine, who is inseparable from her mother, are also still there. So with four generations Christel has considerable additions to all the rest, even though we sit at three different tables, as in a hotel, and each family cooks for itself. As the swarm mostly rushes off to Berlin in the morning and only returns in the evening, the day is fairly quiet. I wish that mother could get some relaxation. Going to and fro, the unaccustomed standing in the kitchen, her desire to help in the many places makes her very tired without her wanting to acknowledge it. A great burden will fall from her spirit when in the spring, as we are certain, at least the family, if not the world at large, is freed from its care.

4 March

Just after I asked for the permission to visit to be speeded up, it arrived. So I expect that this letter will be out of date by the time you get it. Meanwhile the letter from Hans-Christoph and the grandmother at Klein Krössin will be in your hands. Mother keeps wanting to write to you, and is sorry that she is so distracted.

Affectionately, your Father

To Eberhard Bethge   [Tegel] 9 March 1944

Dear Eberhard,
I've heard through my parents again today that you're at least finding things tolerable, and although that's not very much (for

we want life to be more than just 'tolerable'), it is some comfort, as long as we look on our present condition as only a kind of *status intermedius*. If only we knew how long this purgatory is going to last! It seems likely now that I shall have to wait till May. Isn't this dawdling shameful? My parents are now going to Pätzig, where I hope they will have a rest. Sepp is home again; he has fought his way through with all his old resilience and defiance.[166]

I haven't yet answered your remarks about Michelangelo, Burckhardt, and *hilaritas*. I found them illuminating – at any rate, what you say about Burckhardt's theses. But surely *hilaritas* means not only serenity, in the classical sense of the word (Raphael and Mozart); Walther v.d. Vogelweide, the Knight of Bamberg, Luther, Lessing, Rubens, Hugo Wolf, Karl Barth – to mention only a few – also have a kind of *hilaritas*, which I might describe as confidence in their own work, boldness and defiance of the world and of popular opinion, a steadfast certainty that in their own work they are showing the world something *good* (even if the world doesn't like it), and a high-spirited self-confidence. I admit that Michelangelo, Rembrandt and, at a considerable remove, Kierkegaard and Nietzsche, are in quite a different category from those that I've mentioned. There is something less assertive, evident, and final in their works, less conviction, detachment, and humour. All the same, I think some of them are characterized by *hilaritas* in the sense that I've described, as a necessary attribute of greatness. Here is Burckhardt's limitation, probably a conscious one.

I've recently been studying the mature 'worldliness' of the thirteenth century, conditioned, not by the Renaissance, but by the Middle Ages, and presumably by the struggle between the *idea of the emperor* and the papacy. (Walther, the Nibelungen, Parsifal – what surprising tolerance of the Mohammedans in the figure of Parsifal's half-brother Feirefiz! – Naumburg and Magdeburgh cathedrals.) This worldliness is not 'emancipated', but 'Christian', even if it is anti-clerical. Where did this 'worldliness', so essentially different from that of the Renaissance, stop? A trace of it seems to survive in Lessing – in contrast to the Western Enlightenment – and in a different way in Goethe, then later in Stifter and Mörike (to say nothing of Claudius and Gotthelf), but nowhere in Schiller and the Idealists. It would be very useful to draw up a good genealogy here; and that raises the question of the value of classical antiquity. Is this still a real problem and a source of power for us, or not? The modern treatment of it under the heading 'city-state man' is already out of date, and the classicists' treatment of it from the aesthetic point of view has only a limited appeal today, and is something of a museum piece. The fundamental concepts of humanism – humanity, tolerance, gentleness, and moderation – are already present in their finest form in Wolfram von Eschenbach and in the Knight of Bamberg, and they are more accessible to us here than in classical antiquity itself. How far, then, does 'education' still depend on classical antiquity? Is the Ranke-to-Delbrück interpretation of history as a *continuum* consisting of 'classical antiquity', 'the middle ages', and 'modern times' really valid, or isn't Spengler also right with his theory of cultural phases as self-contained cycles, even though he gives too biological a twist to historical events? The idea of the historical *continuum* goes back to Hegel, who sees the whole course of history as culminating in 'modern times' – i.e. in his own system of philosophy. That idea is therefore *idealistic* (in spite of Ranke's assertion that every moment of history is 'immediate to God'; that assertion *might* have supplied a corrective of the whole conception of the *continuum* of development, but it didn't do so). Spengler's 'morphology' is *biological*, and that gives it its limitations (what does he mean by the 'senescence' and 'decline' of a culture?). For the concept of education, this means that we can neither idealistically accept classical antiquity as *the* foundation, nor simply eliminate it, biologically and morphologically, from our pattern of education. Until we can see further into it, it will be as well to base our attitude to the past, and to classical antiquity in particular, not on a general concept of history, but solely on *facts* and *achievements*. Perhaps you will bring back from Italy something important in this direction. Personally, I'm afraid, I've always felt cool towards the Renaissance and classicism; they seem to me somehow alien, and I cannot make them my own. I wonder whether a knowledge of other countries and an intimate contact with them are not more important for education today than a knowledge of the classics. In either case, of course, there is the possibility of philistinism; but perhaps one of our tasks is to see that our contacts with other peoples and countries reach out beyond politics or commerce or snobbishness to something really educational. In that way we should be tapping a hitherto unused source for the fertilizing of our education, and at the same time carrying on an old European tradition.

The wireless is just announcing the approach of strong contingents of aircraft. We could see a good deal of the last two daylight raids on Berlin;[167] there were fairly large formations flying through a cloudless sky and leaving vapour trails behind them, and at times there was plenty of flak. The alert was on for two and a half hours yesterday, longer than at night. Today the sky is overcast. I'm very glad that Renate is in Sakrow; also thinking of you. The siren is just going, so I must break off and write more later.

It lasted two hours. 'Bombs were dropped in all parts of the city,' says the wireless. In my time here I've been trying to observe how far people believe in anything 'supernatural'. Three ideas seem to be widespread, each being partly expressed in some superstitious practice: (1) Time after time one hears 'Keep your fingers crossed', some sort of power being associated with the accompanying thought: people do not want to feel alone in times of danger, but to be sure of some invisible presence. (2) 'Touch wood' is the exclamation every evening, when the question is discussed 'whether they will come tonight or not'; this seems to be a recollection of the wrath of God on the *hubris* of man, a metaphysical, and not merely a moral reason for humility. (3) 'If it's got your number on, you'll get it', and therefore everyone may as well stay where he is. On a Christian interpretation these three points might be regarded as a recollection of intercession and community, of God's wrath and grace, and of divine guidance. To the last-mentioned we might add another remark that is very often heard here: 'Who knows what good may come of it?' There doesn't seem to me to be any trace of a recollection of eschatology. I wonder whether you've noticed anything different. Do write and tell me your thoughts on all this.

This is my second Passiontide here. When people suggest in

their letters . . . that I'm 'suffering' here, I reject the thought. It seems to me a profanation. These things mustn't be dramatized. I doubt very much whether I'm 'suffering' any more than you, or most people, are suffering today. Of course, a great deal here is horrible, but where isn't it? Perhaps we've made too much of this question of suffering, and been too solemn about it. I've sometimes been surprised that the Roman Catholics take so little notice of that kind of thing. Is it because they're stronger than we are? Perhaps they know better from their own history what suffering and martyrdom really are, and are silent about petty inconveniences and obstacles. I believe, for instance, that physical sufferings, actual pain and so on, are certainly to be classed as 'suffering'. We so like to stress spiritual suffering; and yet that is just what Christ is supposed to have taken from us, and I can find nothing about it in the New Testament, or in the acts of the early martyrs. After all, whether 'the church suffers' is not at all the same as whether one of its servants has to put up with this or that. I think we need a good deal of correction on this point; indeed, I must admit candidly that I sometimes feel almost ashamed of how often we've talked about our own sufferings. No, suffering must be something quite different, and have a quite different dimension, from what I've so far experienced.

Now that's enough for today. When shall we be able to talk together again? Keep well, enjoy the beautiful country, spread *hilaritas* around you, and keep it yourself too!

I think of you faithfully each day. With all my heart,

your Dietrich

Do you see any possibility of my coming to your neighbourhood? I hope that you, too, are continuing to be very sensible.[168] Now we have people of all ages from Klausen (the little one) to father. Do you really get enough to eat? Can one send you anything? Maria would love to. I've been waiting three weeks for W.'s[169] visit; he said he was coming and then stayed away without letting me know. Quite inconsiderate, but one is gradually getting used to that, too. I really can't understand it. By contrast, the unwearying loyalty of my parents is a great act of kindness . . . There are situations in which the simplest action is more than the greatest outlines and plans and discussions. I also tell myself that from my present experiences. The real examples I call to mind are your visit that time to Gerhard and your visit (and several attempts) here, and the weekly journey of my parents and Maria's journeys. I really don't want to be unjust to anyone. Each one acts as he has been given. But Matt. 25.36[170] remains the most important thing.

Good-bye. The letter is going off now!

To Eberhard Bethge   [Tegel] Laetare [19 March 1944]

Dear Eberhard,
With the news of the heavy fighting in your neighbourhood, you're hardly ever out of my thoughts; every word that I read in the Bible, and every line of a hymn, I apply to you. You must be feeling particularly homesick . . . in these dangerous days, and every letter will only make it worse. But isn't it characteristic of a man, in contrast to an immature person, that his centre of gravity is always where he actually is, and that the longing for the fulfilment of his wishes cannot prevent him from being his whole self, wherever he happens to be? The adolescent is never wholly in one place; that is one of his essential characteristics, else he would presumably be a dullard. There is a wholeness about the fully grown man which enables him to face an existing situation squarely. He may have his longings, but he keeps them out of sight, and somehow masters them; and the more he has to overcome in order to live fully in the present, the more he will have the respect and confidence of his fellows, especially the younger ones, who are still on the road that he has already travelled. Desires to which we cling closely can easily prevent us from being what we ought to be and can be; and on the other hand, desires repeatedly mastered for the sake of present duty make us richer. Lack of desire is poverty. Almost all the people that I find in my present surroundings cling to their own desires, and so have no interest in others; they no longer listen, and they're incapable of loving their

neighbour. I think that even in this place we ought to live as if we had no wishes and no future, and just be our true selves. It's remarkable then how others come to rely on us, confide in us, and let us talk to them. I'm writing all this to you because I think you have a big task on hand just now, and because you will be glad to think, later on, that you carried it out as well as you could. When we know that someone is in danger, we want to be sure that we know him as he really is. We can have abundant life, even though many wishes remain unfulfilled – that's what I have really been trying to say. Forgive me for putting such 'considerations' before you so persistently, but I'm sure you will understand that considering things takes up a large part of my life here. For the rest, I must add, as a necessary supplement to what I've just written, that I'm more convinced than ever that our wishes are going to be fulfilled, and that there is no need for us to throw up the sponge.

I've just been told about Ursel's visit. I hope she's bringing Renate with her. You will know that Maria is in Bavaria for a few weeks. She's helping to teach the children of her cousin von Truchsess there. It will soon be more than enough for her. Her mother was here again recently; really very touching, on the way from four in the morning to eleven at night! . . .

Once again I'm having weeks when I don't read the Bible much; I never know quite what to do about it. I have no feeling of obligation about it, and I know, too, that after some time I shall plunge into it again voraciously. May one accept this as an entirely 'natural' mental process? I'm almost inclined to think so; it also happened, you know, during our *vita communis*.[171] Of course, there's always the danger of laziness, but it would be wrong to get anxious about it; we can depend upon it that after the compass has wobbled a bit, it will point in the right direction again. Don't you agree? Did that reading Genesis 41.52[172] recently do you as much good as it did me? I hadn't come across it before. It's now a year since we spent those last days and did those last things together, and since I was able to be witness at your engagement. I keep being amazed that I was able to be with you on that day . . . I'm curious as to how the future will lead us on, whether perhaps we shall be together again in our work – which I should very much like, or whether we shall have to be content with what has been. They really were quite wonderful years. If only I could hear something in detail about your present impressions. It would be very important to me! God bless you, Eberhard.

Faithfully, your Dietrich

When do you get leave? I won't be able to get away from here before the middle of May.

To his father   [Tegel] 23 April[173] 1944

Dear father,
The splendid memory of your seventy-fifth birthday a year ago must now last for this year as well. Today it seems almost incredible that only last year we were able to have such a happy gathering of family and friends. We oughtn't to allow ourselves to be deprived of the inner possession of a splendid past by a temporarily troubled present. The great cantata 'Praise the Lord . . .' which we sang on the morning and in the evening of your birthday and the picture of the many children making music together will be very present to us all as a real joy during this year. And the harsh impressions of the past year will only have strengthened what we thought there, adults as well as children. I expect that in the meantime the voice of Christoph, who sang you a couple of Hugo Wolf spring songs in the morning, will have broken, and thanks to Renate you became great-grandparents a few weeks ago. My fate has perhaps brought your future daughter-in-law nearer than would otherwise have been the case and the events of the war have scattered the family during the course of the year. But despite all the changes of an external kind, we've experienced the strong ties that bind our large family probably more stronger this year than ever. The quite decisive reason for this is that you and mother have remained the unchanged centre of the family. There can be no doubt of that, and I'm particularly grateful to you for it today. I also think that you would agree if I told myself to forget the

reproach that I've caused you so much trouble in the past year. Certainly, thinking of me has deprived you of a good deal of peaceful work. But as I know from your letters and visits that you accept and regard the adversities of the past year in the same way as I do, I will continue to be quite calm about all these things. I live daily in the confidence that better days will come again and that the day when we meet again in freedom will be a very splendid one.

I'm very glad that you've gone into the country, at least for a couple of days, and very much hope that you find it refreshing; I'm now eagerly awaiting what you have to tell me. I wonder what you took with you to read? If this letter reaches you while you're still in Pätzig, please give them warmest greetings from me. The one pity is that Maria isn't there. She wrote to me that she was staying in Bavaria over Easter. It's surely better for her not to be torn in several different directions, but to have some peace and quiet. Still, even that is hardly possible as long as my business has not been cleared up and decided.

Will Hans-Walter be able to visit me before he goes off to the front? You told me that he asked to, and I would very much like it. I would also very much like to see one of my brothers or sisters again. But I'm particularly looking forward to my next meeting with you.

I wish you, dear father, a better and more peaceful new year, that will bring us all together again.

With love and many thanks.   Your Dietrich

To Eberhard Bethge   [Tegel] 24 March 1944

Dear Eberhard,

It was a very great joy to hear so much from you. It's really quite wonderful that the dialogue remains intact, and I feel that it's always the most fruitful that I have. I feel that it's one of the laws of spiritual understanding that one's own thoughts, when they are understood by others, at the same time always undergo a transformation and liberation through the medium of the person. To this degree letters are really always 'events', as you write . . . I would understand well if there were only three problems for you at the moment, war, marriage and the church; it's a great joy and a proof of your unchanged frame of mind that the scope of your observations and interests has been extended so much wider in a fine spiritual freedom. I know that for some brothers, doing guard duty at night has been most significant. Is it the same with you? . . .

I expect the question of the baby's baptism is on your mind a good deal now, and that's mainly why I am writing to you, as I think you may be troubled by a certain 'inconsistency' about it. We've sometimes urged that children should be baptized as soon as possible (as it is a question of a sacrament), even if the father cannot be present. The reasons are clear. Yet I'm bound to agree that you will do well to wait. Why? I still think it is right and desirable (especially as an example to the community, and in particular for a pastor) to have one's child baptized soon, assuming that it is done with a sincere faith in the efficacy of the sacrament. At the same time, the father's wish to be present and to take part in the prayers for his child has a claim to be considered. And when I examine my own feelings, I must admit that I'm chiefly influenced by the thought that God also loves the still unbaptized child who is to be baptized later. The New Testament lays down no law about infant baptism; it is a gift of grace bestowed on the church, a gift that may be received and used in firm faith, and can thus be a striking testimony of faith for the community; but to force oneself to it without the compulsion of faith is not biblical. Regarded purely as a demonstration, infant baptism loses its justification. God will not fail to hear our prayers for the child when we ask him to send the day soon when we can bring him to the font together. As long as there is a justifiable hope that that day is not far off, I cannot believe that God is concerned about the exact date. So we can quite well wait a little and trust in God's kindly providence, and do later with a stronger faith what we should at the moment feel simply to be burdensome law . . . So I should wait for a while (without any scruples!); we shall see our way more clearly later. I think it will be better for the actual baptism; what is more important than any purely legal performance is that it should be celebrated in the fullest possible faith.

I expect you say less about your immediate impressions of the war so as not to disquieten us. But I believe that nevertheless I can form an approximate picture, and I think of you every day with a prayer for your protection. Your activity is probably relatively interesting in itself; as far as the matter itself is concerned, it's really the same thing whatever wheel of the great machine one is turning. I can imagine and well understand that interest in commercial concerns, which is so easily associated with it, is irksome to you. In the end, however, the one who is really intact as a person always has the greater authority. I find that here, too. How hard it is for some people really to separate the two spheres; I often feel that it's almost tragic. You're getting to know one of my favourite parts of the world much better than I know it myself. How I should love to sit with you in the car and see the Cecilia Metella or Hadrian's Villa. I've never been able to make much of the Pietà; you must explain some time why it impresses you so much.

25 March

We had another very lively time last night. The view from the roof here over the city was staggering. I've heard nothing yet about the family. Thank God my parents went to Pätzig yesterday; but there wasn't much doing in the West. It seems to me absurd how one can't help hoping, when an air raid is announced, that it will be the turn of other places this time – as the saying goes, 'Holy St Florian, spare my house, set others on fire' – wanting to push off on to others what one fears for oneself: 'Perhaps they will get no further than Magdeburg or Stettin this time'; how often I've heard that fervent wish expressed! Such moments make one very conscious of *natura corrupta* and *peccatum originale*, and to that extent they may be quite salutary. Incidentally, there has been a very marked increase in air activity during the last few days, and it makes one wonder whether it isn't a substitute for the invasion that isn't materializing.

I won't be able to make any plans for the future before May. I'm gradually losing faith in all these forecasts about dates, and I'm attaching less importance to them; who knows whether it will not then be 'in July'? I feel that my own personal future is of quite secondary importance compared with the general situation, though, of course, the two things are very closely connected. So I hope we shall still be able to discuss our plans for the future. I'm amazed . . . at all the fantasies of these supposedly dry-as-dust jurists. The source of sober judgment and actions lies somewhere quite different.

The information that I gave you recently is out of date.[174] Please write to home again. I'm still all right here. One gradually becomes part of the furniture, and sometimes actually has less peace and quiet than one wants.

You're quite right about the rarity of landscape painting in the South generally. Is the south of France an exception – and Gauguin? or perhaps they weren't southerners? I don't know. What about Claude Lorrain? Yet it's alive in Germany and England. The southerner *has* the beauties of nature, while we long for them wistfully, as for a rarity. By the way, to change the subject: Mörike once said that 'where beauty is, there is happiness too'. Doesn't that fit in with Burckhardt? We're apt to acquiesce in Nietzsche's crude alternatives, as if the only concepts of beauty were on the one hand the 'Apolline' and on the other the 'Dionysian', or, as we should now say, the demonic. That's not so at all. Take, for example, Brueghel or Velasquez, or even Hans Thoma, Leopold von Kalckreuth, or the French impressionists. There we have a beauty that is neither classical nor demonic, but simply earthly, though it has its own proper place. For myself, I must say that it's the only kind of beauty that really appeals to me. I would include the Magdeburg virgins and the Naumburg sculptures. May not the 'Faustian' interpretation of Gothic art be on altogether wrong lines? How else would there be such a contrast between the plastic arts and architecture? . . .

That must be all for today, or you would never get through this letter. I'm so glad to remember how you played the cantata 'Praise the Lord' that time. It did us all a lot of good!

Ever faithfully,   your Dietrich

Perhaps I already ought to be sending you my special good wishes for Easter, as I don't know how long it takes for letters to reach you and I would very much like you to know that in the weeks before and after Easter I know that I'm one with you in many good memories. In looking through *Das Neue Lied* these days, I'm constantly reminded that it is mainly to you that I owe my enjoyment of the Easter hymns. It's a year now since I heard a hymn sung. But it's strange how the music that we hear inwardly can almost surpass, if we really concentrate on it, what we hear physically. It has a greater purity, the dross falls away, and in a way the music acquires a 'new body'. There are only a few pieces that I know well enough to be able to hear them inwardly, but I get on particularly well with the Easter hymns. I'm getting a better existential appreciation of the music that Beethoven composed after he had gone deaf, in particular the great set of variations from Opus III, which we once heard played by Gieseking:

By the way, I've sometimes listened lately to the Sunday evening concert from 6 to 7, though on an atrocious wireless set . . .

Easter? We're paying more attention to dying than to death. We're more concerned to get over the act of dying than to overcome death. Socrates mastered the art of dying; Christ overcame death as 'the last enemy' (I Cor. 15.26). There is a real difference between the two things; the one is within the scope of human possibilities, the other means resurrection. It's not from *ars moriendi*, the art of dying, but from the resurrection of Christ, that a new and purifying wind can blow through our present world. *Here* is the answer to δὸς μοὶ ποῦ στῶ καὶ κινήσω τὴν γῆν.[175] If a few people really believed that and acted on it in their daily lives, a great deal would be changed. To live in the light of the resurrection – that is what Easter means. Do you find, too, that most people don't know what they really live by? This *perturbatio animorum* spreads amazingly. It's an unconscious waiting for the word of deliverance, though the time is probably not yet ripe for it to be heard. But the time will come, and this Easter may be one of our last chances to prepare ourselves for our great task of the future. I hope you will be able to enjoy it, in spite of all the hardships that you're having to bear. Good-bye; I must close now, as the letter has to go.

With all my heart, your Dietrich

From Karl-Friedrich Bonhoeffer
[at Charlottenburg] 26 March 1944

Dear Dietrich,

When you get this letter it will probably be exactly a year that you've been in prison. Inconceivable for any of us who has not experienced it. Your letters still keep circulating round our whole family and are a great joy to us. But I would very much like to see you again and talk to you. So I've applied again for permission to visit. With so many members of the family, each individual can only come rarely, and parents and fiancée have priority.

I'm sitting here in the parents' living room. They're now in Pätzig and getting to know the house of your future mother-in-law. I'm very glad that they've finally managed to make the journey. Mother in particular went with a great inner conflict, though she needed the change quite urgently. It's simply too much for her; she must relax. During the bomb attacks she doesn't take the slightest notice, and if anyone advises her to take care in any way she almost regards it as an insult. But of course on top of everything else it will be some relaxation. Unfortunately they don't intend to stay much longer than a week; partly they'll feel they have to come back because they've got permission to visit you. So I expect that you will see them in the week before Easter, even before you get this letter from me.

Meanwhile I've become half a Berliner again. Perhaps not quite 'half', but it looks as if I shall have more to do here in the near future in connection with my new activity with Osram. It may, of course, be that I shall 'evacuate' myself again from here, an idea which has become very topical during the time of your imprisonment. When you come out, you will be amazed at the way in which the world has changed in a year. Academic work has gradually got very difficult. The books in the libraries have all been 'evacuated' and are hard to get at, the Institute has been hit, people are distracted by all sorts of domestic worries. One has to gather up more than all the energy that one has to compel oneself to concentrate. I've left things that were 80% finished lying around for months, but I haven't got them finished. Yet in our area it should be a decisive matter for industry that theoretical questions of pure science should be taken further. In the long run one can't go on living off capital. I would be happy if I could find a quiet, suitable bywater somewhere where I could carry on my scientific and technical investigations and could perhaps bring Grete and the children along. I would then compress my lectures in Leipzig into a few days and so to speak finish up there by making visits. But I'm afraid that this sort of thing can't be found any more.

I'm going to Leipzig again shortly, and am not coming back until Easter. I hope I shall have permission to visit by then. May one wish you a 'happy' festival?

All the best.   Ever your Karl-Friedrich

From Eberhard Bethge   [Rignano, End of March, 1944]

Dear Dietrich,

. . . The chief here and the second in command, both very nice to me personally, are so 'modern'[176] and have such a soldierly approach that I can never talk to them about my problems in the way that would sometimes be desirable. One of those below told me recently, when he was drunk, that in the peace after victory legal proceedings would be taken against people like me and Rainalter (academics), good and proper. Most people found that out of place. When I can come, we shall have to think about a number of things. What will have happened by then? The *Wehrmacht* reports now call for an intrepid and steadfast heart; i.e. only among those who are at all interested in it. I'm very curious to know what all this is that you're now reading in Dilthey about music. . . .

I would very much like to see Sepp.[177] I once had a short talk with his wife. He has surely kept his *hilaritas*. Interesting that you've now become so preoccupied with the Middle Ages. The thirteenth century. Because of the present fashion I've had something of a reaction against this period of the 'Reich'.[178] But your observations on 'worldliness' without an anti- are still very attractive. At the moment I'm sitting here in the country and can't see anything of the Middle Ages and the Renaissance, but only campagna, farmwork, with every now and then an old paving stone and marble remains of old buildings along the road with a frieze.[179] About your observations on what people believe, there is also an interest in fortune-tellers here. Some people keep going to them from time to time while at the same time assuring everyone that they don't believe a word of it . . . I think that I can well understand the business of dramatizing 'suffering', depicting things, making a role out of them. It's probably a form of inner protection against grief and may even be a form of divesting oneself of it . . .

Warmest greetings. It will soon be Palm Sunday and Easter.

Your Eberhard

From his father   Pätzig, 27 March 1943[180]

Dear Dietrich,

When we returned from Tegel last Thursday, we found the permission to visit waiting. That was very sad, because we've now had to put off the visit until our return from Pätzig. The journey here couldn't very well be put off once again. However, Maria is hoping to be able to visit you very soon, probably on the 30th. We arrived here on Friday without any special trouble. Karl-Friedrich went with us to the station. We're being very spoilt here, and I hope that mother will be able to recover a bit during the time while she doesn't have to bother about anything. The weather is cool and windy, with flurries of snow. The advantage

243

of that is that one doesn't go out in the open air much, and is really forced to sit still and rest. We're in very friendly company here. Mother Wedemeyer and the children are a joy to us in every respect, particularly when we can think that you won't find it hard at a later date to feel at home here. Even the many evacuees who are here are nice, considerate people. The unselfish character of the mistress of the house and the way in which she is concerned about everyone has an effect on the whole house. On Saturday we had all sorts of musical offerings from the young people. Cello, piano, flute and recitation. We were reminded very much of our own Saturday musical evenings, when you were all at home. Yesterday Frau von Wedemeyer read aloud to us reminiscences by her husband of his father. They interested me not only because the man evidently had considerable strength of mind, and despite being fettered to a wheel-chair for years kept a tight hand on the reins of his business, but also because despite the quite different sphere of interest, his fundamental attitude to life and to the bringing up of a family hardly differed at all from that of our families in Schwabia. I expect that we shall come back on Tuesday 4 April, and then hope that we shall be able to visit you on Wednesday or Thursday. Mother really wanted to write to you too, but we decided that she shouldn't do so for a couple of days so that you don't get two letters from the same place saying essentially the same thing. I think that the stay here will do mother good. We're rather worried about the last attack on Berlin, about which we've had no further details. One can't get through by telephone. Mother sends much love; she is just writing to Maria. See you soon.   Your Father

To Eberhard Bethge   [Tegel] 2 April 1944

Dear Eberhard,
Now that Easter seems likely to come and go without our being at home and meeting again, I'm putting off hope until Whitsuntide at the latest. What do you think about it? You must be having a glorious spring just now, and you will be longing to be able to

show everything that you're now seeing to Renate one day, in peace. In normal circumstances, I expect that you would have confirmed Klaus and Christoph today. Here it's a clear, but still rather cool Palm Sunday morning. How we would be able to celebrate such a feast day in the family! But how good it is that for years – I believe, since father's seventieth birthday – you've celebrated all the family festivals with us and have added splendour to them. I keep feeling very sorry that Maria has really come to know the family only under the pressure of the last year; she only shared in Hans-Walter's farewell party. She was here a couple of days ago and told very vividly how they had anticipatory celebrations for father's birthday in Pätzig on 29 March. Maria had gone for two days to meet my parents there. In the morning, singing outside the door, birthday breakfast for my parents with Maria and her mother, by themselves, evidently quite an Epicurean banquet with local produce, a great festal board . . . I was really delighted with it all, especially thinking of my parents, who have a very open heart for such spontaneous acts of friendship. Both were said to be cheerful and in a relaxed mood, which pleases me very much after these dreadful months . . .

I got to see Ursel and Dorothee here quite by chance. That H.W. was refused a visit is one of those things which I shall note carefully. I think it an underhand way of acting which should not be allowed to pass without comment. I thought that Dorothee looked well, but Ursel was still rather thin. I've now asked for a picture of the little boy and am waiting for it eagerly . . .

Just fancy, I've suddenly, by an odd chance, taken up graphology again, and am enjoying it very much; I'm now working through Ludwig Klages' book. But I'm not going to try it on my friends and relatives; there are enough people here who are interested in it. I'm convinced of the thing's reliability. I expect you know that I was so successful at it in my student days that it became embarrassing and I gave it up. That was almost 20 years ago. Now, having, I think, got over the dangers of psychology, I'm very interested in it again, and I should like to discuss it with you. If it gets unpleasant again, I shall drop it at once. I think it is possible that you might be very successful at it, as it needs two things, the second of which you have in much greater measure than I: sensitivity, and an acute power of observation. If you like, I will write to you again about it.

In the 800-page biography of Klopstock by Karl Kindt (formerly G[erman] Christian), 1941, I found some very striking extracts from Klopstock's play *Der Tod Adams*, which is about the death of the first man. The idea is interesting enough, and the play itself is powerful. I had sometimes thought of trying to rehabilitate Klopstock, so the book interests me very much.

Maria's birthday is on 23 April. Will you perhaps send her a brief greeting? She would certainly like it very much . . . Well, that was simply a narrative letter which arose solely from a desire to talk to you this morning (in other times we would have made glorious music today) and not to leave you without news.

I have here a very detailed map of the environs of Rome; I often look at it when I'm thinking of you, and imagine you going round the streets with which you are familiar from long acquaintance, hearing the sounds of war not very far away, and looking at the lake from the mountains.

God bless you today wherever you go. Faithfully, with all my heart,   your Dietrich

To Ruth von Wedemeyer   [Tegel] 10 April 1944

Dear mother,[181]
While you are celebrating your birthday in a large circle of family and friends with joy and thankfulness, you must know and feel that from the quietness of a closed cell unceasing good thoughts and wishes go out to you . . . I've looked up the readings for 19 April.[182] They point us towards those who call to us from eternity and are with us, to father and to Max.[183] They will be very much in your thoughts, and yet at the same time you will also be thinking of us and those who need you on this earth. The time between Easter and Ascension has always been particularly important to me. Our gaze is already directed to the last thing of

all, but we still have our tasks, our joys and our sorrows on this earth and the power of living is granted to us by Easter. I say nothing but what I have experienced when I thank you today for going before us on this way between Easter and Ascension; it is the blessing that father and Max have left behind for you and for us. I too want to go this way with Maria, quite prepared for the last thing, for eternity, and yet wholly present for the task, the beauties and the troubles of this earth. Only on this way can we be completely happy and completely at peace together. We want to receive what God bestows on us with open, outstretched hands and delight in it with all our heart, and with a quiet heart we will sacrifice what God does not yet grant us or takes away from us . . .

Thank you for everything that you have done for me in the past year. God preserve you in the coming year for us and your whole house.   Your grateful son, Dietrich

My parents felt so happy with you and you were so particularly good to them that I was very pleased indeed about it. They have the feeling that they get on particularly well with you. Thank you most particularly for those days.

Report on Prison Life
after One Year in Tegel

The formalities of admission were correctly completed. For the first night I was locked up in an admission cell. The blankets on the camp bed had such a foul smell that in spite of the cold it was impossible to use them. Next morning a piece of bread was thrown into my cell; I had to pick it up from the floor. A quarter of the coffee consisted of grounds. The sound of the prison staff's vile abuse of the prisoners who were held for investigation penetrated into my cell for the first time; since then I have heard it every day from morning till night. When I had to parade with the other new arrivals, we were addressed by one of the jailers as 'blackguards', etc. etc. We were asked why we had been arrested, and when I said I did not know, the jailer answered with a scornful laugh, 'You'll find that out soon enough.' It was six months before I got a warrant for my arrest. As we went through the various offices, some NCOs, who had heard what my profession was, wanted now and then to have a few words with me. They were told that no one was to talk to me. While I was having a bath an NCO (I do not know who he was) suddenly appeared and asked me whether I knew Pastor N. [Martin Niemöller]. When I said that I did, he exclaimed, 'He is a good friend of mine', and disappeared again. I was taken to the most isolated single cell on the top floor; a notice, prohibiting all access without special permission, was put outside it. I was told that all my correspondence would be stopped until further notice, and that, unlike all the other prisoners, I should not be allowed half an hour a day in the open air, although, according to the prison rules, I was entitled to it. I received neither newspapers nor anything to smoke. After 48 hours my Bible was returned to me; it had been searched to see whether I had smuggled inside it a saw, razor, or the like. For the next twelve days the cell door was opened only for bringing food in and putting the bucket out. No one said a word to me. I was told nothing about the reason for my detention, or how long it would last. I gathered from various remarks – and it was confirmed later – that I was lodged in the section for the most serious cases, where the condemned prisoners lay shackled.

The first night in my cell I could not sleep much, because in the next cell a prisoner wept loudly for several hours on end; no one took any notice. I thought at the time that that kind of thing would happen every night, but in all the months since then it has only been repeated once. In those first days of complete isolation I could see nothing of how things were run in the building; I could only picture what was going on from the incessant shouting of the warders. My basic impression, which is still unchanged, was that anyone detained for investigation was at once treated as a criminal, and that in practice it was impossible for a prisoner who was treated unjustly to get redress. Later I more than once heard conversations in which warders said quite bluntly that if a prisoner complained of unjust treatment, or of being struck (which is strictly forbidden), the authorities would never believe the prisoner, but always the warder, especially as the latter could be sure of finding a colleague who would testify for him on oath. I have, in fact, known of cases where this evil practice was followed.

After twelve days the authorities got to know of my family connections.[184] While this was a great relief to me personally, it was most embarrassing to see how everything changed from that moment. I was put into a more spacious cell, which one of the men cleaned every day for me; I was offered larger rations, which I always refused, as they would have been at the expense of the other prisoners; the captain fetched me for a daily walk, with the result that the staff treated me with studied politeness – in fact, several of them came to apologize: 'We didn't know', etc. It was painful.

General treatment: The tone is set by those warders who behave in the most evil and brutal way towards the prisoners. The whole building resounds with vile and insulting abuse, so that the quieter and more fair-minded warders, too, are nauseated by it, but they can hardly exercise any influence. During months of detention for investigation, prisoners who are later acquitted have to suffer abuse like criminals, and are absolutely defenceless, since their right to complain exists only in theory. Private means, cigarettes, and promises for later on play an important part. The little man with no connections, etc., has to submit to everything. The same people who rant and rage at the other prisoners show a servile politeness towards me. Attempts to have a quiet word with them about the treatment of all the other prisoners fail because, although they admit everything at the time, they are just as bad as ever an hour later. I must not omit to say that a number of the warders are even-tempered, matter-of-fact, and as far as possible, friendly towards the prisoners; but they mostly remain in subordinate posts.

Food: Prisoners cannot avoid the impression that they do not receive in full the rations due to them. There is often not the slightest trace of the meat that is alleged to be included in the soup. Bread and sausage are divided very unequally. I weighed one sausage ration myself; it was 15 grammes instead of 25. NCOs and others working in the kitchen have plenty of unhappy impressions and observations about this. With 700 prisoners to be fed, even the smallest inaccuracy makes a big difference. I know for a fact that when the doctors or officers inspect the prisoners' food, a nourishing sauce made of meat or cream is added to the plates concerned; and so it is not surprising that the prisoners' food has a high reputation. I also know that the meat intended for the prisoners has all the goodness boiled out of it first in the cauldrons where the staff's food is cooked, and so on. An occasional comparison between the prisoners' food and the staff's is simply staggering. On Sundays and holidays the food is not examined, and the midday meal is beneath all criticism; it consists of cabbage soup made with water and with no fat, meat, or potatoes at all. It seems to me beyond doubt that the food provided is quite inadequate for young people detained for any length of time. No records are kept of the prisoners' weight. Although these prisoners are only being held for investigation, and are, moreover, soldiers, some of whom are sent straight back to their units when they are released, they are told that they are strictly forbidden, on pain of severe punishment, to receive food parcels.[185] No articles of food are allowed in –

not even the eggs and sandwiches that the prisoners' relatives bring them on visiting days. This causes great bitterness among the prisoners and their visitors. Military police who deliver the prisoners are looked after – against standing orders – in the kitchen.

Occupation: By far the greater part of the prisoners detained for investigation spend the day without any work, although most of them ask for work. They receive three books a week from a very mediocre library. Games of every kind, such as chess, are forbidden, even in the communal cells, and if any of the prisoners have managed to make themselves one, it is taken away from them and they are punished. There are no projects for work that would be useful for all the 700 prisoners, such as, for instance, the construction of air-raid shelters. There are no religious services. The prisoners, some of whom are very young (they include anti-aircraft auxiliaries) are bound to suffer in body and soul from the lack of occupation and of supervision, particularly during a long, solitary confinement.

Lighting: During the winter months the prisoners often had to sit in the dark for several hours because the staff were too lazy to switch on the cell lights. When the prisoners, who have a right to lighting in their cells, put out their flags or knocked to get attention, the staff would shout angrily at them, and the light would not be switched on till the next day. The prisoners are not allowed to lie on their beds before the Last Post, so that they had to spend the hours before that sitting in the dark. That is very depressing, and only causes bitterness.

Air-raid warnings: There are no air-raid shelters for the prisoners. With all the labour available here, it would have been quite easy to provide these in good time. A dug-out has been built, but only for the authorities; apart from that, all that happens is that the prisoners on the top floor are locked in with the others in the ground-floor cells. When I asked why the prisoners in the second-floor cells were not moved down to the first floor, I was told that it would make too much work. There is no first-aid shelter. When the sick-bay was put out of action during a heavy attack, they could not start to bandage the injured till after it was over. No one who has experienced it will ever forget the shouting and screaming of the locked-up prisoners during a heavy air raid – some of them are here because of trifling offences, or are actually innocent. Seven hundred soldiers are exposed here to the dangers of a bombing attack with no protection.

Miscellaneous: The only way in which a prisoner can communicate with the staff in case of urgency is by putting out the flag. This is often ignored for hours, or perhaps a passing warder simply pushes it back without finding out what the prisoner wants. If the prisoner then knocks on the door, he gets a volley of abuse. If he reports sick outside the regulation hours, he inconveniences the staff, and is therefore in most cases angrily shouted at; it is only with great difficulty that he manages to gain access to the sick-bay. I have twice known prisoners to be kicked into it; one of them had acute appendicitis and had to be taken to the military hospital at once, and the other was suffering from prolonged hysterical convulsions. – All those who are detained for investigation, even for the most minor offences, appear in chains at their interrogation and trial. This is a great humiliation for a soldier in uniform, and makes the interrogation a more severe ordeal for him. – The men who empty the buckets and bring round the food receive the same small amount of soap for washing as the ordinary prisoners, and even for the latter it is hardly enough.

Lance-Corporal Berg

With a smug and self-satisfied smile, Sergeant-Major Meier takes delivery of a green parcel and hides it away in his brief-case, which he then carefully puts away in his desk. Then he puts on his official face and asks: '. . . and your heart-trouble, Müller?' Müller springs to attention and stutters: 'Sergeant-Major, my wife . . .' 'I'm asking about your heart trouble, Müller. It's – no better? worse?' 'Yes, Sergeant-Major, worse, decidedly worse,' asserts Müller quickly and in a rather flustered way. 'But, Müller, perhaps in three months . . .?' 'Yes, Sergeant-Major, of course, certainly, that is, perhaps, yes, perhaps, Sergeant-Major, in three months. Three months is a long . . .' He breaks off. Müller follows with curious glances the movements of the Sergeant-Major, who takes out a list, makes a brief note after one name and puts the list back in the file. Lance-corporal Müller takes a deep breath. He wants to say thank you, but feels that this is not permissible. 'That's good, Müller, you can go,' says the Sergeant-Major with dignity. Just as Müller has the door-knob in his hand, the Sergeant-Major says almost in passing, without looking at Müller: '. . . and, Müller, you won't forget . . .!' 'But, Sergeant-Major . . .' Müller makes a bow, as though he were standing behind the counter in a shop. Compulsively smiling and bowing again, he goes out.

The telephone rings. 'Wehrmacht Interrogation Prison here, Sergeant-Major Meier speaking – who's there? – I can't hear – ah, Major!' Meier comes to attention, his face fixed as a deferential, smiling mask. 'Pardon me, Major, I had not . . . about a posting?' Meier's voice goes husky. 'Ah, I understand, Major, you want to post a man to us.' Meier's voice is quite clear again. 'Of course, Major, naturally, we have a place here – excellent man – comes from the front – badly wounded – quite capable of duty – understanding treatment – comradely handling – but of course, Major – tremendous comradeship here – of course – the man can come immediately – pardon – understanding treatment? But Major, that goes without saying – fighter at the front – thank you, Major.' He bows, laughs. 'Your obedient servant, Major – the Major can rely on me completely – yours to command, Major.' Meier puts down the receiver quickly and in some disquiet. A new man? I cannot use him. A front-line fighter? These people often introduce such an unattractive tone – they don't fit here – they see everything differently from us – yes, if one had been out there oneself – yes, perhaps not completely fit for duty – badly wounded? Understanding treatment? Comradeship? The same question twice? Meier hesitates, shakes his head. 'No, in the end I have to make the decisions here,' he murmurs to himself complacently. He reaches for the key of the desk and is just about to open the closed packet when there is a knock at the door. The packet vanishes again immediately. Vexed, Meier calls, 'Come in!'

The duty sergeant enters, pushing before him a soldier with handcuffs and chains on his legs, so that he stumbles into the office. 'Today's intake, Sergeant-Major. Deserter. Cell 127.' The prisoner looks round in confusion. He seems overcome with weariness and looks hungry. 'Would you mind taking up a military attitude, you tramp,' roars the Sergeant-Major. 'Have you never seen a parade ground?' The prisoner pulls himself together. 'How old?' 'Eighteen years, Sergeant-Major.' 'Occupation?' 'School-leaver, Sergeant-Major.' 'Where from?' 'The front, Sergeant-Major.' 'From the front, you swine? Do you know what the consequences of that are?' 'Yes, Sergeant-Major.' A slight tremor goes through his body. 'From the front, you cowardly lump? So you're leaving your comrades in the lurch? You're undermining discipline and order? You want to put your personal satisfaction first in the middle of a war? You stuff yourself full and go around with whores while every decent man is sacrificing his blood and his life for the fatherland? You'd run after anything with a skirt on?' 'No, Sergeant-Major.' 'No, you say? Are you a liar as well, you guttersnipe? Why did you desert?' 'I don't know, Sergeant-Major. It just happened.' 'You don't know? It just happened? Don't you know that the German has a will with which he can overcome the swine within himself? It just happened! That's a new one!' The room shakes with the roaring and laughing of the Sergeant-

Major. 'You don't know why you pulled out? Well, I'll tell you. I know. Because you're a miserable piece of scum, who trembles at every shot and who will now get the shot that he deserves on the sand-bags. How many hours were you up at the front, then, you mother's son, you cut above the rest, you school-leaver, you?' 'All the winter, Sergeant-Major.' 'Where?' 'In Russia.' 'All the winter? Why were you called up, then?' 'I volunteered a year ago, Sergeant-Major.' '. . . to hang about out there? Did you ever see a Russian?' 'I have the Iron Cross, class I, Sergeant-Major.' The gaze of the young prisoner involuntarily shifts to the left breast of the Sergeant-Major, which displays only the unspotted, well-pressed, green cloth of a new uniform. Then he looks the Sergeant-Major straight in the face and is amazed that he looks so strikingly young, healthy and well-fed. The Sergeant-Major senses this and becomes uncomfortable. 'The Iron Cross, class I?', he blusters. 'Then why aren't you wearing it?' The Sergeant-Major looks with contempt at the faded, torn uniform of the prisoner. 'I took it off myself after I was arrested.' 'Iron Cross class I? Took it off yourself?' The Sergeant-Major roars with laughter. The sergeant intervenes: 'Sergeant-Major, the Iron Cross class I is entered in his paybook.' 'In his paybook? You fool,' screams the Sergeant-Major, beside himself. 'Don't you know that these jokers forge their paybooks, too? Serious falsification of documents. That, too. You wait, my boy, we'll show you.' The prisoner is silent. He looks dreadfully tired and tormented, but his flickering eyes bore deep into the smug face of the Sergeant-Major. 'Where were you arrested?' 'I don't know, Sergeant-Major. I was lying unconscious in the snow.' 'How long were you on the way?' 'About twelve hours; then I couldn't do any more.' 'Where did you want to go?' 'I don't know. Only away from the front. I simply ran away. I was out of my senses. The others had all run away too.' 'Then how did those who found you know that you were a deserter?' 'Because I told them.' 'Why did you do that, you idiot? Why didn't you say that your unit was on the retreat?' 'Because I had left the post in which I had been placed without orders. Anyone who runs away from the front is cowardly in the face of the enemy and a deserter.' The Sergeant-Major is taken aback. 'What is your father?' 'An officer.' The

Sergeant-Major gives the sergeant a sly glance. 'Take the prisoner back to his cell.' The chains clank as the prisoner comes to attention. The door closes.

Sergeant-Major Meier is ill at ease after this conversation. He wants to forget it. He quickly reaches for the packet again, opens it hastily, cuts off a large slice of sausage and bites into it greedily. Involuntarily he touches the left side of his uniform with his hand, as though the gaze of the young prisoner were still burning there. 'Cursed people, these soldiers from the front,' he mutters to himself.

Heavy knocking. Sergeant-Major Meier jumps. He has become nervous. The door is opened quickly, as Meier is still gulping down his bite. 'Lance-corporal Berg reporting for duty under the Major's orders.' A quiet, firm voice. Meier puts his jacket straight, strokes his careful parting, looks up and remains speechless for a moment. What he sees can hardly be called a human face. Severe burning, as though caused by a flame thrower, has completely destroyed this face. Pieces of strange flesh have been stuck on; the nose is in shreds, the mouth has no lips, only half the ears are there. The Sergeant-Major tries to pull himself together, but he still stares speechlessly at the face of the man standing before him, upright and youthful. 'Did the Major,' he begins finally, 'send you to us?' 'Yes, Sergeant-Major.' The Major's words whirl through Sergeant-Major Meier's head: 'Excellent man – soldier from the front – understanding treatment – comradeship.' 'Are you fully capable of duty?' 'Yes, Sergeant-Major.' 'Are you still having hospital treatment?' 'No, Sergeant-Major, I've been released as cured.' Meier struggles for words. 'So you think . . .?', he falters. 'Yes, Sergeant-Major, I think that I will do my duty here as well as at the front.' The Sergeant-Major shrugs his shoulders. 'Of course, of course, my friend – the Major – are you married?' he asks suddenly. 'No, not yet, Sergeant-Major.' Not yet. What can this man be hoping for? 'How old are you?' 'Twenty-eight.' As old as I am, thinks the Sergeant-Major. He shudders at the thought. 'What's your job?' 'Schoolteacher, Sergeant-Major.' That life's finished. Wouldn't it have been better for such a person if . . .? The Sergeant-Major does not pursue this thought to its conclusion. 'That's good,' he says, 'you can go. The duty sergeant will give you your orders.'

Meier walks up and down his office for a long time without knowing what he is really thinking. He feels an oppressive weight on heart and stomach as though before some imminent evil. He opens the window and takes a deep breath. He walks up and down again. Suddenly he stops in front of the mirror and looks at it for a long time. That comforts him. He finds himself looking neat and good. His new high boots and the close fit of his uniform which he has recently had made give his figure a trim, officer-like look with which he is extremely satisfied. He is at once reminded of the last ladies' social evening at which he made a strong impression on some of the younger women. He sees himself at the head of the table – but as he tries to conjure up the face of a particularly attractive women the gruesome mask of the wounded soldier appears to him. Then some adventures of the last weeks go through his head. He had arranged *Sekt* and an attractive cold dinner. The amazement of his companion. – Again the face. The face – the woman – the dinner – all follow one after the other. He goes to the telephone and asks for the kitchens. 'Send me Müller immediately.'

An hour later, Müller leaves the Sergeant-Major's office. His last words are, 'You can rely on me completely, Sergeant-Major. I quite understand. It is really quite impossible.'

In front of the door he comes across Lance-corporal Berg, who is returning from his first round of the cells. Müller quickly composes himself and asks with a compulsive laugh, just to say something, 'Well, how are our scoundrels?' 'Scoundrels?' replies Berg. 'I've just seen a young man in cell 127 – I would be happy if all soldiers were like him. But it's a shame about him – deserter. If only they would give him one last chance; he would wipe out the disgrace. A shame.' 'No, there's nothing at all to be done,' says Müller with a coarse laugh, and makes a gesture to describe the impending fate of the young soldier. Berg shakes his head. 'Comrade, were you out there in Russia?' Müller is confused. 'No, unfortunately not – I have heart trouble – nervous heart trouble. But in the end we also make our sacrifices here, air attacks, the exhausting work with these scoundrels . . .' 'Hm' – Berg shakes his head again, 'as far as I've seen, those who are sitting here are for the most part comrades who once did a silly thing, but scoundrels – I don't know, I'm afraid that they're to be found elsewhere. I don't want to keep you. I expect you're on your way to the kitchens. See you later! Cook the prisoners something good. We need them outside again. We can't do anything there with skeletons. See you later!' Berg turns away and leaves Müller standing. Müller stammers, wants to say something, but doesn't know what, thinks for a minute and then says to himself, 'Well, a young man like that, one like you.' Instead of going to the kitchens he goes straight into the sick-bay. There he brings the conversation incidentally round to Berg: excellent man, soldier from the front – understanding treatment – certainly, but one cannot ask too much of a man like that. It's not really his concern that he had this hard service, etc., etc. He gets a smooth rebuff; Berg is quite fit for duty. Anyway, they can't understand what it has to do with Müller. Does he have a personal interest? Müller stammers that he only wanted to help; he was a comrade from the front and the Sergeant-Major had had hesitations. He is told that he can report to the Sergeant-Major that his hesitations are groundless.

Lunch time. Müller sits by Berg and begins to talk to him with a mellow, amiable smile. He asks about the front, Berg's injury. Berg is monosyllabic. The Sergeant-Major sits opposite. Berg has to use a straw to drink as there is no feeling in his lips. He does it as unobtrusively as possible. The Sergeant-Major stares at this procedure appalled; Müller turns away. Both think of the next ladies' social evening. It is simply impossible. During the meal Berg praises the food and says that it is unusually good; now he wants to taste the prisoners' food immediately afterwards, as in the end they themselves are simply troops at home, whereas the prisoners for the most part have to go back to the front. This remark meets with an icy silence all round.

After the meal, when everyone has left the mess, the Sergeant-Major exchanges a few words more with Müller.

The next day Müller greets Lance-corporal Berg with special warmth and presses a small packet into his hand. 'You'll need that after all you've been through!' Berg opens it. 'How have I come to deserve a pound of butter?' he says out loud. At the same moment another NCO goes by. 'If it's left over – and I rather wonder about that – I'll share it among the prisoners in my section. By the way, what the prisoners had was muck. Shame on you!' Müller bites his lips and goes. Berg cannot be won over that way.

But Müller is tireless. He knows what it means for himself to put the Sergeant-Major at ease. The next day – breaking a standing rule (but he has the Sergeant-Major behind him!) – he enters into conversation with some of the prisoners from Berg's section. Doesn't the fearful disfigurement of his face have an oppressive effect on the prisoners in a situation which is already so grim? Astonished shaking of the head, incomprehending and even explicitly hostile denials are the answer to his question. Müller has to hasten to wipe out the bad impression of his question again with all sorts of gossip.

At lunch, Berg, whose mouth muscles do not function properly drops the straw while he is drinking and spills the drink on the table. Indignant head-shaking by the Sergeant-Major and cowardly smirking from Müller.

The following day Berg is assigned to supervising visits to the prisoners by their next-of-kin. The Sergeant-Major entertains one of the visiting women in his room afterwards. Later he makes it known through Müller that a visitor has asked him if it is possible to appoint another NCO to supervise the visiting next time; it is impossible for her to utter a word while looking at such a fearfully ravaged face.

Berg feels that people are talking about him. He begins to suspect why.

At meal time Müller sits next to him. 'These month-long stretches of imprisonment are nonsense for people who have played foolish pranks. It only corrupts them. A short sharp punishment would be much better,' says Berg. 'And then what would become of us?', Müller bursts out. 'I mean . . .' He now tries in vain to gloss over his previous words. 'I mean – in the end the people must have committed some offence, otherwise they wouldn't be here, and in that case it does them no harm to stew for a couple of months.' 'On the contrary, I think that you're wrong in every respect,' shouts Berg, aroused. 'Be careful, Berg, be careful,' Müller now protests, 'You criticize here, and if the Sergeant-Major hears . . .' 'Quite different people from the Sergeant-Major will hear what is going on here, I can assure you,' shouts Berg. Müller goes pale.

The next day, Berg is summoned to the Sergeant-Major. 'Unfortunately I have to tell you, Berg, that you have been called away with immediate effect. I'm very sorry. I would very much have liked to keep a soldier from the front like you here.' 'May I ask on what grounds I've been posted away, Sergeant-Major?' 'There is no reason why I should answer that question.' 'But I insist on an answer, Sergeant-Major,' says Berg stubbornly. 'Now take it easy, my dear Berg, I'll make an exception and tell you. It was an official order.' Berg goes pale. He does not believe what the Sergeant-Major is saying, indeed he is convinced that the Sergeant-Major is lying, but he has no chance of proving it. Berg comes to attention and leaves the office.

When the formalities have been settled, he opens the cell of the school-leaver once more and sees the traces of tears in his eyes. However, the face of the young deserter lights up when he sees Berg. 'What's the matter, lad?' asks Berg. 'I want to go back to the front,' the boy says, and tears spring from his eyes. 'So do I,' says Berg, and clenches his teeth. 'Keep your chin up, lad, I'll go to the General for you. You'll get out again. But I have to say good-bye to you now. I'm going.' 'You're going?,' cries the young man, aghast and in dismay. 'You're going? Why? Why only you? You were the only one here . . .' 'I'll tell you: the Sergeant-Major didn't like my face.' Shaken, both are silent. Berg goes to the door. 'Good-bye, comrade!' 'Good-bye, comrade!'

NOTES

1. In the outline of the letter he also wrote: '. . . in the morning I have a great longing for coffee, and for some alcohol after food, to refresh the heart a little. In the end, a storm will come.'

2. With an eye to the censor.

3. The beginning of August saw the three heavy air attacks on Hamburg, after which Goebbels intensified his great evacuation plan, moving families and offices from Berlin.

4. 'And across the surging ocean that has conspired against me, not one note of your song is lost to me, although it is muffled.'

5. Pätzig.

6. Hope that a date for the trial will be fixed soon.

7. Prof. Harteck, a physicist. He is mentioned in the German edition of the Bonhoeffer biography, p. 71, but not in the English translation.

8. In Sakrow, near Potsdam.

9. City commandant of Berlin; his mother's cousin.

10. Lawyer and friend of Klaus Bonhoeffer.

11. The Reich War Court was partly transferred to Torgau.

12. Susanne Dress.

13. Eberhard Bethge.

14. Waiting in vain for news of the date of his trial. Dr Roeder went on long leave and was then transferred.

15. Published in German in *Gesammelte Schriften* II, pp. 478ff.

16. The outline reads: 'The death of the three young pastors affects me very much. All three were specially esteemed among the young theologians; many hundred young pastors will grieve deeply over Klapproth, who combined unusual spiritual gifts with a firm leadership of men. Winfried Krause was with us only a few months ago; I liked his straightforward manner very much. I would be glad if his wife could be told in some way that I cannot write to her now. Also Grosch's father; he was my schoolteacher. These three were among the closest of my pupils. It is a great loss to me and to the church.'

17. H. Chr. von Hase, at that time an army chaplain, son of Bonhoeffer's mother's brother, Superintendent Hans von Hase in Frankfurt/Oder.

18. General Paul von Hase, see p. 92.

19. Lev. 26.6.

20. Because of the expected date of the trial.

21. The family's summer house in the Harz mountains.

22. His father added a note: 'arrived 1 October.'

23. Added in the margin: 'Would you please order for me there a book that's just appeared, *Das Zeitalter des Marius und Sulla*, Diederich Verlag (16 RM).'

24. The home of Walter and Susanne Dress was, as mentioned in his mother's letter of 9 September, damaged by bombs.

25. Berlin families evacuated to Pätzig.

26. The next estate to Pätzig.

27. The lawyer Dr Otto John.

28. Eberhard Bethge's home village.

29. This letter was partly dictated by Eberhard Bethge as it seemed advisable not to let correspondence of any kind between him and Dietrich Bonhoeffer go through the hands of the censor. Even Renate Bethge was to appear as rarely as possible. The illegal correspondence between the two only began at the end of November, when Dr Roeder's term of office expired.

30. In the Burchhardthaus in Dahlem, destroyed by a direct hit.

31. Onnasch, formerly inspector of studies in the preachers' seminary at Finkenwalde.

32. The Russian counter-offensive, the overthrow of Badoglio in Italy, the air-attacks on Hamburg and the evacuation of Berlin.

33. Friedrichsbrunn.

34. In the meantime Eberhard Bethge had been released from his exempt status by the *Abwehr* and had been called up for military training.

35. Cf. the letter from Christoph von Dohnanyi, 7 September 1943.

36. A joiner and opponent of the Nazis; occasionally went to the Bonhoeffer's house to help.

37. On the envelope (for his lawyer, Dr Wergin): 'In case of my death to be handed to my next of kin.'

38. Onnasch.

39. Dress.

40. In view of a date for his trial, which he still confidently expected.

41. 'And however crazy, or Christian, or unchristian things may be outside, this world, this beautiful world is quite indestructible.'

42. His fiancée's brother, who fell on the Eastern front in 1942.

43. Household help.

44. Hans-Christoph von Hase.

45. Ruth-Alice von Bismarck, wife of Klaus von Bismarck.

46. Help in the Schleicher house.

47. German proverb: 'Good work takes time.'

48. So-called 'bombing leave' because of the damage done to the Burckhardthaus in August.

49. Christine Schleicher.

50. The following correspondence between Bonhoeffer and Bethge was all smuggled. The exchange of letters began during the first leave from the army that Bethge was able to spend in Berlin.

51. During the transition from the intelligence branch (following his exempt status with the *Abwehr*) to normal military service.

52. 'For what credit is it, if when you do wrong and are beaten for it you take it patiently? But if when you do right and suffer for it you take it patiently, you have God's approval.' 'But even if you do suffer for righteousness' sake, you will be blessed. Have no fear of them, nor be troubled.'

53. Unfortunately lost.

54. Part of it is printed, in German, in *Gesammelte Schriften* III, pp. 478–512.

55. Printed in *Ethics*, pp. 326ff. (Fontana ed., pp. 363ff.).

56. See pp. 139ff.

57. For further military training Bethge was posted to Lissa (Poland).

58. 'Thereupon I awoke and looked, and my sleep was pleasant to me.'

59. The 'men of the inner line' were churchmen who disliked Hitler's anti-Christian dictatorship but who, under pressure, abandoned their opposition to it.

60. A pastor from Brandenburg, who belonged to the Finkenwalde group.

61. Pastors from Saxony, the latter from the Finkenwalde seminary.

62. The former was a Nazi daily paper, the latter a Nazi weekly.

63. In Switzerland in the summer of 1943 (to justify his exemption for the *Abwehr*).

64. Sonata for flute and piano by J. S. Bach.

65. A hint that the relationship between Bonhoeffer and Bethge had been kept out of the interrogations. If necessary, 'licenciate studies' were to have been given as the reason for Bethge's exempt status during the first months of the war, had the interrogation moved in this direction.

66. Lost; presumably they were hymn verses.

67. Being smuggled, it had to be completely concealed or destroyed.

68. The letters of 18–23 November 1943 were smuggled out as one letter.

69. End of March 1943.

70. Hymn-book for Protestant youth.

71. Bethge had let Bonhoeffer know that the Confessing Synod in Breslau had prayed for him by name at its service on 17 November 1943.

72. At this time there began the massed night attacks with saturation bombing of Berlin suburbs – surprisingly, for the people, not on moon-lit nights, but at new moon and in bad weather.

73. Captain Maetz would be generous in supervising the visit.

74. On the envelope: 'For Eberhard Bethge personally'.

75. His parents, Maria von Wedemeyer and Eberhard Bethge.

76. A present from Karl Barth, whom Bethge had been able to visit and inform on a visit to Switzerland in summer 1943 under the auspices of the *Abwehr*.

77. Visser 't Hooft.

78. Fritz Onnasch, imprisoned in Stettin for some weeks in winter 1937–38.

79. Locomotive works in Tegel.

80. Klaus von Dohnanyi.

81. Dr Roeder.

82. Christine von Dohnanyi, who was visiting her husband in prison (Lehrter Strasse).

83. Rev. 10.9f.

84. Soldiers who had been given political screening for service in military units of the *Abwehr*.

85. Dr Roeder.

86. Prof. J. Zutt, at that time Director of a private psychological and neurological clinic in the West End.

87. See p. 130

88. Dr Roeder.

89. Leibholz in Oxford.

90. G. K. A. Bell, Bishop of Chichester; addresses in case of being taken prisoner by the English.

91. *Abwehr*.

92. Code word for listening to English news bulletins.

93. Karl Barth.

94. Monsignor Johannes Schönhöffer in the Vatican.

95. Bonhoeffer had learnt that Bethge had been given further leave before leaving for active service.

96. *Church Dogmatics*, II, 1 and 2, sent from Switzerland without title and cover, as they were banned in Germany.

97. A holiday trip to Rome made by Bonhoeffer and Bethge following the ecumenical conference in Chamby.

98. Dr Cesare Gay (former member of the Youth Commission of the World Alliance) or Prof. Ernesto Comba.

99. Superintendent in Berlin, president of the German group of the World Alliance concerned with co-operation between churches.

100. 'There is a friend who sticks closer than a brother.'

101. Because of the outward appearance of Bonhoeffer's case, family and friends were working together to ensure that Bonhoeffer's trial, if it materialized at all, would be held only in conjunction with that of von Dohnanyi, because of fears that the case might not be limited to the relatively harmless details of the charge.

102. 'Yea, by thee I can crush a troop; and by my God I can leap over a wall.'

103. 'With God we shall do valiantly; it is he who will tread down our foes.'

104. Return from America in July 1939.

105. Hans von Dohnanyi was in the Charité with an embolism from 24 November 1943 to 22 January 1944 and was treated there by Prof. Sauerbruch (DB, pp. 711f.).

106. The Dohnanyis' house in Sakrow.

107. Daily texts, published yearly since 1731.

108. 'And when the shepherds saw it, they made known the saying which had been told them concerning this child.'

109. A. von Weymarn, working in the World Council in Geneva.

110. From Paul Gerhardt's hymn, 'Nun lasst uns gehn und treten.'

111. Garrison in Poland.

112. Hans Lokies, at that time Director of the Gossner mission and a member of the Berlin Council of Brethren.

113. The second part of the letter is lost.

114. In Munich.

115. Christine, Countess Kalckreuth, who had allowed Bonhoeffer to use her house as an accommodation address for reporting to the police in Munich; see DB, pp. 589, 604.

116. For the attempted overthrow in March 1943, see DB, pp. 684ff.

117. The Munich hotel which Bonhoeffer used most frequently to stay in while travelling through during his time at Ettal.

118. Rignano, below Monte Soratte on the Via Flaminia. A reminiscence of the trip to Rome in 1936 after the ecumenical conference at Chamby.

119. Rüdiger Schleicher.

120. Karl-Friedrich Bonhoeffer on 13 January, Rüdiger Schleicher on 14 January.

121. Lost.

122. Dr Wergin, the defence lawyer.

123. 'And I will lead the blind in a way that they know not, in paths that they have not known I will guide them.'

124. The Allies had established a bridgehead from the sea at Nettuno and Anzio, south of Rome.

125. In case of being taken prisoner of war in the West.

126. In charge of the German congregation of St Paul in London in 1939.

127. On the tour of the Finkenwalde Preachers' Seminary to Sweden in March 1936.

128. Niemöller.

129. Meaning the Jewish problem.

130. Wolf-Dieter Zimmermann, formerly a member of the seminary at Finkenwalde.

131. Christine von Dohnanyi, whose husband had just been transferred again from the Charité to prison (22 January 1944); see DB, p. 712.

132. In the Dohnanyis' house in Sakrow.

133. A South German S-shaped Christmas biscuit.

134. Two air attacks on the Borsig factory, immediately next to the prison.

135. According to notes in Bonhoeffer's book of readings, a Herr Engel.

136. A type of novel which depicts an actual situation, but in which all the characters are disguised.

137. It never came, and is lost.

138. 'O thou who hearest prayer! To thee shall all flesh come' (Ps. 65.2): 'The prayer of a righteous man has great power in its effects' (James 5.16).

139. Dr Hans Schönfeld in Geneva.

140. William Paton in London.

141. Visit by Bethge.

142. The Leibholz family had emigrated from there to England in 1938.

143. At the Finkenwalde seminary.

144. Martin Luther's first complete translation of the Bible.

145. 'Ich danke Gott und freue mich' ('I thank God and rejoice').

146. A beautiful little rosewood cupboard, which came from Minna Herzlieb, through the von Hases, to the Bonhoeffers (see p. 197).

147. 'The Lord will judge the ends of the earth; he will give strength to his king' (I Sam. 2.10). 'Humble yourselves therefore under the mighty hand of God, that in due time he may exalt you' (I Peter 5.6).

148. Again hopes for a date for the trial.

149. Martin Niemöller in Dachau concentration camp.

150. Military bishop.

151. Monte Soratte, within whose slopes Kesselring's headquarters lay.

152. To Monsignore Leiber and Schönhöffer in the *Propaganda Fide*, who had been let in on the conspiracy.

153. Velletri, in front of the allied bridgehead at Anzio-Nettuno, south of Castel Gandolfo.

154. Hans von Dohnanyi.

155. Bach's uncompleted *Art of Fugue* was handed down with this chorale as a conclusion.

156. J. Rainalter.

157. Artillery duel at Anzio-Nettuno.

158. A reference to National Socialist convictions and caution because of the conspiracy.

159. Via Appia (1936).

160. From Velletri, south of Rome, to Rignano.

161. The expected trial.

162. According to notes in the book of readings, 8–10 February.

163. His cousin. H. Chr. von Hase, at the time divisional pastor, and Maria Czeppan, née Horn, for a long time nanny in the Bonhoeffer house.

164. Censorship by the Reich War Court, which had been transferred to Torgau.

165. Alerts were expected less on full moon nights because of strengthened defence by night-fighters.

166. Dr Josef Müller's trial was taken separately and ended with an acquittal, but not a release, which Dietrich Bonhoeffer did not know at this time. See DB, p. 713.

167. Bonhoeffer noted the first daylight raid on Berlin in his book of readings on 6 March 1944.

168. Meaning, not doing or saying anything that might be politically dangerous, above all in connection with the illegal correspondence; probably something of the sort had been discovered in Tegel.

169. The defence lawyer, Dr Wergin.

170. 'I was in prison and you visited me.'

171. In the 'house of brethren' at the Finkenwalde seminary.

172. 'For God has made me fruitful in the land of my affliction', 17 March 1944.

173. A slip of the pen; it should be March.

174. Probably refers to the warning of 9 March, see p. 232, n. 168 above.

175. 'Give me somewhere to stand, and I will move the earth' (Archimedes).

176. I.e. National Socialist.

177. Dr Josef Müller, after his supposed release following his acquittal.

178. This is a reference to the weekly paper created by Goebbels, named *Das Reich*, which was especially directed at the intellectuals.

179. The Via Flaminia.

180. A slip of the pen; it should be 44.

181. Ruth von Wedemeyer, née von Kleist-Retzow, his fiancée's mother.

182. 'Into thy hand I commit my spirit; thou hast redeemed me, O Lord, faithful God' (Ps. 31.6). 'My desire is to depart and be with Christ, for that is far better' (Phil. 1.23).

183. Both killed on the Eastern front in 1942.

184. The City Commandant of Berlin, who was also responsible for the military prisons, Paul von Hase, a cousin of his mother, had asked after him.

185. The prohibition was constantly evaded, partly by bribery and partly thanks to the friendliness of individual guards.

III

Holding Out until the Overthrow

April to July 1944

Dear Eberhard,
I really intended to write to you at Easter, but I had so many well-
meaning visitors that I had less peace and quiet than I should have
liked. I didn't even manage to get a letter to Maria finished. I've
got so used to the silence of solitude by now that after a short time
I long for it again. I can't imagine myself spending the day as I
used to, or even as you have to spend it now. You know that even
earlier I couldn't take family festivals very well; I hope that this
tendency hasn't grown too much now. I would certainly like to
have a good talk with someone, but aimless gossip gets on my
nerves terribly. The same is true of the usual music on the wireless; I just don't feel that it's music at all, but a quite empty racket.
There's surely a danger in all this. Nevertheless, I expect that you
often feel the same way. Feelings of quality just cannot be killed,
but grow stronger from year to year.

How did you spend Easter? Were you in Rome? How did you
get over your homesickness? I should imagine that that is more
difficult in your position than in mine, for it cannot be done
merely through diversion and distraction. You need to get right
down to fundamentals, to come to terms with life, and for that
you need plenty of time to yourself. I find these first warm days of
spring rather trying, and I expect you do too. When nature is
rediscovering herself, and the actual communities in which we
live remain in unresolved tension, we feel the discord particularly keenly. Or it may be really nothing but homesickness, which
it's good for us to feel keenly. At any rate, I must say that I myself
have lived for many, many years quite absorbed in aims and tasks
and hopes without any personal longings; and perhaps that has
made me old before my time. It has made everything too 'matter-
of-fact'. Almost everyone has aims and tasks, and everything is
objectified, reified to such a tremendous extent – how many
people today allow themselves any strong personal feeling and real
yearning, or take the trouble to spend their strength freely in
working out and carrying out that yearning, and letting it bear
fruit? Those sentimental radio hits, with their artificial naïveté

and empty crudities, are the pitiful remains and the maximum that people will tolerate by way of mental effort; it's a ghastly desolation and impoverishment. By contrast, we can be very glad when something affects us deeply, and regard the accompanying pains as an enrichment. High tensions produce big sparks (isn't that a physical fact? If it isn't, then translate it into the right kind of language). I've long had a special affection for the season between Easter and Ascension Day. Here's another great tension. How can people stand earthly tensions if they know nothing of the tension between heaven and earth? Have you by chance a copy of *Das Neue Lied* with you? I well remember learning the Ascension hymns with you, among them the one that I'm fondest of today: 'On this day we remember . . .' Just about now, by the way, we are beginning the tenth year of our friendship; that's a fairly large slice of one's life, and in the past year we've shared things together almost as closely as in the previous years of our *vita communis*.

23 April is Maria's birthday. She will have to celebrate it alone again, and I have the impression that the two of us – I mean you and I – will only get back home at the same time.[1] I've been told that I had better not, for the time being, expect any change in my present position – and that is after they've been giving me fresh promises every fortnight. I don't think that is either right or clever, and I have my own ideas about it; I should very much like to tell them to you, but as I can't have my own way, I must just make the best of it, and go on hoping for Whitsuntide.

I heard someone say yesterday that the last years had been completely wasted as far as he was concerned. I'm very glad that I have never yet had that feeling, even for a moment. Nor have I ever regretted my decision in the summer of 1939,[2] for I'm firmly convinced – however strange it may seem – that my life has followed a straight and unbroken course, at any rate in its outward conduct. It has been an uninterrupted enrichment of experience, for which I can only be thankful. If I were to end my life here in these conditions, that would have a meaning that I think I could understand; on the other hand, everything might be a thorough preparation for a new start and a new task when peace comes.

A letter has just come from Rüdiger. I see from it that you too are not exactly leading a base-camp existence. I would very much like to know more about your day-to-day life. Is the billeting really tolerable? But you're to some degree used to that from boarding-school. With great delight I've seen the pictures of the seventy-fifth birthday party again, with you among the grandchildren; my parents brought them along recently . . . I'm very pleased that they were so happy at Pätzig. Maria's mother seems to have looked after them quite touchingly, and even father spoke very warmly about the stay . . . Now I'm going to close for today; I must do another graphological analysis; that is the way in which I now spend the hours in which I cannot work properly. This letter is somewhat disjointed, as it was written with constant interruptions. Nevertheless, I expect that you will find it better than nothing. I often think of you each day and commend you to God. With all my heart,   your Dietrich

From Ursula Schleicher   [Klein-Krössin] 18 April 1944

Dear Dietrich,

A week ago . . . I came to aunt Ruth's with Dorothee to get some rest . . . We're very spoilt here; Dorothee is delighted at last to have enough to eat. She has to keep working . . . She's hoping to leave school in the autumn; I'm less sure, as she will only be sixteen in May. Christine is now to begin confirmation classes . . . We shall probably send her to Potsdam for instruc-tion. Hans-Walter is not yet on active service, but will be trained for another three to six months as a long-range wireless operator. He is near Leipzig, so we shall certainly be able to visit him there sometime. He was very disappointed to be refused permission to visit when Klaus Dohnanyi is a nephew and was allowed to see you; *he* was expecting to go on active service. The letter that you wrote him[3] when he was called up has often been a help to him; he would very much have liked to speak to you, and perhaps that will happen one day. All is well with little Dietrich; he's growing and is soon to have a photograph taken. You will also be getting a copy. The pictures that we've taken have been rather bad, but Eberhard thinks that he can detect a hundred similarities, although one can see more cot than baby.

I hope that I will soon be granted permission to visit, so that we shall be able to see each other again at last. Rüdiger has already applied twice for me.

Meanwhile, good-bye. All the very, very best from the bottom of my heart. Your Ursula

Love from everyone here.

From Eberhard Bethge [Rignano] 21 April 1944

Dear Dietrich,
As we were not able to see each other at Easter, but will have to put off our hope to the next festival, you've sent me greetings again and I'm gladly advised by you of the new dates for the important work. I spent Easter very quietly here with letters from Renate and beautiful flowers; I did some walking and read some Burckhardt (*Culture of the Renaissance*). Do you know Cardano's[4] autobiography from that period? That must be a rather special instance of objective self-consideration; he's a doctor. Does your father have it? The spring is already very beautiful, above all in valleys with streams running through; I hardly ever get into other areas now. But we like even the bad weather, as then there is general quietness in the air.

I must now also think of what will happen with Klaus' and Christoph's confirmation. How difficult these things have become. It's Maria's birthday the day after tomorrow; I've written to her. I wonder whether she will be able to come to see you? Instead of festivals like that we had promotions yesterday, and then celebrated 20 April by drinking the Führer's good health in a glass of wine. The conversation was very turgid . . . It's a pity that now there is hardly any possibility of Renate visiting you. . . .

I've never had anything to do with graphology and have always been suspicious of it, perhaps from anxiety at not being able to consider it with sufficient detachment . . . The report of that death[5] was new to me. I'm very sorry. I too had sent greetings a while ago. Will I probably get them back again?

I'm struck by the way in which the Catholics among the comrades here see religion as consisting entirely in laws and commands. This is very deeply rooted in them, in spite of all the overlay. That's where they get the standards by which they judge. By the way, Whit Sunday plays a great part in their consciousness; some sent greetings and garlands of roses home or to godparents. I hope all goes well with you. Don't lose courage about the final date.

Faithfully, your Eberhard

To Eberhard Bethge [Tegel] 22 April 1944

Dear Eberhard,
I've just heard through my parents again about how things are going with you; I would always like to know much more, but it's a great comfort even to know that you are well. Father was very pleased with your letter, and so was Maria with the one of 5 April. Many thanks, it was a *very* good, friendly thought on your part.

When you say that my time here will be very important for my practical work, and that you're very much looking forward to what I shall have to tell you later, and to what I've written, you mustn't indulge in any illusions about me. I've certainly learnt a great deal, but I don't think I have changed very much. There are people who change, and others who can hardly change at all. I don't think I've ever changed very much, except perhaps at the time of my first impressions abroad and under the first conscious influence of father's personality. It was then that I turned from phraseology to reality. I don't think, in fact, that you yourself have changed much. Self-development is, of course, a different matter. Neither of us has really had a break in our lives. Of course, we have deliberately broken with a good deal, but that again is something quite different. Even our present experiences probably don't represent a break in the passive sense. I sometimes used to long for something of the kind, but today I think differently about it. Continuity with one's own past is a great gift, too. Paul wrote II Tim. 1.3a as well as I Tim. 1.13.[6] I'm often surprised how little (in contrast to nearly all the others here) I grub among my past mistakes and think how different one thing or another would be today if I had acted differently in the past; it doesn't worry me at all. Everything seems to have taken its natural course, and to be determined necessarily and straightforwardly by a higher providence. Do you feel the same?

I've often wondered lately why we grow insensitive to hardships in the course of time. When I think how I felt for weeks a year ago, it strikes me very much. I now see the same things quite differently. To put it down to nature's self-protection doesn't seem to me adequate; I'm more inclined to think that it may come from a clearer and more sober estimate of our own limitations and possibilities, which makes it possible for us genuinely to love our neighbour; as long as we let our imagination run riot, love of one's neighbour remains something vague and abstract. Today I can take a calmer view of other people, their predicaments and needs, and so I'm better able to help them. I would speak of clarification rather than of insensitiveness; but of course, we are always having to try to change one into the other. I don't think we need reproach ourselves just because our feelings grow cooler and calmer in the course of time, though, of course, we must always be alive to the danger of not seeing the wood for the trees and keep a warm heart as well as a cool head. Will these thoughts be of any use to you?

I wonder why it is that we find some days so much more oppressive than others, for no apparent reason. Is it growing pains – or spiritual trial? Once they're over, the world looks quite a different place again.

The other day I heard the angel scene from *Palestrina* on the wireless, and thought of Munich. Even then, that was the only part that I specially liked. There is a great *Palestrina* fan here who cannot understand why I didn't specially care for it, and he was quite thrilled when I enjoyed the angel scene . . .

After a rather long unproductive period, I feel in better form for work now that spring is coming. I'll tell you something about it next time. Meanwhile keep well and in good spirits. I hope that in spite of everything we shall soon have the joy of meeting again. With all my heart.　　　　　　　　　　Your faithful Dietrich

To his parents　　　　　　　　　　　　　　[Tegel] 26 April 1944

Dear parents,
As it will presumably be a while after your last visit until I can talk to you, I would like to let you have at least a letter so that you know that things are well with me. This is my second spring in prison, but it's very different from last year's. Then all my impressions were fresh and vivid, and privations and pleasures were felt more keenly. Since then something has happened which I should never have thought possible – I've got used to things; and the only question is which has been greater, the growth of insensitivity or the clarification of experience – it probably varies in different connections. The things towards which we become insensitive are soon forgotten, as they're of no great consequence; but there are other things, which we have consciously or unconsciously assimilated and cannot forget. Intense experience forges them into convictions, resolutions, and plans, and as such they're important for our lives in the future. It certainly makes a great difference whether one is in prison for a month or a year; in the latter case one absorbs not only an interesting or intense impression, but a radically new kind of life. At the same time I think that certain inward preconditions are necessary to enable one to assimilate this particular aspect of life without danger, and I think a long imprisonment is extremely dangerous for very young people as far as their spiritual development is concerned. The impressions come with such violence that they may well sweep a great deal overboard.

I must thank you very much for the way you're continually making things easier for me by your regular visits, letters, and parcels. The great joy that your greetings give me has remained constant from the first, and always encourages me afresh to use my time here to the full. Thank you, too, for all the letters from the family – I had very nice letters again from Ursel and Karl-Friedrich. I wonder whether you could try to get me Ortega y Gasset's new book, *The Nature of Historical Crises* (Deutsche Verlagsanstalt Stuttgart–Berlin) and, if possible, his earlier work, *History as a System*; also H. Pfeffer, *The British Empire and the USA* (1944, Dünnhauptverlag)? Perhaps Ursel might look after something from me for Dorothee's birthday, if that's possible. It's the last birthday before her *abitur*, and I'm sure that there are books that she wants.

I hope that you will soon decide to go into the country again for a while; I would be very pleased about that.

I hope we shall see each other again soon. With much love,
your grateful Dietrich

To Eberhard Bethge   [Tegel] 30 April 1944

Dear Eberhard,

Another month gone. Does time fly as fast with you as it does with me here? I'm often surprised at it myself – and when will the month come when you and Renate, I and Maria, and we two can meet again? I have such a strong feeling that great events are moving the world every day and could change all our personal relationships, that I should like to write to you much oftener, partly because I don't know how much longer I shall be able to, and even more because we want to share everything with each other as often and as long as we can. I'm firmly convinced that, by the time you get this letter, great decisions will already be setting things moving on all fronts. During the coming weeks we shall have to keep a stout heart, and that is what I wish you. We shall have to keep all our wits about us, so as to let nothing scare us. In view of what is coming, I'm almost inclined to quote the biblical δεῖ, and I feel that I 'long to look', like the angels in I Peter 1.12,[7] to see how God is going to solve the apparently insoluble. I think God is about to accomplish something that, even if we take part in it either outwardly or inwardly, we can only receive with the greatest wonder and awe. Somehow it will be clear – for those who have eyes to see – that Ps. 58.11b and Ps. 9.19f.[8] are true; and we shall have to repeat Jer. 45.5[9] to ourselves every day. It's harder for you to go through this separated from Renate and your boy than it is for me, so I will think of you especially, as I am already doing now.

How good it would seem to me, for both of us, if we could go through this time together, helping each other. But it's probably 'better' for it not to be so, but for each of us to have to go through it alone. I find it hard not to be able to help you in anything – except by thinking of you every morning and evening when I read the Bible, and often during the day as well. You've no need to worry about me at all, as I'm getting on uncommonly well – you would be surprised, if you came to see me. People here keep on telling me (as you can see, I feel very flattered by it) that I'm 'radiating so much peace around me', and that I'm 'always so cheerful', – so that the feelings that I sometimes have to the contrary must, I suppose, rest on an illusion (not that I really believe that at all!). You would be surprised, and perhaps even worried, by my theological thoughts and the conclusions that they lead to; and this is where I miss you most of all, because I don't know anyone else with whom I could so well discuss them to have my thinking clarified. What is bothering me incessantly is the question what Christianity really is, or indeed who Christ really is, for us today. The time when people could be told everything by means of words, whether theological or pious, is over, and so is the time of inwardness and conscience – and that means the time of religion in general. We are moving towards a completely religionless time; people as they are now simply cannot be religious any more. Even those who honestly describe themselves as 'religious' do not in the least act up to it, and so they presumably mean something quite different by 'religious'.

Our whole nineteen-hundred-year-old Christian preaching and theology rest on the 'religious *a priori*' of mankind. 'Christianity' has always been a form – perhaps the true form – of 'religion'. But if one day it becomes clear that this *a priori* does not exist at all, but was a historically conditioned and transient form of human self-expression, and if therefore man becomes radically religionless – and I think that that is already more or less the case (else how is it, for example, that this war, in contrast to all previous ones, is not calling forth any 'religious' reaction?) – what does that mean for 'Christianity'? It means that the foundation is taken away from the whole of what has up to now been our 'Christianity', and that there remain only a few 'last survivors of the age of chivalry', or a few intellectually dishonest people, on whom we can descend as 'religious'. Are they to be the chosen few? Is it on this dubious group of people that we are to pounce in fervour, pique, or indignation, in order to sell them our goods? Are we to fall upon a few unfortunate people in their hour of need and exercise a sort of religious compulsion on them? If we don't want to do all that, if our final judgment must be that the western form of Christianity, too, was only a preliminary stage to a complete absence of religion, what kind of situation emerges for us, for the church? How can Christ become the Lord of the religionless as well? Are there religionless Christians? If religion is only a garment of Christianity – and even this garment has looked very different at different times – then what is a religionless Christianity?

Barth, who is the only one to have started along this line of thought, did not carry it to completion, but arrived at a positivism of revelation, which in the last analysis is essentially a restoration. For the religionless working man (or any other man) nothing decisive is gained here. The questions to be answered would surely be: What do a church, a community, a sermon, a liturgy, a Christian life mean in a religionless world? How do we speak of God – without religion, i.e. without the temporally conditioned presuppositions of metaphysics, inwardness, and so on? How do we speak (or perhaps we cannot now even 'speak' as we used to) in a 'secular' way about 'God'? In what way are we 'religionless-secular' Christians, in what way are we the ἐκ-κλησία, those who are called forth, not regarding ourselves from a religious point of view as specially favoured, but rather as belonging wholly to the world? In that case Christ is no longer an object of religion, but something quite different, really the Lord of the world. But what does that mean? What is the place of worship and prayer in a religionless situation? Does the secret discipline, or alternatively the difference (which I have suggested to you before) between penultimate and ultimate, take on a new importance here?

I must break off for today, so that the letter can go straight away. I'll write to you again about it in two days' time. I hope you see more or less what I mean, and that it doesn't bore you. Goodbye for the present. It's not easy always to write without an echo, and you must excuse me if that makes it something of a monologue.

I'm thinking of you very much. Your Dietrich

I'm not really reproaching you for not writing. You have too much else to do.

I find, after all, that I can write a little more. – The Pauline question whether περιτομή [circumcision] is a condition of justification seems to me in present-day terms to be whether religion is a condition of salvation. Freedom from περιτομή is also freedom from religion. I often ask myself why a 'Christian instinct' often draws me more to the religionless people than to the religious, by which I don't in the least mean with any evangelizing intention, but, I might almost say, 'in brotherhood'. While I'm often reluctant to mention God by name to religious people – because that name somehow seems to me here not to ring true, and I feel myself to be slightly dishonest (it's particularly bad when others start to talk in religious jargon; I then dry up almost completely and feel awkward and uncomfortable) – to people with no religion I can on occasion mention him by name quite calmly and as a matter of course. Religious people speak of God when human knowledge (perhaps simply because they are too lazy to think) has come to an end, or when human resources fail – in fact it is always the *deus ex machina* that they bring on to the scene, either for the apparent solution of insoluble problems, or as strength in human failure – always, that is to say, exploiting human weakness or human boundaries. Of necessity, that can go on only till people can by their own strength push these boundaries somewhat further out, so that God becomes superfluous as a *deus ex machina*. I've come to be doubtful of talking about any human boundaries (is even death, which people now hardly fear, and is sin, which they now hardly understand, still a genuine boundary today?). It always seems to me that we are trying anxiously in this way to reserve some space for God; I should like to speak of God not on the boundaries but at the centre, not in weaknesses but in strength; and therefore not in death and guilt but in man's life and goodness. As to the boundaries, it seems to me better to be silent and leave the insoluble unsolved. Belief in the resurrection is *not* the 'solution' of the problem of death. God's 'beyond' is not the beyond of our cognitive faculties. The transcendence of epistemological theory has nothing to do with the transcendence of God. God is beyond in the midst of our life. The church stands, not at the boundaries where human powers give out, but in the middle of the village. That is how it is in the Old Testament, and in this sense we still read the New Testament far too little in the light of the Old. How this religionless Christianity looks, what form it takes, is something that I'm thinking about a great deal, and I shall be writing to you again about it soon. It may be that on us in particular, midway between East and West, there will fall a heavy responsibility.

Now I really must stop. It would be fine to have a word from you about all this; it would mean a great deal to me – probably more than you can imagine. Some time, just read Prov. 22.11, 12;[10] there is something that will bar the way to any escapism disguised as piety.

All the very best.   Your Dietrich

Dear Dietrich,

I got your letter of 11 April a few days ago. Many thanks for it . . . In the meantime I've been given the electrifying hope that I may be able to bring you this greeting myself in a couple of days. That is, if nothing gets in the way. That would be quite terrible, as I've already been feeding my hopes at home. But surely it will come off. In that case are we really to have the baptism without you? It won't be very good if it has to come to that. I hope that at least I shall get to see you. How much I would like to discuss the question of army chaplaincies with you; it's been going through my head for a few days. I have the six-month 'trial period' almost immediately after my leave. I simply can't imagine it, and perhaps the question will not in fact arise. But I would like to be more oriented about it. I'll discuss it with Justus.[11]

Many thanks for your long letter. Where do you get the marvellously good notepaper from? Renate and I are sometimes worried at being so brief . . . Do you get the chance, then, to listen to the radio all day? . . .

Can you tell me anything about the fact that all my feeling and thinking is now really concentrated on personal experience, and that excitement over church affairs, love for its cause, has been caught up in a degree of stagnation? My conscious missionary impulse, which in earlier years was there perhaps more or less naïvely, has given way to the attempt to understand things, people and circumstances and to grasp them in a 'human' way. A few days ago the lawyer here asked me whether I would like to take my Bible with me on a walk and read him something aloud, gospel and epistle or something else good. And we did that. But I can't record it as anything special or report it with special hopes and exclamations. It was 'very nice'; but matter of fact. By the way, how difficult some circumstances and attitudes are to explain at the time! . . .

When will we get home? Our Major has a fabulous attitude. Recently Spiess, he, Rainalter (the lawyer) and I sat drinking wine in the office until two in the morning. Towards midnight he talked about the end of the war. He said it could only be positive, otherwise we wouldn't experience what went on later. We would concentrate somewhere, 'dig in', hold out to the last man and fall. 'Isn't that so, Rainalter and Bethge?' That is really soldierly and honourable to the last degree! I think that I shall now be home at Whitsun. You were asking about my billet. We even have a bath which we heat up now and then; it's a great amenity. We sleep in camp beds with mattresses and blankets. Of course there aren't any sheets. It's all very tolerable.

I would really be very excited about the life of an army chaplain? What is one to say?

Monday evening – 8 May

I got your letter of 30 April today. It came very quickly. I'm delighted about the things which, I must say, excite me very much. Some of it is echoed in the questions that I've written above, though they're put more naïvely and primitively.

I'm rather disturbed that you seem to hear from me so rarely. I can't say more exactly just when I wrote, except that I've answered each of your letters more or less in length. Renate's exact words to me (about handing on letters) were: 'But I'm always a bit worried, first of all about the grandparents, and if I've happily given them letters, I'm afraid that they don't pass them on . . .'

These last days before my departure get on my nerves intolerably. First of all there's the anxiety that the great events will put some hindrance in the way, and secondly there are the day and night attacks on the roads by bombers and low-flying planes which have now grown colossally. They rob me of all composure.

What do you think of the Ascension Day reading as a text for the baptism? I found the picture particularly attractive. Maria has written me another very nice letter. At the moment I've no time to answer it properly. I hope I can talk to you.

Faithfully, and with great gratitude.   Your Eberhard

Dear Eberhard,

I keep hoping that you will already be on leave – you must be about due for it by now so that you can see your son – and that my letter will be sent on to you (and so be out of date). However, everything is so uncertain nowadays – and long experience suggests that everything is more likely to remain as it is than to change soon – that I'll write to you all the same. I learnt from Christel, who visited me yesterday, that things are going relatively well with you, and that you can at least delight Renate with a letter. It's really worth a great deal that Renate can be in Sakrow all the time and that you are at least spared worry for her with the alerts here. I would very much like to talk to Renate myself one day, but it doesn't seem possible to arrange that at the moment. I'm only glad that at least we were able to see each other in December. That was a good piece of work by your father-in-law . . . I so much wish that you could come soon, though it will be sad that presumably we shall still not be able to see each other. I'm getting along quite well and so is the case, but the question of the date is still quite open. But all good things come over night, and I'm waiting and hoping confidently. In my earlier letter there was an address[12] that you can use if you want; but it isn't necessary; I simply wanted to let you know.

A few more words about 'religionlessness'. I expect you remember Bultmann's essay on the 'demythologizing' of the New Testament?[13] My view of it today would be, not that he went 'too far', as most people thought, but that he didn't go far enough. It's not only the 'mythological' concepts, such as miracle, ascension, and so on (which are not in principle separable from the concepts of God, faith, etc.), but 'religious' concepts generally, which are problematic. You can't, as Bultmann supposes, separate God and miracle, but you must be able to interpret and proclaim *both* in a 'non-religious' sense. Bultmann's approach is fundamentally still a liberal one (i.e. abridging the gospel), whereas I'm trying to think theologically.

What does it mean to 'interpret in a religious sense'? I think it means to speak on the one hand metaphysically, and on the other hand individualistically. Neither of these is relevant to the biblical message or to the man of today. Hasn't the individualistic question about personal salvation almost completely left us all? Aren't we really under the impression that there are more important things than that question (perhaps not more important than the *matter* itself, but more important than the *question*!)? I know it sounds pretty monstrous to say that. But, fundamentally, isn't this in fact biblical? Does the question about saving one's soul appear in the Old Testament at all? Aren't righteousness and the Kingdom of God on earth the focus of everything, and isn't it true that Rom. 3.24ff. is not an individualistic doctrine of salvation, but the culmination of the view that God alone is righteous? It is not with the beyond that we are concerned, but with this world as created and preserved, subjected to laws, reconciled, and restored. What is above this world is, in the gospel, intended to exist *for* this world; I mean thàt, not in the anthropocentric sense of liberal, mystic pietistic, ethical theology, but in the biblical sense of the creation and of the incarnation, crucifixion, and resurrection of Jesus Christ.

Barth was the first theologian to begin the criticism of religion, and that remains his really great merit; but he put in its place a positivist doctrine of revelation which says, in effect, 'Like it or lump it': virgin birth, Trinity, or anything else; each is an equally significant and necessary part of the whole, which must simply be swallowed as a whole or not at all. That isn't biblical. There are degrees of knowledge and degrees of significance; that means that a secret discipline must be restored whereby the *mysteries* of the Christian faith are protected against profanation. The positivism of revelation makes it too easy for itself, by setting up, as it does in the last analysis, a law of faith, and so mutilates what is – by Christ's incarnation! – a gift for us. In the place of religion there now stands the church – that is in itself biblical – but the world is in some degree made to depend on itself and left to its own devices, and that's the mistake.

I'm thinking about how we can reinterpret in a 'worldly' sense – in the sense of the Old Testament and of John 1.14[14] – the concepts of repentance, faith, justification, rebirth, and sanctification. I shall be writing to you about it again.

Forgive me for writing all this in German script; normally I do this only when my writing is for my own use – and perhaps what I've written was more to clear my own mind than to edify you. I really don't want to trouble you with problems, for you may well have no time to come to grips with them, and they may only bother you; but I can't help sharing my thoughts with you, simply because that is the best way to make them clear to myself. If that doesn't suit you at present, please say so. – Tomorrow is Cantate, and I shall be thinking of you and enjoying very pleasant memories.

My parents were here recently and said how nice and healthy the little boy is . . .

Good-bye. Be patient, as we are, and keep well.

With all my heart – you're daily in my thoughts.

Your Dietrich

To Eberhard Bethge   [Tegel] 6 May 1944

Dear Eberhard,
It was a quite extraordinary delight today that you thought of me so nicely and well on 24 April.[15] I haven't anything special to tell you today except that it's wonderful to catch an echo occasionally. I'm very grateful to you for it.

. . . More about graphology soon, as it interests you. Unfortunately your letter failed to reach me because of the casualty. Did it come back to you, and what was its date? Did you put your own name on the back?

I shall be writing next time about Christians' 'egoism' ('selfless self-love'). I think we agree about it. Too much altruism is oppressive and exacting; 'egoism' can be less selfish and less demanding.

I hope that you always get all my letters, roughly every 1–2 weeks. Enough for today. Good-bye, dear Eberhard. Thank you for everything, and keep well.   Your Dietrich

I've just heard some good morning-music by Reger and Hugo Distler; it was a good beginning for Sunday. The only jarring note was an interruption announcing that 'enemy air squadrons are moving towards . . .' The connection between the two is not immediately obvious.

I thought last night about what mothers-in-law should do. . . I'm sure that they should not try to teach; what right have they to undertake anything of the kind? It is their privilege to have a *grown-up* daughter or son, and they ought to regard that as an enrichment of their family, not as an occasion for criticism. They may find joy in their children, and give them help and advice if they're asked to, but the marriage completely relieves them of any responsibility for upbringing; that is really a privilege. I believe that when a mother-in-law sees that her child is really loved . . . she should just be glad of it and let everything else take a back seat, especially any attempts to alter character! There are few people who know how to value reticence. I think mother and father can. The siren is just going; more later.

Well, it was pretty heavy again, and I'm always glad to know that Renate is out of Berlin. With regard to reticence, it all depends on *what* we are keeping to ourselves, and on whether there is one person with whom we can share everything . . . I think it would be going too far to speak of the jealousy of mothers-in-law; it would be truer to say that there are two kinds of love, a mother's and a wife's; and that gives rise to a great deal of mis-understanding. Incidentally, it's much easier for sons-in-law than for daughters-in-law to get on peacefully with a mother-in-law – although the Bible gives a unique example to the contrary in Naomi and Ruth . . .

One more thing: the letters to my dead friend[16] should all go back to the sender. Was the sender given? In any case, would you write again to the new address or to home? I would be very sorry to have to miss a letter. I almost assume that the letter returned to you in the meanwhile. I'll also make further inquiries here.

I don't know Cardano. Is he translated into German?

You write so incidentally that the bad weather is welcome because of the fliers; I infer from this that otherwise you usually have unwelcome experiences. In this respect I still can't form any accurate picture of your situation at all. You're pretty taciturn about it, and that also suggests conclusions to be drawn, as of course you don't want to disturb Renate; but you could tell me how things really are.

Just lately I've been in the city again a few times;[17] the result has been quite satisfactory. But as the question of the date is still unresolved, I am really losing interest in my case; I often quite forget it for weeks on end. That's all for now. God keep you and all of us.   Your faithful Dietrich

How's your Italian getting on? And how are the thoughts about Dohrmann?[18]

To Renate and Eberhard Bethge   [Tegel] 9 May 1944

Dear Renate and Eberhard,
Your hope that leave may be near is also a great piece of good news for me. If you really manage to be together again in a few days – though in all these hopes one must always keep the joyful anticipation damped down a bit until the last minute – and if you can also have your child baptized then, I shouldn't like the thought of my absence to cast the least shadow on your happiness and particularly on you personally, Eberhard. I shall try to write you something for the occasion, and you know that I shall be with you in spirit. It's painful to me, to be sure, that the improbable has happened, and that I shall not be able to celebrate the day with you; but I've quite reconciled myself to it. I believe that nothing that happens to me is meaningless, and that it is good for us all that it should be so, even if it runs counter to our own wishes. As I see it, I'm here for some purpose, and I only hope I may fulfil it. In the light of the great purpose all our privations and disappointments are trivial. Nothing would be more unworthy and wrongheaded than to turn one of those rare occasions of joy, such as

you're now experiencing, into a calamity because of my present situation. That would go entirely against the grain, and would undermine my optimism with regard to my case. However thankful we may be for all our personal pleasures, we mustn't for a moment lose sight of the great things that we're living for, and they must shed light rather than gloom on your joy. I couldn't bear to think that your few weeks of happiness, which you've had difficulty enough in getting, should be in the very least clouded by my present circumstances. That would be a real calamity, and the other is not. My only concern is to help you, as far as I can, to keep the lustre of these spring days – I expect you're celebrating your first wedding anniversary together – as radiant as may be. Please don't think for a moment that you're missing something through my not being with you – far from it! And above all, please don't think I'm finding it difficult to get these words out for your sake; on the contrary, they are my most earnest request to you, and its fulfilment would simply make me pleased and happy. If we did manage to meet while you're on leave, I should be only too delighted; but please don't put yourself out over it – I still have vivid memories of 23 December! And please don't lose a single day for the sake of spending a little time with me here. I know you would willingly do so, but it would only distress me. Of course, if your father could arrange for you to visit me, as he did in December, I should be extremely grateful. Anyway, I know we shall be thinking of each other every morning as we read the daily texts, and I'm very glad you'll be able to read the Bible together again morning and evening; it will be a great help to you, not only for these present days, but for the future. Don't let the shortness of your time together and the thought that you must soon part overshadow the happiness of your leave. Don't try to do too much; let other people come and see you, instead of your going round everywhere to them, and enjoy every hour of the day peacefully as a great gift. My own opinion is that the next few weeks will bring such great and surprising events that when you start your leave you won't really know how it's all going to turn out. However much these events may affect our own personal destinies, I do hope they won't rob either of you of the peace and quietness that you need during your time together. It's a good thing that you've the chance of meeting now and deciding on all your plans together. If something edible is sent to you from Silesia in the next few days,[19] please adorn your days with it!

How I should have loved to baptize your little boy; but that's of no great consequence. Above all, I hope the baptism will help to assure you that your own lives, as well as the child's, are in safe keeping, and that you can face the future with confidence. Are you going to choose the text for the baptism yourself? If you're still looking for one, what about II Tim. 2.1, or Prov. 23.26 or 4.18?[20] (I only came across the last of these recently; I think it's beautiful.)

I don't want to bother you with too long a letter just at the beginning of your reunion; all I wanted to do was to send you my good wishes and tell you that I'm sharing your pleasure. Mind you have plenty of good music!

I wish you all imaginable good things with all my heart.

Your Dietrich.

To Eberhard Bethge   [Tegel] 16 May 1944

Dear Eberhard,

I've just heard that you've sent a message saying that you hope to arrive this morning. You can't imagine how glad and relieved I am that you can be here just now.[21] For once I was almost ready to talk about 'providence' and 'an answer to prayer'; and perhaps you feel the same. It would have been very hard for Renate if things had turned out otherwise, and for you, of course, as well. Since I received your letter today – to some extent as a welcome – at the same time as the news of your arrival, I think that it's much better that your superior is now looking after himself for a while without you. I would hardly have been up to the kind of situation that you describe on that wine evening. However, things often seem rather different under the influence of alcohol than in naked reality, and there is a *façon de parler* among these people which often stands in an astonishing contradiction to their actual behaviour. I keep noting this here with a mixture of amusement and embarrassment during the air raids. Still – it's so much better that way.

So today you're seeing your son for the first time . . . I expect that my letter to welcome you has arrived in the meantime. Your letter today once again aroused a strong desire to have a thorough talk with you again, but joy at your being here is so great that all personal wishes completely disappear behind it.

I think it would be right if you discussed the question of an army chaplaincy here at least once, preferably with Dohrmann himself. Mother can easily arrange that . . . I would think that one can proclaim the gospel very freely today and that one will at least find an attentive audience. If it came off, I would write to you very fully and would gladly also send you sermon meditations . . .

I don't think that you really need to have any worry about my running out of notepaper. Quite apart from my stock of rough paper, I have the possibility of getting some more if necessary. Just let me know when it's really short with you. Your letters really mustn't be abbreviated any further. I hope the parcel for Renate will soon come from Upper Silesia. I *don't* want you to bring me any of it; you're to enjoy it together. Now that waiting here has become my only task, I don't need so much, and it is one of my greatest joys to be able to see to a little something for you even from here. Now enjoy the coming days to the full. With all best wishes, from my heart.   Your faithful Dietrich

I'm still writing something for the baptism. What would you think of Ps. 90.14 as a text? I might have suggested Isa. 8.18,[22] but I thought it was rather too general.

To Renate and Eberhard Bethge   [Tegel] 18 May 1944

Dear Renate and Eberhard,
I very much wanted to write you something for the day of the baptism. It's not come out right. I'm sending it just to show you

that I'm thinking very much about you. Thank you once again for choosing me as godfather for your child and for calling him after me. I hope you will always have specially happy memories of this day, and that it will give your short time together that essential quality that will endure across the time of your separation (which I trust will be brief). Some memories are painful, and others strengthen one; this day will strengthen you.

Who is baptizing him? Who will be sponsor? How will you celebrate it? I hope to hear everything soon, preferably from you yourselves. Please harbour no regrets about me. Martin[23] has had nearly seven years of it, and that is a very different matter. The 21st will also be a day of great joy for me. How splendid that you returned on exactly your first wedding anniversary! I wish you much joy and peace.   Your faithful Dietrich

I've just heard the great news that I'm likely to see you here tomorrow – I had given up hoping for it. So I'm spending today getting ready for your visit. Who managed to arrange it? Whoever it was, I'm really *very* grateful.

Thoughts on the Day of the Baptism of Dietrich Wilhelm Rüdiger Bethge

May 1944

You are the first of a new generation in our family, and therefore the oldest representative of your generation. You will have the priceless advantage of spending a good part of your life with the third and fourth generation that went before you. Your great-grandfather will be able to tell you, from his own personal memories, of people who were born in the eighteenth century; and one day, long after the year 2000, you will be the living bridge over which your descendants will get an oral tradition of more than 250 years – all this *sub conditione Jacobea*, 'if the Lord wills'. So your birth provides us with a suitable occasion to reflect on the changes that time brings, and to try to scan the outlines of the future.

The three names that you bear refer to three houses with which your life is, and always should be, inseparably connected. Your grandfather on your father's side lived in a country parsonage. A simple, healthy life, with wide intellectual interests, joy in the most homely things, a natural and unaffected interest in ordinary people and their work, a capacity for self-help in practical things, and a modesty grounded in spiritual contentment – those are the earthly values which were at home in the country parsonage, and which you will meet in your father. In all the circumstances of life you will find them a firm basis for living together with other people, and for achieving real success and inward happiness.

The urban middle-class culture embodied in the home of your mother's parents has led to pride in public service, intellectual achievement and leadership, and a deep-rooted sense of duty towards a great heritage and cultural tradition. This will give you, even before you are aware of it, a way of thinking and acting which you can never lose without being untrue to yourself.

It was a kindly thought of your parents that you should be known by the name of your great-uncle, who is a pastor and a great friend of your father's; he is at present sharing the fate of many other good Germans and Protestant Christians, and so he has only been able to participate at a distance in your parents' wedding and in your own birth and baptism, but he looks forward to your future with great confidence and cheerful hope. He is striving to keep up the spirit – as far as he understands it – that is embodied in his parents' (your great-grandparents') home. He takes it as a good omen for your future that it was in that home that your parents got to know each other, and he hopes that one day you will be thankful for its spirit and draw on the strength that it gives.

By the time you have grown up, the old country parsonage and the old town villa will belong to a vanished world. But the old spirit, after a time of misunderstanding and weakness, withdrawal and recovery, preservation and rehabilitation, will produce new forms. To be deeply rooted in the soil of the past makes life harder, but it also makes it richer and more vigorous. There are in human life certain fundamental truths to which men will always return sooner or later. So there is no need to hurry; we have to be able to wait. 'God seeks what has been driven away' (Eccles. 3.15).

In the revolutionary times ahead the greatest gift will be to know the security of a good home. It will be a bulwark against all dangers from within and without. The time when children broke away in arrogance from their parents will be past. Children will be drawn into their parents' protection, and they will seek refuge, counsel, peace, and enlightenment. You are lucky to have parents who know at first hand what it means to have a parental home in stormy times. In the general impoverishment of intellectual life you will find your parents' home a storehouse of spiritual values and a source of intellectual stimulation. Music, as your parents understand and practise it, will help to dissolve your perplexities and purify your character and sensibility, and in times of care and sorrow will keep a ground-bass of joy alive in you. Your parents will soon be teaching you to help yourself and never to be afraid of soiling your hands. The piety of your home will not be noisy or loquacious, but it will teach you to say your prayers, to fear and love God above everything, and to do the will of Jesus Christ. 'My son, keep your father's commandment, and forsake not your mother's teaching. Bind them upon your heart always; tie them about your neck. When you walk, they will lead you; when you lie down, they will watch over you; and when you awake, they will talk with you' (Prov. 6.20–22). 'Today salvation has come to this house' (Luke 19.9).

I wish you could grow up in the country; but it will not be the countryside in which your father grew up. People used to think that the big cities offered the fullest kind of life and lots of pleasure, and they used to flock to them as though to a festival; but those cities have now brought on themselves death and dying, with all imaginable horrors, and have become fearsome places from which women and children have fled. The age of big cities on our continent seems to have come to an end. According to the Bible, Cain founded the first city. It may be that a few world metropolises will survive, but their brilliance, however alluring it may be, will in any case have something uncanny about it for a European. On the other hand, the flight from the cities will mean that the countryside is completely changed. The peace and seclusion of country life have already been largely undermined by the radio, the car, and the telephone, and by the spread of bureaucracy into almost every department of life; and now if millions of people who can no longer endure the pace and the demands of city life are moving into the country, and if entire industries are dispersed into rural areas, then the urbanization of the country will go ahead fast, and the whole basic structure of life there will be changed. The village of thirty years ago no more exists today than the idyllic South Sea island. In spite of man's longing for peace and solitude, these will be difficult to find. But with all these changes, it will be an advantage to have under one's feet a plot of land from which to draw the resources of a new, natural, unpretentious, and contented day's work and evening's leisure. 'There is great gain in godliness and contentment; . . . if we have food and clothing, with these we shall be content' (I Tim. 6.6f.). 'Give me neither poverty nor riches; feed me with the food that is needful for me, lest I be full, and deny thee, and say, "Who is the Lord?", or lest I be poor, and steal, and profane the name of my God' (Prov. 30.8f.). 'Flee from the midst of Babylon . . . She was not healed . . . Forsake her, and let us go each to his own country' (Jer. 51.6, 9).

We have grown up with the experience of our parents and grand-parents that a man can and must plan, develop, and shape his own life, and that life has a purpose, about which a man must make up his mind, and which he must then pursue with all his strength. But we have learnt by experience that we cannot plan even for the coming day, that what we have built up is being destroyed over-night, and that our life, in contrast to that of our parents, has become formless or even fragmentary. In spite of that, I can only say that I have no wish to live in any other time than our own, even though it is so inconsiderate of our outward well-being. We realize more clearly than formerly that the world lies under the wrath and grace of God. We read in Jer. 45: 'Thus says the Lord: Behold, what I have built I am breaking down, and what I have planted I am plucking up . . . And do you seek great things for yourself? Seek them not; for, behold, I am bringing evil upon all flesh; . . . but I will give your life as a prize of war in all places to which you may go.' If we can save our souls unscathed out of the wreckage of our material possessions, let us be satisfied with that. If the Creator destroys his own handiwork, what right have we to lament the destruction of ours? It will be the task of our generation, not to 'seek great things', but to save and preserve our souls out of the chaos, and to realize that it is the only thing we can carry as a 'prize' from the burning building. 'Keep your heart with all vigilance; for from it flows the spring of life' (Prov. 4.23). We shall have to keep our lives rather than shape them, to hope rather than plan, to hold out rather than march forward. But we do want to preserve for you, the rising generation, what will make it possible for you to plan, build up, and shape a new and better life.

We have spent too much time in thinking, supposing that if we weigh in advance the possibilities of any action, it will happen automatically. We have learnt, rather too late, that action comes, not from thought, but from a readiness for responsibility. For you thought and action will enter on a new relationship; your thinking will be confined to your responsibilities in action. With us thought was often the luxury of the onlooker; with you it will be entirely subordinated to action. 'Not every one who *says* to me, "Lord, Lord", shall enter the kingdom of heaven, but he who *does* the will of my Father who is in heaven', said Jesus (Matt. 7.21).

For the greater part of our lives pain was a stranger to us. To be as free as possible from pain was unconsciously one of our guiding principles. Niceties of feeling, sensitivity to our own and other people's pain are at once the strength and the weakness of our way of life. From its early days your generation will be tougher and closer to real life, for you will have had to endure privation and pain, and your patience will have been greatly tried. 'It is good for a man that he bear the yoke in his youth' (Lam. 3.27).

We thought we could make our way in life with reason and justice, and when both failed, we felt that we were at the end of our tether. We have constantly exaggerated the importance of reason and justice in the course of history. You, who are growing up in a world war which ninety per cent of mankind did not want, but for which they have to risk losing their goods and their lives, are learning from childhood that the world is controlled by forces against which reason can do nothing; and so you will be able to cope with those forces more successfully. In our lives the 'enemy' did not really exist. You know that you have enemies and friends, and you know what they can mean in your life. You are learning very early in life ways (which we did not know) of fighting an enemy, and also the value of unreserved trust in a friend. 'Has not man a hard service upon earth?' (Job 7.1.) 'Blessed be the Lord, my rock, who trains my hands for war, and my fingers for battle; my rock and my fortress, my stronghold and my deliverer, my shield and he in whom I take refuge' (Ps. 144.1f.). 'There is a friend who sticks closer than a brother' (Prov. 18.24).

298

Are we moving towards an age of colossal organizations and collective institutions, or will the desire of innumerable people for small, manageable, personal relationships be satisfied? Must they be mutually exclusive? Might it not be that world organizations themselves, with their wide meshes, will allow more scope for personal interests? Similarly with the question whether we are moving towards an age of the selection of the fittest, i.e. an aristocratic society, or to uniformity in all material and spiritual aspects of human life. Although there has been a very far-reaching equalization here, the sensitiveness in all ranks of society for the human values of justice, achievement, and courage could create a new selection of people who will be allowed the right to provide strong leadership. It will not be difficult for us to renounce our privileges, recognizing the justice of history. We may have to face events and changes that take no account of our wishes and our rights. But if so, we shall not give way to embittered and barren pride, but consciously submit to divine judgment, and so prove ourselves worthy to survive by identifying ourselves generously and unselfishly with the life of the community and the sufferings of our fellow-men. 'But any nation which will bring its neck under the yoke of the king of Babylon and serve him, I will leave on its own land, to till it and dwell there, says the Lord' (Jer. 27.11). 'Seek the welfare of the city . . . and pray to the Lord on its behalf' (Jer. 29.7). 'Come, my people, enter your chambers, and shut your doors behind you; hide yourselves for a little while until the wrath is past' (Isa. 26.20). 'For his anger is but for a moment, and his favour is for a lifetime. Weeping may tarry for the night, but joy comes with the morning' (Ps. 30.5).

Today you will be baptized a Christian. All those great ancient words of the Christian proclamation will be spoken over you, and the command of Jesus Christ to baptize will be carried out on you, without your knowing anything about it. But we are once again being driven right back to the beginnings of our understanding. Reconciliation and redemption, regeneration and the Holy Spirit, love of our enemies, cross and resurrection, life in Christ and Christian discipleship – all these things are so difficult and so remote that we hardly venture any more to speak of them. In the traditional words and acts we suspect that there may be something quite new and revolutionary, though we cannot as yet grasp or express it. That is our own fault. Our church, which has been fighting in these years only for its self-preservation, as though that were an end in itself, is incapable of taking the word of reconciliation and redemption to mankind and the world. Our earlier words are therefore bound to lose their force and cease, and our being Christians today will be limited to two things: prayer and righteous action among men. All Christian thinking, speaking, and organizing must be born anew out of this prayer and action. By the time you have grown up, the church's form will have changed greatly. We are not yet out of the melting-pot, and any attempt to help the church prematurely to a new expansion of its organization will merely delay its conversion and purification. It is not for us to prophesy the day (though the day will come) when men will once more be called so to utter the word of God that the world will be changed and renewed by it. It will be a new language, perhaps quite non-religious, but liberating and redeeming – as was Jesus' language; it will shock people and yet overcome them by its power; it will be the language of a new righteousness and truth, proclaiming God's peace with men and the coming of his kingdom. 'They shall fear and tremble because of all the good and all the prosperity I provide for it' (Jer. 33.9). Till then the Christian cause will be a silent and hidden affair, but there will be those who pray and do right and wait for God's own time. May you be one of them, and may it be said of you one day, 'The path of the righteous is like the light of dawn, which shines brighter and brighter till full day' (Prov. 4.18).

Dear Eberhard and Renate,
I can't tell you how delighted I was with your visit; and your
courage in deciding to come in, just the two of you together, was
splendid. If Maetz wasn't such a pedant, it might perhaps have
lasted even longer. But even so it was quite marvellous . . . To
talk to you again was glorious. I would like to know whether two
other people could say as much and make themselves understood
as well as the two of us in an hour and a half; it takes practice,
which is now entering its tenth – I'm right, it *is* the tenth – year;
I'm really proud of that.

I'm deeply moved by what you told me about your recent
experiences. I'm in too great a hurry to go into details today.
Above all, I hope you will find the peace, both within and without,
that you need after your upsetting experiences. I'm so sorry
that the alert was on just when you came, and I breathed a
sigh of relief when the commandant brought your telephone
message. The question of the 'meaning' of things is often burdensome; but don't you think it is very important that we
at least know *why* all this is necessary and has to be endured,
although the 'what for' is problematical? That is clearer for me
here.

The person who brings this letter[24] will also bring you my
warmest greetings for the day of the baptism and instructions for
a baptismal present – perhaps even the present itself. I'm very glad
that this is possible and you will certainly get on very well with
the friendly messenger. Just tell him a great deal and let him make
notes, so that I can learn everything. He will also be glad to tell
you about me and my life here. I think that it's very nice of him
to arrange this contact between us on this particular day. By the
way, he is a great musician. Perhaps you can arrange something
together. (Later I would very much like to see the 'Schütz' which
pleased you so much.) . . .

I've always been eager for the day when you came home for
the first time from the front, and I never doubted that you would
come back the same person who went and that we would

understand each other in everything without any change. That this is really the case is a quite indescribable joy to me.

I wonder whether it will be possible to arrange a second meeting on the grounds that today's had to be broken off because of air-raid warnings (Maetz certainly doesn't know how long it lasted; he was much too agitated for that!). It would be quite marvellous if it came off. There is still so much to discuss.

That's all for today. I've had to write very quickly in the sick-bay. That's how it got rather messy. So, once again, much love to all and good wishes for you, your son and a fine day . . .

With all my heart, Dietrich

I'm colossally pleased about your position over the Catholic confessor.

How good that you're baptizing him yourself. I would very much like to have the sermon!

To Eberhard Bethge   [Tegel] 20 May [1944]

Dear Eberhard,

Once again this letter is intended only for you . . . I must say to begin with that everything that you told me[25] has moved me so much that I couldn't stop thinking of it all day yesterday and had a restless night; I'm infinitely grateful to you for it; for it was a confirmation of our friendship, and moreover reawakens the spirit for life and for battle, and makes it stubborn, clear and hard. But I can't completely escape the feeling that there is a tension in you which you can't get rid of completely, and so I would like to help you as a brother. Accept it as it is intended. If a man loves, he wants to live, to live above all, and hates everything that represents a threat to his life. You hate the recollection of the last weeks, you hate the blue sky, because it reminds you of them, you hate the planes, etc. You want to live with Renate and be happy, and you have a good right to that. And indeed you must live, for the sake of Renate and the little – and also the big – Dietrich. You haven't the right to speak as your chief did recently. On the contrary, you couldn't be responsible for that at all. Sometime you must argue it out with him quite quietly; it is obvious what is necessary, but you mustn't act as a result of any personal emotion. There's always a danger in all strong, erotic love that one may love what I might call the polyphony of life. What I mean is that God wants us to love him eternally with our whole hearts – not in such a way as to injure or weaken our earthly love, but to provide a kind of *cantus firmus* to which the other melodies of life provide the counterpoint. One of these contrapuntal themes (which have their own complete independence but are yet related to the *cantus firmus*) is earthly affection. Even in the Bible we have the Song of Songs; and really one can imagine no more ardent, passionate, sensual love than is portrayed there (see 7.6).[26] It's a good thing that the book is in the Bible, in face of all those who believe that the restraint of passion is Christian (where is there such restraint in the Old Testament?). Where the *cantus firmus* is clear and plain, the counterpoint can be developed to its limits. The two are 'undivided and yet distinct', in the words of the Chalcedonian Definition, like Christ in his divine and human natures. May not the attraction and importance of polyphony in music consist in its being a musical reflection of this Christological fact and therefore of our *vita christiana*? This thought didn't occur to me till after your visit yesterday. Do you see what I'm driving at? I wanted to tell you to have a good, clear *cantus firmus*; that is the only way to a full and perfect sound, when the counterpoint has a firm support and can't come adrift or get out of tune, while remaining a distinct whole in its own right. Only a polyphony of this kind can give life a wholeness and at the same time assure us that nothing calamitous can happen as long as the *cantus firmus* is kept going. Perhaps a good deal will be easier to bear in these days together, and possibly also in the days ahead when you're separated. Please, Eberhard, do not fear and hate the separation, if it should come again with all its dangers, but rely on the *cantus firmus*. – I don't know whether I've made myself clear now, but one so seldom speaks of such things . . .[27]

Dear Eberhard,

I've just written the date of this letter as my share in the baptism
and the preparations for it. At the same moment the siren went,
and now I'm sitting in the sick-bay and hoping that today at any
rate you will have no air raid. What times these are! What a
baptism! And what memories for the years to come! What
matters is that we should direct these memories, as it were, into
the right spiritual channels, and so make them harder, clearer, and
more defiant, which is a good thing. There is no place for sentimentality on a day like this. If in the middle of an air raid God
sends out the gospel call to his kingdom in baptism, it will be quite
clear what that kingdom is and what it means. It is a kingdom
stronger than war and danger, a kingdom of power and authority,
signifying eternal terror and judgment to some, and eternal joy
and righteousness to others, not a kingdom of the heart, but one
as wide as the earth, not transitory but eternal, a kingdom that
makes a way for itself and summons men to itself to prepare its
way, a kingdom for which it is worth while risking our lives. –

The shooting is just beginning, but it doesn't seem likely to be
very bad today. I should so like to hear you preaching in a few
hours' time . . . At eight this morning I heard a chorale prelude
on 'What God does is well done' – a good beginning to the day;
as I listened to it, I thought of you and my godson. I hadn't heard
an organ for a long time, and the sound of it was like a refuge in
time of trouble. I'm really very sad indeed that your letter to me
as godfather has gone astray. I'm sure that you will have said a few
very good and beneficial and encouraging words to me in it, and
I would have been and am very grateful for them. Will it still be
possible to find it? And will you write me a few words instead?
I suppose you'll have to make an after-dinner speech today, and
that you'll be thinking of me as you do so. I should very much
like to hear what you said. The very fact that we so rarely say such
words to one another makes one long for them from time to time.
Do you understand that? Perhaps one feels it all the more strongly
through being cut off from other people here. I used to take such

things for granted, and in fact I still do, in spite of everything. Did you find here recently that it's now 'harder to speak' than before? I didn't. I only ask because you said this in a recent letter.

Perhaps you were surprised that yesterday's letter was on the one hand intended to say something to *you*, but on the other was itself so helpless. But isn't this what happens? One tries to help and is oneself the person most in need of help. What is said about the *cantus firmus* was written more for Renate's sake than for your own; i.e. for the sake of your shared life rather than because I felt that you didn't know it all well enough. The image of polyphony is still pursuing me. When I was rather distressed today at not being with you, I couldn't help thinking that pain and joy are also part of life's polyphony, and that they can exist independently side by side. The day before yesterday you said something to the effect that perhaps I had things better than I knew. Certainly, Eberhard, I'm in much less danger than you, and I would therefore give a great deal to be able to change places with you in this respect. That's not just empty speaking; it keeps entering into my prayers quite automatically; I've already seen more of life and experienced more than you . . . but perhaps that is precisely why I'm more 'tired of life' than you may be. So the advantage that you see in my position is relatively small. Isn't it rather the case that you experience life in all its sides, in happiness and in danger, and that that is better than when one is to some degree cut off from the breath of life, as I am here? I certainly don't want to be pitied, and I don't want to grieve you in any way, but I do want you to be *glad* about what you have: it really *is* the polyphony of life (excuse this riding round on my little invention!).

All clear. I'm glad for your sake. – I have on my desk two wonderful sprigs of lilac which a kind man brought me. The photographs that you brought I have put in front of me, and I'm looking at the baby who is being baptized today. I've also lit the large candle and am enjoying it very much. Many thanks. Who does he look like? I think Renate and you! The forehead is quite clearly yours, the rest Renate's. I think he's lovely, and if he is to take after me at all physically, I only hope he will have my freedom from toothache and headache, and my leg muscles and sensitive palate (though the latter is not an unmixed blessing). For other things he can do better elsewhere . . . He has also inherited the best thing about me, my name. I've always been satisfied with it, and as a boy I was actually proud of it. Believe me, I shall always be a good godfather to him and do all I possibly can to help him. I don't think he could choose a better one! . . .

I'm still completely under the influence of your story. If only we could experience all this together! I would much prefer to be with you there than all alone here in 'security'! When I think how many dangers you've been through in your life . . . and how until recently you've had tangible proofs of your preservation, and how good things have kept happening to you unexpectedly . . . I'm quite at ease and believe that you are well taken care of in the plans of God. At times now you may only see death in your thoughts about the war, but if you do so, you underestimate the number of ways in which God operates. The hour of a man's death is determined, and it will find him no matter where he may turn. We must be ready for it. But

> He knows ten thousand ways
> To save us from death's power.
> He gives us food and meat,
> A boon in famine's hour.

That's something we mustn't forget. – Another alert.

It's the 22nd. A good thing that you're out there. I've learnt a good deal about yesterday and am very glad about it. Maria liked your sermon very much; I found even the brief outline that I was given very revealing. And what splendid hymns! You were also thinking of me when you sang Schütz . . . I like both hymns very much. You gave my notes very much their due in doing that; it wasn't really my intention. But I'm glad if you were pleased. It must have been remarkable for father to read this text. I would very much like to hear more about it.

I'm very glad that Perels and mother are taking up the Dohrmann business immediately. Can't Klaus do anything? If it's necessary at all, legalization would have to be direct for service as an army chaplain. One can't very well demand more. The whole question now looks rather different from five years ago.[28] Nevertheless there are, of course, conditions which one could not accept. In that case it would be God's sign not to go further along this way. For God alone protects; otherwise there is nothing. I'm sending you a letter to give to Niebuhr, in case of need. Also in case of need, we must arrange a rendezvous. Later on I expect we shall be able to keep in touch through N. and Uncle George.[29] Good-bye for today. Can I do anything for you? How attractive the pictures of the little one are. God protect us all! From my heart.

Your faithful Dietrich

How did the surprise visit come off?

Dear Eberhard,
Here is the letter which you can always use as identification. Isn't it true that you were with me when I was visiting there?[30] (I hope it is clear that the letter is addressed to Prof. von Dietze-Freiburg.[31]) I think it right that you should be well and safely introduced. He's a very likable, lively and interesting man, a good friend of Paul Tillich, and his chief interest is ethics. Well, I won't bother you with more today. It's one o'clock at night and I'm waiting in the sick-bay for the alert that has been announced. *Quousque tandem?*
Good-bye for today. Your Dietrich

22 May

To Renate and Eberhard Bethge   [Tegel] 24 May [1944]

Dear Eberhard and Renate,
I don't know any better way of expressing my wishes for your Whitsun than by using a word which my lips frame only rarely – my wish is that you celebrate a blessed Whitsun, a Whitsun with God and with prayer, a Whitsun on which you feel the touch of the Holy Spirit, a Whitsun which will be a *rocher de bronce* in your

memories for the coming weeks and months. You need days whose memory is not painful because of something that was lacking, but a source of strength because of something that endures. I've been trying to write you a few words on the readings[32] – in fact, I was at it today while the alert was on, and so they are rather inadequate, and not as well thought out as I could wish. But perhaps you will read them together in the morning and find them some small substitute for the service that you might perhaps miss. Eberhard, is the recollection of Whit Sunday morning at Finkenwalde also so splendid and important for you?

In addition I hope that you have fine weather, much joy in little Dietrich, many peaceful hours and good music! With the alerts like this, I don't really dare to ask you to pay yet another visit. I will understand *very* well if you remain in Sakrow. You mustn't feel that if you do you are neglecting me in any way. It was so very splendid the other day, and the possibility of writing is also a very great help.

I'm now reading with great interest Weizsäcker's book about the 'world-view of physics', and I hope to learn a great deal from it for my own work. If only one had the chance to exchange ideas! In earlier days we always used to read and discuss such things together. The most recent news from Italy has again moved me very much. Whatever will happen in the next couple of weeks? One cannot think too much of the last verse which you sang at the baptism.[33]

Now good-bye, have a good festival and do not forget

your faithful Dietrich

To Eberhard Bethge   [Tegel 26 May 1944]

Dear Eberhard,

It's a week today since you were here. I wonder how you're spending your time. I often think that – objectively – it's very good for the two of you that I'm not there, so that you can be together without a third party. How are things now with Dohrmann?

I would dearly like to know. If you can come again, it would be best in the afternoon after 4; then I can see that we are more undisturbed. I would then let you know the appropriate day. In that case an early application is unnecessary. It would be wonderful if it came off. As Maria hasn't been now for at least six weeks, perhaps it will really work.

I don't expect that in any circumstances you will find things as you left them.[34] How grateful Renate will be that you are spared the unrest of these days and weeks. I think that it's a pity that you didn't draw more landscapes down there. The one page is quite vividly before my eyes . . . and all this is an untrained gift of yours! With me, on the other hand, training is almost everything. Without training I would be a quite tedious don! If the two things come together in your son, we are really in for it . . .

On the duties of godparents: in the old books the godparents often played a special part in a child's life. Growing children often want sympathy, kindness, and advice from grown-up people other than their parents; and the godparents are the people chosen by the parents to help in this way. The godparent has the right to give good advice, whereas the parents give orders. I didn't have any godparents of this kind . . . but I can imagine that I would very much have liked to have had one and could have used one very well. Did you? But this is the direction in which I see one of my future duties as a godparent . . . I would give boys chiefly male and girls chiefly female godparents. I'm asking father to see to some Pervitin – or Isophan – for me and for you. I'm writing to him myself. I very much hope to hear from you soon. All the very, very best.

Love to you and Renate and the little one,   your Dietrich

To Eberhard Bethge   [Tegel] 27 May 1944

Dear Eberhard,
Many thanks for your greeting. But don't you see that too short a letter is like someone for whose visit one has waited for a long

time opening the door slightly just for a moment, looking round into the room with a smile and then vanishing again? I think that you ought to write again so that I don't feel out of place with my letters and questions; at any rate, it would make things much easier for me. Do you understand?

If you can still visit me, Thursday 1 June after 4 or Sunday 3 June after 1.30 would be possible. I'll leave you to work it out. But some things can in fact be said more easily by letters than by word of mouth, so please don't set everything on the uncertain possibility of a visit . . .

The mention of Velletri[35] was strangely moving, and, I'm sure, most of all to you. Have you got the thing about the *cantus firmus* and my questions and the Whitsun meditations?

Once again many thanks for your greeting and all good wishes,

ever your Dietrich

To Eberhard Bethge   [Tegel] 29 May 1944

Dear Eberhard,

I hope that, in spite of the alerts, you are enjoying to the full the peace and beauty of these warm, summer-like Whitsuntide days. One gradually learns to acquire an inner detachment from life's menaces–although 'acquire detachment' seems too negative, formal, artificial, and stoical; and it's perhaps more accurate to say that we assimilate these menaces into our life as a whole. I notice repeatedly here how few people there are who can harbour conflicting emotions at the same time. When bombers come, they are all fear; when there is something nice to eat, they are all greed; when they are disappointed, they are all despair; when they are successful, they can think of nothing else. They miss the fullness of life and the wholeness of an independent existence; everything objective and subjective is dissolved for them into fragments. By contrast, Christianity puts us into many different dimensions of life at the same time; we make room in ourselves, to some extent, for God and the whole world. We rejoice with those who rejoice, and weep with those who weep; we are anxious (– I was again interrupted just then by the alert, and am now sitting out of doors enjoying the sun –) about our life, but at the same time we must think about things much more important to us than life itself. When the alert goes, for instance: as soon as we turn our minds from worrying about our own safety to the task of helping other people to keep calm, the situation is completely changed; life isn't pushed back into a single dimension, but is kept multi-dimensional and poly-phonous. What a deliverance it is to be able to *think*, and thereby remain multi-dimensional. I've almost made it a rule here, simply to tell people who are trembling under an air raid that it would be much worse for a small town. We have to get people out of their one-track minds; that is a kind of 'preparation' for faith, or some-thing that makes faith possible, although really it's only faith itself that can make possible a multi-dimensional life, and so enable us to keep this Whitsuntide, too, in spite of the alarms.

At first I was a bit disconcerted, and perhaps even saddened, not to have a letter from anyone this Whitsuntide. Then I told myself that it was perhaps a good sign, as it meant that no one was worry-ing about me. It's a strange human characteristic that we like other people to be anxious about us – at least just a trifle anxious.

Weizsäcker's book *The World-View of Physics* is still keeping me very busy. It has again brought home to me quite clearly how wrong it is to use God as a stop-gap for the incompleteness of our knowledge. If in fact the frontiers of knowledge are being pushed further and further back (and that is bound to be the case), then God is being pushed back with them, and is therefore continually in retreat. We are to find God in what we know, not in what we don't know; God wants us to realize his presence, not in unsolved problems but in those that are solved. That is true of the relation-ship between God and scientific knowledge, but it is also true of the wider human problems of death, suffering, and guilt. It is now possible to find, even for these questions, human answers that take no account whatever of God. In point of fact, people deal with these questions without God (it has always been so), and it is simply not true to say that only Christianity has the answers to them. As to the idea of 'solving' problems, it may be that the Christian answers are just as unconvincing – or convincing – as any others. Here again, God is no stop-gap; he must be recognized at the centre of life, not when we are at the end of our resources; it is his will to be recognized in life, and not only when death comes; in health and vigour, and not only in suffering; in our activities, and not only in sin. The ground for this lies in the revelation of God in Jesus Christ. He is the centre of life, and he certainly didn't 'come' to answer our unsolved problems. From the centre of life certain questions, and their answers, are seen to be wholly irrelevant (I'm thinking of the judgment pronounced on Job's friends). In Christ there are no 'Christian problems'. – Enough of this; I've just been disturbed again.

30 May evening

I'm sitting alone upstairs. Everything is quiet in the building; a few birds are still singing outside, and I can even hear the cuckoo in the distance. I find these long, warm evenings, which I'm now living through here for the second time, rather trying. I long to be outside, and if I were not so 'reasonable', I might do something foolish. I wonder whether we have become too reasonable. When you've deliberately suppressed every desire for so long, it may have one of two bad results: either it burns you up inside, or it all gets so bottled up that one day there is a terrific explosion. It is, of course, conceivable that one may become completely selfless, and I know better than anyone else that that hasn't happened to me. Perhaps you will say that one oughtn't to suppress one's desires, and I expect you would be right. But look, this evening for example I couldn't dare to give really full rein to my imagination and picture myself and Maria at your house, sitting in the garden by the water and talking together into the night etc. etc. That is simply self-torture, and gives one physical pain. So I take refuge in thinking, in writing letters, in delighting in your good fortune, and curb my desires as a measure of self-protection. However paradoxical it may sound, it would be more selfless if I didn't need to be so afraid of my desires, and could give them free rein – but that is very difficult. – Just now I happened to hear Solveig's Song on the wireless in the sick-bay. It quite got hold of me. To wait loyally a whole lifetime – that is to triumph over the hostility of space, i.e. separation, and over time, i.e. the past. Don't you think that such loyalty is the only way to happiness, and that disloyalty leads to unhappiness? – Well, I shall go to bed now, in case we have another disturbed night. Good-bye.

I'm thinking of you a great deal.   Your Dietrich

Maetz has gone away for the moment and has been replaced by a man with whom I get on less well. Both from the standpoint of security from alerts and for other reasons an afternoon visit is more opportune; Sunday afternoon (3 June) would be best. But I don't want to suggest the long journey here to you *immediately* before your departure. In the afternoon you must ask straight away to speak to the OvD (not the UvD) – he is an officer or a sergeant. If permission still hasn't come by Saturday, perhaps Maass[36] could be asked to allow a continuation of the visit broken off by the alarm, because you have to go back to the front. It's only a purely technical question. Maass would have to be rung on Friday or Saturday early, so that things were still all right for Saturday afternoon.

To Hans-Walter Schleicher   [Tegel] 2 June [1944]

Dear Hans-Walter,
I heard of your unexpected leave through Eberhard; I'm very pleased for you yourself and for all of you that you can now be together for a week as in the old days. So we do still keep having pleasant surprises! It's really a very nice thought of yours to want to visit me, despite the short time that you have here. Of course I would be especially pleased to see you. But you know that without express permission the most that is possible is a very short greeting without the chance of being able to tell each other anything. I quite definitely don't want you to make the journey here just for that, specially as it isn't even completely certain that we should be able to see each other. Unfortunately they're very mean with the permissions.

If I could have seen you and talked with you I would have had a great deal to ask you, above all what your views now are, after your experiences, about the generation of young people about the same age as you. Do you feel very isolated and strange among them? On what basis do you get together with them? Do your conversations ever go beyond the usual soldier's themes – which have probably always been the same in every corner of the earth – and if so, in what respect? What are they interested in – or if this word sounds too high-flown and intellectual, what do they depend on? What do they want and what do they wish for themselves? What do they believe and by what points of view do they arrange their lives? It has probably always been the minority to whom these questions apply at all. But on the other hand they are the only ones who count for the future. Do you have the feeling that the way of life that you've brought with you from home gives you any advantage in living together with other people, or does it have the opposite effect, that it chiefly causes you difficulties? Do you have the feeling that perhaps either too little or too much importance has been attached to certain things in our homes? In short, I would like to discuss all such questions, which I'm sure that you keep putting to yourself, with you. The most important question for the future is how we can find a basis for human life together, what spiritual realities and laws we accept as the foundations of a meaningful human life. If (after your leave!) you have a quiet hour and the inclination to do so, do write to me; I would like it very much. Renate can give you the right address. If you give me your field post number, I will write to you again. That's enough for today. Enjoy the free days as much as you can! I often think of you and wish you all the very, very best for the time to come. Love to parents and family, and warmest greetings from your

Uncle Dietrich

314

To Eberhard Bethge

Dear Eberhard,

The enclosed meditations[37] are only meant for the two of you. But if at present you don't want to hear any 'strange' voice, just put them on one side. Your own thoughts will be more help to Renate in these days. You wrote that time before your last departure that you were still reading the daily texts in the train. I was very glad about that then, and now I've had to think about it again.

I'm delighted at the enthusiasm with which Herr Linke[38] keeps speaking of you; he was particularly amazed that you 'hadn't flattered me at all', which is what he says other people usually do in such situations. I told him that that sort of thing wasn't necessary, and that was the good thing about it. He was evidently also very impressed in other respects. This sort of conversation is a new world to him, and I myself believe that quite objectively it is something unique . . .

While you're in Italy I shall write to you about the Song of Songs. I must say I should prefer to read it as an ordinary love song, and that is probably the best 'Christological' exposition. I must think again about Eph. 5. I hope that by now you have found something about Bultmann, if it has not been lost. Do you get on well enough with your colleague Rainalter there that you can talk to him about the miracle of the correspondence?[39] I'm quite amazed at it. Thank you very much for all your help in my personal questions.[40] Even when you simply say 'That's not so', it means a great deal to me. But the proof will only come at a moment when everything will depend on whether what you said is right. That's the difficulty. Quite apart from this purely personal problem, which was originally quite unexpected, there are also the objective problems of the child and the possibility of feeding his family . . . It makes a difference whether the facts are already accomplished or whether one can begin to have some responsibility over shaping them. That things simply 'fall back on me' is certainly the greatest comfort in everything and a support for faith – quite apart from the fact that I couldn't conceive of them *not* falling back on me!! – but in the end I am the one who is responsible, and I'm no longer twenty-five years old, so that I simply might and could stagger into something. Delay over the present status is in many respects a very questionable matter. But perhaps one day it will turn out to have been the right thing. I don't want to bother you any longer with these questions now. You have plenty of other things to think about. I will only have something else to say when I've heard from you again.

All the best for the last days; please keep me up to date with developments in your concern. With all my heart,

your faithful Dietrich

The baptism sermon follows tomorrow. Once again, many thanks!

[On the page with the manuscript interpretations of the daily texts for the 7 and 8 June 1944, added to the letter of 2 June]

Dear Eberhard and Renate,
These words flowed from my pen when I was meditating on the texts for the days before you with you in mind. They've only been thrown off in haste and not worked out beforehand; they are simply meant to accompany your own reading of the texts and if possible to be a little help. I've plucked up courage to send them to you from the fact that you, Eberhard, said that you liked the Whitsun meditations. Now good-bye, be of good confidence, and hope with me for a happy reunion soon.   Your Dietrich

From Eberhard Bethge   [Sakrow] 3 June 1944

Dear Dietrich,
Delight over that unique visit has remained with me for a long time. Questions and observations struck me afterwards in an electrifying way, and now I have the earlier letter and a new one. All that is missing now is the discussion of Bultmann. You were really very much in order, on the mark and stimulating; the whole situation had something refreshing and cheering about it in every

respect. But it's good if one attaches importance to technical details and feels experienced in them. When I got home, I first had a meal with Justus,[41] his wife and Renate, and then we all sat for a while with the grandparents (i.e. your parents) and Karl-Friedrich, who is very warm-hearted and always extremely interested in you. There was a message of congratulation from Sabine, 'Congratulations to the great grandmother',[42] and also the even older greeting from Gert: 'Can I do anything?' The grandparents have now gone off to Pätzig. I hope they have fine warm weather.

. . . many thanks for your parting words. You always speak to me instead of vice versa. These three weeks have been incomparably splendid, and I'm glad to have found you so well despite all my fears to the contrary. Then I'm glad that we've baptized the boy. And that you were able to say so much at it.

When I was telling Justus in passing that evening that you were preoccupied with the problem of Bultmann, he immediately said that he thought that it had been settled and that Bultmann was a man who would have to be 'excommunicated'. He might be a philosopher, but not a theological teacher. It's remarkable that the problem doesn't trouble him; people want to have fixed conceptions – despite everything. I'm eager to see what you've written to me. How do we Protestants avoid the actual surrender of 'ground' from generation to generation or along the line (to put it crudely) Barth-Bultmann-Bonhoeffer, which *in fact* has made tremendous progress in contrast to the liberal period, despite all new beginnings and restitutions? What has attracted people to Barth and to the Confessing Church? The feeling that they can find a certain hoard of truth here, 'Old Testament, prophetic', the perception of a certain support for the oppressed? The reasons for all this were left undiscussed; they were not understood any more than at an earlier time or were tacitly rejected, indeed they were lamented as a retrogression into dogma; and anyone who ventured to leap into them soon became sterile . . .

So, what are we to do about making particular claims on 'ground' in the world? What is the role of the cult and the prophet? Finally, what is the significance of the Christian tradition in which we stand? Of the 'conceptions' of people with which they are to be nourished and in which they have been nourished? But I expect that you're thinking about all this.

In Italy, things seem to have developed to the point that I expect it will no longer be possible to reach the area in the north.[43] In that case I shall have to investigate where to find my people again . . .

Won't anyone give you the Dostoievski? I think that you would very much like to read it. An essential part of the liberation to think and so to share in a multiplicity of dimensions is that one knows of a meaning, of tasks, of goals; otherwise it is the one who doesn't think who has to be envied. What do you mean when you say that only faith truly makes life in many dimensions possible? And you ought to explain a bit more how the basis for 'God in health, power and action' lies in the 'revelation in Jesus Christ'; what does the 'midst of life' mean?[44] . . .

[Note by Bonhoeffer on the other side of the page:]

Without God – Cath. Protest. united in rejection! God not there. 'Crisis! Exist. philos. psychother., Barth, Bultmann; lib. theology; Schlatter; Althaus; Tillich 'sinner' not the righteous Aristocratic Christianity?

To Eberhard Bethge[45]   [Tegel, 5 June 1944]

Dear Eberhard,
That really was something special,[46] didn't you think? I was sorry to have been so abrupt in the morning and that you had to get everything ready so quickly; but you can understand that I didn't want to let this opportunity slip past . . .

One question . . . On the other hand keep . . . to Ps. 37.3b . . . will also to Justus . . .

Warmest greetings and again many, many thanks for everything!   Your Dietrich

Dear Eberhard,

I should be behaving like a shy boy if I concealed from you the fact that I'm making some attempts here to write poetry. Up to now I've been keeping it dark from everyone, even Maria, who would be most concerned with it – simply because it was somehow painful to me and because I didn't know whether it wouldn't frighten her more than please her. You are the . . . to whom I can talk with a certain matter-of-factness; I hope that if need be you will tick me off and tell me clearly not to meddle with it. So today I'm sending you a sample,[47] first, because I think it would be silly to have any secrets from you, secondly, so that you can have something you didn't expect to read on your journey, and thirdly, because the subject of it is a good deal in your mind at the moment, and what I've written may be on the lines of what you're already thinking as you part from Renate. This dialogue with the past, the attempt to hold on to it and recover it, and above all, the fear of losing it, is the almost daily accompaniment of my life here; and sometimes, especially after brief visits, which are always followed by long partings, it becomes a theme with variations. To take leave of others, and to live on past memories, whether it was yesterday or last year (they soon melt into one), is my everrecurring duty, and you yourself once wrote that saying good-bye goes very much against the grain. In this attempt of mine the crucial part is the last few lines. I'm inclined to think they are too brief – what do you think? Strangely enough, they came out in rhyme of their own accord. The whole thing was composed in a few hours, and I didn't try to polish it.

Now that I've talked about it to someone for the first time, I see that I can and must also send it to Maria. If some of the things in it frighten her, she must work out what is meant. I would be glad to hear a word from you about it. Perhaps I shall suppress these impulses in future, and use my time to better advantage; but that might well depend on your opinion. If you like, I'll send you some more to look at.

Is the Dohrmann affair[48] now quite excluded? Of course I'm very preoccupied with it and yet I can't say that it oppresses me particularly; I've too strong a feeling that your ways are being directed from above and that this is better than everything that we undertake. Certainly one must try everything, but only to become more certain what God's way is and to be able to pray Psalm 91 with great confidence. But if there's anything else that I can do, let me know.

I've again seen from our conversation recently that no one can interpret my thoughts better than you can. That is always a great satisfaction to me. How and where will you find your unit again after the move from Rome? God bless you, wherever you are.

In faithfulness and gratitude.　　　　　　　　　　Your Dietrich

THE PAST

O happiness beloved, and pain beloved in heaviness,
you went from me.
What shall I call you? Anguish, life, blessedness,
part of myself, my heart – the past?
The door was slammed;
I hear your steps depart and slowly die away.
What now remains for me – torment, delight, desire?
This only do I know: that with you, all has gone.
But do you feel how I now grasp at you
and so clutch hold of you
that it must hurt you?
How I so rend you
that your blood gushes out,
simply to be sure that you are near me,
a life in earthly form, complete?
Do you divine my terrible desire
for my own suffering,
my eager wish to see my own blood flow,
only that all may not go under,
lost in the past?

Life, what have you done to me?
Why did you come? Why did you go?
Past, when you flee from me,
are you not still my past, my own?
As o'er the sea the sun sinks ever faster,
as if it moved towards the darkness,
so does your image sink and sink and sink
without a pause
into the ocean of the past,
and waves engulf it.
As the warm breath dissolves
in the cool morning air,
so does your image vanish from me,
and I forget your face, your hands, your form.
There comes a smile, a glance, a greeting;
it fades, dissolves,
comfortless, distant,
is destroyed, is past.

I would inhale the fragrance of your being,
absorb it, stay with it,
as on hot summer days the heavy blossoms welcoming the bees
intoxicate them,
as privet makes the hawk-moths drunken –
but a harsh gust destroys both scent and blossoms,
and I stand like a fool
seeking a past that vanished.

It is as if parts of my flesh were torn out with red-hot pincers,
when you, a part of my life that is past, so quickly depart.
Raging defiance and anger beset me,
reckless and profitless questions I fling into space.
'Why, why, why?' I keep on repeating –
why cannot my senses hold you,
life now passing, now past?
Thus I will think, and think anew,
until I find what I have lost.

But I feel
that everything around me, over, under me
is smiling at me, unmoved, enigmatic,
smiling at my hopeless efforts
to grasp the wind,
to capture what has gone.

Evil comes into my eye and soul;
what I see, I hate;
I hate what moves me;
all that lives I hate, all that is lovely,
all that would recompense me for my loss.
I want my life; I claim my own life back again,
my past, yourself.
Yourself. A tear wells up and fills my eye;
can I, in mists of tears,
regain your image,
yourself entire?
But I will not weep;
only the strong are helped by tears,
weaklings they make ill.

Wearily I come to the evening;
welcome are bed and oblivion
now that my own is denied me.
Night, blot out what separates, give me oblivion,
in charity perform your kindly office;
to you I trust myself.
But night is wise and mighty,
wiser than I, and mightier than day,
What no earthly power can do,
what is denied to thoughts and senses, to defiance, to tears,
night brings me, in its bounty overflowing.
Unharmed by hostile time,
pure, free, and whole,
you are brought to me by dream,
you, my past, my life,

you, the day and hour but lately gone.

Close to you I waken in the dead of night,
and start with fear –
are you lost to me once more? Is it always vainly that I seek you,
you, my past?
I stretch my hands out,
and I pray –
and a new thing now I hear:
'The past will come to you once more,
and be your life's enduring part,
through thanks and repentance.
Feel in the past God's forgiveness and goodness,
pray him to keep you today and tomorrow.'

To Eberhard Bethge   [Tegel] 6 June 1944

Dear Eberhard,
I'm sending you this hurried greeting, simply because I want in
some way to share the day[49] with you yourself and with all of you.
The news didn't come as a surprise to me, and yet things turn out
differently from what we expect. Today's texts take us to the heart
of the gospel – 'redemption' is the key word to it all. Let us face
the coming weeks in faith and in great assurance about the general
future, and commit your way and all our ways to God. Χάρις καὶ
εἰρήνη!   Your Dietrich

From Eberhard Bethge   [Sakrow] 6 June 1944

Dear Dietrich,
Many thanks for your letter. The sermon has come. Above all,
thank you for the two meditations. I've read them once for myself
and thank you very much for the helpful, brotherly word . . .

Frau von Kleist writes today that she has heard that the grand-parents gave me their permission to visit. She's so pleased about it: 'How heart-rending it will have been for the two of you.' Yes, of course it was 'heart-rending', but that's an aspect that one didn't notice so much. Instead, we get down to things very quickly in a cheerful and concentrated way. The reason for that is that you aren't sorry for yourself, and don't seek recognition of your 'role'. The Bultmann letter is still missing. As far as I can tell I can rely on comrade R[ainalter]. Things got going in the West today. I hadn't expected it yet; but I'm glad you've at last won a bet. I've heard from the wife of a comrade here that the Velletri people have all settled well in the northern place.[50] Meanwhile they will have gone further. And I must search. Many greetings and thanks; keep cheerful.   Your Eberhard

Wednesday evening. Many thanks for the further letter which I found here with the parents. Also for the one to Justus, which he will get tomorrow. Off early tomorrow.   Your Eberhard

To Eberhard Bethge   [Tegel] 8 June 1944

Dear Eberhard,
While you're spending your first hours in the train and moving further away from us hour by hour, my thoughts are going with you; perhaps this letter will meet up with you just at the time when you reach your new destination. It was a special delight to get another letter from you early this morning. That you were as glad about our meeting as I was is reassuring, as I'd already been thinking that I had robbed you of this whole afternoon . . . In some respects at least, you will have left with a lighter heart than you had feared at first. We had put off our meeting from Christmas to Easter, and then from Easter to Whitsuntide; one feast went by, and then another. But the next feast is sure to be ours; I've no doubt about that now. It's good that you saw Karl-Friedrich. He's written me such a good letter again. It's probably

hard for Klaus to find a starting point after so long a time.[51] I really know that it isn't a lack of warm-heartedness . . . Klaus has inherited mother's tendency to complicate things and her natural need to help, together with father's uncommonly wise foresight . . . There is hardly anything more stimulating than to have a conversation with him, and I can't think of a more kind-hearted and generous, more distinguished character than he is, but he is not the man for the simple . . . decisions of life . . .

There are always reasons for not doing something; the question is whether one does them nevertheless. If one only wants to do something that has *everything* in its favour, one will never get round to doing anything, or rather, the action will no longer be necessary because other people will already have anticipated one in it. Every real action is of such a kind that no one other than oneself can do it. I am, however, clear that I must first have this conversation with myself, for you know best how difficult I often find it to make up my mind in little things. This must be a legacy of my grandfather Bonhoeffer.

I was very pleased about Sabine's and G.'s[52] greetings (I hadn't known anything about either of them . . . I had often asked!).

You now ask so many important questions on the subjects that have been occupying me lately, that I should be happy if I could answer them myself. But it's all very much in the early stages; and, as usual, I'm being led on more by an instinctive feeling for questions that will arise later than by any conclusions that I've already reached about them. I'll try to define my position from the historical angle.

The movement that began about the thirteenth century (I'm not going to get involved in any argument about the exact date) towards the autonomy of man (in which I should include the discovery of the laws by which the world lives and deals with itself in science, social and political matters, art, ethics, and religion) has in our time reached an undoubted completion. Man has learnt to deal with himself in all questions of importance without recourse to the 'working hypothesis' called 'God'. In questions of science, art, and ethics this has become an understood thing at which one now hardly dares to tilt. But for the last hundred years or so it has also become increasingly true of religious questions; it is becoming evident that everything gets along without 'God' – and, in fact, just as well as before. As in the scientific field, so in human affairs generally, 'God' is being pushed more and more out of life, losing more and more ground.

Roman Catholic and Protestant historians agree that it is in this development that the great defection from God, from Christ, is to be seen; and the more they claim and play off God and Christ against it, the more the development considers itself to be anti-Christian. The world that has become conscious of itself and the laws that govern its own existence has grown self-confident in what seems to us to be an uncanny way. False developments and failures do not make the world doubt the necessity of the course that it is taking, or of its development; they are accepted with fortitude and detachment as part of the bargain, and even an event like the present war is no exception. Christian apologetic has taken the most varied forms of opposition to this self-assurance. Efforts are made to prove to a world thus come of age that it cannot live without the tutelage of 'God'. Even though there has been surrender on all secular problems, there still remain the so-called 'ultimate questions' – death, guilt – to which only 'God' can give an answer, and because of which we need God and the church and the pastor. So we live, in some degree, on these so-called ultimate questions of humanity. But what if one day they no longer exist as such, if they too can be answered 'without God'? Of course, we now have the secularized offshoots of Christian theology, namely existentialist philosophy and the psychotherapists, who demonstrate to secure, contented, and happy mankind that it is really unhappy and desperate and simply unwilling to admit that it is in a predicament about which it knows nothing, and from which only they can rescue it. Wherever there is health, strength, security, simplicity, they scent luscious fruit to gnaw at or to lay their pernicious eggs in. They set themselves to drive people to inward despair, and then the game is in their hands. That is secularized methodism. And whom does it touch? A small number of intellectuals, of degenerates, of people who regard themselves as the most important thing in the world, and who therefore like to busy themselves with themselves. The ordinary man, who spends his everyday life at work and with his family, and of course with all kinds of diversions, is not affected. He has neither the time nor the inclination to concern himself with his existential despair, or to regard his perhaps modest share of happiness as a trial, a trouble, or a calamity.

The attack by Christian apologetic on the adulthood of the world I consider to be in the first place pointless, in the second place ignoble, and in the third place unchristian. Pointless, because it seems to me like an attempt to put a grown-up man back into adolescence, i.e. to make him dependent on things on which he is, in fact, no longer dependent, and thrusting him into problems that are, in fact, no longer problems to him. Ignoble, because it amounts to an attempt to exploit man's weakness for purposes that are alien to him and to which he has not freely assented. Unchristian, because it confuses Christ with one particular stage in man's religiousness, i.e. with a human law. More about this later.

But first, a little more about the historical position. The question is: Christ and the world that has come of age. The weakness of liberal theology was that it conceded to the world the right to determine Christ's place in the world; in the conflict between the church and the world it accepted the comparatively easy terms of peace that the world dictated. Its strength was that it did not try to put the clock back, and that it genuinely accepted the battle (Troeltsch), even though this ended with its defeat.

Defeat was followed by surrender, and by an attempt to make a completely fresh start based on the fundamentals of the Bible and the Reformation. Heim sought, along pietist and methodist lines, to convince the individual man that he was faced with the alternative 'despair or Jesus'. He gained 'hearts'. Althaus (carrying forward the modern and positive line with a strong confessional emphasis) tried to wring from the world a place for Lutheran teaching (ministry) and Lutheran worship, and otherwise left the world to its own devices. Tillich set out to interpret the evolution of the world (against its will) in a religious sense – to give it its shape through religion. That was very brave of him, but the world unseated him and went on by itself; he, too, sought to understand the world better than it understood itself; but it felt that it was completely misunderstood, and rejected the imputation. (Of course, the world *must* be understood better than it understands itself, but not 'religiously' as the religious socialists wanted.)

Barth was the first to realize the mistake that all these attempts (which were all, in fact, still sailing, though unintentionally, in the channel of liberal theology) were making in leaving clear a space for religion in the world or against the world. He brought in against religion the God of Jesus Christ, '*pneuma* against *sarx*'. That remains his greatest service (his *Epistle to the Romans*, second edition, in spite of all the neo-Kantian egg-shells). Through his later dogmatics, he enabled the church to effect this distinction, in principle, all along the line. It was not in ethics, as is often said, that he subsequently failed – his ethical observations, as far as they exist, are just as important as his dogmatic ones –; it was that in the non-religious interpretation of theological concepts he gave no concrete guidance, either in dogmatics or in ethics. There lies his limitation, and because of it his theology of revelation has become positivist, a 'positivism of revelation', as I put it.

The Confessing Church has now largely forgotten all about the Barthian approach, and has lapsed from positivism into conservative restoration. The important thing about that church is that it carries on the great concepts of Christian theology; but it seems as if doing this is gradually just about exhausting it. It is true that there are in those concepts the elements of genuine prophecy (among them two things that you mention: the claim to truth, and mercy) and of genuine worship; and to that extent the Confessing Church gets only attention, hearing, and rejection. But both of them remain undeveloped and remote, because there is no interpretation of them. Those who, like e.g. Schütz or the Oxford Group or the Berneucheners, miss the 'movement' and the 'life', are dangerous reactionaries; they are reactionary because they go right back behind the approach of the theology of revelation and seek for 'religious' renewal. They simply haven't understood the problem at all yet, and their talk is entirely beside the point. There is no future for them (though the Oxford Group would have the best chance if they were not so completely without biblical substance).

Bultmann seems to have somehow felt Barth's limitations, but he misconstrues them in the sense of liberal theology, and so goes off into the typical liberal process of reduction – the 'mythological' elements of Christianity are dropped, and Christianity is reduced to its 'essence'. – My view is that the full content, including the 'mythological' concepts, must be kept – the New Testament is not a mythological clothing of a universal truth; this mythology (resurrection etc.) is the thing itself – but the concepts must be interpreted in such a way as not to make religion a precondition of faith (cf. Paul and circumcision). Only in that way, I think, will liberal theology be overcome (and even Barth is still influenced by it, though negatively) and at the same time its question be genuinely taken up and answered (as is *not* the case in the Confessing Church's positivism of revelation!). Thus the world's coming of age is no longer an occasion for polemics and apologetics, but is now really better understood than it understands itself, namely on the basis of the gospel and in the light of Christ.

Now for your question whether there is any 'ground' left for the church, or whether that ground has gone for good; and the other question, whether Jesus didn't use men's 'distress' as a point of contact with them, and whether therefore the 'methodism' that I criticized earlier isn't right.

9 June

I'm breaking off here, and will write more tomorrow. A letter to Maria also has to go off. Many thanks for your greeting of 6 June, so shortly before your departure . . . The Bultmann letter went several weeks ago to Italy (shortly before you left). I expect that you will find it there . . . By the way, if we're talking about 'roles', yours is undoubtedly much more difficult, and I was very glad that you were going into the future so cheerfully and bravely. In short, it was very splendid for both of us to be together and I can't imagine that anything will change in the years that are to come. That is a real possession, perhaps acquired slowly and laboriously, but how worthwhile have been all the sacrifices that we have made for it!

That's all. All the very, very best. I'm thinking of you faithfully and with gratitude. Ever your Dietrich

Dear Dietrich,

I was very surprised to get another letter from you with the
verses. I find in them once again the compactness of your style,
the clarity with which you say a thing and some very vivid
imagery.

I wonder what Maria will say to it? Is the conclusion perhaps
too short for others, as you yourself fear? . . . I wonder whether
you oughtn't to find a more 'propitious' title if you give it to her.
In other words, you oughtn't to send her just this, or only something in this tenor. You express yourself so vividly and compel-
lingly in the poem that one might feel (and she certainly can't read
it objectively) that you were alone in the situation. You certainly
are, but you also live, feel and think in other dimensions – and in a
very lively way . . .

It's so easy for those who are near to a person to react painfully
and sensitively to any work he may produce of this kind. But my
immediate reaction was one of great joy and wonderment . . . I
shall be getting out at Munich and have the break of journey certi-
fied. They must have the latest news of the new position in
Munich, at Theresienstrasse,[53] because of radio links, etc. Perhaps
they will also give me a military pass to cover all eventualities, so
that I don't get whisked off.

Evening

I'm now lying in white sheets once again at the Europäische Hof
and living once again on your connections. The same sister always
sits in reception; she had a couch prepared for me because they
were full up.

Friday morning, early

This morning I spoke to Renate on the telephone and heard that
all was going well. There's another letter there. A pity that it came
a day too late. Now I'll have to wait longer for it. I wonder
whether it's the one with the Bultmann thing? . . . With loyal
thoughts,   your Eberhard

[Munich] 16 June 1944
Friday

Dear Dietrich,

Before I finally leave the country, one quick letter . . . The attempt of that place that you know to find my unit took a marvellously long time. It was unsuccessful, so I must find other ways of achieving my end . . .

The best thing of all was that Renate was able to come, with the help of my parents and Bärbel. And thanks to your person, the Europäische Hof was very helpful and generous about everything that one needed. This time parting was more horrible for me, as I returned to the room and had to wait almost the whole day. The departing train and an over-full carriage are more merciful. Then this evening came the OKW report of the flying-bomb attacks on England.⁵⁴ One can't envisage them at all. What immediate effects, what further consequences? Anxiety; will you feel any? . . . When I arrive, I hope that I shall find post there before too long. Greetings and loyal thoughts,   your Eberhard

Notes⁵⁵

[End of June 1944]

Aphrodite –	Embracing nature. Longing in the world. Man and beast.
Hermes –	The escort, lord of the ways (*hermein*). Spirit of the night, night is the mother of mysteries, nothing far and nothing near
The world of Hermes	Not a heroic world, cheerfulness, god of highwaymen and thieves, laughter, villainy, roguery, devil-may-care

'God' – is not a demonstrable entity
'Hades' – what has been

'Man' – not a beast
Dionysus – not Homeric
'He who has thought most deeply, loves most vigorously'
    Hölderlin on Socrates/Alcibiades
Human form – animal form unspiritual, tremendous, boundless against the world of care, the longings that cannot be stilled, the delight in death. Against the trend towards the *supernatural* as *hubris*. Therefore 'instead of a symbol for the absolute, instead of bewildering monstrosity, the perfect human form'.

Guilt and freedom, not the humility of putting the blame on one-self, but the alternative of knowing that one is not the only cause of what has happened.
'Ye gods, to meet again, then, is a God!' (Helen and Menelaus)

The divine not in absolutes, but in the natural form of man.

'Theomorphism, not anthropomorphism' (Goethe)

No self-revelation of the gods. Apollo reveals 'the right', but not himself.

To Eberhard Bethge   [Tegel] 21 June [1944]

Dear Eberhard,
Many thanks for your last letter from Munich before your departure. I can imagine that returning to the empty room was a wrench. But once again it was unexpectedly splendid that you had another couple of days together. You must have been very pleased that everything happened so conveniently to make it possible for you. Now you're somewhere looking for your unit, and I hope that when you reach it you will find some letters there to greet you – assuming that your old field post number is still correct. All I want to do today is to send you a greeting. I daren't

enclose the next instalment of theological argument, or any poetry, as I don't know whether the old field post number will still get you. As soon as I hear about that, there will be some more to follow. I'm very grateful for your opinion and criticism of the poem. I hardly know yet what to make of these new children of mine, as I've no standard to judge them by. I think that you're quite right in all your criticisms. But I'm rather in despair at being able to find anything else for the verse 'And a new thing now I hear' that doesn't destroy the whole construction of the last verse. Still, perhaps an idea will occur to me.

This morning we had the worst of all the air raids so far. For several hours my room was so dark with the cloud of smoke that hung over the city that I almost switched the light on. I've just heard that all is well at home. I expect that Renate is continuing to stay in Sakrow with the little boy; she could do any shopping that she needed in Potsdam. Nothing has happened there yet. I'm not pleased that my parents are coming back at just this moment. They, too, ought to go to Sakrow for the time being. I'm very confident and assured about the use of our new weapon.[56]

It often seems hard to have to spend the beautiful long summer days here for the second time; but one just can't choose where one has to be. So we must keep on trying to find our way through the petty thoughts that irritate us, to the great thoughts that strengthen us. – I'm at present reading the quite outstanding book by W. F. Otto, the classics man at Königsberg, *The Gods of Greece*. To quote from his closing words, it's about 'this world of faith, which sprang from the wealth and depth of human existence, not from its cares and longings'. Can you understand my finding something very attractive in this theme and its treatment, and also – *horribile dictu* – my finding these gods, when they are so treated, less offensive than certain brands of Christianity? In fact, that I almost think I could claim these gods for Christ? The book is most helpful for my present theological reflections. By the way, there's a good deal about Cardano in Dilthey.

Good-bye for today. I'm waiting daily for news of your whereabouts and am always with you in my thoughts.

With all my heart.   Your Dietrich

SORROW AND JOY

Sorrow and joy,
striking suddenly on our startled senses,
seem, at the first approach, all but impossible
of just distinction one from the other,
even as frost and heat at the first keen contact
burn us alike.

Joy and sorrow,
hurled from the height of heaven in meteor fashion,
flash in an arc of shining menace o'er us.
Those they touch are left
stricken amid the fragments
of their colourless, usual lives.

Imperturbable, mighty,
ruinous and compelling,
sorrow and joy
– summoned or all unsought for –
processionally enter.
Those they encounter
they transfigure, investing them
with strange gravity
and a spirit of worship.

Joy is rich in fears;
sorrow has its sweetness.
Indistinguishable from each other
they approach us from eternity,
equally potent in their power and terror.

From every quarter
mortals come hurrying,
part envious, part awe-struck,
swarming, and peering
into the portent,

where the mystery sent from above us
is transmuting into the inevitable
order of earthly human drama.

What, then, is joy? What, then, is sorrow?
Time alone can decide between them,
when the immediate poignant happening
lengthens out to continuous wearisome suffering,
when the laboured creeping moments of daylight
slowly uncover the fullness of our disaster,
sorrow's unmistakable features.

Then do most of our kind,
sated, if only by the monotony
of unrelieved unhappiness,
turn away from the drama, disillusioned,
uncompassionate.

O you mothers and loved ones – then, ah, then
comes your hour, the hour for true devotion.
Then your hour comes, you friends and brothers!
Loyal hearts can change the face of sorrow,
softly encircle it with love's most gentle
unearthly radiance.

To Eberhard Bethge   [Tegel] 27 June 1944

Dear Eberhard,
Maria has just been with me; I heard from her that the last news
of you was from Verona and since then there has been nothing
more. Although I've no idea whether or when the post is reaching
you, I'm still writing to you under the old field post number.
Before I go on with the theological reflections, I should prefer to
wait till I hear from you; and the same goes for the verses –
especially my latest, a rather long poem[57] about my impressions

here – which are more suitable for an evening's talk than for a long journey by post . . .

I'm at present writing an exposition of the first three commandments.[58] I find No. 2 particularly difficult. The usual interpretation of idolatry as 'wealth, sensuality, and pride' seems to me quite unbiblical. That is a piece of moralizing. Idols are worshipped, and idolatry implies that people still worship something. But we don't worship anything now, not even idols. In that respect we're truly nihilists.

Now for some further thoughts about the Old Testament. Unlike the other oriental religions, the faith of the Old Testament isn't a religion of redemption. It's true that Christianity has always been regarded as a religion of redemption. But isn't this a cardinal error, which separates Christ from the Old Testament and interprets him on the lines of the myths about redemption? To the objection that a crucial importance is given in the Old Testament to redemption (from Egypt, and later from Babylon – cf. Deutero-Isaiah) it may be answered that the redemptions referred to here are *historical*, i.e. on *this* side of death, whereas everywhere else the myths about redemption are concerned to overcome the barrier of death. Israel is delivered out of Egypt so that it may live before God as God's people on earth. The redemption myths try unhistorically to find an eternity after death. Sheol and Hades are no metaphysical constructions, but images which imply that the 'past', while it still exists, has only a shadowy existence in the present.

The decisive factor is said to be that in Christianity the hope of resurrection is proclaimed, and that that means the emergence of a genuine religion of redemption, the main emphasis now being on the far side of the boundary drawn by death. But it seems to me that this is just where the mistake and the danger lie. Redemption now means redemption from cares, distress, fears, and longings, from sin and death, in a better world beyond the grave. But is this really the essential character of the proclamation of Christ in the gospels and by Paul? I should say it is not. The difference between the Christian hope of resurrection and the mythological hope is that the former sends a man back to his life on earth in a wholly new way which is even more sharply defined than it is in the Old Testament. The Christian, unlike the devotees of the redemption myths, has no last line of escape available from earthly tasks and difficulties into the eternal, but, like Christ himself ('My God, why hast thou forsaken me?'), he must drink the earthly cup to the dregs, and only in his doing so is the crucified and risen Lord with him, and he crucified and risen with Christ. This world must not be prematurely written off; in this the Old and New Testaments are at one. Redemption myths arise from human boundary-experiences, but Christ takes hold of a man at the centre of his life.

You see how my thoughts are constantly revolving round the same theme. Now I must substantiate them in detail from the New Testament; that will follow later.

That's enough for today. Good-bye, Eberhard, God bless you every day. In loyalty and gratitude,   ever your Dietrich

I read in the paper about tropical heat in Italy – you poor man! It reminds me of August 1936. Ps. 121.6![59]

From Eberhard Bethge   'Il Balcone'
                                                         Montevettolini
                                                         (Pistoia)
                                                         27 June 1944

Dear Dietrich,
By now I hope that you will have heard that all has gone well with me, with the journey, its interruption and finally the arrival at my unit. The pass which was finally handed out to me in Munich brought me through the dangerous rocks of the assembly points in Verona and Bologna. So I spent only one day in Verona and had a splendid tour of the city with a corporal as guide. I've not had such a good introduction before . . . People seemed very friendly, and despite being over-tired I was very happy. Of course there was a certain amount of chaos in Bologna and I spent a night on a bare stone floor without any covering. After that things

turned out very well. The following day the heavens threw down all the moisture they had at their disposal, collected over a long period. So I could happily hitch-hike the next day to reach our new position in glorious Tuscany without seeing a single plane. At first we were told here that we would be going northwards again very soon, but we're still here. So far I've had to plunge into the records, which have got into complete disorder, and haven't had any time . . . Now I'm almost through. The retreat of our people must have been quite chaotic and dreadful. Nevertheless, they all got safely through the traps with all the vehicles. Everything happened so quickly that the military hospitals in Rome and Civitacastellana (near us) had to be surrendered to the enemy; only very light casualties were sent away on foot. It's much quieter and more beautiful here than in the last months in Rignano. The road is a long way away, and so we see the planes only at a considerable distance, above all in the morning and in the evening . . . I've a good office with a northward aspect, i.e. that's good because of the heat. The only unpleasant thing is when one has to make a car journey by day. In that case one takes a comrade on the running board who has to act as observer. On my arrival, on the very first morning I was surprised by an unusual 'parade'. The reason: I've been promoted to lance-corporal. The reason was given as my skilful work in returning to my unit. I'd already thought of that in Munich . . .

There was letter upon letter from you here to meet me and make everything nice. Some from before my leave, 22 April, 5 and 6 May, and some after it, 6 and 8 June. The latter with the very good and detailed theological definitions of your thoughts on religionlessness. I'll now try to give at least some reply . . . First of all, however, I must say again that my leave, as a really successful whole, is still a source of joy and comfort; the days with Renate . . . the hours with you which we enjoyed without any wasted time . . . your good letters, which put me back on the right lines (the unrest and sense of oppression which wouldn't go away after the experiences of the first days are now really only a memory and no longer have any power); the baptism and the boy . . .

Unfortunately I quite forgot to ask you about your novel and the short work for myself. And I would so like to see them.

The letter with the discussion about Bultmann about which you spoke is surely that of the 5 May, which I found waiting here, so it's not lost. Would you allow me to give extracts from these letters, above all the longer passages, to people like Albrecht Schönherr, Winfried Maechler, Dieter Zimmermann[60] some time? It would certainly please them very much – or are you against that? Tell me some time. I find everything in them much clearer than previous remarks of yours on the question, and your location of the position in the history of doctrine is very interesting . . . I wait eagerly for the continuation which you promised about the non-religious interpretation of the great Christian concepts.

Now the great events develop from day to day, and one delights in every day that one can spend in a degree of peace and quiet, glad of news from home.

My writing has been very disturbed, but I want to send it off so that the report doesn't reach you late.

Keep your spirits up. Many greetings.   Your Eberhard

To Eberhard Bethge   [Tegel] 30 June 1944

Dear Eberhard,
Today was a hot summer's day here, and I could enjoy the sun only with mixed feelings, as I can imagine what ordeals you're having to go through. Probably you're stuck somewhere or other, tired and up to your eyes in dust and sweat, and perhaps with no chance of washing or cooling down. I suppose you sometimes almost loathe the sun. And yet, you know, I should like to feel the full force of it again, making the skin hot and the whole body glow, and reminding me that I'm a corporeal being. I should like to be tired by the sun, instead of by books and thoughts. I should like to have it awaken my animal existence – not the kind that

degrades a man, but the kind that delivers him from the stuffiness and artificiality of a purely intellectual existence and makes him purer and happier. I should like, not just to see the sun and sip at it a little, but to experience it bodily. Romantic sun-worshipping that just gets intoxicated over sunrise and sunset, while it knows something of the power of the sun, does not know it as a reality, but only as a symbol. It can never understand why people worshipped the sun as a god; to do so one needs experience, not only of light and colours, but also of heat. The hot countries, from the Mediterranean to India and Central America, have been the intellectually creative countries. The colder lands have lived on the intellectual creativeness of the others, and anything original that they have produced, namely technology, serves in the last resort the material needs of life rather than the mind. Is that what repeatedly draws us to the hot countries? And may not such thoughts do something to compensate for the discomforts of the heat?

But I expect you're feeling that that is all the same to you, and that you're just longing to be out of that hell, back to Grunewald and a glass of Berlin beer. I remember very well how I longed to get out of Italy in June 1923, and didn't breathe freely again till I was out on a day's ramble in pouring rain in the Black Forest. And there was no war on then, and all I had to do was to enjoy myself. I remember, too, how in August 1936 you rejected in horror the idea of going to Naples. How are you standing up to it now physically? Formerly one simply couldn't do without the 'espresso', and Klaus, to my youthful annoyance, threw away a lot of money on it. Besides that, we took a coach even for the shortest distances, and consumed vast quantities of *granitos* and *cassatas* on the way.

I've just had the most welcome news – that you have written, and that you've kept your old field post number, from which I conclude that you've rejoined your old unit. You can't think how reassuring – relatively, at any rate – that is for me . . .

A few hours ago Uncle Paul[61] called here to inquire personally about my welfare. It's most comical how everyone goes about flapping his wings and – with a few notable exceptions – tries to outdo everyone else in undignified ways. It's painful, but some of them are in such a state now that they can't help it.

Now I will try to go on with the theological reflections that I broke off not long since. I had been saying that God is being increasingly pushed out of a world that has come of age, out of the spheres of our knowledge and life, and that since Kant he has been relegated to a realm beyond the world of experience. Theology has on the one hand resisted this development with apologetics, and has taken up arms – in vain – against Darwinism, etc. On the other hand, it has accommodated itself to the development by restricting God to the so-called ultimate questions as a *deus ex machina*; that means that he becomes the answer to life's problems, and the solution of its needs and conflicts. So if anyone has no such difficulties, or if he refuses to go into these things, to allow others to pity him, then either he cannot be open to God; or else he must be shown that he is, in fact, deeply involved in such problems, needs, and conflicts, without admitting or knowing it. If that can be done – and existentialist philosophy and psychotherapy have worked out some quite ingenious methods in that direction – then this man can now be claimed for God, and methodism can celebrate its triumph. But if he cannot be brought to see and admit that his happiness is really an evil, his health sickness, and his vigour despair, the theologian is at his wits' end. It's a case of having to do either with a hardened sinner of a particularly ugly type, or with a man of 'bourgeois complacency', and the one is as far from salvation as the other.

You see, that is the attitude that I am contending against. When Jesus blessed sinners, they were real sinners, but Jesus did not make everyone a sinner first. He called them away from their sin, not into their sin. It is true that encounter with Jesus meant the reversal of all human values. So it was in the conversion of Paul, though in his case the encounter with Jesus preceded the realization of sin. It is true that Jesus cared about people on the fringe of human society, such as harlots and tax-collectors, but never about them alone, for he sought to care about man as such. Never did he question a man's health, vigour, or happiness, regarded in themselves, or regard them as evil fruits; else why should he heal the sick and restore strength to the weak? Jesus claims for himself and the Kingdom of God the whole of human life in all its manifestations.

Of course I have to be interrupted just now! Let me just summarize briefly what I'm concerned about – the claim of a world that has come of age by Jesus Christ.

I can't write any more today, or else the letter will be kept here another week, and I don't want that to happen. So: To be continued!

Uncle Paul has been here. He had me brought downstairs at once, and stayed – Maetz and Maass were there – more than five hours! He had four bottles of *Sekt* brought – a unique event in the annals of this place – and was nicer and more generous than I should ever have expected. He probably wanted to make it clear to everyone what good terms he is on with me, and what he expects from the jittery and pedantic M. Such independence, which would be quite unthinkable in a civilian, was most remarkable. By the way, he told me this story: At St Privat a wounded ensign shouted loudly, 'I am wounded; long live the king.' Thereupon General von Löwenfeld, who was also wounded, said, 'Be quiet, ensign; we die here in silence!' – I'm curious to know what will be the effect of his visit here; I mean what people will think of it.

Well, good-bye, and forgive me for breaking off. But I think you would sooner have this than nothing at all. I hope we shall be together again early in the autumn.

I think of you faithfully and with gratitude and pray for you each day. With all my heart,   your Dietrich

1 July   Seven years ago today we were at Martin's[62] together!

Notes

1. Truth and interpretation of scripture; *testim spiritus sancti*? Pp? *sui ipsius interpres*? Authority outside God?
2. Conscience, the voice of the general and the necessary. But agreement, command, recognition by another man is more convincing than a good conscience.
3. To what degree can Christ claim a man's decision?
4. A confession of faith does not express what another man 'must' believe, but what a man believes himself. (Episcopius at the Synod of Dordrecht for the Arminians) Dilthey 102.[63]
5. Concept of tolerance.
6. Men go to God in their distress
   Men go to God in his distress
7. Something new can always happen in conversation.
   Why so foolish? I don't know:
   I wait and always disappointment
   I wait for God.
8. When I read the poems of poets

To Eberhard Bethge   [Tegel] 8 July [1944]

Dear Eberhard,

If I could assume that you were continuing in the cheerful and contented mood which was expressed by your last letter, I would be really glad. Many thanks for it. It's a great thing that you're managing to enjoy memories and not to be troubled by them; I would be glad if I always succeeded. How remarkable and unexpectedly good things have been with you again in the last weeks; first Munich, then Verona, then the day of rain and finally the recognition of your fortune as a special merit. Your advancement is so disquieteningly fast that I certainly can't catch up with you now; I wouldn't even have been able to keep pace with you . . .

A little while ago I wrote you a letter with some very theoretical philosophy about heat. In the last few days I've been trying it on my own body. I feel as if I were in an oven, and I'm wearing only a shirt that I once brought you from Sweden, and a pair of shorts (has someone really walked off somewhere with your shirts? I'm sure that you will get them back again later), and the only reason why I don't complain about it is that I can imagine how badly you must be suffering from the heat, and how frivolous my former letter must have seemed to you. So I will try to squeeze a few thoughts out of my sweating brain, and let you have them. Who knows – it may be that it won't have to be too often now, and that we shall see each other sooner than we expect.[64] The other day I read a fine and striking remark in Euripides, in a scene of reunion after a long separation- 'So, then, to meet again is a god.'

Now for a few more thoughts on our theme. Marshalling the biblical evidence needs more lucidity and concentration than I can command at present. Wait a few more days, till it gets cooler! I haven't forgotten, either, that I owe you something about the non-religious interpretation of biblical concepts. But for today, here are a few preliminary remarks:

The displacement of God from the world, and from the public part of human life, led to the attempt to keep his place secure at least in the sphere of the 'personal', the 'inner', and the 'private'. And as every man still has a private sphere somewhere, that is where he was thought to be the most vulnerable. The secrets known to a man's valet – that is, to put it crudely, the range of his intimate life, from prayer to his sexual life – have become the hunting-ground of modern pastoral workers. In that way they resemble (though with quite different intentions) the dirtiest gutter journalists – do you remember the *Wahrheit* and the *Glocke*,[65] which made public the most intimate details about prominent people? In the one case it's social, financial, or political blackmail and in the other, religious blackmail. Forgive me, but I can't put it more mildly.

From the sociological point of view this is a revolution from below, a revolt of inferiority. Just as the vulgar mind isn't satisfied till it has seen some highly placed personage 'in his bath', or in other embarrassing situations, so it is here. There is a kind of evil

344

satisfaction in knowing that everyone has his failings and weak spots. In my contacts with the 'outcasts' of society, its 'pariahs', I've noticed repeatedly that mistrust is the dominant motive in their judgment of other people. Every action, even the most un-selfish, of a person of high repute is suspected from the outset. These 'outcasts' are to be found in all grades of society. In a flower-garden they grub around only for the dung on which the flowers grow. The more isolated a man's life, the more easily he falls a victim to this attitude.

There is also a parallel isolation among the clergy, in what one might call the 'clerical' sniffing-around-after-people's-sins in order to catch them out. It's as if you couldn't know a fine house till you had found a cobweb in the furthest cellar, or as if you couldn't adequately appreciate a good play till you had seen how the actors behave off-stage. It's the same kind of thing that you find in the novels of the last fifty years, which do not think they have depicted their characters properly till they have described them in their marriage-bed, or in films where undressing scenes are thought necessary. Anything clothed, veiled, pure, and chaste is presumed to be deceitful, disguised, and impure; people here simply show their own impurity. A basic anti-social attitude of mistrust and suspicion is the revolt of inferiority.

Regarded theologically, the error is twofold. First, it is thought that a man can be addressed as a sinner only after his weaknesses and meannesses have been spied out. Secondly, it is thought that a man's essential nature consists of his inmost and most intimate background; that is defined as his 'inner life', and it is precisely in those secret human places that God is to have his domain!

On the first point it is to be said that man is certainly a sinner, but is far from being mean or common on that account. To put it rather tritely, were Goethe and Napoleon sinners because they weren't always faithful husbands? It's not the sins of weakness, but the sins of strength, which matter here. It's not in the least neces-sary to spy out things; the Bible never does so. (Sins of strength: in the genius, *hubris*; in the peasant, the breaking of the order of life – is the decalogue a peasant ethic?—; in the bourgeois, fear of free responsibility. Is this correct?)

On the second point: the Bible does not recognize our distinction between the outward and the inward. Why should it? It is always concerned with *anthrōpos teleios*, the *whole* man, even where, as in the Sermon on the Mount, the decalogue is pressed home to refer to 'inward disposition'. That a good 'disposition' can take the place of total goodness is quite unbiblical. The discovery of the so-called inner life dates from the Renaissance, probably from Petrarch. The 'heart' in the biblical sense is not the inner life, but the whole man in relation to God. But as a man lives just as much from 'outwards' to 'inwards' as from 'inwards' to 'outwards', the view that his essential nature can be understood only from his intimate spiritual background is wholly erroneous.

I therefore want to start from the premise that God shouldn't be smuggled into some last secret place, but that we should frankly recognize that the world, and people, have come of age, that we shouldn't run man down in his worldliness, but confront him with God at his strongest point, that we should give up all our clerical tricks, and not regard psychotherapy and existentialist philosophy as God's pioneers. The importunity of all these people is far too unaristocratic for the Word of God to ally itself with them. The Word of God is far removed from this revolt of mistrust, this revolt from below. On the contrary, it reigns.

Well, it's time to say something concrete about the secular interpretation of biblical concepts; but it's too hot!

If you want of your own accord to send Albrecht,[66] etc., extracts from my letters, you can, of course, do so. I wouldn't do it myself as yet, because you're the only person with whom I venture to think aloud, as it were, in the hope of clarifying my thoughts. But please yourself about it.

The novel has got stuck, and the little work for you is also not completely finished – I had such an unproductive time between January and March. I'm enclosing two poems.[67] I would prefer to show you a long one (about this place) here[68]; I don't think that it's too bad. Perhaps one day it will get out.

I'm so glad that you're away from the street and that you have a north room and that the countryside is so beautiful where you are. We shall very soon now have to be thinking a great deal about our journey together in the summer of 1940, and my last sermons.[69]

Now good-bye, and many thanks for every thought and greeting that comes to me. Don't give yourself too much trouble with them. I know how hard it is for you now. God bless you, dear Eberhard, and bring you back to us safely and soon. With all my heart.   Your Dietrich

By the way, it would be very nice if you didn't throw away my theological letters but sent them on to Renate from time to time, as I'm sure they're too much of a burden for you. Perhaps I might want to read them again later for my work. One writes some things more freely and more vividly in a letter than in a book, and often I have better thoughts in a conversation by correspondence than by myself. But it isn't at all important! By the way, H. Linke, Berlin-Friedrichshagen, Wilhelmstr. 58 will be glad of a greeting from you from time to time.[70]

9 July   That's all. I think that we shall meet again soon. All the very best until then!   Your Dietrich

WHO AM I?

Who am I? They often tell me
I would step from my cell's confinement
calmly, cheerfully, firmly,
like a squire from his country-house.

Who am I? They often tell me
I would talk to my warders
freely and friendly and clearly,
as though it were mine to command.

Who am I? They also tell me
I would bear the days of misfortune

347

equably, smilingly, proudly,
like one accustomed to win.

Am I then really all that which other men tell of?
Or am I only what I know of myself,
restless and longing and sick, like a bird in a cage,
struggling for breath, as though hands were compressing my
    throat,
yearning for colours, for flowers, for the voices of birds,
thirsting for words of kindness, for neighbourliness,
trembling with anger at despotisms and petty humiliation,
tossing in expectation of great events,
powerlessly trembling for friends at an infinite distance,
weary and empty at praying, at thinking, at making,
faint, and ready to say farewell to it all?

Who am I? This or the other?
Am I one person today, and tomorrow another?
Am I both at once? A hypocrite before others,
and before myself a contemptibly woebegone weakling?
Or is something within me still like a beaten army,
fleeing in disorder from victory already achieved?

Who am I? They mock me, these lonely questions of mine.
Whoever I am, thou knowest, O God, I am thine.

CHRISTIANS AND PAGANS

I

Men go to God when they are sore bestead,
Pray to him for succour, for his peace, for bread,
For mercy for them sick, sinning, or dead;
All men do so, Christian and unbelieving.

2

Men go to God when he is sore bestead,
Find him poor and scorned, without shelter or bread,

Whelmed under weight of the wicked, the weak, the dead;
Christians stand by God in his hour of grieving.

3
God goes to every man when sore bestead,
Feeds body and spirit with his bread;
For Christians, pagans alike he hangs dead,
And both alike forgiving.

NIGHT VOICES IN TEGEL[71]

Stretched out on my cot
I stare at the grey wall.
Outside, a summer evening
That does not know me
Goes singing into the countryside.
Slowly and softly
The tides of the day ebb
On the eternal shore.
Sleep a little,
Strengthen body and soul, head and hand,
For peoples, houses, spirits and hearts
Are aflame.
Till your day breaks
After blood-red night –
Stand fast!

Night and silence.
I listen.
Only the steps and cries of the guards,
The distant, hidden laughter of two lovers.
Do you hear nothing else, lazy sleeper?

I hear my own soul tremble and heave.
Nothing else?

I hear, I hear
The silent night thoughts
Of my fellow sufferers asleep or awake,
As if voices, cries,
As if shouts for planks to save them.
I hear the uneasy creak of the beds,
I hear chains.

I hear how sleepless men toss and turn,
Who long for freedom and deeds of wrath.
When at grey dawn sleep finds them
They murmur in dreams of their wives and children.

I hear the happy lisp of half-grown boys,
Delighting in childhood dreams;
I hear them tug at their blankets
And hide from hideous nightmares.

I hear the sighs and weak breath of the old,
Who in silence prepare for the last journey.
They have seen justice and injustice come and go;
Now they wish to see the imperishable, the eternal.

Night and silence.
Only the steps and cries of the guards.
Do you hear how in the silent house
It quakes, cracks, roars
When hundreds kindle the stirred-up flame of their hearts?

Their choir is silent,
But my ear is open wide:
'We the old, the young,
The sons of all tongues,
We the strong, the weak,
The sleepers, the wakeful,
We the poor, the rich,
Alike in misfortune,

The good, the bad,
Whatever we have been,
We men of many scars,
We the witnesses of those who died,
We the defiant, we the despondent,
The innocent, and the much accused,
Deeply tormented by long isolation,
Brother, we are searching, we are calling you!
Brother, do you hear me?'

Twelve cold, thin strokes of the tower clock
Awaken me.
No sound, no warmth in them
To hide and cover me.
Howling, evil dogs at midnight
Frighten me.
The wretched noise
Divides a poor yesterday
From a poor today.
What can it matter to me
Whether one day turns into another,
One that could have nothing new, nothing better
Than to end quickly like this one?
I want to see the turning of the times,

When luminous signs stand in the night sky,
And over the peoples new bells
Ring and ring.
I am waiting for that midnight
In whose fearfully streaming brilliance
The evil perish for anguish
And the good overcome with joy.

The villain
Comes to light
In the judgment.

Deceit and betrayal,
Malicious deeds –
Atonement is near.

See, O man,
Holy strength
Is at work, setting right.

Rejoice and proclaim
Faithfulness and right
For a new race!

Heaven, reconcile
The sons of earth
To peace and beauty.

Earth, flourish;
Man, become free,
Be free!

Suddenly I sat up,
As if, from a sinking ship, I had sighted land,
As if there were something to grasp, to seize,
As if I saw golden fruit ripen.
But wherever I look, grasp, or seize,
There is only the impenetrable mass of darkness.

I sink into brooding;
I sink myself into the depths of the dark.
You night, full of outrage and evil,
Make yourself known to me!
Why and for how long will you try our patience?
A deep and long silence;
Then I hear the night bend down to me:
'I am not dark; only guilt is dark!'

Guilt! I hear a trembling and quaking,
A murmur, a lament that arises;
I hear men grow angry in spirit.
In the wild uproar of innumerable voices
A silent chorus
Assails God's ear:

'Pursued and hunted by men,
Made defenceless and accused,
Bearers of unbearable burdens,
We are yet the accusers.

'We accuse those who plunged us into sin,
Who made us share the guilt,
Who made us the witnesses of injustice,
In order to despise their accomplices.

'Our eyes had to see folly,
In order to bind us in deep guilt;
Then they stopped our mouths,
And we were as dumb dogs.

'We learned to lie easily,
To be at the disposal of open injustice;
If the defenceless was abused,
Then our eyes remained cold.

'And that which burned in our hearts,
Remained silent and unnamed;
We quenched our fiery blood
And stamped out the inner flame.

'The once holy bonds uniting men
Were mangled and flayed,
Friendship and faithfulness betrayed;
Tears and rue were reviled.

353

'We sons of pious races,
One-time defenders of right and truth,
Became despisers of God and man,
Amid hellish laughter.

'Yet though now robbed of freedom and honour,
We raise our heads proudly before men.
And if we are brought into disrepute,
Before men we declare our innocence.

'Steady and firm we stand man against man;
As the accused we accuse!

'Only before thee, source of all being,
Before thee are we sinners.

'Afraid of suffering and poor in deeds,
We have betrayed thee before men.

'We saw the lie raise its head,
And we did not honour the truth.

'We saw brethren in direst need,
And feared only our own death.

We come before thee as men,
As confessors of our sins.

'Lord, after the ferment of these times,
Send us times of assurance.

'After so much going astray,
Let us see the day break.

'Let there be ways built for us by thy word
As far as eye can see.

'Until thou wipe out our guilt,
Keep us in quiet patience.

'We will silently prepare ourselves,
Till thou dost call to new times.

'Until thou stillest storm and flood,
And thy will does wonders.

'Brother, till the night be past,
Pray for me!'

The first light of morning creeps through my window pale
    and grey,
A light, warm summer wind blows over my brow.
'Summer day,' I will only say, 'beautiful summer day!'
What may it bring to me?
Then I hear outside hasty, muffled steps;
Near me they stop suddenly.
I turn cold and hot,
For I know, oh, I know!
A soft voice reads something cuttingly and cold.
Control yourself, brother; soon you will have finished it,
soon, soon.
I hear you stride bravely and with proud step.
You no longer see the present, you see the future.
I go with you, brother, to that place,
And I hear your last word:
'Brother, when the sun turns pale for me,
Then live for me.'

Stretched out on my cot
I stare at the grey wall.
Outside a summer morning
Which is not yet mine
Goes brightly into the countryside.

Brother, till after the long night
Our day breaks
We stand fast!

From Eberhard Bethge   [S. Polo d'Enza, Reggio Emilia]
                                                    8 July 1944

Dear Dietrich,
Yesterday I received your letter of 27 June, and assume that
another one is on the way which should have arrived first . . .
Our detour to the north side of the Apennines went well; it was
full of experiences for me as I had to transport an old 1921 Fiat
car; after a number of patches I eventually simply drove on the
rims, which caused merriment everywhere. Anyway, I got over
the dreaded pass successfully . . . The partisans are now active
in the Apennines. A few days ago they killed a war court lawyer
10 kilometres from us, close to the event of 1077.[72] They occupy
whole villages, set up headquarters, requisition, occupy built-up
places (which are intended later for our front), and are hard to get
hold of . . .

   The requisition of the well-kept house of an educated family in
which we now live (with a bath, on a breezy height), the throwing
out of the people, the sniffing through all the chests, larders and
cupboards by our men, was the most nauseating thing that I've
experienced recently. I hadn't had anything to do with that sort of
thing before. Greed for expected enjoyment makes people nervous; they just wait for the slightest provocation by those concerned to find righteous anger and justification for their own
conduct in such a house; then all restraint is abandoned. The
officers root around for '*Abwehr* reasons'; the NCOs to provide
the troops with everything that they 'need', the men – they're
the best. Together they spread themselves out on the carved
tables and in the armchairs and drink the cellar dry. And you
stand by.

   Two days ago we had a marvellous experience in the early

morning. After thunder showers at night, the chain of the Alps suddenly appeared clearly in front of us; Monte Rosa and behind it the Finsteraarhorn group; they were about 120–150 miles away as the crow flies.

But now I must thank you for your good letter. I had been waiting for news. But it didn't happen. I hope that you won't wait with the poems until that long evening together, though you may be right . . .

What is 'worshipping' idols? Is it the fact that for some people there is still something that cannot be discussed, sacrosanct, something different from worship? Do you now have new insights into the absence of life after death in the OT; fourth commandment; ways of describing future existence; the difficulty we have with all eschatology? It seems to me unbiblical to regard eschatology as an evasion. What about the hymns and the attitude of Paul Gerhardt, the Thirty Years' War? Many greetings, keep heart and don't surrender to sorrow and hopelessness.

Faithfully, your Eberhard

What about the 'apolitical character' of the New Testament?
Staemmler got three years.[73]
Early Sunday: as a result of your letter I'm reading today's epistle and gospel with renewed perception.

To Eberhard Bethge [Tegel] 16 July [1944]

Dear Eberhard,

I heard yesterday from my parents that you had been moved again. I hope to hear soon how you're getting on. The historic atmosphere[74] sounds attractive, anyway. Only ten years ago we should hardly have realized that the symbolic crozier and ring, claimed by both emperor and pope, could lead to an international political struggle. Weren't they really *adiaphora*? We have had to learn again, through our own experience, that they were not. Whether

Henry IV's pilgrimage to Canossa was sincere or merely diplomatic, the picture of Henry IV in January 1077 has left its mark permanently on the thought of European peoples. It was more effective than the Concordat of Worms of 1122, which formally settled the matter on the same lines. We were taught at school that all these great disputes were a misfortune to Europe, whereas in point of fact they are the source of the intellectual freedom that has made Europe great.

There's not much to report about myself. I heard lately on the wireless (not for the first time) some scenes from Carl Orff's operas (and also *Carmina Burana*). I liked them very much; they were so fresh, clear, and bright. He has also produced an orchestral version of Monteverdi. Did you know that? I also heard a *concerto grosso* by Handel, and was again quite surprised by his ability to give such wide and immediate consolation in the slow movement, as in the *Largo*, in a way in which we wouldn't dare to any more. Handel seems to be more concerned than Bach with the effect of his music on the audience; that may be why he sometimes has a façade-like effect. Handel, unlike Bach, has a deliberate purpose behind his music. Do you agree?

I am very interested to read *The House of the Dead*, and I'm impressed by the non-moral sympathy that those outside have for its inhabitants. May not this amorality, the product of religiosity, be an essential trait of these people, and also help us to understand more recent events? For the rest, I'm doing as much writing and composing as much poetry as my strength allows. I've probably told you before that I often get down to a bit of work[75] in the evening, as we used to. Of course, I find that pleasant and useful. That's all the news that I have about myself. They say that all is going normally at home; i.e. things are not going at all well with Hans.[76] I'm really very sorry indeed about that. I sometimes think that if he had had a good pastor to visit him at the right time, perhaps physically he wouldn't have had such a bad time of it. I'm glad that Klaus is in such good spirits;[77] he was so depressed for some time. I think all his worries will soon be over; I very much hope so for his own and his family's sake. H. Walter has been made an officer! I'm now having my books sent from Pätzig to Friedrichsbrunn. I often have to think of grandmother Kleist now; she has become so immobilized.[78] Perhaps we shall be able to celebrate our wedding in Friedrichsbrunn. Maria, too, can't travel any more after the new restrictions. Perhaps it's a good thing for her, but it's a shame for me. Unfortunately she was quite depressed the last time that I saw her; I can well understand it . . . It's time that we were able to be together.

If you have to preach in the near future, I should suggest taking some such text as Ps. 62.1; 119.94a; 42.5; Jer. 31.3; Isa. 41.10; 43.1; Matt. 28.20b; I should confine myself to a few simple but vital thoughts. One has to live for some time in a community to understand how Christ is 'formed' in it (Gal. 4.19); and that is especially true of the kind of community that you would have. If I can help in any way, I should be glad to.

Now for a few more thoughts on our theme. I'm only gradually working my way to the non-religious interpretation of biblical concepts; the job is too big for me to finish just yet.

On the historical side: There is one great development that leads to the world's autonomy. In theology one sees it first in Lord Herbert of Cherbury, who maintains that reason is sufficient for religious knowledge. In ethics it appears in Montaigne and Bodin with their substitution of rules of life for the commandments. In politics Machiavelli detaches politics from morality in general and founds the doctrine of 'reasons of state'. Later, and very differently from Machiavelli, but tending like him towards the autonomy of human society, comes Grotius, setting up his natural law as international law, which is valid *etsi deus non daretur*, 'even if there were no God'. The philosophers provide the finishing touches: on the one hand we have the deism of Descartes, who holds that the world is a mechanism, running by itself with no interference from God; and on the other hand the pantheism of Spinoza, who says that God is nature. In the last resort, Kant is a deist, and Fichte and Hegel are pantheists. Everywhere the thinking is directed towards the autonomy of man and the world.

(It seems that in the natural sciences the process begins with Nicolas of Cusa and Giordano Bruno and the 'heretical' doctrine of the infinity of the universe. The classical *cosmos* was finite, like the created world of the Middle Ages. An infinite universe, however it may be conceived, is self-subsisting, *etsi deus non daretur*. It is true that modern physics is not as sure as it was about the infinity of the universe, but it has not gone back to the earlier conceptions of its finitude.)

God as a working hypothesis in morals, politics, or science, has been surmounted and abolished; and the same thing has happened in philosophy and religion (Feuerbach!). For the sake of intellectual honesty, that working hypothesis should be dropped, or as far as possible eliminated. A scientist or physician who sets out to edify is a hybrid.

Anxious souls will ask what room there is left for God now; and as they know of no answer to the question, they condemn the whole development that has brought them to such straits. I wrote to you before about the various emergency exits that have been contrived; and we ought to add to them the *salto mortale* [death-leap] back into the Middle Ages. But the principle of the Middle Ages is heteronomy in the form of clericalism; a return to that can be a counsel of despair, and it would be at the cost of intellectual honesty. It's a dream that reminds one of the song *O wüsst' ich doch den Weg zurück, den weiten Weg ins Kinderland*.[79] There is no such way – at any rate not if it means deliberately abandoning our mental integrity; the only way is that of Matt. 18.3,[80] i.e. through repentance, through *ultimate* honesty.

And we cannot be honest unless we recognize that we have to live in the world *etsi deus non daretur*. And this is just what we do recognize – before God! God himself compels us to recognize it. So our coming of age leads us to a true recognition of our situation before God. God would have us know that we must live as men who manage our lives without him. The God who is with us is the God who forsakes us (Mark 15.34).[81] The God who lets us live in the world without the working hypothesis of God is the God before whom we stand continually. Before God and with God we live without God. God lets himself be pushed out of the world on to the cross. He is weak and powerless in the world, and that is precisely the way, the only way, in which he is with us and helps us. Matt. 8.17[82] makes it quite clear that Christ helps us, not by virtue of his omnipotence, but by virtue of his weakness and suffering.

Here is the decisive difference between Christianity and all religions. Man's religiosity makes him look in his distress to the power of God in the world: God is the *deus ex machina*. The Bible directs man to God's powerlessness and suffering; only the suffering God can help. To that extent we may say that the development towards the world's coming of age outlined above, which has done away with a false conception of God, opens up a way of seeing the God of the Bible, who wins power and space in the world by his weakness. This will probably be the starting-point for our 'secular interpretation'.

18 July

I wonder whether any letters have been lost in the raids on Munich. Did you get the one with the two poems? It was just sent off that evening, and it also contained a few introductory remarks on our theological theme. The poem about Christians and pagans contains an idea that you will recognize: 'Christians stand by God in his hour of grieving'; that is what distinguishes Christians from pagans. Jesus asked in Gethsemane, 'Could you not watch with me one hour?' That is a reversal of what the religious man expects from God. Man is summoned to share in God's sufferings at the hands of a godless world.

He must therefore really live in the godless world, without attempting to gloss over or explain its ungodliness in some religious way or other. He must live a 'secular' life, and thereby share in God's sufferings. He *may* live a 'secular' life (as one who has been freed from false religious obligations and inhibitions). To be a Christian does not mean to be religious in a particular way, to make something of oneself (a sinner, a penitent, or a saint) on the basis of some method or other, but to be a man – not a type of man, but the man that Christ creates in us. It is not the religious act that makes the Christian, but participation in the sufferings of God in the secular life. That is *metanoia*: not in the first place thinking about one's own needs, problems, sins, and fears, but allowing oneself to be caught up into the way of Jesus Christ, into the messianic event, thus fulfilling Isa. 53. Therefore 'believe in the gospel', or, in the words of John the Baptist, 'Behold, the Lamb of God, who takes away the sin of the world' (John 1.29). (By the way, Jeremias has recently asserted that the Aramaic word for 'lamb' may also be translated 'servant'; very appropriate in view of Isa. 53 !)

This being caught up into the messianic sufferings of God in Jesus Christ takes a variety of forms in the New Testament. It appears in the call to discipleship, in Jesus' table-fellowship with sinners, in 'conversions' in the narrower sense of the word (e.g. Zacchaeus), in the act of the woman who was a sinner (Luke 7) – an act that she performed without any confession of sin, in the healing of the sick (Matt. 8.17; see above), in Jesus' acceptance of children. The shepherds, like the wise men from the East, stand at the crib, not as 'converted sinners', but simply because they are drawn to the crib by the star just as they are. The centurion of Capernaum (who makes no confession of sin) is held up as a model of faith (cf. Jairus). Jesus 'loved' the rich young man. The eunuch (Acts 8) and Cornelius (Acts 10) are not standing at the edge of an abyss. Nathaniel is 'an Israelite indeed, in whom there is no guile' (John 1.47). Finally, Joseph of Arimathea and the women at the tomb. The only thing that is common to all these is their sharing in the suffering of God in Christ. That is their 'faith'. There is nothing of religious method here. The 'religious act' is always something partial; 'faith' is something whole, involving the whole of one's life. Jesus calls men, not to a new religion, but to life.

But what does this life look like, this participation in the powerlessness of God in the world? I will write about that next time, I hope. Just one more point for today. When we speak of God in a 'non-religious' way, we must speak of him in such a way that the godlessness of the world is not in some way concealed, but rather revealed, and thus exposed to an unexpected light. The world that has come of age is more godless, and perhaps for that very reason nearer to God, than the world before its coming of age. Forgive me for still putting it all so terribly clumsily and badly, as I really feel I am. But perhaps you will help me again to make things clearer and simpler, even if only by my being able to talk about them with you and to hear you, so to speak, keep asking and answering.

The address[83] is now H. Linke, Berlin-Friedrichshagen, Wilhelmstrasse 58. I'm very glad that you've now got over the mountain passes. We're getting up at 1.30 almost every night here; it's a bad time, and it handicaps work rather.

I hope I shall hear from you soon. All best wishes and faithful and grateful thoughts.   Ever your Dietrich

NOTES

1. After a successful overthrow or the end of the war.

2. To return home from the USA, see DB, pp. 557ff.

3. The German text is printed in *Gesammelte Schriften* II, pp. 422–25.

4. Geronimo Cardano, philosopher, doctor and mathematician (1501–1576), who gave his name to 'cardan joints' (universal joints).

5. According to an entry in his book of readings one of the soldiers of the guard who was acting as a go-between was killed on 31 March. Bonhoeffer gave a new address. Letters from Eberhard Bethge to the earlier address have been lost.

6. 'I thank God whom I serve with a clear conscience, as did my fathers.' 'I formerly blasphemed and persecuted and insulted him; but I received mercy because I had acted ignorantly in unbelief.'

7. 'Things into which angels long to look.'

8. 'Surely there is a God who judges on the earth.' 'Arise, O Lord! Let not man prevail; let the nations be judged before thee.'

9. 'And do you seek great things for yourself? Seek them not; for, behold, I am bringing evil upon all flesh, says the Lord; but I will give you your life as a prize of war in all places to which you may go.'

10. He probably means Prov.24.11f.: 'Rescue those who are being taken away to death; hold back those who are stumbling to the slaughter. If you say, "Behold, we did not know this." does not he who keeps watch over your soul know it, and will he not requite man according to his work?'

11. Friedrich Justus Perels, justitiary of the Confessing Church.

12. Corporal Knobloch, a member of the Tegel guard; see DB, p.751.

13. 'New Testament and Mythology', Whitsun 1941, first printed in the supplements to *Evangelische Theologie* the same year; there is an

English translation in *Kerygma and Myth* (ed. H. W. Bartsch), SPCK 1953, pp. 1–41.

14. 'The Word became flesh.'

15. A slip of the pen; should probably be 21 April.

16. See pp. 275.

17. For interrogation at the Reich War Court.

18. The attempt to obtain a post for Bethge as army chaplain from the military bishop, Dohrmann.

19. Through the mother of a fellow-prisoner.

20. 'You then, my son, be strong in the grace that is in Christ Jesus.' 'My son, give me your heart, and let your eyes observe my ways.' 'But the path of the righteous is like the light of dawn, which shines brighter and brighter until full day.'

21. The allied offensive in Central Italy was beginning; the bases at Velletri and Rignano, near Róme, were threatened.

22. 'Behold, I and the children whom the Lord has given me are signs and portents in Israel from the Lord of hosts, who dwells on Mount Zion.'

23. Martin Niemöller, in Dachau concentration camp.

24. Corporal Linke.

25. About the travelling on leave which was delayed and endangered by heavy bomb attacks by the Allies on the transport routes and passes of northern Italy in preparation for their offensive.

26. 'How fair and pleasant you are, O loved one, delectable maiden.'

27. The continuation of the letter has been lost.

28. In 1939, Bonhoeffer had still uncompromisingly rejected 'legalization' and submission to the official church authorities, as it represented the surrender of the function of the Councils of Brethren in governing the church; see DB, pp. 513ff., 596ff.

29. George Bell, Bishop of Chichester.

30. A letter of introduction to Reinhold Niebuhr, whom Bonhoeffer had met in England, in Sussex, in March 1939, to be used if Bethge were taken prisoner.

31. In case the letter, which did not, of course, bear Niebuhr's name, was discovered by the Gestapo.

32. The German text is in *Gesammelte Schriften* IV, pp. 588–92.

33. 'Why are your senses sick? Why do you grieve day and night? Take your sorrow and cast it on him who made you . . . He has provided for everything in his rule; what he does and allows to happen has a good ending. So let him continue and do not chide him; in that

way you will rest in peace here and be eternally happy' (Paul Gerhardt).

34. The front in Central Italy was moving rapidly northwards.

35. In the *Wehrmacht* report.

36. Commandant of the officers' section of the military prison in Lehrter Strasse, 64 (where Hans von Dohnanyi was held prisoner).

37. German text printed in *Gesammelte Schriften* IV, pp. 592–96.

38. The NCO who had supervised the visit.

39. The illegal correspondence between Bonhoeffer and Bethge.

40. Wondering whether to marry immediately if he was released.

41. Friedrich Justus Perels.

42. News of his twin sister and her husband from Oxford, obtained via Zürich through Erwin Sutz.

43. Rignano on the Via Flaminia.

44. Parts of the letter have been lost.

45. As a result of weather conditions, this letter was damaged in its hiding place and has become largely illegible.

46. A telephone call from the prison made possible a very extended, illegal visit at short notice.

47. The poem 'The Past'.

48. See p. 289.

49. The day of the allied landing in Normandy.

50. Rignano.

51. Klaus Bonhoeffer avoided, especially now, so soon before the attempted overthrow, anything in spoken words or writing that might draw attention to himself; so he did not keep in touch with his brother in Tegel.

52. Sabine and Gerhard Leibholz in Oxford.

53. Military office for *Abwehr* units in Italy.

54. News of the firing of the first V-1 rockets against Southern England.

55. These are key-words and quotations which Bonhoeffer jotted down while reading W. F. Otto's book *The Gods of Greece*.

56. An ironic reference to the first V-1 rocket attacks on England and the hopes of a decisive turning point in the war which official propaganda expected as a result.

57. 'Night Voices in Tegel', see pp. 349ff.

58. German text printed in *Gesammelte Schriften* IV, pp. 597–612.

59. 'The sun shall not smite you by day, nor the moon by night.'

60. Former students from the time when Bonhoeffer was a lecturer in Berlin, 1931–33, and then candidates at Finkenwalde.

61. General Paul von Hase, City Commandant of Berlin, executed on 8 August 1944.

62. At the vicarage in Dahlem on the day when Martin Niemöller was arrested.

63. See W. Dilthey, *Weltanschauung und Analyse des Menschen seit Renaissance und Reformation* in his *Gesammelte Schriften* II, ⁷1964.

64. An allusion to the imminent *Putsch*.

65. Berlin papers from the Weimar period.

66. Albrecht Schönherr.

67. 'Who am I?' and 'Christians and Pagans'.

68. 'Night Voices in Tegel'.

69. Recollection of the prohibition against preaching during the visit to Eastern Prussia in 1940 (see DB, pp. 602ff.), is meant to be a reference to Hitler's headquarters, Wolfsschanze, in East Prussia and the coming attempt.

70. A further accommodation address for correspondence.

71. This translation, by Keith R. Crim, was originally printed in: Dietrich Bonhoeffer, *I Loved this People*, SPCK and John Knox Press 1964, pp. 51–9. © M. E. Bratcher 1965. It has been reprinted here, with alterations to conform to the present text of *Letters and Papers from Prison*, by permission.

72. Canossa.

73. W. Staemmler, at that time president of the Old Prussian Council of Brethren, was put on trial for political statements.

74. Near Canossa.

75. Codeword for listening to foreign broadcasts, e.g. the BBC.

76. In June 1944 Hans von Dohnanyi got diphtheria with peripheral paralysis.

77. Meaning good progress in preparing the *Putsch*.

78. A reference to the possible penetration of the Soviet front into Further Pomerania (Klein-Krössin).

79. 'If only I knew the way back, the long way into the land of childhood.'

80. 'Unless you turn and become like children, you will never enter the kingdom of heaven.'

81. 'My God, my God, why hast thou forsaken me?'

82. 'This was to fulfil what was spoken by the prophet Isaiah, "He took our infirmities and bore our diseases." '

83. See note 70.

IV

After the Failure

July 1944 to February 1945

To Eberhard Bethge   [Tegel] 21 July [1944]¹

Dear Eberhard,

All I want to do today is to send you a short greeting. I expect you
are often with us here in your thoughts and are always glad of any
sign of life, even if the theological discussion stops for a moment.
These theological thoughts are, in fact, always occupying my
mind; but there are times when I am just content to live the life of
faith without worrying about its problems. At those times I simply
take pleasure in the days' readings² – in particular those of yesterday and today; and I'm always glad to go back to Paul Gerhardt's
beautiful hymns.

During the last year or so I've come to know and understand
more and more the profound this-worldliness of Christianity. The
Christian is not a *homo religiosus*, but simply a man, as Jesus was a
man – in contrast, shall we say, to John the Baptist. I don't mean
the shallow and banal this-worldliness of the enlightened, the
busy, the comfortable, or the lascivious, but the profound this-
worldliness, characterized by discipline and the constant knowledge
of death and resurrection. I think Luther lived a this-worldly life
in this sense.

I remember a conversation that I had in America thirteen years
ago with a young French pastor.³ We were asking ourselves quite
simply what we wanted to do with our lives. He said he would
like to become a saint (and I think it's quite likely that he did
become one). At the time I was very impressed, but I disagreed
with him, and said, in effect, that I should like to learn to have faith.
For a long time I didn't realize the depth of the contrast. I thought
I could acquire faith by trying to live a holy life, or something like
it. I suppose I wrote *The Cost of Discipleship* as the end of that path.
Today I can see the dangers of that book, though I still stand by
what I wrote.

I discovered later, and I'm still discovering right up to this
moment, that is it only by living completely in this world that one
learns to have faith. One must completely abandon any attempt to
make something of oneself, whether it be a saint, or a converted
sinner, or a churchman (a so-called priestly type!), a righteous man

or an unrighteous one, a sick man or a healthy one. By this-world-liness I mean living unreservedly in life's duties, problems, successes and failures, experiences and perplexities. In so doing we throw ourselves completely into the arms of God, taking seriously, not our own sufferings, but those of God in the world – watching with Christ in Gethsemane. That, I think, is faith; that is *metanoia*; and that is how one becomes a man and a Christian (cf. Jer. 45!). How can success make us arrogant, or failure lead us astray, when we share in God's sufferings through a life of this kind?

I think you see what I mean, even though I put it so briefly. I'm glad to have been able to learn this, and I know I've been able to do so only along the road that I've travelled. So I'm grateful for the past and present, and content with them.

You may be surprised at such a personal letter; but if for once I want to say this kind of thing, to whom should I say it? Perhaps the time will come one day when I can talk to Maria like this; I very much hope so. But I can't expect it of her yet.

May God in his mercy lead us through these times; but above all, may he lead us to himself.

I was delighted to hear from you, and am glad you're not finding it too hot. There must be a good many letters from me on the way. Didn't we go more or less along that way in 1936?

Good-bye. Keep well, and don't lose hope that we shall all meet again soon. I always think of you in faithfulness and gratitude.

Your Dietrich

STATIONS ON THE ROAD TO FREEDOM

Discipline

If you set out to seek freedom, then learn above all things
to govern your soul and your senses, for fear that your passions
and longing may lead you away from the path you should follow.
Chaste be your mind and your body, and both in subjection,

obediently, steadfastly seeking the aim set before them;
only through discipline may a man learn to be free.

Action

Daring to do what is right, not what fancy may tell you,
valiantly grasping occasions, not cravenly doubting –
freedom comes only through deeds, not through thoughts taking
    wing.
Faint not nor fear, but go out to the storm and the action,
trusting in God whose commandment you faithfully follow;
freedom, exultant, will welcome your spirit with joy.

Suffering

A change has come indeed. Your hands, so strong and active,
are bound; in helplessness now you see your action
is ended; you sigh in relief, your cause committing
to stronger hands; so now you may rest contented.
Only for one blissful moment could you draw near to touch
    freedom;
then, that it might be perfected in glory, you gave it to God.

Death

Come now, thou greatest of feasts on the journey to freedom
    eternal;
death, cast aside all the burdensome chains, and demolish
the walls of our temporal body, the walls of our souls that are
    blinded,
so that at last we may see that which here remains hidden.
Freedom, how long we have sought thee in discipline, action, and
    suffering;
dying, we now may behold thee revealed in the Lord.

371

[Accompanying note]

Dear Eberhard,

I wrote these lines in a few hours this evening. They are quite unpolished, but they may perhaps please you and be something of a birthday present for you.   Your Dietrich

I can see this morning that I shall again have to revise them completely. Still, I'm sending them to you as they are, in the rough. I'm certainly no poet!

To Eberhard Bethge   [Tegel] 25 July 1944

Dear Eberhard,

I like to write to you as often as I can now, because I think you're always glad to hear from me. There's nothing special to report about myself nor about the family, as far as I know . . . I expect that aunt Elisabeth will soon be visiting my parents.[4]

During the last few nights it's been our turn again round here. When the bombs come shrieking down, I always think how trivial it all is compared with what you're going through out there. It often makes me downright angry to see how some people behave in such situations, and how little they think of what is happening to other people. The danger here never lasts more than a few minutes. I wonder how things are with Jochen Kanitz[5] now? He was on the central front.

I've now finished *Memoirs from the House of the Dead*. It contains a great deal that is wise and good. I'm still thinking about the assertion, which in his case is certainly not a mere conventional dictum, that man cannot live without hope, and that men who have really lost all hope often become wild and wicked. It may be an open question whether in this case hope = illusion. The importance of illusion to one's life should certainly not be underestimated; but for a Christian there must be hope based on a firm foundation. And if even illusion has so much power in people's lives that it can keep life moving, how great a power there is in a hope that is based on certainty, and how invincible a life with such a hope is. 'Christ our hope' – this Pauline formula is the strength of our lives.

They've just come to take me off to my exercise, but I will just finish this letter, to make sure that it goes today. I think of you every day with true gratitude. God bless you and Renate and your boy and all of us.   Your Dietrich

To Eberhard Bethge   [Tegel, postmark 27 July 1944]

Dear Eberhard,
Just a brief note and thanks for your letter of the 16th.[6] I'm glad that you're not suffering too much with the heat. It's become almost cool here. It must be a relief to your mind that you have plenty to do; at any rate, I should suppose so.

Your summary of our theological theme is very clear and simple. The question how there can be a 'natural piety' is at the same time the question of 'unconscious Christianity', with which I'm more and more concerned. Lutheran dogmatists distinguished between a *fides directa* and a *fides reflexa*. They related this to the so-called children's faith, at baptism. I wonder whether this doesn't raise a far-reaching problem. I hope we shall soon come back to it.

Things are unchanged in the family. You can go on writing as you've been doing so far. Everyone is glad of a letter. Have you got the poems (3)?[7] Enough for today.

All best wishes. Keep well. Watch out for malaria with those mosquitoes!

All the very best, always.   Your Dietrich

Dear Eberhard,

I haven't thanked you yet for the nice little photograph which gave me great pleasure in its Italian frame. Quaint – can one photograph in Italian and in German? and the most remarkable thing is that this can be the case with such a nondescript picture. Why don't you get a comrade to take a picture some time that shows all of you in your natural surroundings. It's very reasonable that you're now working in shirt sleeves.

You think the Bible hasn't much to say about health, fortune, vigour, etc. I've been thinking over that again. It's certainly not true of the Old Testament. The intermediate theological category between God and human fortune is, as far as I can see, that of blessing. In the Old Testament – e.g. among the patriarchs – there's a concern not for fortune, but for God's blessing, which includes in itself all earthly good. In that blessing the whole of the earthly life is claimed for God, and it includes all his promises. It would be natural to suppose that, as usual, the New Testament spiritualizes the teaching of the Old Testament here, and therefore to regard the Old Testament blessing as superseded in the New. But is it an accident that sickness and death are mentioned in connection with the misuse of the Lord's Supper ('The cup of *blessing*', I Cor. 10.16; 11.30), that Jesus restored people's health, and that while his disciples were with him they 'lacked nothing'? Now, is it right to set the Old Testament blessing against the cross? That is what Kierkegaard did. That makes the cross, or at least suffering, an abstract principle; and that is just what gives rise to an unhealthy methodism, which deprives suffering of its element of contingency as a divine ordinance. It's true that in the Old Testament the person who receives the blessing has to endure a great deal of suffering (e.g. Abraham, Isaac, Jacob, and Joseph), but this never leads to the idea that fortune and suffering, blessing and cross are mutually exclusive and contradictory – nor does it in the New Testament. Indeed, the only difference between the Old and New Testaments in this respect is that in the Old the blessing includes the cross, and in the New the cross includes the blessing.

To turn to a different point: not only action, but also suffering is a way to freedom. In suffering, the deliverance consists in our being allowed to put the matter out of our own hands into God's hands. In this sense death is the crowning of human freedom. Whether the human deed is a matter of faith or not depends on whether we understand our suffering as an extension of our action and a completion of freedom. I think that is very important and very comforting.

I'm getting on all right, and there's nothing fresh to report about the family. Hans is completely laid up with his diphtherial paralysis but there seems to be good hope for him. Good-bye, and keep your spirits up as we're doing; and look forward, as we're doing, to meeting soon.

With all my heart.   Your faithful Dietrich

Neues Lied, no. 370, 3–4.[8]

Miscellaneous Thoughts

Giordano Bruno: 'There can be something frightening about the sight of a friend; no enemy can be so terrifying as he' – Can you understand that? I'm trying hard, but I can't really understand it. Does 'terrifying' refer to the inherent danger of betrayal, inseparable from close intimacy (Judas?)?
Spinoza: Emotions are not expelled by reason, but only by stronger emotions.

It is the nature, and the advantage, of strong people that they can bring out the crucial questions and form a clear opinion about them. The weak always have to decide between alternatives that are not their own.

We are so constituted that we find perfection boring. Whether that has always been so I don't know. But I can't otherwise explain why I care so little for Raphael or for Dante's *Paradiso*. Nor am I charmed by everlasting ice or everlasting blue sky. I should seek the 'perfect' in the human, the living, and the earthly, and therefore not in the Apolline, the Dionysian, or the Faustian. In fact, I'm all for the moderate, temperate climate.

The beyond is not what is infinitely remote, but what is nearest at hand.

Absolute seriousness is never without a dash of humour.

The essence of chastity is not the suppression of lust, but the total orientation of one's life towards a goal. Without such a goal, chastity is bound to become ridiculous. Chastity is the *sine qua non* of lucidity and concentration.

Death is the supreme festival on the road to freedom.

Please excuse these rather pretentious *'pensées'*. They are fragments of conversations that have never taken place, and to that extent they belong to you. One who is forced, as I am, to live entirely in his thoughts, has the silliest things come into his mind – i.e. writing down his odd thoughts!

From his parents to Eberhard Bethge   [Sakrow] 30 July 1944

Dear Eberhard,
On this peaceful Sunday morning which we're enjoying here on the veranda at Sakrow with our great grandson contentedly beside us wriggling and chattering in his cot . . . we want to send you a good letter and tell you that your offspring is getting on very well and is delighting us with his attractive temperament and that all is well with Renate, too.

You will be getting regular news of the goings on of the rest of the family. I was able to see Hans last week. He is in a pitiful state as a result of the dreadful paralysis from his diphtheria; his face and throat have improved somewhat, but it is still advanced in his arms, legs and back, making him almost impossible to move. One can certainly expect that he will recover again, but it's a severe affliction and trial of patience for both him and Christel. Dietrich's health is good; we hope to talk to him very soon. He will be suffering very much from his isolation in this fast-moving time and have trouble in concentrating on Dilthey, which he is now studying for his ethics. Of course our thoughts are very much with you and your comrades in Italy, and we are very much preoccupied with the movement of the fronts in East and West. I hope that the V-1 will soon bring us peace, before winter comes.[9] I myself think that we ought to get a cease-fire this year, but I can't say that my prophecies have always been right. I hope that this year will then bring us together again. One can't begin to imagine in detail what that will be like. I wonder whether we shall be able to celebrate such fine family feasts as in previous years? But perhaps you will surprise us by an unexpected leave before then, and we shall celebrate that as far as the times still allow.

Grandmother wants to write, too. So I'll stop and keep the rest of the news until we can talk about it. Keep well and God bless you.   The Great-grandfather

Dear Eberhard,

. . . Everything was already going well, but now Perels thinks that prospects have become much more difficult, if not impossible.[10] In any case, it would have been a great exception. But one never knows what things are good for. We've seen that now with our two.[11] Man thinks and God directs. That now seems so clear to one, and yet we go on thinking and thinking how we can do everything in the best and wisest way. It's the same with the various young families and their children. The women don't know how to divide themselves between their children and their husbands. Is it right to leave the children in Friedrichsbrunn or Stawedda or is it better now for the families to stay together in Berlin or Leipzig? These are the questions which occupy us a great deal. We recently took Dietrich some patience cards! It's a hard time for the two of them.

I hope that everything won't last too long now and that God will allow us to keep our heads up. When you come home you will have enormous delight in your wonderful son. My thoughts are very much with you. God bless you.　　　　Your Grandmother

To Eberhard Bethge　　　　　　　　　　　　　[Tegel] 3 August [1944]

Dear Eberhard,

Today your child is six months old. You will be at home by the time he begins to speak. What a good thing that you know where you're going on your return. It's better to wait for something definite than for something indefinite. I expect that Maria will go back to the Red Cross again when her foot is right. Where we shall see each other then one can't know. Sometimes I think that I've laid too heavy a burden on her. But who could have guessed that? And if things had gone as I wanted, my situation even today would have long been a different one. But you mustn't think that I feel any bitterness about it. I sometimes wonder myself at how 'composed' (or should I say 'blunted'?) I am.

I wonder whether you will be moved again soon, and if so, where to. I should like to know whether you've read my poems. You must read the very long one (in rhyme), 'Night Voices in Tegel', some time later. I'm enclosing the outline of a book that I've planned. I don't know whether you can get anything from it, but I think you more or less understand what I'm driving at. I hope I shall be given the peace and strength to finish it. The church must come out of its stagnation. We must move out again into the open air of intellectual discussion with the world, and risk saying controversial things, if we are to get down to the serious problems of life. I feel obliged to tackle these questions as one who, although a 'modern' theologian, is still aware of the debt that he owes to liberal theology. There will not be many of the younger men in whom these two trends are combined. How very useful your help would be! But even if we are prevented from clarifying our minds by talking things over, we can still pray, and it is only in the spirit of prayer that any such work can be begun and carried through.

I've been reading about 'tropical heat' in Italy. Is it very bad? How will you be celebrating your birthday? Do you remember the evening ice in Florence on 28 August 1936? At that time I don't think that I had given you a present, because we didn't have any money. Have you seen San Gimigniano this time? And do you remember that on that occasion too you also went on strike about making the detour because of the heat? Or won't you admit that nowadays? Or could my memory really be so wrong? There's nothing to report about the family. I'm always glad when I can write that. Good-bye. When you've got through the Cicerone, you will later be a glorious guide to Italy. I'm looking forward to that.

All the very, very, best, each day and for ever. God bless you.

Faithfully, your Dietrich

Notes

[July/August 1944]

The forcing of God out of the world is the disqualification [?] of religion
live without God
But how, if Chr[istianity] were not a religion at all?
Worldly, non-religious interpretation of Christian concepts.
Christianity arises from the enco[unter] with a particular man:
Jesus. Experience of transcendence
The educated? Col[lap]se of Christian ethics

No social ethics
Confessional

'I only believe what I see'
God – not a relig. concept [?]
Return to the M[iddle] A[ges]

Unconscious Christianity: the left hand does not know what the
right hand is doing. Matt. 25.
We know not what to pray.
Motto: Jesus said to him: 'What is it that you want me to do?'

Outline for a Book

I should like to write a book of not more than 100 pages, divided
into three chapters:

1. A Stocktaking of Christianity.
2. The Real Meaning of Christian Faith.
3. Conclusions.

Chapter 1 to deal with:

(*a*) The coming of age of mankind (as already indicated). The
safeguarding of life against 'accidents' and 'blows of fate'; even if
these cannot be eliminated, the danger can be reduced. Insurance
(which, although it lives on 'accidents', seeks to mitigate their
effects) as a western phenomenon. The aim: to be independent of
nature. Nature was formerly conquered by spiritual means, with
us by technical organization of all kinds. Our immediate environ-
ment is not nature, as formerly, but organization. But with this
protection from nature's menace there arises a new one – through
organization itself.

But the spiritual force is lacking. The question is: What protects us against the menace of organization? Man is again thrown
back on himself. He has managed to deal with everything, only
not with himself. He can insure against everything, only not
against man. In the last resort it all turns on man.

(*b*) The religionlessness of man who has come of age. 'God' as a working hypothesis, as a stop-gap for our embarrassments, has become superfluous (as already indicated).

(*c*) The Protestant church: Pietism as a last attempt to maintain evangelical Christianity as a religion; Lutheran orthodoxy, the attempt to rescue the church as an institution for salvation; the Confessing Church: the theology of revelation; a δὸς μοὶ ποῦ στῶ over against the world, involving a 'factual' interest in Christianity; art and science searching for their origin. Generally in the Confessing Church: standing up for the church's 'cause', but little personal faith in Christ. 'Jesus' is disappearing from sight. Sociologically: no effect on the masses – interest confined to the upper and lower middle classes. A heavy incubus of difficult traditional ideas. The decisive factor: the church on the defensive. No taking risks for others.

(*d*) Public morals – as shown by sexual behaviour.

Chapter 2.

(*a*) God and the secular.

(*b*) Who is God? Not in the first place an abstract belief in God, in his omnipotence etc. That is not a genuine experience of God, but a partial extension of the world. Encounter with Jesus Christ. The experience that a transformation of all human life is given in the fact that 'Jesus is there only for others'. His 'being there for others' is the experience of transcendence. It is only this 'being there for others', maintained till death, that is the ground of his omnipotence, omniscience, and omnipresence. Faith is participation in this being of Jesus (incarnation, cross, and resurrection). Our relation to God is not a 'religious' relationship to the highest, most powerful, and best Being imaginable – that is not authentic transcendence – but our relation to God is a new life in 'existence for others', through participation in the being of Jesus. The transcendental is not infinite and unattainable tasks, but the neighbour who is within reach in any given situation. God in human form – not, as in oriental religions, in animal form, monstrous, chaotic, remote, and terrifying, nor in the conceptual forms of the absolute, metaphysical, infinite, etc., nor yet in the Greek divine-human form of 'man in himself', but 'the man for others', and therefore the Crucified, the man who lives out of the transcendent.

(c) Interpretation of biblical concepts on this basis. (Creation, fall, atonement, repentance, faith, the new life, the last things.)

(d) Cultus. (Details to follow later, in particular on cultus and 'religion'.)

(e) What do we really believe? I mean, believe in such a way that we stake our lives on it? The problem of the Apostles' Creed? 'What *must* I believe?' is the wrong question; antiquated controversies, especially those between the different sects; the Lutheran versus Reformed, and to some extent the Roman Catholic versus Protestant, are now unreal. They may at any time be revived with passion, but they no longer carry conviction. There is no proof of this, and we must simply take it that it is so. All that we can prove is that the faith of the Bible and Christianity does not stand or fall by these issues. Karl Barth and the Confessing Church have encouraged us to entrench ourselves persistently behind the 'faith of the church', and evade the honest question as to what we ourselves really believe. That is why the air is not quite fresh, even in the Confessing Church. To say that it is the church's business, not mine, may be a clerical evasion, and outsiders always regard it as such. It is much the same with the dialectical assertion that I do not control my own faith, and that it is therefore not for me to say what my faith is. There may be a place for all these considerations, but they do not absolve us from the duty of being honest with ourselves. We cannot, like the Roman Catholics, simply identify ourselves with the church. (This, incidentally, explains the popular opinion about Roman Catholics' insincerity.) Well then, what do we really believe? Answer: see (b), (c), and (d).

Chapter 3.

Conclusions:

The church is the church only when it exists for others. To make a start, it should give away all its property to those in need. The clergy must live solely on the free-will offerings of their congregations, or possibly engage in some secular calling. The church must share in the secular problems of ordinary human life, not dominating, but helping and serving. It must tell men of every calling what it means to live in Christ, to exist for others. In particular, our own church will have to take the field against the vices of *hubris*, power-worship, envy, and humbug, as the roots of all evil. It will have to speak of moderation, purity, trust, loyalty, constancy, patience, discipline, humility, contentment, and modesty. It must not under-estimate the importance of human example (which has its origin in the humanity of Jesus and is so important in Paul's teaching); it is not abstract argument, but example, that gives its word emphasis and power. (I hope to take up later this subject of 'example' and its place in the New Testament; it is something that we have almost entirely forgotten.) Further: the question of revising the creeds (the Apostles' Creed); revision of Christian apologetics; reform of the training for the ministry and the pattern of clerical life.

All this is very crude and condensed, but there are certain things that I'm anxious to say simply and clearly – things that we so often like to shirk. Whether I shall succeed is another matter, especially if I cannot discuss it with you. I hope it may be of some help for the church's future.

To Eberhard Bethge   [Tegel] 10 August [1944]

Dear Eberhard,
That really was a . . . surprise . . .: your [essay][12] . . . I'll send it . . . back to you, although I would very much like to keep it, but for the moment I'm not keeping anything here . . .

By the way, you can do what you think best with my things (poems etc.). The only thing to be careful about is that nothing gets into the wrong hands. I think that your corrections are good ('contemptible' can be omitted. 'Stand by God' probably arose from thinking about the cross).

I can understand your no longer finding your memories 'nourishing'. But the strength of thankfulness continually gives strength to memories. It is in just such times that we should make an effort to remember in our prayers how much we have to be thankful for. Above all, we should never allow ourselves to be consumed by the present moment, but should foster that calmness that comes from great thoughts, and measure everything by them. The fact that most people can't do this is what makes it so difficult to bear with them. It is weakness rather than wickedness that perverts a man and drags him down, and it needs profound sympathy to put up with that. But all the time God still reigns in heaven.

I'm now working on the three chapters that I wrote about. It's as you say: 'knowing' is the most thrilling thing in the world, and that's why I'm finding the work so fascinating. I think of you a great deal in your 'solitude'. I'm so glad that now you've found a sideline to occupy all your attention . . . Maria is coming to my parents permanently, as an assistant receptionist. I'm very glad about that! Now let's continue to remain confident and patient; I hope that we shall celebrate Renate's birthday together again. God bless you and all of us each day and give us strong faith.

From my heart, your faithful Dietrich

To Eberhard Bethge [Tegel] 11 August [1944]

Dear Eberhard,

The fact that you've managed to produce a little . . . work from your solitude, in the last few weeks, much to my amazement, leaves me so restless that I must write again straight away. Reading this couple of closely-packed pages was the most pleasant surprise I've had for a long time. I always felt that one day you would achieve something in the way of productive work and I'm now experiencing the joy which you've perhaps had already, the joy when a friend succeeds in a work . . . Many people write today about life in a country village, but they either lay things on too much or write with a false romanticism or with a deliberate harshness (as in *The Fishers of Lissau*). Who does it as simply as you? . . . You say that you had to wrestle very hard for simplicity; that I can believe. Simplicity is an intellectual achievement, one of the greatest. I believe that with a sure touch you've found the appropriate form for yourself – narrative, first person – and the right subject-matter – what you yourself have experienced, seen, observed, been through, felt, thought. Your gift of *seeing* seems to me to be the most important thing. And precisely *how* and *what* you see. This is no urgent, analytical, curious seeing, that wants to pry into everything, but clear, open and reverent seeing. *This* kind of seeing, with which I'm concerned in the problems of theology – *theoretically* – is now leading you to . . . descriptive writing. I think that here perhaps our strong spiritual affinity – with me it's a matter of seeing with the intellect, whereas you use your eyes and all your senses, but the manner of seeing is related – or the most important result of our long spiritual fellowship is to be found . . .

Perhaps before long you will get a letter from one or two Italian officers who are friends of mine; Professor Latmiral[13] is a very refined and cultured man; if by any chance a meeting were possible, it would certainly be a great joy for both you and him; he speaks German well. Gilli is also a very nice boy. Anyway, you can always turn to them.

All is well in the family. When will I get the photos of the baptism? And a new picture of little Dietrich? I really can't understand why Oster acted like I Samuel 31.4.[14] I still remember how it was *he* who one summer evening at home was interested in your missionary work and wouldn't keep off the subject, although you weren't really enjoying it very much. Don't you also know Gisevius?[15]

The new travel restrictions mean that my parents unfortunately won't be able to travel. I'm sorry about that. Maria is not at all well . . .

What shall I send you for your birthday? I've already been thinking about it a great deal. Until then, all the best and above all keep your spirits up!

With all my heart.   Your faithful Dietrich

Dear Eberhard,

For the first time, this birthday will be marked only by letters for you; at present they will be on their way by many means and I hope that they will reach you at about the right time. Perhaps you yourself will have a quiet hour on your birthday to write letters home. *Epistula non erubescit* – and then one sometimes learns more from letters than is usually said at an ordinary birthday party. You will see from the letters how many people are fond of you, how they share in your life and depend on you. There is hardly anything that can make one happier than to feel that one counts for something with other people. What matters here is not numbers, but intensity. In the long run, human relationships are the most important thing in life; the modern 'efficient' man can do nothing to change this, nor can the demigods and lunatics who know nothing about human relationships. God uses us in his dealings with others. Everything else is very close to *hubris*. Of course, one can cultivate human relationships all too consciously in an attempt to mean something to other people, as I've been realizing lately in the letters of Gabriele von Bülow-Humboldt; it may lead to an unrealistic cult of the human. I mean, in contrast to that, that people are more important than anything else in life. That certainly doesn't mean undervaluing the world of things and practical efficiency. But what is the finest book, or picture, or house, or estate, to me, compared to my wife, my parents, or my friend? One can, of course, speak like that only if one has found others in one's life. For many today man is just a part of the world of things, because the experience of the human simply eludes them. We must be very glad that this experience has been amply bestowed on us in our lives. . .

[You] strive to live up to the highest demands. I've often noticed how much depends on what sort of demands we make on ourselves. Some people are spoilt by being satisfied with mediocrity, and so perhaps getting results more quickly; they have fewer hindrances to overcome. I've found it one of the most potent educative factors in our family that we had so many hindrances to overcome (in connection with relevance, clarity,

naturalness, tact, simplicity, etc.) before we could express ourselves properly. I think you found it so with us at first. It often
takes a long time to clear such hurdles, and one is apt to feel that
one could have achieved success with greater ease and at less cost
if these obstacles could have been avoided . . . But one can
never go back behind what one has worked out for oneself. That
may be inconvenient for others and even for oneself sometimes,
but those are the inconveniences of education . . .

For your new year I wish you − after you've returned to your
family and into the ministry − a really great task and responsibility
and at the same time the necessary calm to be able to write something very good from time to time. For myself, my wish is that
our spiritual exchanges will continue to make it possible for our
thoughts to arise, be expressed and clarified, and still more important, that in each other we shall always have someone in whom
we can place unlimited trust. The readings for the 28th are splendid.[16] When I think of you that morning, I shall keep to them. The
question 'Is thy hand . . .?' Num. 11.23 may perhaps remind us
of some unfulfilled wishes and hopes. Over against this, II Cor.
1.20 says: God does not give us everything we want, but he does
fulfil all his promises, i.e. he remains the Lord of the earth, he preserves his church, constantly renewing our faith and not laying on
us more than we can bear, gladdening us with his nearness and
help, hearing our prayers, and leading us along the best and
straightest paths to himself. By his faithfulness in doing this, God
creates in us praise for himself . . .

I'm sorry that I've been interrupted so much in writing this
letter that it wasn't as tranquil and profound as I wanted it to be.
But you know how much I'm thinking of you and how I'm
always with you with good wishes. What shall I give you for your
birthday? Would you like the ikon that I once brought back from
Sofia?[17] Or is there something else that you would like? The
interpretation of I Sam. 31 somehow does not seem to fit.[18] Perhaps you can hide my letters somewhere. Nothing new about the
family. Let us go forward into the future in patience and confidence. God bless and protect you and all of us.

In loyalty and gratitude,   your Dietrich

THE FRIEND

Not from the heavy soil,
where blood and sex and oath
rule in their hallowed might,
where earth itself,
guarding the primal consecrated order,
avenges wantonness and madness –
not from the heavy soil of earth,
but from the spirit's choice and free desire,
needing no oath or legal bond,
is friend bestowed on friend.

Beside the cornfield that sustains us,
tilled and cared for reverently by men
sweating as they labour at their task,
and, if need be, giving their life's blood –
beside the field that gives their daily bread
men also let the lovely cornflower thrive.
No one has planted, no one watered it;
it grows, defenceless and in freedom,
and in glad confidence of life untroubled
under the open sky.
Beside the staff of life,
taken and fashioned from the heavy earth,
beside our marriage, work, and war,
the free man, too, will live and grow towards the sun.
Not the ripe fruit alone –
blossom is lovely, too.
Does blossom only serve the fruit,
or does fruit only serve the blossom –
who knows?
But both are given to us.
Finest and rarest blossom,
at a happy moment springing
from the freedom of a lightsome, daring, trusting spirit,
is a friend to a friend.

Playmates at first
on the spirit's long journeys
to distant and wonderful realms
that, veiled by the morning sunlight,
glitter like gold;
when, in the midday heat
the gossamer clouds in the deep blue sky
drift slowly towards them –
realms that, when night stirs the senses,
lit by the lamps in the darkness,
like treasures prudently hidden
beckon the seeker.

When the spirit touches
man's heart and brow
with thoughts that are lofty, bold, serene,
so that with clear eyes he will face the world
as a free man may;
when then the spirit gives birth to action
by which alone we stand or fall;
when from the sane and resolute action
rises the work that gives a man's life
content and meaning –
then would that man,
lonely and actively working,
know of the spirit that grasps and befriends him,
like waters clear and refreshing
where the spirit is cleansed from the dust
and cooled from the heat that oppressed him,
steeling himself in the hour of fatigue –
like a fortress to which, from confusion and danger,
the spirit returns,
wherein he finds refuge and comfort and strengthening,
is a friend to a friend.

And the spirit will trust,
trust without limit.

Sickened by vermin
that feed, in the shade of the good,
on envy, greed, and suspicion,
by the snake-like hissing
of venomous tongues
that fear and hate and revile
the mystery of free thought
and upright heart,
the spirit would cast aside all deceit,
open his heart to the spirit he trusts,
and unite with him freely as one.
Ungrudging, he will support,
will thank and acknowledge him,
and from him draw happiness and strength.

But always to rigorous
judgment and censure
freely assenting,
man seeks, in his manhood,
not orders, not laws and peremptory dogmas,
but counsel from one who is earnest in goodness
and faithful in friendship,
making man free.

Distant or near,
in joy or in sorrow,
each in the other
sees his true helper
to brotherly freedom.

At midnight came the air-raid siren's song;
I thought of you in silence and for long –
how you are faring, how our lives once were,
and how I wish you home this coming year.

We wait till half past one, and hear at last
the signal that the danger now is past;

so danger – if the omen does not lie –
of every kind shall gently pass you by.

To Eberhard Bethge   [Tegel 21 August 1944]

Dear Eberhard,

It's your birthday in a week's time. Once again I've taken up the readings and meditated on them. The key to everything is the 'in him'. All that we may rightly expect from God, and ask him for, is to be found in Jesus Christ. The God of Jesus Christ has nothing to do with what God, as we imagine him, could do and ought to do. If we are to learn what God promises, and what he fulfils, we must persevere in quiet meditation on the life, sayings, deeds, sufferings, and death of Jesus. It is certain that we may always live close to God and in the light of his presence, and that such living is an entirely new life for us; that nothing is then impossible for us, because all things are possible with God; that no earthly power can touch us without his will, and that danger and distress can only drive us closer to him. It is certain that we can claim nothing for ourselves, and may yet pray for everything; it is certain that our joy is hidden in suffering, and our life in death; it is certain that in all this we are in a fellowship that sustains us. In Jesus God has said Yes and Amen to it all, and that Yes and Amen is the firm ground on which we stand.

In these turbulent times we repeatedly lose sight of what really makes life worth living. We think that, because this or that person is living, it makes sense for us to live too. But the truth is that if this earth was good enough for the man Jesus Christ, if such a man as Jesus lived, then, and only then, has life a meaning for us. If Jesus had not lived, then our life would be meaningless, in spite of all the other people whom we know and honour and love. Perhaps we now sometimes forget the meaning and purpose of our profession. But isn't this the simplest way of putting it? The unbiblical idea of 'meaning' is indeed only a translation of what the Bible calls 'promise'.

I feel how inadequate these words are to express my wish, namely to give you steadfastness and joy and certainty in your loneliness. This lonely birthday need not be a lost day, if it helps to determine more clearly the convictions on which you will base your life in time to come. I've often found it a great help to think in the evening of all those who I know are praying for me, children as well as grown-ups. I think I owe it to the prayers of others, both known and unknown, that I have often been kept in safety.

Another point: we are often told in the New Testament to 'be strong' (I Cor. 16.13; Eph. 6.10; II Tim. 2.1; I John 2.14). Isn't people's weakness (stupidity, lack of independence, forgetfulness, cowardice, vanity, corruptibility, temptability, etc.) a greater danger than evil? Christ not only makes people 'good'; he makes them strong, too. The sins of weakness are the really human sins, whereas the wilful sins are diabolical (and no doubt 'strong', too!). I must think about this again. Good-bye; keep well, and don't lose confidence. I hope we shall celebrate Renate's birthday[19] together again. Thank you for everything. I keep thinking faithfully of you.

Your Dietrich

To Eberhard Bethge   [Tegel] 23 [August 1944]

Dear Eberhard,

It's always an almost indescribable joy to get letters from you. The peace and quiet in which your last letter was written was especially splendid . . . The quotation about 1077 is really fine. So you're giving yourself the chore of making selections from my very provisional thoughts. I'm sure that when you pass them on you will remember everything that ought to be remembered, won't you . . . The thoughts all come from a period about 3–4 years ago![20] You can imagine how pleased I am that you're bothering about them. How indispensable I would now find a matter-of-fact talk to clarify this whole problem! When that comes about, it will be one of the great days of my life. I think that the poem about 'Sorrow and Joy' isn't at all bad. But isn't it a bit too contrived and literary? . . . You can also show Rainalter the other products with an easy conscience, if you want to talk about them. He doesn't know me. Perhaps it would be best if he were to keep all these things. Renate will have written to you that Hans has meanwhile gone into the hospital in Brother Scharf's community.[21] I'm very sorry for him and Christel, but perhaps he will have the advantage of quicker treatment.

Please don't ever get anxious or worried about me, but don't forget to pray for me – I'm sure you don't! I am so sure of God's guiding hand that I hope I shall always be kept in that certainty. You must never doubt that I'm travelling with gratitude and cheerfulness along the road where I'm being led. My past life is brim-full of God's goodness, and my sins are covered by the forgiving love of Christ crucified. I'm most thankful for the people I have met, and I only hope that they never have to grieve about me, but that they, too, will always be certain of, and thankful for, God's mercy and forgiveness. Forgive my writing this. Don't let it grieve or upset you for a moment, but let it make you happy. But I did want to say it for once, and I couldn't think of anyone else who I could be sure would take it aright.

Did you get the poem on freedom? It was very unpolished, but it's a subject about which I feel deeply.

I'm now working at the chapter on 'A Stocktaking of Christianity'. Unfortunately my output of work has come to depend increasingly on smoking, but I'm lucky enough to have a good supply from the most varied sources, so that I'm getting on more or less. Sometimes I'm quite shocked at what I say, especially in the first part, which is mainly critical; and so I'm looking forward to getting to the more constructive part. But the whole thing has been so little discussed that it often sounds too clumsy. In any case, it can't be printed yet, and it will have to go through the 'purifier' later on. I find it hard work to have to write everything by hand, and it seems hardly legible. (Amusingly enough, I have to use German script, and then there are the corrections!) We shall see; perhaps I shall write out a fair copy.

Maria was here today, so fresh and at the same time steadfast and tranquil in a way I've rarely seen . . . You ask how the smaller and the large work fit together. Perhaps one might say that the smaller work is a prelude to and in part an anticipation of the larger. By the way, H[ans] and O[ster] were very interested in your missionary work; I had nothing to do with it. Nothing was said about it previously. Our connection is essentially through church music and academic theology; in addition, Renate was the great point of attraction . . .[22]

Now with all my heart I wish you further peace and quiet, outwardly and inwardly. God protect you and all of us and grant us a speedy reunion. With gratitude and loyalty and daily prayers. I'm always thinking of you.   Your D.

From Eberhard Bethge   S. Polo d'Enza, 24 August 1944

Dear Dietrich,
I really write to you much more often than I get words down on paper . . . Aroused by your thoughts, I'm reading Proverbs, The Song of Songs, Ecclesiastes with new delight. I can understand the complex much better. Proverbs 25.2[23] is remarkable and really quite comforting. Job has become difficult for me again. Ecclesiastes 5.2–3[24] is splendid, but has it been translated rightly? . . .

I well remember the conversations that time in your garden and my own resistance.[25] What are your latest thoughts about 'unconscious Christianity'? That's very important. Please give best wishes to Linke and also thank him in my name. That's all for today.

With many affectionate greetings.   Your Eberhard

Dear Dietrich,

I would like to begin today to reply to your birthday letter and to thank you already for your thoughts and the way in which you've made the event such a fine one . . . You can't give anything more personal than a poem.[26] And you could hardly give me greater joy. There is no greater self-sacrifice, no better way of signifying an otherwise unattainable nearness than in a poem. And it is probably *the* form, because it makes visible the inwardness that is bound up and held in check within it. Unlimited surrender of the spirit awakens anxiety in the receiver. But this restrained surrender seems to me to be the highest degree of friendship and understanding. And as a result there is something very cheering and stimulating about it. Its touch is steadier and more far-reaching than that of a letter. Many thanks.

The parts of the construction that you think you ought to transpose and alter haven't yet occurred to me. I find the language very finished. It's splendid to see how whole complexes of shared experiences, insights and convictions are aroused in such strophes . . .

Your first three strophes are close to me in every phrase. Most striking and least comprehensible to me so far is the thought of the fourth, which you also expressed to me quite recently . . .

Accepting your present is a delicate matter. You know that I'm very fond of your lovely possessions and also of this ikon, and feel very much at home with them. They, and above all the pictures, are almost part of my everyday atmosphere. But each time that your gift in your present situation is more generous than before, in your effort to spread even more joy despite the hindrances, something in me protests that perhaps you're parting with too much – so I would like to postpone acceptance until the time of the new freedom . . . It's quite certain, of course, that it would hang *very* beautifully on our walls and that you would be able to enjoy it when you came, as it awoke all the memories of the rooms in Finkenwalde, Schlönwitz, Sigurdshof and Berlin. So you see, I've already half accepted it . . .

Do keep on writing to me, in such an exciting and cheering way. Very, very many thanks.   Your Eberhard

29 August . . . During the night there was some fighting here between partisans and Fascists. We're making ourselves secure. They're now getting more lively. But all is well with us. Greetings and many thanks.   Your Eberhard

Winfried Maechler wrote for my birthday. He's been in a military hospital since July and has therefore been preserved from the worst developments in France. The splendid meditation on the readings has just come. Many thanks for it . . .

From Eberhard Bethge   [S.Polo d'Enza] 21 September [1944]

Dear Dietrich,
What will you think of me! I don't know what to do, as I've been given such violently conflicting advice.[27] But perhaps it's superfluous. So I haven't said anything about the poem on friendship, which particularly attracted me . . . Could you omit the 'lovely' in the line 'the lovely cornflowers thrive', as at that point you suddenly move from a continuous viewpoint into a value judgment? All that follows about it says it better and at greater length. Afterwards, 'blossom is lovely, too' is different. Perhaps, too, the superlatives 'Finest and rarest blossom' are unnecessary? The occasional over-short and over-long lines match the very thoughtful content well. Anyway, it was a unique form of birthday celebration and I can only say in return that it has been a great source of strength for the others to see how the threats to your situation lead to such concentration. Many, many thanks . . .

You took the death of Moses as a subject? It interests me very much that you say 'in verse', as otherwise it would have been too explosive! . . .

Horst Thurmann's[28] wife wrote to me very nicely that he sent you warmest greetings. After a letter from Fritz, A. Schönherr has to be sought in my direction, as has Otto Kunze. When I pulled his leg about his work being 'l'église c'est moi', he wrote about collaboration on all sides from Gehlhoff, Lutschewitz, Knorr, de Boor, Block, Kehrl, Strecker, Rendtorff (who, by the way, often drops a short note to me in his capacity as director of the People's Mission Bible Weeks), Frau Ohnesorge and Sup. Krause. But on the whole it all seems too optimistic to me. August Tetsch is a lieutenant, has a second child, is in Russia; Jensen (also a second child) in Lyons, as is Otto Range, Gerh. Krause (small daughter) by the Pleskauer See, Eugen Rose (of whom Rainalter tells nice stories from their time at the interpreters' school) is an Indian interpreter in France. Voelz (little son) is at the front after a long time in a garrison, as is Wolfg. Schmidt, having often been with Walter Schmidt in Saxony. Wapler wrote to him in the middle of June, but is now missing in Russia. Karl Ferdinand Müller has another son (Sebastian, of course), Willi Rott is still in Athens, a short while ago he had special leave. W. Kärgel is still home guard in Prenzlau. Derschau and K. H. Reimer in Bojak's home country. Bernh. Onnasch wounded in Weimar. Fritz Vater very fit and serviceable. St. Jakobi in Stettin has collapsed. Fritz is leader of a group of air-raid wardens with the Stahlhelm in Stettin, his house in Stettin is continually filled up with casualties. He sent me a sermon from Marahrens' former adjutant . . . The poorest one has vanished, as have the two in the church office for foreign affairs.[29] Only Pompe is still there. I heard that from Lokies.

Things are still going remarkably well with us here. But there has been shooting by the partisans, and the Lieutenant (unfortunately the Major has been transferred) makes us mad with foolish reconnaissances and other such things. Ecclesiasticus 13.11.[30] He's all too fond of involving me in long conversations; he eats with us and lectures us constantly; the atmosphere has lost much of its freedom as a result. Some time there will certainly be a row (not with me). He recently forced me to give a lecture and presumably thought that it was going to be some sort of sermon; I refused that, and talked about India, which I still remembered a bit about; he's as old as I am, with an addiction to commerce. We're now very expectant about when the move will take place and how we shall cross the Po.

Very many greetings and thanks. You will understand my silence. It's quite dreadful for me. With loyal thoughts,

your Eberhard.

30 September

Another ten days have passed, and I kept waiting for something from you. Moses[31] came yesterday, and today the letter with the 'abstract concept of the future'. With it were the fifteen letters from Renate which have been missing for so long.

I'm really *very* sorry to have been silent for so long, but it was the result of really urgent thoughts. Now, however, I shall break silence again. Did you get my letter of the 28th? You don't seem to have done . . . Many thanks for Moses. I got it yesterday evening before going on guard and read it afterwards; it moved me very much, but I'm not sure what to make of it. The language is fine, but with the fetters of the rhyme it didn't seem quite like your other things . . . I haven't come across anything that seems to me to need alteration. Once again we're living in a great pause. I find your thoughts about the future bold and perhaps even comforting. This letter ought to go now, so that you hear something at last.

Many greetings. Your Eberhard

If only I could tell you of my latest spiritual and worldly experiences!

JONAH[32]

In fear of death they cried aloud and, clinging fast
to wet ropes straining on the battered deck,
they gazed in stricken terror at the sea
that now, unchained in sudden fury, lashed the ship.

'O gods eternal, excellent, provoked to anger,
help us, or give a sign, that we may know
who has offended you by secret sin,
by breach of oath, or heedless blasphemy, or murder,

who brings us to disaster by misdeed still hidden,
to make a paltry profit for his pride.'
Thus they besought. And Jonah said, 'Behold,
I sinned before the Lord of hosts. My life is forfeit.

Cast me away! My guilt must bear the wrath of God;
the righteous shall not perish with the sinner!'
They trembled. But with hands that knew no weakness
they cast the offender from their midst. The sea stood still.

To his mother [Prinz-Albrecht-Strasse]
28 December 1944

Dear mother,
I'm so glad to have just got permission to write you a birthday
letter. I have to write in some haste, as the post is just going. All I
really want to do is to help to cheer you a little in these days that
you must be finding so bleak. Dear mother, I want you to know
that I am constantly thinking of you and father every day, and
that I thank God for all that you are to me and the whole family.
I know you've always lived for us and haven't lived a life of your
own. That is why you're the only one with whom I can share all
that I'm going through. It's a very great comfort to me that Maria
is with you. Thank you for all the love that has come to me in my
cell from you during the past year, and has made every day easier
for me. I think these hard years have brought us closer together
than we ever were before. My wish for you and father and Maria
and for us all is that the New Year may bring us at least an occasional glimmer of light, and that we may once more have the joy
of being together. May God keep you both well.

With most loving wishes, dear, dear mother, for a happy
birthday. Your grateful Dietrich

POWERS OF GOOD

With every power for good to stay and guide me,
comforted and inspired beyond all fear,
I'll live these days with you in thought beside me,
and pass, with you, into the coming year.

The old year still torments our hearts, unhastening;
the long days of our sorrow still endure;
Father, grant to the souls thou hast been chastening
that thou hast promised, the healing and the cure.

Should it be ours to drain the cup of grieving
even to the dregs of pain, at thy command,
we will not falter, thankfully receiving
all that is given by thy loving hand.

But should it be thy will once more to release us
to life's enjoyment and its good sunshine,
that which we've learned from sorrow shall increase us,
and all our life be dedicate as thine.

Today, let candles shed their radiant greeting;
lo, on our darkness are they not thy light
leading us, haply, to our longed-for meeting? –
Thou canst illumine even our darkest night.

When now the silence deepens for our hearkening,
grant we may hear thy children's voices raise
from all the unseen world around us darkening
their universal paean, in thy praise.

While all the powers of good aid and attend us,
boldly we'll face the future, come what may.
At even and at morn God will befriend us,
and oh, most surely on each newborn day!

To his parents   [Prinz-Albrecht-Strasse]
                                             17 January 1945

Dear parents,

I'm also writing today because of the People's Sacrifice.[33] I would
like to ask you to take complete control of my things. I'm told
that even a dinner jacket would be accepted; please give mine
away; also a 'pepper and salt' suit which is too small for me and a
pair of brown shoes; you, mother, now know better than I do
what I still have. *In short, give away whatever anyone might need, and
don't give it another thought.* If you have any doubts about anything,
you might perhaps telephone Commissar Sonderegger! The last
two years have taught me how little we can get along with . . .
In the inactivity of a long imprisonment one has above all a great
need to do whatever is possible for the general good within the
narrow limits that are imposed. You'll be able to understand that.
When one thinks how many people lose everything each day, one
really has no claim on possessions of any kind. I know that you
think the same way, and only want to play my part. Is Hans-
Walter actually flying in the East now? And Renate's husband?
Thank you very much for your letter, and thank Maria *very*
much for her Christmas letter! I read my letters here till I know
them by heart.

Now for a few more requests: unfortunately there were no
books handed in here for me today; Commissar Sonderegger
would be willing to accept them every now and then if Maria
could bring them. I should be very grateful for them. There were
no matches, face-cloths, or towel this time. Excuse my mentioning
that; everything else was splendid. Could I please have some
tooth-paste and a few coffee beans? Father, could you get me
from the library *Lienhard* and *Abendstunden eines Einsiedlers* by

H. Pestalozzi, *Sozialpädagogik* by P. Natorp, and Plutarch's *Lives of Great Men*?

I'm getting on all right. Do keep well. Many thanks for everything.   With all my heart, your grateful Dietrich

Please leave some writing paper with the Commissar!

From his father   [Charlottenburg] 2 February 1945

Dear Dietrich,

To make things easier for the censor, I'm writing this birthday letter with the typewriter. I hope that you can receive it. Of course, it would be better if we could visit you. We don't need to tell you what we wish for you and for this new year of your life. Our thoughts are with you every day in any case, but the day after tomorrow they will be especially so. Maria will be thinking of you particularly. She has gone with her little sister to relatives, and therefore isn't here at present. Aunt Elisabeth has gone to Warmbrunn. Suse is here with her children and wants to stay if possible. Hans-Walter is in the West.

Unfortunately I've had no luck with the library. Pestalozzi was only issued for the reading room; why, I don't know, but I will ask a library assistant I know. Natorp is out. Karl-Friedrich had thought of the Plutarch for you for your birthday. Only the cakes come from us. Maria will certainly be very sorry that she can't bring anything herself. Whatever happens, we two old ones want to stay here. As a doctor, there is always a chance that I can help someone, and mother has to help me. I'm hoping that I shall be able to visit you soon. At my age one has an obligation to regulate one's concerns as far as possible . . .

Affectionate greetings. The memory of many good things that you have experienced and the hope of a near end to your time of trial will make your birthday tolerable for you.   Your Father

From his father   [Charlottenburg] 7 February 1945[34]

Dear Dietrich,

Because of the attack, our birthday letter for the 4th, which we
wanted to bring on Saturday, didn't get into your hands. We sat
in Anhalt station in the S-Bahn during the attack; it wasn't very
attractive. Nothing happened, except that afterwards we looked
like chimney-sweeps. Afterwards, however, when we tried to
visit you, we were very disturbed because we weren't allowed in
because of the blind shells. The next day we heard that nothing had
happened to the prisoners. We hope that that is true.

Now about the family. Maria has gone with her sister from
Pätzig to the West. Aunt Elisabeth is in Warmbrunn. Suse is here
with the children and wants to remain here. Hans-Walter is in the
West. Unfortunately I had no luck at the library. Pestalozzi is
issued only for the reading room. Natorp is out. Karl-Friedrich had
thought of the Plutarch for you for your birthday. I hope this
letter reaches you. We hope that we shall be able to visit you soon.
At our age some things have to be arranged which need discussion
with our children. I'm writing this on a typewriter to make it more
legible. Affectionate greetings.   Your Father

From Maria von Wedemeyer to her mother

                                   Flossenbürg, 19 February 1945

Dear mother,

Unfortunately my whole journey to Bundorf and Flossenbürg has
been completely unsuccessful. Dietrich just isn't there. Who knows
where he is? In Berlin they wouldn't tell me anything, and in
Flossenbürg they don't know. Quite a hopeless business. But what
am I to do now? If I remain in Berlin, our Pätzig[35] friends will
come and that's no help to Dietrich! If I arrive too early, I shall be
called up into the anti-aircraft force or who knows what? If I stay
in Bundorf, I'm so awfully far from you all and I don't know how
I shall be able to get back to you. I really think that there's relatively little sense in going back to Berlin now. If I can't even do

anything for Dietrich any more . . . I've got a touch of the screaming miseries, but that's only because I've spent two days now on the train, had to walk seven kilometres today and then seven kilometres back again without any prospect. And now it will probably be two days again before I'm back in Bundorf . . . I'm sure you've written, but it hasn't come. What's the news of Hans-Werner? Love and kisses to everyone, and especially to my fugitive. Your Maria

From his parents [Charlottenburg] 28 February 1945[36]

Dear Dietrich,

We've heard nothing of you since your departure from Berlin, and I expect that you've heard nothing from us. Nothing has happened to us during the many recent raids apart from the breakage of a couple of panes of glass. So you needn't worry. All the rest of the family are still in good health. Maria is at present taking her sister, who has fled from the East, to relations, so mother is doing my appointments as well as the house. It's a lot for her on top of all the other things that a large family involves. We're worried about your health. We would like to send your washing and the other things that we could otherwise send, but so far we haven't found any way of doing it. I hope that Christel will bring some news from the Prinz-Albrecht-Strasse today. If it's possible, do send us some message soon. Old people like ourselves ought to have permission to write more frequently. Affectionately,

your Father

My dear Dietrich,

My thoughts are with you day and night. I'm worried how things may be going with you. I hope that you can do some work and some reading, and don't get too depressed. God help you and us through this difficult time. Your old Mother

We are staying in Berlin, come what may.

1. The day after the unsuccessful attempt on Hitler's life.

2. 20 July: 'Some boast of chariots, and some of horses; but we boast of the name of the Lord our God' (Ps. 20.7); 'If God is for us, who can be against us?' (Rom. 8.31). 21 July: 'The Lord is my shepherd, I shall not want' (Ps. 23.1); 'I am the good shepherd; I know my own and my own know me' (John 10.14).

3. Jean Lasserre.

4. This means that his mother's sister will be giving up her home in Breslau because of the approach of the eastern front.

5. A student from Bonhoeffer's time as a lecturer, and a member of the Finkenwalde seminary.

6. Lost.

7. 'Night Voices in Tegel', 'Sorrow and Joy', 'Stations on the Road to Freedom'.

8. 'Oh, that I might hear the word soon resounding on the earth, that freedom might be everywhere that Christians dwell. Oh, that God would say to us the end of war, the abandonment of weapons, the end of all unhappiness. Oh, that this evil time might soon give way to good days, that we might not completely waste away in great sorrow. But God's help is near and his grace is there for all who fear him' (Paul Gerhardt).

9. Meant ironically.

10. To obtain an army chaplaincy for Eberhard Bethge.

11. The meaning is that ten days after the unsuccessful attempt on Hitler's life on 20 July there had still been no change in the position of Hans von Dohnanyi and Dietrich Bonhoeffer. Thus hopes had been raised that early imprisonment might prove to be their salvation, as no connection with the attempt of 20 July could be proved.

12. A sketch by Eberhard Bethge of his dead father, for Dietrich Bethge.

13. Italian officers, who were held prisoner in Tegel after the overthrow of Badoglio; see DB, pp. 735ff., 765f. and plate 35.

14. 'Therefore Saul took his own sword, and fell upon it.' Bonhoeffer had heard the rumour of the suicide of General Oster, but it had not yet been confirmed.

15. An indication of what to say if Bethge were interrogated and the subject of the August 1940 conversation about work for the *Abwehr* came up; see DB, p. 601.

16. Num. 11.23: 'Is the Lord's hand shortened?'; II Cor. 1.20: 'For all the promises of God find their Yes in him. That is why we utter the Amen through him, to the glory of God.'

17. Ecumenical conference in September 1933, see DB, pp241ff.

18. The rumour of General Oster's suicide.

19. End of October.

20. If the extracts fell into the hands of the Gestapo, at interrogations it was to be claimed by both sides that they came from the time of the journeys of inspection or the stay at Ettal.

21. On the previous day, 22 August, Gestapo commissar Sonderegger had transferred Hans von Dohnanyi from the isolation hospital at Potsdam to Sachsenhausen concentration camp; thus regular contact with his wife had been broken off.

22. Again a direction for possible new interrogations in which Bethge might be involved because he too had once been granted exemption by the *Abwehr*. 'Mission work' refers to connections with India which Bethge had through his appointment with the Gossner mission.

23. 'It is the glory of God to conceal things, but the glory of kings is to search things out.'

24. 'Be not rash with your mouth, nor let your heart be hasty to utter a word before God, for God is in heaven and you upon earth; therefore let your words be few. For a dream comes with much business, and a fool's voice with many words.'

25. Agreement for possible remarks about connections with the *Abwehr* in August 1940.

26. 'Stations on the Road to Freedom'.

27. Dietrich Bonhoeffer was urging a continuation of the illegal correspondence, but on the ground of new discoveries by the Reich Security Head Office, Christine von Dohnanyi intimated that the situation should not be further endangered by the continuation of the correspondence.

28. Largely news of former members of Finkenwalde and friends of the Confessing Church.

29. News of the arrest of Hanns Lilje, Eugen Gerstenmaier and – probably – Wilhelm Bachmann.

30. 'Do not try to treat him as an equal, nor trust his abundance of words; for he will test you through much talk, and while he smiles he will be examining you.'

31. 'The Death of Moses'; a German version is printed in *Gesammelte Schriften* IV, pp. 613–20.

32. On 22 September the discovery of documents by the Gestapo (see DB, pp. 730f.) made the situation worse for the family. At the beginning of October Dietrich Bonhoeffer gave up a plan of escape; this poem was written soon afterwards, about the 5th. On 8 October he was transferred to the Gestapo bunker in Prinze-Albrecht-Strasse and subjected to a new series of interrogations by the Reich Security Head Office. Klaus Bonhoeffer, Rüdiger Schleicher and Eberhard Bethge were imprisoned in the Reich Security Head Office prison in Lehrter Strasse 3 the same month.

33. During the series of interrogations by the Reich Security Head Office, which were partly open ones, this 'People's Sacrifice', a bit of Goebbels' propaganda, made this last letter possible; see DB, p. 803.

34. A new attempt to reach his son by letter after it proved impossible to deliver the previous letter of 2 February, hence the repetitions; this letter, too, could not be delivered. On 7 February, Dietrich Bonhoeffer was transferred to the concentration camp at Buchenwald.

35. A reference to the Soviet troops which had overrun Pätzig some weeks before.

36. A copy of the letter, which presumably never reached its destination.

EPILOGUE

Memories of a Survivor

Karl-Friedrich Bonhoeffer to his children, June 1945

. . . I want to tell you all about it. Why? Because my thoughts are there now, there in the ruins from which no news comes to us, where I visited uncle Klaus, condemned to death, in prison three months ago.

The Berlin prisons! What did I know of them a few years ago, and with what different eyes I've looked upon them since! The Charlottenburg Interrogation Prison in which aunt Christel was held for some time; the Tegel Interrogation Prison in which uncle Dietrich sat for eighteen months; the Moabit Military Prison with uncle Hans; the SS Prison in the Prinz-Albrecht-Strasse where uncle Dietrich was held for six months in a bunker behind bars, and the prison in the Lehrter Strasse where uncle Klaus was tortured and uncle Rüdiger went through agony, where they lived for two months after being sentenced to death.

I waited in front of the harsh iron doors of all these prisons while I was in Berlin in the last years and had 'official business' there. I've accompanied aunt Ursel and aunt Christel, aunt Emmi and Maria there. They often went daily to bring things or take them away. They often went in vain; they often had to suffer the taunts of supercilious commissars; but sometimes they also found a friendly porter who showed some humanity and passed on a greeting, accepted something outside the prescribed time or gave the prisoners something to eat against the rules.

Yes, taking food! In the last years it wasn't very easy, and aunt Ursel in particular could hardly do enough. She starved herself until she was a skeleton. There were tragedies, as when uncle Rüdiger sent the food back and said that he had enough. Who believed him? Aunt Ursel sent it in again and it came out again. Uncle Klaus was different. He always devoured everything that he was sent. Uncle Dietrich didn't have things too bad as long as he was in Tegel. He got on well with the prison staff there and the commandant of the prison was human. Uncle Hans didn't have things too bad at first, either. The commandant of his prison was almost a friend to him. But then he became ill, and went into the Charité Surgical Clinic under Sauerbruch, where I saw him for the last time. When he had been returned to prison he caught scarlet fever and diphtheria, and spent almost six months in bed, with severe post-diphtheria paralysis, lastly in the concentration camp at Oranienburg and in the State Hospital in Berlin. And now! The last time I was in Berlin was at the end of March; I had to go back shortly before grandfather's seventy-seventh birthday. Uncle Klaus and uncle Rüdiger were still alive; uncle Hans gave news through the doctor which was not completely hopeless; there was no trace of uncle Dietrich, who had been taken away by the SS at the beginning of February. I think it was on 8 April, shortly before my departure to you at Friedrichsbrunn, that I telephoned to the grandparents for the last time from Leipzig. At that time everything was still unchanged. That is more than two months ago. What may have happened since the capture of Berlin by the Russians? A man came from there who said that they had executed 4000 political prisoners beforehand. What may have happened during the attack and afterwards? Is everyone still alive? Have the grandparents been able to survive these bitter days? Both were already at the end of their tether. Grandmother often had attacks of weakness and loss of memory in the last years as a consequence of over-exertion, excitement and under-nourishment. They had no able-bodied help in the house. Uncle Dietrich spoke to someone at length on 5 April, in the neighbourhood of Passau. [On this day the prison transport containing Bonhoeffer was making an intermediary stop at Regensburg prison.] From there he is said to have gone to the concentration camp at Flossenbürg. Why isn't he here yet? . . .

Dietrich Bonhoeffer was executed in the concentration camp at Flossen-
bürg on 9 April. With the capitulation, all communications in Germany
were broken off for months. Maria von Wedemeyer received the news in
June, in West Germany. His parents in Berlin only heard it at the end
of July.

Hans von Dohnanyi was killed on 9 April in the concentration camp
at Sachsenhausen. His wife only heard more from trials of members of
the Reich Security Head Office.

Klaus Bonhoeffer and Rüdiger Schleicher were taken out of the prison
at Lehrter Strasse 3 with others, on 23 April, and shot. At the end of
May, the investigations of Eberhard Bethge, who was released from the
same prison, confirmed this to the family. Only a farewell letter from
Klaus Bonhoeffer has been preserved (Auf dem Wege zur Freiheit,
Poems and letters from prison, 1946).

His parents died in the Marienburger Allee, his father in December
1948 and his mother in February 1951.

APPENDIX
The Other Letters from Prison
by Maria von Wedemeyer-Weller

It would be presumptuous to think that I could add anything to the picture of the theologian and man Dietrich Bonhoeffer that has been drawn so aptly and diligently by Eberhard Bethge in his recently published biography, *Dietrich Bonhoeffer*.[1] I write only because of my knowledge that our engagement was a source of strength to Dietrich. He was able to convert painful longing into gratitude for the fact that there was something to anticipate; he was able to convert self-reproach for the suffering he may have caused others into a joy that those relationships existed at all. Yes, he even had the ability to convert his annoyance at the limitations of our relationship, and the misunderstandings that resulted from them, into a hopeful and eager expectation and challenge. He was able to transform the fumblings and erratic emotions of a young girl into the assured certainty that this was an addition and a source of strength to his own life. These lines can be nothing more than the recollections of a girl, then nineteen years old, who very undeservedly had gained his love.

Early life together

My first encounter with Dietrich Bonhoeffer was in the home of my grandmother, Ruth von Kleist-Retzow. I was twelve years old and had asked to be included in the confirmation classes which Bonhoeffer conducted for my older brother and two cousins. The interview was held in the presence of my grandmother. I flunked. Whatever the reason may have been, I remember that it caused Dietrich considerable amusement and my grandmother none at all. Sunday church services were attended regularly by my grand-

This article originally appeared in the Fall 1967 issue of the Union Theological Seminary *Quarterly Review* (Vol. XXIII, No. 1).

mother at Finkenwalde, Dietrich's seminary. This involved lengthy commuting and was not always appreciated by her six grand-children. We were, however, participants in many conversations with Dietrich that left us with little detailed information, but with an admiration and healthy respect for him. I remember one occasion when he told us about an exceptionally good sermon of one of his students, but voiced the criticism that the sermon was not recited from memory. He claimed that he had learned his first ten sermons by heart. At this point I quietly left the room for fear he might be tempted to prove his statement!

I saw him again after I graduated from high school and the *rapport* was immediate. Dietrich had the great gift of putting a person utterly at ease by accepting the level of the other with sincerity and commitment. We talked about mathematics. Neither of us knew much about the subject, but we managed to fill an evening with animated discussion of it. During the next fall I was in Berlin taking care of my grandmother, and Dietrich had ample opportunity to visit and talk. It amused him to take me to lunch at a small restaurant close to the hospital which was owned by Hitler's brother. He claimed there was no safer place to talk.

There was no urgency on his part, although he had great sensitivity to the changing levels of our friendship and to my willingness to receive his attention. When he wanted to present me to his family he had his niece, Renate Schleicher, later the wife of Eberhard Bethge, issue the invitation. It was a memorable evening of music-making and the only time I ever saw the entire family together. After our engagement Dietrich became less cautious. He had at first accepted a waiting period out of respect to my family, but soon he objected clearly, decisively, and repeatedly in letters and telephone calls to me. When we succeeded in changing the dictum, it was too late; he had been imprisoned.

Visiting the prisoner

Our first meeting thereafter took place in the *Reichskriegsgericht* and I found myself being used as a tool by the prosecutor Roeder. I was brought into the room with practically no forewarning, and Dietrich was visibly shaken. He first reacted with silence, but then carried on a normal conversation; his emotions showed only in the pressure with which he held my hand. Thereafter I saw him fairly regularly, at least once a month. He was given permission to write a one-page letter every four days and alternated between his parents and me. There was no limitation on the number of letters I wrote other than the patience of the censor. Finally he found a friendly guard who smuggled letters in both directions. Most of Dietrich's letters to me are now in the Houghton Library at Harvard.[2] A few were lost in the hurried flight from the Russian invasion.

Dietrich often mentioned his reluctance to express his feelings. He pondered the differences between our two families and his own feelings of propriety and privacy. Yet when he felt the need to express them in a smuggled letter (or on those few times during my visits when the attending officer would tactfully leave the room), he did so with an intensity that surprised him more than it did me. When I decided to live with his parents in order to be closer, he wrote:

It happens to be the case that certain things remain unsaid in my family, while they are expressed in yours. There is no point discussing what is the 'right' way. It involves different people who act as they inwardly must. I can imagine that at first it will be hard for you that many things, especially in religious matters, remain unexpressed at home. But I would be very glad if you could succeed in adjusting to the ways of my parents as I have tried through your grandmother to adjust to the ways of your family. I have become increasingly grateful for this (undated).

From my visits I recall that his reaction to imprisonment took one of two forms, either confident hope that the end was clearly in sight, or utter annoyance at the fact that not enough pressure was applied to drive his case ahead. In connection with the latter he wrote: 'How many "scruples" (*Bedenklichkeiten*) repeatedly prevent our class from acting. I believe that the weakness of our class is based on its justified or unjustified scruples. Simple people are different. They make more mistakes, but they also do more good, because their road to action does not lead through scruple' (undated).

After one of my early visits he wrote:

You cannot imagine what it means in my present situation to have you.

I am certain of God's special guidance here. The way in which we found each other and the time, so shortly before my imprisonment, are a clear sign for this. Again, it was a case of *hominum confusione et dei providentia*. Everyday I am overcome anew at how undeservedly I received this happiness, and each day I am deeply moved at what a hard school God has led you through during the last year. And now it appears to be his will that I have to bring you sorrow and suffering . . . so that our love for each other may achieve the right foundation and the right endurance. When I also think about the situation of the world, the complete darkness over our personal fate and my present imprisonment, then I believe that our union can only be a sign of God's grace and kindness, which calls us to faith. We would be blind if we did not see it. Jeremiah says at the moment of his people's great need 'still one shall buy houses and acres in this land' as a sign of trust in the future. This is where faith belongs. May God give it to us daily. And I do not mean the faith which flees the world, but the one that endures the world and which loves and remains true to the world in spite of all the suffering which it contains for us. Our marriage shall be a yes to God's earth; it shall strengthen our courage to act and accomplish something on the earth. I fear that Christians who stand with only one leg upon earth also stand with only one leg in heaven (12 August 1943).

Dietrich encouraged me to plan the practical aspects of our future together. It helped him to envision a specific piece of furniture in our future apartment, a particular walk through the fields, a familiar spot on the beach. He never tired of urging me to learn better English or to resume practising the violin, although both of these seemed irrelevant to me at the time. He was thoroughly and justifiably convinced that he was the better cook, but refused to think this important, or rather considered it just as unimportant as my interest in mathematics. But he enjoyed talking about details of our wedding; he had chosen the 103rd psalm as a text and claimed that he was working on the menu.

He advised me about what I should read and carefully indicated which of the books he had returned from prison were worth my reading. Yet he patiently read my favourites and commented on them with understanding. For example, he questioned my enthusiasm for Rilke. Discussing *Letters to a Young Poet* he wrote: 'To me – and I trust also to you – Rilke would have written quite differently (though I am quite certain he would not have bothered to write to me at all). To make a musical comparison: I have to transpose Rilke continually from d-sharp major to c-major, and his pianissimo I would disregard at times – so would you' (8 October 1943). I did make a dutiful attempt to read his books, starting from the beginning with *Sanctorum Communio*. When I admitted my frustration, it amused him thoroughly. He claimed that the only one of concern to him at that moment was *Life Together*, and he preferred that I wait until he was around to read it.

At least once a week we delivered books, laundry, and food, and picked up what he chose to return. It was important to Dietrich that he knew the day and time in advance, and because of air raids and disrupted transportation this was not always easy. He especially asked to be informed of a visit as far in advance as possible. 'You cheat me out of the joy of anticipation,' he would say, 'and that is a very necessary part of your visit.' There were some happy times during these visits. The fact that I brought a sizable Christmas tree all the way from home created great hilarity with both the guards and Dietrich. He remarked that maybe if he moved his cot out of his cell and stood up for the Christmas season he could accommodate the tree comfortably. It ended up in the guards' room where Dietrich was invited to enjoy it. He teased me about it often and complained that I had not brought an Easter bunny for Easter. But he also wrote: 'Isn't it so that even when we are laughing, we are a bit sad.'

Life in prison

He lived by church holidays and by seasons, rather than by the calendar month, and the dates on his letters were sometimes approximations at best. He voiced his disappointment that he had not received a letter from me or anyone else expressly for Whit Sunday. About Advent he wrote: 'A prison cell, in which one waits, hopes, does various unessential things, and is completely dependent on the fact that the door of freedom has to be opened *from the outside*, is not a bad picture of Advent' (21 November 1943).

Once, during the summer, he was permitted to sit in the prison yard while writing a letter to me:

The sun is a special favourite of mine and has reminded me often of the fact that man is created from earth and does not consist of air and thoughts. This went so far that once, when I was asked to preach in Cuba at Christmas time, coming from the ice of North America into the blooming vegetation, I almost succumbed to the sun cult and hardly knew what I should have preached. It was a real crisis, and something of this comes over me every summer when I feel the sun. To me the sun is not an astronomical entity, but something like a living power which I love and fear. I find it cowardly to look past these realities rationally. . . . So must patience, joy, gratitude and calm assert themselves against all sorts of resistance. It says in the psalm 'God is sun and shield.' To recognize and experience and believe this is a moment of great grace and by no means an everyday wisdom (20 August 1943).

He looked forward to being included in the life that was led at my home. We made a bet about whether I would be able to teach him to dance: he thought that I could, while I considered him a hopeless case. It would have been a private exercise anyway, because he did not think that a minister should dance in public. He also wanted to learn horseback riding, yet hunting was not to his taste. 'Did you know that Friedrich Wilhelm the First would ask any minister he met if hunting was a sin – he was a passionate hunter – and I think all of them, including A. H. Franke, were reasonable enough to declare that it was not. Yet it is, like many other things, not everyone's business' (21 November 1943).

He also looked forward to big family events, albeit with a certain reluctance:

You can hardly imagine how I long for everyone: after these long months of solitude, I have a real hunger for people. I am afraid, however, that at first I shall have trouble enduring long gatherings of many people. Even in times past I could endure family festivities, which in fact I love dearly, only if I could escape into my room for half an hour from time to time. From now on I hope you will escape with me. Yet you must not think me unsociable. Unfortunately, I find people extremely exhausting. But of these social vices and virtues you will learn soon enough (1 December 1943).

As time went on there were, of course, moments of discouragement:

It would be better if I succeeded in writing to you only of my gratitude, my joy, and my happiness in having you and in keeping the pressure and the impatience of this long imprisonment out of sight. But that would not be truthful, and it would appear to me as an injustice to you. You must know how I really feel and must not take me for a pillar saint (*Säulenheiligen*) . . . I can't very well imagine that you would want to marry one in the first place – and I would also advise against it from my knowledge of church history (20 August 1943).

Slowly it gets to be a waiting whose outward sense I cannot comprehend; the inward reason must be found daily. Both of us have lost infinitely much during the past months; time today is a costly commodity, for who knows how much more time is given to us? And yet I do not dare to think that it was or is lost time either for each of us individually or for both of us together. We have grown together in a different way than we have thought and wished, but these are unusual times and will remain so a while longer, and everything depends on our being one in the essential things and on our remaining with each other. Your life would have been quite different, easier, clearer, simpler had not our path crossed a year ago. But there are only short moments when this thought bothers me. I believe that not only I, but you too, had arrived at the moment in life when we had to meet, neither of us basically has any desire for an easy life, much as we may enjoy beautiful and happy hours in this life, and much as we may have a great longing for these hours today. I believe that happiness lies for both of us at a different and hidden place which is incomprehensible to many. Actually both of us look for challenges (*Aufgaben*), up to now each for himself, but from now on together. Only in this work will we grow completely together when God gives us the time for it (20 September 1943).

Stifter once said 'pain is a holy angel, who shows treasures to men which otherwise remain forever hidden; through him men have become greater than through all joys of the world.' It must be so and I tell this to myself in my present position over and over again – the pain of longing which often can be felt even physically, must be there, and we shall not and need not talk it away. But it needs to be overcome every time, and thus there is an even holier angel than the one of pain, that is the one of joy in God (21 November 1943).

The last letter

Dietrich was moved to the Gestapo prison in October, 1944. It was then impossible to obtain visitation permits, and it is improbable that any of my letters reached him there. When the prison was badly damaged during an air raid in February he was moved out of Berlin and my attempts to find him in either Dachau, Buchenwald, or Flossenbürg failed. In his last letter to me at Christmas, 1944, he wrote:

These will be quiet days in our homes. But I have had the experience over and over again that the quieter it is around me, the clearer do I feel the connection to you. It is as though in solitude the soul develops senses which we hardly know in everyday life. Therefore I have not felt lonely or abandoned for one moment. You, the parents, all of you, the friends and students of mine at the front, all are constantly present to me. Your prayers and good thoughts, words from the Bible, discussions long past, pieces of music, and books, – [all these] gain life and reality as never before. It is a great invisible sphere in which one lives and in whose reality there is no doubt. If it says in the old children's song about the angels: 'Two, to cover me, two, to wake me,' so is this guardianship (*Bewahrung*), by good invisible powers in the morning and at night, something which grown ups need today no less than children. Therefore you must not think that I am unhappy. What is happiness and unhappiness? It depends so little on the circumstances; it depends really only on that which happens inside a person. I am grateful every day that I have you, and that makes me happy (19 December 1944).

NOTES

1. Anyone who knew Dietrich Bonhoeffer must be filled with admiration and gratitude to Bethge for his outstanding biography. No matter how well one may have known Dietrich Bonhoeffer, this work offers an abundance of new facts, insights, and explanations which could have been uncovered only by thorough and painstaking research throughout the years of utter dedication. And no one but Bethge could have produced it. He is unique in his knowledge of Bonhoeffer, his background, and the thoughts with which he lived. Bethge has welded the three into a whole.

2. The Houghton Library has 38 letters (and other papers) which are not, however, accessible to the public. The following quotations are from these letters. Translation is the author's.

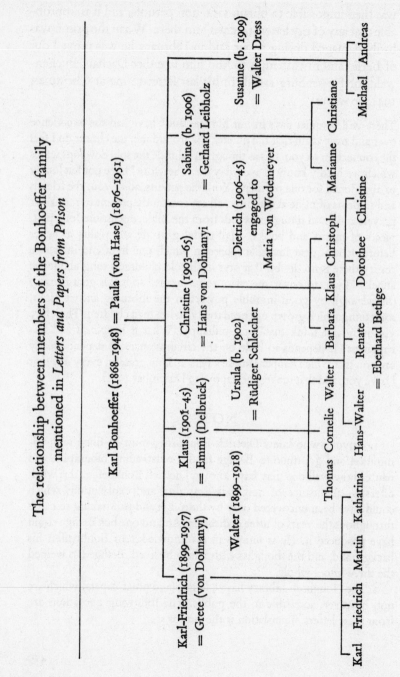

The relationship between members of the Bonhoeffer family mentioned in *Letters and Papers from Prison*

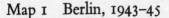

Map 1 Berlin, 1943-45

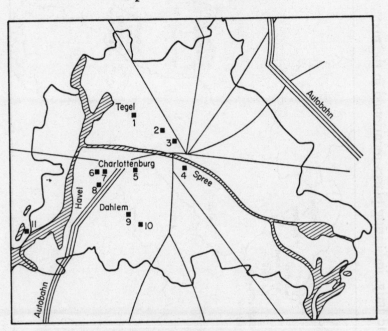

1 Dietrich Bonhoeffer's prison, Seidelstrasse 39
2 H. von Dohnanyi's and J. Müller's prison, Lehrter Strasse 64
3 Klaus Bonhoeffer's, R. Schleicher's and E. Bethge's prison, Lehrter Strasse 3
4 Reich Security Head Office. Prinz-Albrecht-Strasse 8
5 Reich War Court, Witzlebenstrasse 4–10
6 Schleicher home, Marienburger Allee 42
7 The Bonhoeffer parents' home, Marienburger Allee 43
8 Home of Klaus Bonhoeffer, Alte Allee 11
9 Dress home, Helferrichstrasse 18
10 Burckhardthaus, Rudeloffweg 27
11 Von Dohnanyi home, Sakrow, Am Hemphorn

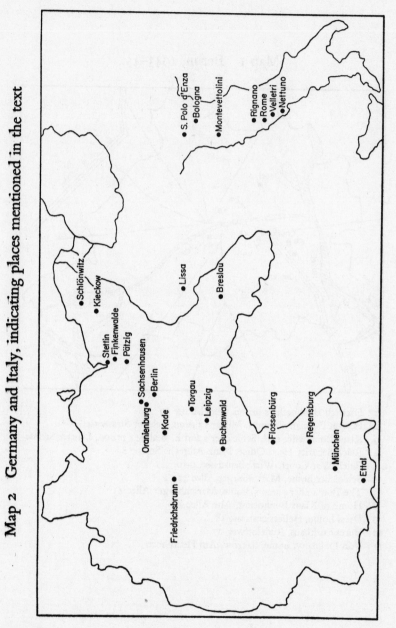

Map 2   Germany and Italy, indicating places mentioned in the text

Index of Biblical References

Index of Names

Because of the frequency with which they occur, no listing is given in this index of the names of Dietrich Bonhoeffer, his parents Karl and Paula Bonhoeffer, his fiancée Maria von Wedemeyer, or Renate, Eberhard and Dietrich Bethge.

425

Index of Subjects

God—*cont.*
  honour of, 43f., 157
  inexpressibility of, 135, 137
  judgment of, 194, 199, 299, 304
  kingdom of, 43, 46, 135, 142, 286,
    300, 304, 342
  language of, 53, 328
  name of, 135, 157, 281
  omnipotence of, 210, 381
  ordinance of, 46
  revelation of, 312, 318
  righteousness of, 11, 210, 286, 300,
    304
  vengeance of, 157
  verdict of, 166
  will of, 41f., 167, 168f., 297, 306
  word of, 300, 346
  wrath of, 46, 147, 157, 199, 231, 297,
    299
  apostasy from, 326
  life before, 9, 32, 43, 45f.
  rest in, 44
  trust in, 32, 62
  and history, 6, 11, 32, 231
  and Jesus, 312, 318, 328, 391
  and man, 10, 41, 140, 168f., 174,
    192, 282, 303, 311ff., 341, 362, 381
  and marriage, 41ff., 303
  and religion, 281ff., 362
  and the world, 344, 346, 362
  as a working hypothesis, 325, 360, 381
  in human form, 381f.
Godless, 146, 333
Godparents, 117, 195, 209, 304, 309
Good, 7, 11, 16, 42, 139f., 169, 210,
  229, 282, 285, 300, 346, 390, 392
Good Friday, 25, 126, 218
Gospel, 286, 292, 304
Grace, 3, 137, 143, 156, 174, 231, 237
Graphology, 245, 273, 274f.
Gratitude, 3, 22, 25f., 32, 34, 42, 73,
  109, 112, 129, 131, 139f., 141, 166,
  176, 179, 187, 190, 203, 208, 272,
  323, 370, 384, 394, 400, 412, 417f.
Guidance, 173, 217, 272f., 276, 299,
  370, 393
Guilt, 11, 32, 35, 186, 282, 300, 311,
  332, 353ff.

Heart, 11, 13, 26, 87, 146, 163, 169,
  178, 202, 209, 247, 296, 297, 320,
  324, 328, 289, 394, 402
Heaven, 46, 352
Heritage, spiritual (see also Home),
  165, 194f.
Heroic, 7, 16, 146, 331
History, 4, 6, 7, 9, 11, 14, 33, 101, 193,
  203, 215, 219, 227, 229–232, 271,
  278, 280, 294.ff, 298, 299, 325ff.,
  337, 344–347, 359ff.
Home, 38, 44ff., 49, 60, 67, 70, 112,
  130, 159, 165, 215, 219, 275, 294ff.,
  314
Homesickness (see also Longing), 168,
  184
Homo religiosus, 135, 154
Honesty, 17, 40, 78, 294, 360, 382, 385,
  387
Honour, 14, 45, 336, 354
Hope, 15, 25, 30, 140, 146, 149, 160,
  208, 220f., 223, 237, 269, 271,
  294f., 297, 370, 372, 387, 414
Hubris, 231, 332, 345, 383, 386
Human, 3, 8, 43, 46, 125, 145, 191,
  230, 281f., 295, 311, 325f., 337,
  341f., 344f., 376, 381f., 386, 392
Humility, 232, 332, 383
Hypocrisy, 11, 129, 348

Idealism, 6, 230
Illness, 35, 168, 362, 374
Illusions, 33, 117, 215, 275, 372f.
Impatience, 35, 132, 174
Imprisonment, 22, 49, 53, 134, 248ff.
Incarnation, 286, 381
India, 340
'Inner line', 132
Insensitiveness, 13, 35, 192, 222, 276,
  378
Intellectual, 8, 145, 280, 327, 360
Intercession, 112, 128, 130, 137, 198f.,
  231, 279, 290, 392, 394
Interpretation, non-religious, 203,
  285–7, 328, 339, 344–7, 359–62
  individualistic, 286
Invasion, 218f., 238f., 324
Inwardness, 280, 344f.

433